A History of the Korean People in Modern Times

Books by Robert T. Oliver

On Asia and Korea

Leadership in Twentieth Century Asia
Leadership in Asia: Persuasive Communication in the Making of Nations
Syngman Rhee: The Man Behind the Myth
Syngman Rhee and American Involvement in Korea, 1942–1960: A Personal Narrative
Korea: Forgotten Nation
Why War Came in Korea
The Truth About Korea
Divided Korea: Its Economic Resources, Potentials, and Needs
Verdict in Korea

On Leadership and Speech Communication

Communication and Culture in Ancient India and China
History of Public Speaking in America
The Influence of Rhetoric in the Shaping of Great Britain
Public Speaking in the Reshaping of Great Britain
The History of Public Speaking in Pennsylvania (with Dewitt Holland)
Four Who Spoke Out: Burke, Fox, Sheridan and Pitt
The Psychology of Persuasive Speech
The Healthy Mind in Communion and Communication (with Dominick Barbara)
Becoming an Informed Citizen
Culture and Communication
Effective Speech (with Rupert Cortright)
Communicative Speaking and Listening (with P. D. Holtzman and Harold Zelko)
Effective Speech for Democratic Living
Making Your Ideas Effective
Training for Effective Speech

A History of the Korean People in Modern Times

1800 to the Present

Robert T. Oliver

DELAWARE

Newark: University of Delaware Press
London and Toronto: Associated University Presses

Associated University Presses
440 Forsgate Drive
Cranbury, NJ 08512

Associated University Presses
25 Sicilian Avenue
London WC1A 2QH, England

Associated University Presses
P.O. Box 338, Port Credit
Mississauga, Ontario
Canada L5G 4L8

The paper used in this publication meets the requirements of the American National Standard for Permanence of Paper for Printed Library Materials Z39.48-1984.

Library of Congress Cataloging-in-Publication Data

Oliver, Robert Tarbell, 1909–
A history of the Korean people in modern times : 1800 to the present / Robert T. Oliver.
p. cm.
Includes bibliographical references and indexes.
ISBN 0-87413-477-3
1. Korea History—1864–1910. 2. Korea History—20th century. 3. Korea (South) History. I. Title.
DS915.2.045 1993
951.9'02—dc20 92-50486
CIP

SECOND PRINTING 1993

PRINTED IN THE UNITED STATES OF AMERICA

[redacted]

Dedicated to my wife, Margaret,
whose support never wavers

[redacted]

Guidelines

"One of the most important research subjects in the modern history of nations of the world must be on how the medieval *ancien regime* was dismantled and how a new modern system was established in its place."

—Sin Yong Ha
The Tonghak Peasant Army of 1894

"Our roots go deep into the soil. If those roots are pulled out, we wither, but if those roots remain strong and we allow the winds from the four quarters to blow in upon us, then they will yield branch and flower and fruit."

—Jawaharlal Nehru
Speech at the United Nations

"Respect for the word—to employ it with scrupulous care and incorruptible heartfelt love of truth—is essential if there is to be any growth in a society or in the human race."

—Dag Hammarskjold
Markings

Contents

Preface

This history of the Korean people in modern times is drawn from both primary and secondary sources. The secondary sources are listed in the References and to these scholars who have assembled facts and presented their own interpretations I gratefully give my thanks. Sources are generally noted in the text. The primary sources are complicated and personal. They consist of my unusual opportunities, in the years since 1942, to observe Korean affairs and to participate in many of them.

My effort in this history is to present a balanced interpretation. As the extensive references indicate, I have searched laboriously through the writings of specialists who have patiently examined the nooks and the crannies as well as the mainstream of Korean developments, from many perspectives, and from a broad diversity of viewpoints. Korea's modern history is beset by controversies. Interpretations vary widely. Amidst all the controversies about "who was to blame for what," I have sought to sift out the realities.

Facts are the building blocks of history. But they do not and cannot explain themselves. They must be organized, viewed from some particular perspectives, and evaluated by the historian. Evaluations and interpretations of Korean history differ, as they do for all histories. More than for most others, the meanings of circumstances, events, and leading individuals during the two centuries of Korean modernization have been confused and distorted by controversies. For all that has gone wrong (and much has) opinions differ sharply as to who and what should be blamed. Conclusions are so diverse that disagreement seems to be the rule concerning such vital matters as how Korea lost its independence, the nature and the effects of its rule by Japan, the reasons for the division of the peninsula, responsibility for its long continuing separation, the nature and effects of the North and South governments, and the personality and character of the principal successive political leaders. On these and many lesser matters, there is as yet no clarifying consensus.

My own interpretation of modern Korean history has changed and evolved during the five decades of my widely differing experiences. As a friend, counsellor, and publicist for President Syngman Rhee and the Republic of Korea government, I not only had from 1942 to 1960 an inside view of Korean affairs but also some responsibility for explaining and defending them. As all counsellors and spokesmen understand, this position necessitated sharp attention to both the faults and the achievements of the ROK government in both its domestic and its international operations. After my direct involvement ended, I continued my study of its circumstances through correspondence and successive visits. My understanding has been broadened by increasing knowledge and my earlier judgments have been modified by hindsight as well as by the shift from personal involvement.

During all the years since 1942, my evolving views of Korean affairs and of the Korean people have been clarified and sometimes illuminated by associations and discussions with a wide array of individuals whose perspectives have differed from mine and from one another's. These include Koreans from both inside and outside of their government, ranging from the wealthy and the powerful to the very poor and the rebellious dissidents. I have been privileged, also, to hold discussions on Korean problems with top-ranking American and United Nations officials, with diplomats and generals, with both Korean and foreign newsmen, and with scholarly specialists in Korean studies. These are among my original primary sources.

To list all who have been truly helpful is impossible. But there are some to whom I am most especially grateful. At the higher levels of government, I have been enabled to share views meaningfully with Chiang Kai-shek, Ernest Bevin, and John Foster Dulles during the crucial years of 1945–53, and through the longer span—up to 1960—with U.S. Assistant Secretaries of State John R. Hilldring and Walter Robertson. Concerning military matters, close association with generals James A. Van Fleet, John Coulter, Archer L. Lerch, and Albert C. Wedemeyer were helpful. So was my regrettably adverse relationship with General John R. Hodge. It was my good fortune to enjoy friendly relations with Admiral C. Turner Joy, while he headed the U.N. delegation to the Panmunjom peace negotiations. Among the successive U.S. aid administrators, my closest personal ties were with William Warne, who firmly maintained American policies while also sympathetically understanding why those of the Korean government differed from them.

Special insights into Korean problems were provided by such long-time friends as Ben C. Limb, Pyun Yung-tae, Walter Jhung, Lee Insoo and his family, Kim Young-shik, Pyo-Wook and Chungnim Han, General (later Prime Minister) Chung Il-kwon, Admiral Sohn Won-yil, Prime Minister Paek Tujin and Education Minister George Paik (translitering their names as they did themselves).

Over the years my discussions of Korean affairs with Dr. Chong-sik Lee have helped clarify murky issues. Dr. Benjamin Weems has helped me to see objectively problems in which my personal involvement slanted my perspective. The late Gregory Henderson generously shared with me his special insights in Korean-American relations. With Bruce Cumings I have fruitfully argued over some of our diverse interpretations. Professor Yur-bok Lee has helped me to thread my way through the quagmire of the late monarchical period. To the many more who remain unlisted to spare the readers' patience, I gratefully extend my thanks and apologies.

Very tangible help in the writing of this history has been provided by three institutions. Over a span of two decades, Pennsylvania State University generously allowed me months of freedom from campus duties so that I could pursue my Korean studies and responsibilities. The International Cultural Institute of Korea (renamed The Korea Foundation in January 1992) twice provided travel costs and facilities throughout south Korea to facilitate my information gathering. The East-West Center in Honolulu awarded me Fellowship grants over a period of four years in order that I might utilize the resources of its libraries and those of the University of Hawaii. Dr. Lee-Jay Cho, vice-president of the East-West Center and director of its Population Institute, encouraged the initiation of this study and provided essential research and secretarial assistance as it has progressed. Always thoughtfully helpful were staff members of the East-West Center, notably my research assistant Ban Byung-yool, administrative assistants LeNora Wee and Joan Choi, librarians Alice Harris and Phyllis Tabusa, and secretaries Karen Hee and Wenda Tsurjimura, who patiently and skillfully transcribed my successive manuscripts through many revisions on their word-processors.

My special appreciation goes to Dr. Woo-chul Kang of Ewha University, who generously and thoughtfully revised my interpretation through the early chapters; to Dr. Lew Young Ik of Hallim University, who read the entire manuscript and offered helpful correctives; to Dr. Joon-Mann Kang of Chunbak National University whose thoughtful and alert reading of the entire text eliminated several damaging errors; and to Dr. Yoon H. Kim, Professor of Economics of Hankook University of Foreign Studies, whose questions and comments were helpful. My highest gratitude is owing to Dr. John Merrill, whose doctoral dissertation on Korea was awarded the Council of Graduate Schools in the United States highest award in 1982, who graciously and wisely pointed the way to my final reconstruction of the history.

On a different plane, seeking ways to enhance interest among readers who are unknowledgeable about Korea and not especially interested in it, I induced readings of the manuscript by my brother, Dr. Kenneth A. Oliver, my sister, Leah Sherman, and my wife's niece, Margaret Graham, whose reactions led to many stylistic improvements and the elimination of distracting qualifications. Ultimately, without the tolerance, faith, encouragement and critical superintendence of my wife, Margaret Knoll Oliver, this history would not have been undertaken and could not have been completed. I appreciate also her faithful assistance in proof reading.

I extend my gratitude also to the editorial staffs of the University of Delaware Press and the Associated University Presses—particularly to Ms. Regina M. Phair, production editor at AUP.

Indispensable as all such help has been, the general plan of this history, its interpretations, and its judgments are my own and for them I accept full responsibility. This is a history of the Korean people in modern times as I know them.

Names

The transliteration of Korean names into English from their Chinese ideographic and Korean hangul originals is far from standardized. Diacritical markings, to represent sounds not duplicated in English, confuse rather than help foreign readers. For this reason, they often are omitted by both foreign and Korean writers. Thus P'yongyang is rendered as Pyongyang and In'chŏn as Inchon. T'oegye becomes Toegye and Po-sŏn Yun is more familiar as Yun Po-sun. Individual choices guide the transliteration of family names. Thus Yi Seungman became first Lee Seungman and then Syngman Rhee. Noh Tae-woo becomes Roh Tae Woo. Chang Myun appears as John Myun Chang, Shin Ik-I as Shinicky, Yŏ Un-hyŏng as Lyuh Woon-heung or Lyuh Woon-Hyung. In context there is little likelihood of confusion of identities. In this history diacritical markings of Korean place and family names are omitted. They are retained for infrequently-cited Chinese and Japanese names. All of this accords with general practice. Diacritical markings are restored in the two indexes.

A History of the Korean People in Modern Times

Introduction: What Is Korea Really Like?

What is Korea, what are Koreans, really like?

There are almost as many opinions as there are foreign commentators, and scholars who specialize in examining Korean affairs.

In one view South Korea is a battleground of sometimes violent disorders. Labor unions seize and occupy industrial plants, defying the police. College students march in their thousands, shouting anti-government slogans and "Yankees go home!" This is like taking photographs in a thunder storm, when the lightning flashes. It is far from an accurate picture.

In another view, the Republic of Korea is a sheer miracle of economic and social success. Within a single generation the people have emerged from wide-spread illiteracy to universal education, and from a quagmire of near starvation and epidemic diseases into the upper tier of modernized society. This is a view that emphasizes the achievements while ignoring their costs.

Both the pessimists and the optimists are only partly right. A proper perspective demands consideration of the enormity of obstacles that had to be overcome. Both failures and success are relative to their circumstances.

For a century and a half after the West began its penetration into the East, Korea's Confucian monarchy and aristocracy held modernity at bay through an isolationism so strict that the peninsula came to be called the Hermit Kingdom. Korea's government clung to its past, glorifying its four thousand years of culture and of special privileges for those who held power. The people had neither voice nor choice of their own. This is what had to be overcome.

Whatever else "modernization" implies, its most essential component is democracy. Becoming modern had to mean increasing the equality of rights, of justice, and of opportunities. In addition to these safeguards for individuals, democracy also implies equality of judgment. Decisions concerning the nation are less and less to be made by the powerful and more and more by the mass of the people. However uninformed or uneducated the majority might be, the democratic assumption is that these masses do unerringly know what is good for their own welfare—and that they are entitled to have it. This transformation of government from the entrenched minority to the majority did not occur quickly or easily. As in other nations all around the world, the shift has been gradual and (also as elsewhere) has by no means as yet become complete. Nevertheless, from traditional acceptance of monarchical and aristocratic dominance, the ruling faith has shifted to belief in universal inalienable rights. This is the fundamental meaning of "modernization" as it has progressed in Korea—less rapidly and less than fully ideal, but basically and with ever increasing effect. "Power to the people," once only a slogan, has become the irreversible trend.

Without strength enough to resist the imperialism that marked the closing years of the nineteenth century and the opening of the twentieth, Korea's location as "the strategic heart of northeast Asia" made it the centerpiece of contention among China, Russia, and Japan. In this struggle Japan won, and it converted the peninsula into its vital and tragically used corridor for militant entry into the continent of Asia.

The defeat of Japan in 1945 resulted in the "liberation" of Korea from Japan's generation-long rule. But the continuing division of the peninsula into two zones made it, along with Eastern Europe, one of the costliest effects of the Cold War.

During the bitterly destructive Korean War, the entire peninsula was devastated. Some three millions of its population were killed and more than ten million more were left homeless and jobless. And despite the enormous sacrifices not only by Koreans but also by the U.N. allies, this "land of morning calm" remained split apart.

Half of its territory and a third of its population were left under a communist dictatorship so impenetrable that it continues to be seemingly unaffected by the shattering collapse of the imposing Euro-Asian communist empire. In the south, a neo-democracy confronted the problems of constructing a modern society with few resources and no national experience in societal freedoms.

Today both Koreas are members of the United Nations, tentatively searching for some practical means of reconciliation, pending their eventual reunification.

The question remains: what is Korea really like? Amid all the disagreements, and over-riding the complexities and inconsistencies, there is an answer, though not a quick and easy one. The answer has to be sought from an understanding of what Korea has been and of how it has emerged, haltingly, often uncertainly, but persistently, through the past two centuries of both internal and external turmoil. Nothing for modern Korea has come easily. To know what Koreans are like it is necessary to know what they have been and how, step by step, they have got from where they were to where they now are.

Commonly, history is the story of government. This book relates the story of the half dozen generations of the Korean people as their country emerged, buffetted and battered, into the new world of Westernized modernity. The structural framework has to be the policies and actions of both the Korean governments and the external powers that assailed the peninsula. But the focus is on the people of Korea as a unique ethnic group and upon key individuals who are important for what they did or failed to do or whose experiences illuminate feelings and thoughts, shortcomings, aspirations, and attitudes, that are peculiarly Korean.

By any standard of measurement, Koreans are a sturdy people with a stubborn core of undefeatable Koreanism. They are zealous individuals who are united in pride in their traditions yet who are also passionately divided by clannish and regional contentiousness. Their strength derives from their proud sense of having been a significant factor in the creation of Asian civilization. Their weaknesses derive largely from their high self-regard, which resists compromises or accommodation of long unreconciled differences among themselves.

Socrates and Aristotle posited self-actualization as the central aim of life, for individuals, even for vegetation, and for communities. To be, in this view, is to become. Success is fulfillment of innate potentials. What any people or any nation is truly like is a developmental question. What Koreans ultimately are like is a question calling for exploration through the six-generation gestation period of their modernization. This era unfolds a fascinating drama that is illuminated by individual and communal heroic endeavors as well as being marred or misdirected by misjudgments and misconduct.

In a generalized sense, there are many Koreas. More truly, however, there is only one—multifaceted, but unique. To depict what this one is like is why this book was written. In the detailed chapters that follow, this aim is pursued.

1

Prelude: Approaching Modernity

Korea's medieval or middle period, bridging from antiquity to modernity, was briefer than the same period in Europe. It was shaken by contention between the old and the new. Western historians have commonly treated the advent of modernity in Korea as just another example of the general Westernization of northeast Asia, which gathered impetus in the nineteenth century. There was much else.

Significant internal changes were introduced early in the seventeenth century by King Sonjo and his son and successor, King Kwanghae, notably through the *Taedong* law.[1] Changes in the tax structure were instituted which resulted in changing the social and economic structure of the society. This blow to traditionalism was intensified in 1627 and again in 1636 by devastating invasions by the Manchus, while they were conquering China. In 1637 King Injo made peace with the Manchus by agreeing to a treaty that formalized Korea's status as a subordinate (or "younger brother") relationship within the Chinese family of nations. This treaty was less a surrender than an accommodation.

To preserve Korea's sovereignty, King Injo created the Office of Border Defense, as part of a general policy of isolationism. This defense council established an Army Training Center and also instituted, in agreement with China, a neutral zone, running along the northern side of the Yalu River. In order to prevent undue Chinese interference in Korea's domestic affairs, Chinese were forbidden, on pain of death, to cross through this zone. Those Chinese who lived in Korea were confined within a designated residential area on the outskirts of Seoul. For trading purposes, a two-week-long annual market was conducted within the neutral zone. Trade with Japan was brisker, conducted through a trading center at Waegwan, near Pusan, in which Japanese merchants were permitted to reside but from which they could not travel, even locally. Principal imports from Japan included tobacco and potatoes—American products that entered Japan through its port of Nagasaki, which was open to Chinese and Dutch merchants.

Korea's foreign relations were exclusively with China and Japan. As part of the elder brother–younger brother relationship with China, the Korean king sent annual emissaries to Peking, bearing large quantities of Korean goods, including gold, ginseng, and cotton cloth, and received in return comparable gifts. Trade with Japan, throughout the Tokugawa period, was more systematic. In addition to the exchange of goods, Japanese welcomed and sought the artifacts, knowledge, and ideas that derived from Korea's higher cultural attainments. Koreans also welcomed and sought Japanese goods and ideas that were brought into the islands through Nagasaki. Between 1607 and 1811, Korean envoys accompanied by as many as five hundred attendants visited Japan twelve times. By a trade agreement signed in 1609, some twenty Japanese trading ships operated between Pusan and Tsushima. To further enforce isolationism, the Koreans created a system of beacon fires along the coasts, to be lighted as warning signals when foreign vessels were sighted. Thus began the period in which Korea attempted to hold Westernized modernity at bay and came therefore to be known as the Hermit Kingdom.

Along with isolationism, the monarchy also imposed measures to strengthen the influence of established customs. The maintenance of traditionalism was esteemed the highest virtue. Social change was not tolerated. Stability, which tends to deteriorate into stagnation, was the hallmark of the society. Confucianism, along with lending authority to the rejection of change, also encouraged ethical, intellectual, and hierarchical values. It became debased in practice, however, as nepotism, factionalism, and corruption characterized official conduct at all levels, from the court down into the small communities. Intrigue, with its accompaniments of deception and betrayal, characterized the competitive struggles among the major clans and also affected the behavior of the citizenry, as a necessity for protection against the exactions of officials.

To understand any society, it is necessary to know both its ideals and its weaknesses. Korea today is not merely a culmination of its modernity but also a reflection of its whole history, one of the longest of any nation. During so long a period, strong roots develop. A national character gradually takes form. The present draws from the basic nature of the past. The starting point for any great historical renovation (such as the fall of the Roman Empire, the rise of the European renaissance, the democratization of England, or, similarly, the modernization of Korea) cannot be precisely dated. A new current begins to flow. It gains its force from the confluence of many sources. To interpret the transition requires a broad view of how these changes came together, of how they influenced one another, and of how new elements came to be integrated with the old.

In theory, the Confucian virtues of *in* and *ye* (the Chinese terms are *jen* and *li*) were the guides for all conduct, public and private, from the highest to the lowest levels of society.[2] *In,* variously translated as gentility, benevolence, or goodness, marked the superior man and was supposed to govern all behavior that was not otherwise ritualistically prescribed. *Ye* may be interpreted as propriety, conformity to established customs, and appropriateness of behavior. More explicitly, *ye* prescribed a five-fold set of instructions: the duties of subject and sovereign, of son and father, of younger and elder brothers, of wife and husband, and of the relations among friends.

The acceptable personality pattern was conformity, so that everyone would know what to expect from others, in all manner of dealings and relationships. To be innovative or individualistic was an eccentricity strictly condemned. Progress was undreamed of and new thoughts or new modes of behavior were not tolerated. This, to repeat, was the theory. But (like religious ethics) while it was highly praised, it was not fully practiced. What it presumed was ideal relationships within a well-ordered society. Instead, the laws bore unjustly upon the poor and the weak, and the legal system was decisively favorable to the aristocracy and the wealthy.

This was the harsh side of Old Korea. It was far from being a uniform pattern. As the history of the transitional period is examined, it will become clear that while isolationism and conservatism were gradually giving way to modernity, the resiliency and the strength which mark present day Koreans was already deeply rooted.

There is much in Korea's long history to foster patriotic pride. The peninsular people were among the prime shapers of Asian civilization. During the Ming dynasty, Korea was known among Chinese as "the land of scholars and gentlemen." Japan's Buddhism, its Confucianism, its ceramic arts, and many other rudiments of its civilization came partly by way of Korea. Specialists in oriental art have high praise for Korean accomplishments. The German orientalist Andreas Eckhardt, in his precursory *A History of Korean Art,* declared it to be "no exaggeration to aver that Korea is responsible for the production of by far the most beautiful, or rather, the most classical works of art in the Far East." Similarly, W. H. Honey, keeper of the prestigious Department of Ceramics in London's Victoria and Albert Museum, in his monograph *Corean Pottery* judged Korea's Koryo dynasty ceramics to be "unsurpassed for beauty of form," expressive of an "easeful serenity and grace, flowing and seemingly effortless, yet never lapsing into facility or trivial prettiness." Then, elaborating his belief that art reflects the character of its makers, Dr. Honey added: "Like the Corean people, even today, they have strength and dignity, as well as great charm." Not less celebrated is Korean architecture, especially as represented in its temples and palaces, for its combination of massive sturdiness and delicacy, for its harmonious and brightly hued coloring, and for its heavily tiled roofs, which are lightened by gracefully uplifted eaves that display aerily posed figurines guarding the premises.

By no means was art the only or the principal achievement of Old Korea. During the Silla period—which extended from 57 B.C.to 935 A.D.,with an especially brilliant creative greatness in the years 660–780—Korean commerce was dominant throughout eastern Asia. With an unprecedented mastery of navigation, Korean ships plied the coastal Pacific as far south as the East Indies, stimulating both trade and the expansion of knowledge. In Kyongju, the Silla capital, there still stands the oldest remaining solar observatory in northeast Asia. Silla pottery, Silla golden jewelry, Silla poetry, and attainment of unrivalled artistry in architecture and in statuary art attest the accomplishment of tasteful luxury, at least for the ruling class.

In 918, while much of Europe was still a wilderness peopled by warring tribes, a new dynasty, the Koryo, brought fundamental changes to Korea. For one thing, Buddhism was sponsored by the court and was emphasized over Confucianism as the dominant social pattern. For another, the Koryo kings (after 949) acknowledged a relationship to the Chinese emperors much like that of Canada and Australia in the present day British Commonwealth. Buddhist concepts of the unity of all life and of the special responsibility of each individual for his own destiny, transformed not only the intellectual but also the social character of the nation. For the first time, so far as the very limited communication facilities permitted, the whole country was knit into an integrated community. Buddhist monasteries located in all parts of the peninsula, and the continual travel among them of Buddhist monks, helped to develop a high sense of national unity. The marauding Khitan tribes, invading from Manchuria, were decisively defeated in 1019, ushering in a brief period of peace, prosperity and exultant patriotism.

In 1067 the Sung edition of the *Tripitaka,* one of the world's great compilations of literary, philosophical, and religious writings, was brought into Korea. When Korea was invaded and devastated by the Mongols in the thirteenth century, Korea's Buddhist scholars rescued and re-edited the mutilated texts of the Tripitaka and in 1251 completed the publication of a carefully accurate text that was acclaimed all through Asia. The text was carved onto 81,258 hardwood blocks, from which the 162,516-page edition was printed, two hundred years before the start of European printing. These blocks, still preserved in fine condition in the Buddhist monastery at Haein-sa, a few miles from Taegu, are among the early examples of extensive book publication.

On the darker side, in the passage of time, during the latter Koryo period, the Buddhist officials became so corrupt, so autocratic, and so inefficient that the state was unable to protect the people from incursions by northern tribes and Japanese pirates. The standard of living severely declined. In 1392 General Yi Song-ye revolted against the monarchy and established his own rule as King Taejo, founder of the Choson (or Yi) dynasty, with its capital at Seoul just below the 38th parallel in mid-Korea. His son, who ascended to the throne in 1401, as King Taejong, recruited a brilliant assemblage of Confucian scholar-officials to replace the former Buddhist advisors.

With a new Confucian emphasis upon governing through ability and virtue, and upon the importance of scholarship and education, Old Korea's brightest century began. Under King Taejong, the metal movable type which had been first cast in Korea in 1234, was brought into widespread use in 1403.

He also established schools throughout the peninsula and founded four universities, one in each quarter of the kingdom. The next King, Sejong—generally hailed as Korea's greatest monarch and called the democratic king—directed his scholars in the invention of a twenty-four-letter phonetic alphabet, first called *Onmun* and, later, *Hangul,* so simple that all Koreans could easily learn to read and write. His reign was a remarkable period of progress and innovation. His scholars devised water clocks, improved instruments for astronomical observation, and invented the iron rain gauge—which was used for the annual recording of rainfall, valuable in managing agriculture. He also instituted a graduated land tax, in six grades, which for centuries served as a method of taxation based on land productivity.

Predictably, the scholars, who enjoyed high status and special privileges because of their mastery of the Chinese ideograms, rejected the Onmun alphabet as being "too simple" for any use except the printing of brochures on agriculture and the production of folk tales, riddles, and other popular writings designed for the amusement of women and children. Hence the educational advantage offered by King Sejong's alphabet was postponed until the new emphasis upon literacy after the 1945 liberation of Korea from Japan.

Nevertheless, King Sejong's stimulation to learning had important effects. The most influential was the re-establishment of Confucianism as a transforming factor in the whole panoply of Korean affairs. As rightly noted by the English scholar, James H. Grayson, a specialist in Confucian influences, "Confucianism in no other society in East Asia took as strong a hold on the culture as it did in Korea during the Choson dynasty. . . . It is only in Korea that we find a society in which the predominant political, cultural, and social influence was Confucian." The effects of this influence stemmed from its broadly educational nature. It led to a freshened examination of old ideas and a search for new insights through fuller knowledge. This impulse, fortified by the means to print books, led to numerous extensive compilations.

In 1394 a Confucian scholar named Chong To-jon compiled the *Code for the Administration of Choson,* which defined lawful government as consisting of five principles: (1) the law should be derived from the ancient statutes; (2) the law should be good; (3) the law should not be amended or repealed in a rash manner; (4) the law should follow folk faith and the will of the people; and (5) the king, too, is restricted by law. This was succeeded in 1474 by a comprehensive volume entitled *Complete Library of the Laws of Government.* Music, which was important in Confucian rites and ceremonies, was systemized in a set of nine volumes, *Rules and Patterns of Music,* in 1493. Medical scholarship resulted in an 85-volume *Library of Folk Medicine* and in 266 pamphlet-size volumes entitled *Classification of Pathologies,* published in 1445. Several histories of prior dynasties were written, designed as guides for the ruling monarch. A book on farming, reporting the results of scientific experiments, appeared in 1429. A *Book of Filial Piety,* written in the new Onmun alphabet, became the most widely read Korean book during the fifteenth century.

These books were basically backward-looking, seeking guidance from the past. Confucianism in effect merged politics, scholarship, and economics—since the *yangban,* or nobility, consisted of scholars who won political positions, along with grants of land and other emoluments, through success in the examinations that were based on the Chinese classics. To be successful resulted in high social standing, political authority, and rental income as a landholder. Ambitious young men might aim either to win status in the *munban,* or literary class of yangban, or in the *muban,* the military branch. Each of these yangban classes entitled its members to own land, as the sole landlords along with the royal family. This meant that their loyalty went first of all to the court. Since their appointments extended into every district of every province, the network of yangban officialdom proved an effective means of knitting the whole nation into a unified organization. One effect was to reduce the internal disorders that had distraught the preceding Koryo era. An adverse effect was that progressive innovation was discouraged.

Confucianism was particularly suited to a village society, in which the people lived closely together and knew one another, and where all across the land there was a similarity of problems that must be dealt with. In such communities precedent was a safe guide. New knowledge, new insights, new understanding, and new ways were accepted only cautiously. What had been learned through generations of experience was dependable. "This is how grandfather, and all his ancestors, did it." There was seldom need to reshape old wisdom to fit new circumstances, for from generation to generation there was little change. Whether the circumstance at a given time might be a drought or a flood, good crops or bad, the rapacity of a corrupt official or the happy chance of a fortunate marriage, there always was a precedent to guide what should be thought and what should be done. In such village communities, what was needed was stability and harmony. The people must know what to depend upon. And they must have confidence that they could depend on one another. The desirable behavior was conformist and ritualistic.

The society was far from egalitarian. The Korean language, which is the index to how the people lived, is strongly marked by its hierarchical levels. There are some six or eight different levels of civility in the vocabulary and in the grammar—and they were strictly observed. A child, a servant, a neighbor, a friend, a stranger, a scholar, an official, an elder, and a younger person was each in turn to be spoken to in terms that reflected the relative status of the speaker and the one spoken to. The equality of all was a concept too ludicrous to be thought of.

Instead, what gave structure and meaning to the society was *particularization.* Each person was in some respects special. And it was this specialism that mattered. A child should behave like a child, an elder son like an elder son, a wife like a wife, a stranger like a stranger. Similarly, a farmer, a merchant, a soldier, a student, a scholar, a newcomer in the community, an official, each should carefully observe and exemplify the requirements of his own role. The reason was well stated by Confucius in his *Analects:* "Build up your character so as to inspire the people with assurance." There should be no reason to doubt what behavior was suitable.

The particularization of individuals was given social significance in the formation of guilds (mutual financial associations similar to those in medieval Europe), of which more than one hundred kinds were organized during the Choson dynasty. There was a special guild for each vocation—and also guilds for such occasions as weddings, funerals, births, and celebrations of the sixtieth birthday. The elaborate costumes and paraphernalia required for these special days were far too costly to be owned individually by farmers. The guilds owned them, and they could be used again and again. Similarly, farm guilds assured mutual helpfulness in the spring planting and fall harvesting seasons. It was through guilds that the people supported one another in their predictable needs, and it was through guilds that they celebrated together with singing, dancing, and feasting in harvest festivals and on unexpected occasions of good fortune.

The guilds manifested the social choice of particularization rather than democratic equality. There was a need for teaching, so teachers must teach. There were needs for butchers, for harness-makers, for shoe-makers, for midwives. The guilds, one for each vocation, set and enforced standards, provided training, and sought to protect the special needs of the workers. Along with their other functions, the guilds also served as a social bond for the members—with good results and bad. The good side assured the members of mutual help and comradeship; the bad effect was to emphasize divisiveness, differences, cliquishness, and competitive disunity. On balance, the guilds served such real needs that they long persisted as major structural factors of the society.

Confucianism, too, had both bad and good effects. The Confucian examinations that were supposed to select meritorious individuals for public offices were degraded in practice by nepotism, favoritism, and corruption. But since Confucianism exalted scholarship and prescribed virtue and learning as the highest attributes of the good life, many idealistic scholars deliberately distanced themselves from self-seeking officialdom.

These scholars, known as *sonbi,* launched a new movement called *Silhak,* or "practical learning."[4] They not only avoided government service but also took up residence in rural areas, away from the influence of the court and of the capitals of provinces. They scorned the formalistic scholarship of those yangban who studied only in order to advance their own political careers. They also developed, at least in intellectual circles, a practical search for new workable solutions to problems of government and of community life. In 1498, 1504, 1519, and 1545 there occured purges that drove from Seoul such remaining idealistic Confucian scholars as the king and his nobles considered to be lacking in loyalty to them and their administrations. Thus the remote and rural areas of the kingdom were enriched by both scholars who chose such abodes and by others who came because they had no other choice.

In general, these scholars remained loyal to the throne, but less so to the person of successive kings. They were not revolutionists, but they did have reformist influence. Their ideal was the pursuit of knowledge as something good in itself. They believed that officials, including the king, were entitled to govern only so long as they did so virtuously. As they became well-acquainted with local conditions and problems, they came to espouse governmental reforms. They identified themselves with the peasantry and turned their minds to the solution of social problems. One such scholar, Yun Chun (1629–1714) boldly advocated "a break with tradition if the government were to deal effectively with the harsh realities of the times."

One significant effect was the revival of *hyanggyo,* or local schools. Along with them, on a higher level, were *sowon* centers, which were higher academies or colleges. These were primarily devoted to the study of Confucian classics, but before long they took on also, in varying degrees, the character of discussion clubs or town meetings. Along with the study of Confucian ethics and customs, problems were discussed that ritualistic behavior did not solve, but which called for specific action.[5] Articulate individuals spoke up to advocate their own ideas. For those who felt unable to speak out, suggestion boxes were placed in market squares, in which they could express themselves anonymously.

The need for social justice was acute, and during the seventeenth century the overtaxed and mistreated peasantry commenced a series of protest demonstrations. In 1662 these protests coalesced into an attempted revolution. Hundreds of thousands of villagers, most of them armed only with clubs or with farmer's tools, advanced on government centers. Their revolt was disorganized, without central leadership, and the lack of both training and arms made the demonstrators resemble a mob more than an army. The uprisings were rather quickly and easily suppressed. Nevertheless, they made their point. It was clear that improvements were urgently needed.

Well before and independent of Western influences, Koreans began to develop their own type of modernity and of village democracy. The driving force behind it was stated clearly by an eighteenth century historian, An Chong-bok, in a book he wrote for the proper guidance of local magistrates, in which he concluded: "If the people, after talking it over among themselves, do not want a thing, the ruler must not enforce it. Let this be known to all people so that there will be none who is ignorant of the fact." Thus, he not only stated the principle of self-rule but also advocated discussion, propaganda, and agitation to popularize it.

For a time the anger and resentment of the people were dealt with only by increasing the severity of police controls. But two reform-minded kings, Yongjo (1725–76) and his well-taught grandson, Chongjo (1777–1800), undertook to make public opinion a strong force in government. They placed stress upon receiving and then acting on reports from provincial and local administrators, concerning what the people complained about and what it was they wanted. Since it was clear that the reports from administrators were self-serving, these kings also created an inspection system. Inspectors, who maintained anonymity by dressing as farmers or even as beggars, went quietly into provincial capitals and into villages, where they observed the conduct of tax-gatherers, police, and judges. Under their robes they carried bronze identification plaques that confirmed their authority, signed by the king's own seal. When they were ready to do so, they showed these plaques to establish their authority and demanded such reforms as they deemed just.

This inspection system improved the honesty of the local administrators and the accuracy of the reports that they rendered to the court. But it had the negative effect of arousing the aristocracy to take stern measures to protect its own special privileges. One of King Chongjo's advisers wrote a memorandum to the king protesting that the efforts to govern according to the will of the people did more harm than good. "I have heard," he wrote, "that even the ignorant men and women of the provinces, upon hearing about the recent happening [a public opinion poll that was ordered by the government] turn their heads toward the north,[6] saying 'we have appealed to heaven to look into our sorrows but it has never answered our appeals. Yet today the answer has come to us. Our king is going to save us.' Since the people's expectations are thus great, how could we appease their resentments when abuses continue? The prestige of the state also will be lost then. Rather than this, it would have been better not to have taken such a measure or dug out wrong-doing."

This advice, that it was wiser to ignore discontent than to try to allay it, prevailed during the next three reigns; meanwhile, gradually expanding influences from the West were pointing the way toward the end of Korea's isolation and initiating the period of transition from traditionalism to modernity. The reformation of Korean society was propelled from inside the country as well as from the West: this domestic force was the arousal of intellectuals to befriend the oppressed commoners.

Among the early liberals was a Confucian scholar named Yi Ik (1681–1763) who lived through the early years of the reign of the liberal King Yongjo, a period when Korea was obtaining some knowledge of the West, and England and France were enthusiastically learning about orientals. Yi Ik's father was an emissary to China, where he became excited by the new ideas from the West. Accordingly, Yi Ik grew up in a home that was alive with expanded knowledge and with liberalizing discussions of faraway and hitherto wholly-unknown peoples and customs. The most stimulating of the new ideas was humanitarianism—concern for the underprivileged, along with a sense of responsibility to improve their lot in life. Accordingly, he wrote a book entitled *Concern for the Underprivileged,* in which he advocated a broad range of social and political reforms.

This book, along with the general liberalism of the Yongjo-Chongjo reigns, united the *Silhak* movement with Western ideas, contrasting with and repudiating the established *Tonghak* learning, which was devoted to traditional Confucian and Buddhist classics and philosophy. *Silhak* was a bridging movement; one of its interpreters, Ch'on Kwan-u, has called it "the womb in which the modern spirit was conceived." Its adherents sought to reanimate the morality of Confucianism and to "reform the society into a more progressive one in which all individuals will be guaranteed opportunities to obtain social positions in accordance with their abilities and efforts." To Yi Ik, and to a growing body of other scholars, it was becoming evident that Chinese culture was not the only form of civilization and that, in many respects, it was inferior to what little they knew of Western culture.

Both *progress* and *modernity* were strange and ambiguous new terms and new concepts. They were neither welcomed nor well understood. For thousands of years, all through eastern Asia, China was the Middle Kingdom, the fountainhead of civility; and the world outside its sphere was inhabited by uncultivated barbarians. The way of life in which Asians lived was civilization itself. Their driving moral force, their social and political systems, and their aspirations were shaped and animated by Shamanism, Taoism, Confucianism, and Buddhism. These idea systems were distinct and competitive with one another. Yet they also were complementary, each having its own special emphasis and utility. Shamanism taught its believers to venerate and to feel close to nature. The same god-spirit that was in human beings was also in all forms of creation. How could it be otherwise, their *mudangs* (shamans) taught, since divine creation accounted for it all? Taoism, equally devoted to naturalism, taught that all of life is a unified flow and that individuals should seek to be a part of it, rather than seeking separately for their own individual satisfactions through individualistic assertiveness. Buddhism taught the great truth of *kharma,* that all one's faults and virtues, all good fortune and all that was bad, derived ultimately from one's own inward thoughts and outward conduct. Confucianism, meanwhile, provided a dependable and detailed guidance for all familial and social relationships, defining the individual's political rights and duties.

Underlying and supporting these belief systems was a general acceptance of the principle of mutualism, consisting of the *um* (*yin* in Chinese) and the *yang,* the opposites that were not antagonistic but complementary. Where there is life there is death, where there is wrong there is right, where there is failure there is success, where there is hatred there is love. Throughout life one accepts what is and looks beyond it to what will be. Also fully accepted in all the belief systems and codes of conduct was the guiding reverence for ancestors, which was the ultimate duty of individuals.

With the new and different Silhak emphasis upon practicality and attention to the realities of current conditions, a quite different movement commenced under the name of the School of Governing the Country and Saving the People. It was initiated, as a revolt against Chu Hsi Confucianism, by Yi Hyong-won (1622–1673). Yi Ik's writings, and the spread of the Silhak learning, gave great impetus to it. But it was another scholar, a rebellious and liberal-minded philosopher named Chong Yag-yong (1762–1836), who brought this movement into its full maturity of influence. Chong took the pen name of Tasan, by which he is remembered. Tasan lived much of his life in rural isolation, where his ideas gradually developed. One of his great achievements was in finding a way of reconciling the teachings of Confucianism with the Western religion, Catholic Christianity, which in the eighteenth and nineteenth centuries was finding its way into Korea.

As a mere youth, a twenty-three-year-old university student, Tasan wrote down his first rounded philosophical ideas. His ambitious aim was to reinterpret and reinvigorate Confucianism by demonstrating that there was no conflict between self-interest and social duties. Self and society are both best served, he wrote, when it is understood that the needs of both are so thoroughly intertwined that there is no conflict of interest between them.

Under the slogan "Self cultivation and good government," he developed the theme that man is not an isolated being but, rather, is consistently and essentially social. From birth he is subject to the relationship between parents and their offspring. He grows up as a member of a closely-knit family. As a citizen, he is bound by the normal ties beween ruler and subject. All through his life, the individual is restrained, guided, and deeply influenced by the relationship of husband and wife, of senior and junior, of teacher and student, of friend to friend, and of employee to employer. To conceive of the needs of an individual as something that is separate and distinct from his social needs and his social duties is unrealistic. To think that an individual's personal needs and his social duties are in different categories, and are basically antithetic, is a violation of reason. Practically speaking, there is no divergence between "self cultivation" and "mutuality." What is good for others, especially for the members of our own community and for those in our intimate circle, is good for us—and vice versa. The goal is well-developed individuals in a well-regulated society. Consequently, the old Confucian social regulations known as *ye* had to be reconsidered. Tasan accepted the five-fold relations (sovereign-subject, husband-wife, father–elder son, elder–younger siblings, and friend-to-friend) as self-evident. But he rejected the tradition that they were vertical and he redefined them horizontally. They were not hierarchical, he concluded, but reciprocal. Obligations and duties flowed both ways, each way equally important. Friends must trust and help one another; elder sons give as well as receive respect; husbands expect obedience from wives but also have the duty of caring for them, just as kings should rule only so long as they rule well. These were the convictions Tasan developed during his student years. This was his interpretation of the meaning of Confucianism. This was the Silhak way. The year in which he wrote them down was 1784.

Shortly thereafter his philosophy underwent a stormy reconsideration, after he was introduced to Catholic theology, which he studied and meditated about with the same devotion he had given to Confucianism. What he found in Christianity was a concentration upon self—upon the salvation of the individual, upon a one-to-one relationship between the individual and his Savior. For three decades, Tasan underwent a difficult intellectual struggle. Then he published a considerably revised version of his youthful manuscript, in which he sought to harmonize Confucian and Christian teachings. How he did so, and with what effects, belongs in chapter 2, depicting how "Old Korea" came into its first vital relationships with the West.

What was Korea like in its social pattern before the intrusion of the West? Its social and political circumstances may be variously interpreted, for they were both bad and good. For one thing, despite the homogeneity of their race and language, and their sharing of a long and proud history, the Koreans were also deeply divisive. The ruling and influential classes were beset by clan rivalries and factionalism. The leading yangban officials contended, often bitterly, with one another in their ambitious pursuit of wealth and power. Competitive clans were organized partly around family relationships (like the Pungyang Chos, the Yohung Mins, and the Andong Kims). Other factions were reflective of geographic separation, which was especially potent because of poor transportation and communication facilities, enhanced by ecological differences, such as the contrast between the mountainous and heavily forested north and the rice paddy flatlands of the south. Still other rivalries stemmed from the long history of discrimination that favored Seoul at the expense of Pyongyang, Kwangju, Taegu, Masan, and other cities.

The living standard was low and both the causes and the effects bore heavily upon the people. Both Buddhism and Confucianism prescribed elaborate ritualism that was costly and nonproductive, and the hierarchical rigidity that extended throughout the population was unjust and also inefficient. Diseases, especially cholera and malaria, were endemic. High infant and child mortality kept life expectancy low. Women were exploited, as they were in most of the world. Men who could afford to do so took concubines. Widowed or divorced wives became social outcasts. Some of them, in order to survive, became slaves, as did also the unfortunate debtors who were unable to pay their debts.

Agriculture was unscientific and arable lands were depleted. There were virtually no schools except a few for scholarly members of the upper and middle nobility and of the gradually expanding *hyanggyo* centers. Roads were virtually nonexistent, except for gravelled or clay city streets and narrow, unbridged paths between major communities. Taxation bore almost exclusively upon the poor. The corruption of officials and heavy, even random, exactions by landlords were additional burdens.

The deplorable condition of the peasantry in that time was much later highlighted in a cry of anguish by an early twentieth-century writer Yi In-jik, in his novel entitled *Tears of Blood.*[7] In basic respects, the society was in urgent need of being rectified and modernized. But this was far from the whole character of premodern Korea. The arts, especially ceramics and painting, reached new heights of aesthetic appeal. The many world-famous ceramic pieces, all anonymous, that have been preserved in museums include unrivalled celadon glazed wine bottles, drinking cups, food bowls, and vases. Painting also reached new heights, with typical Korean styles predominating over the Chinese models. One of the most celebrated is a portrait of Song Si-yol, whom King Chongjo praised as "the center of the scholarly world," painted by an unknown artist. Exquisite, idealistic portraits of women were painted by Yun To-so (1668–?), who flourished in the late seventeenth and early eighteenth centuries, and is honored as one of the best Choson dynasty painters. Landscapes and mountain scenes by Chong son (1676–1759), Sim Sa-jong (1707–1770), and Yi In-mun (1746–1825) are especially evocative of strong feelings in their combination of realism with elements of traditional symbolism. Sin Yun-bok, who was born in 1758, and died about 1820, specialized in painting multiple figures of Koreans in varied poses and activities that suggested "ten thousand feelings in the mind," each of which, as a contemporary critic averred, represented "the spirit as well as a figure." Under the pen names of Hyewon and Ippu, he originated four different forms of genre painting in which he has never been excelled.

The premodern society also had the virtues of primitive ruralism, including neighborliness, family responsibility and solidarity, mutual helpfulness, and widespread quality of acceptance that was undisturbed by unrealistic expectations. Conditions were to be accepted as they were, for they were as their ancestors had known them and as they probably always would be. Along with this resigned fatalism there was also a high degree of self-respect. Every individual had a recognized role and an individualized niche in the community. In sharp contrast with the court circles and provincial officialdom, throughout the general population personal competitiveness was minimized. Their concepts of proper understanding and behavior included emphasis upon individual responsibility, high endeavor, and belief that what is both natural and inevitable is also probably right. Such basic beliefs are well-imbedded in their proverbs, through which the true nature of the villagers is well revealed. Down-trodden and exploited as the peasants undoubtedly were, nevertheless these proverbs reveal they had an enriching understanding of what life is like and of what it can be for those who adhere to nature. A representative selection of these proverbs tells much of what

Old Korea was truly like. Each proverb is an epitome of rationalized shared experience:

Even the hedgehog thinks her young are smooth.

Pinch yourself and you will know the pain another feels when pinched.

The water downstream will not be clear if the water upstream is muddied.

Blame yourself, not the stream, if you fall in the water.

A virtuous character is needed even when driving a cow.

You cannot carry a stone up a mountain without getting red in the face.

Where there are no tigers, wild cats will be very self-important.

To make a mountain, you must carry every load of earth.

A finger prick will demand attention though worms may be eating the heart unknown.

What looked like blossoms on the dead tree turned out to be only the white mold of decay.

Give a peck and get a bushel.

Kick a stone in anger and you will hurt your own foot.

You can mend with a trowel today what it will take a spade to mend tomorrow.

If you love your own children, love also those of others.

You cannot eat the picture of a loaf of bread.

You cannot catch even one rabbit if you chase two at once.

You cannot sit in the valley and see the new moon set.

Do not try to cut water with a sword.

Don't kill a bullock for a feast when a hen would suffice.

A fellow who has ten faults sneers at another for having one.

Neither these proverbs, nor any other simple pen portrait, can show fully what the Koreans, in their premodern time, were really like. They were both admired by their nearest neighbors, the Chinese and the Japanese, and harassed by them. Either way, they were very definitely considered to be different: weaker, surely; superior, perhaps, at least in their arts and in some portions of their philosophy; in any event, not well understood, because of their stubborn isolationism. Stubborness, clannishness, and a persistent clinging to old ways and ancestral patterns seemed to be their hallmarks. As China was, however reluctantly, receiving some Westernized influences, and as Japan, through its treaty port of Nagasaki, was allowing some Western goods and ideas to trickle in, Korea remained tightly closed. It was still some two and three generations after its leading scholars began meditating about the significance of what little they learned of Western ways before the isolationism of the Hermit Kingdom was decisively punctured.

2

The Entry of Modernity into Korea

In the transformation of traditional Korea into modern Korea, Christian missionaries and the Silhak scholars combined to provide the energizing impetus. The reasons were only partially theological. The liberal-minded and pragmatic Silhak scholars found in Christianity much for which they were searching. To become Christian, in addition to religious conversion, usually meant accepting such values as egalitarianism, social and political reforms, humanitarianism, and efforts to improve the lot of the poor, and of women and children. All of these goals were part of what Silhak had been endeavoring for more than a century to accomplish. The Christian missionaries were welcomed by Silhak scholars as allies. And for these same reasons, the missionaries regarded the Silhak movement as preparatory for their evangelism.

It was through this kind of thinking that the missionary enterprise initially developed in China. The first Catholic evangelists, in order to make conversion all the more acceptable, wisely accommodated themselves as best they could to Chinese culture. The Jesuit priests who came to China in the early years of the seventeenth century sought to win converts by two indirect methods. For one, they learned the Chinese language, they adopted Chinese dress, and they conformed to the inclusive and intricate Confucian patterns of social etiquette. More importantly, they brought in, along with the Bible, a wide selection of Western scientific knowledge.

Father Matteo Ricci, the Portuguese priest who led the movement to Christianize northeastern Asia, won permission to build a church in Peking by teaching mathematics and geography, and by assisting the Chinese in the manufacture of guns. His epochal treatise on *The True Principles of Christianity* won interest because he also wrote books on Western science, including *An Outline of Arithmetic* and *An Original Text of Geometry.*

Treatises of this nature attracted the interest of Korean envoys during their annual tributary missions to China. They were especially impressed by European knowledge of astronomy, of mathematics, and of geography. The world, they came quickly to realize, was vastly bigger than they had ever known and, out beyond the oceans, vastly different. To a small but influential number of Korean yangban, the scholarly officials, it soon became increasingly evident that Chinese civilization was not, as they had been taught to believe, the only true culture. And they also began to believe that it was not in all respects the best.

It was in 1630 that Western modernity made its first significant impact upon Korea. In that year one of the envoys to Peking, Chong Tu-won, took with him, on his return home, an enlightening accumulation of books and Western artifacts. Among them was a book on astronomy. For many centuries astrology had been a central study by both Chinese and Koreans because of their belief that human life is much influenced by the stars. This book was different, for it was reenforced by considerable astronomical data that surpassed their own extensive knowledge. Envoy Chong also brought back the European calendar, a geography, an alarm clock, a telescope, two pistols, and a cannon. They were impressive evidence of a civilization well worth learning about. Fourteen years later, a more prestigious envoy, Prince Sohyon, returned to Seoul from Peking with a statue of the Virgin Mother and a collection of Christian books. As Korean scholars studied these books and maps drawn by Europeans, they readily accepted the evidence that the earth is round. And they had to question the traditional belief that China was the center of the world.

An important step in the modernization of Korea, however, might be dated as late as 1794—the year in which for the first time an ordained Catholic priest entered Korea. By that time there had been, at least in scholarly circles, a century and a half of increasing familiarity with some aspects of the Christian religion. As the eighteenth century drew toward its close, there were already implanted in areas adjacent to Seoul and in northeastern Korea several small but vigorously devout bodies of self-taught Christians. One was Yi Sung-hun, who, in the winter of 1783 went to Peking with the annual tribute mission, was converted, was baptized under the name of Pierre or Peter, to signify his role as the first foundation stone of the Korean Christian Church, and began after his return home to organize a Catholic hierarchy inside Korea. In 1790, these self-made Catholics were sternly ordered by the papacy to discontinue such unauthorized conduct. Peking's Bishop, Alexandre do Govea, informed them that the only rite they could perform was baptism. He also ordered that they abandon absolutely the most sacred duty that a Korean owed to his family, to the society, and to the state, that is, the reverence accorded to ancestors. This led to the martyrdom of two devoted converts, Paul Yun and James Kwon, who, on 18 December 1791 were executed for refusing to honor their ancestral tablets.

Then, in 1794 Bishop Govea dispatched to Korea a young Chinese priest, James Chu (Chu Mun-Mo), to minister to the Korean converts. Seven years later Chu was beheaded. A convert, Alexander Hwang (Hwang Sa-Yong), wrote a letter to the Peking Bishop urging that some sixty or seventy thousand European soldiers be sent to conquer Korea. This sensational letter, sewn into the garment of the messenger, was discovered by a government agent and, naturally, caused deep concern. The Korean king sent a letter to the Chinese Emperor protesting against the dispatch of Christian missionaries to Korea. He also unleashed, in 1801, a persecution designed to eradicate the heretical religion. At least three hundred converts were put to death, but enough survived by 1811 to implore the Bishop of Peking to send them help. By then, the Catholic Church was also suffering from persecution in China, and no help for Korea was available.

The Koreanization of this Western religious influence owed much to the scholar Tasan. Tasan held a central place, as the Great Renovator, in the early stages of the transformation of traditionalism into modernity. He was a meditative scholar, rather than an activist. In 1776, at the age of fifteen, and newly married, he came to Seoul to take up university studies, in the course of which he learned about Catholicism. Like all yangban his central interest was Confucianism, which he studied with enthusiasm. Among his fellow students was a man eight years older, the brother-in-law of Tasan's elder brother. This man, Yi Pyok, had just returned from the annual embassy to Peking. While there, he was converted and baptized, and he was filled with evangelistic zeal. During a boat ride on the Han River, Yi Pyok talked ardently with Tasan about the Catholic religion. Tasan listened intently and, as he afterward attested, "for the first time I was joyful and my mind became interested." Yi Pyok organized a series of meetings for the study of the Catholic faith. These meetings Tasan did not attend. Nevertheless, he kept closely in touch with the new ideas. During the 1801 persecutions of the Catholics, Tasan was among those considered sufficiently heretical to be banished from the capital. He took refuge in the small town of Kangjin, down on the southern coast. There he remained for eighteen years, developing his own philosophy. One problem that chiefly concerned him was how to interpret Christianity from the perspectives of Confucianism, Shamanism, and Buddhism, in a way that would make it intellectually comprehensible and acceptable to Koreans.

In 1818, at the age of fifty-seven, Tasan came out of his rural retreat and returned to his birthplace, the town of Yanggun, near Seoul. Despite periodically renewed outbreaks of persecution, he declared openly his interest in Catholicism. For yet another eighteen years until his death in 1836, he poured out a succession of books. In them he advocated a broad range of political reforms, one being the freedom to believe in and to practice and propagate Christianity.

The themes Tasan dealt with were central and vital in traditional Korean culture. He challenged and rejected the *Um-Yang* (Yin-Yang) dualistic view that all of life is governed by reciprocal and complementary aspects, maintaining a balanced overall pattern within which things that seem to be evil must be accepted as an integral part of man's destiny. He also denied that the four fundamental Confucian virtues—compassion, righteousness, propriety, and wisdom—are innate. On the contrary, he insisted, virtue consists of actions and general behavior that derive from right thinking and from socially helpful conduct. Moreover, he attacked the shamanistic belief that all living forms, including animals and plants, share a common divine spirit. Instead, he insisted, mankind is invested with a unique kind of spirit, which induces the pursuit of idealistic goals. He also rejected Buddhism because of its identification of individual minds with the whole universe (so that reincarnation may be animalistic as well as humanistic). Rather, he argued, man stands apart from nature, and relates to it much as a servant to his master. That is, man must not violate nature and must neither ignore nor deny its implacable laws. He must, instead, do as nature demands. But we are not a part of nature, for we differ from all the rest of it.

Actually, Tasan's philosophical views were so inclusive and so complex that Korea's scholars are still disputing about what he meant.[8] What is clear is that he centered his thinking around the relationships between Christianity and Neo-Confucianism. He sought to show that they both are intellectually acceptable and are compatible rather than antagonistic.

If he ever converted to Catholicism it was on his deathbed, where he did, as he lay dying, receive the last sacraments. Tasan did not accept the insistence of the Catholic Church that ancestor reverence must be disavowed. Far from it. Instead, throughout his life he remained devoted to ancestor reverence, considering it, in Confucian terms, to be the binding force in society.[9] His influence helped greatly to make Christianity—at that time, in northeastern Asia, meaning Catholicism—to be socially acceptable to the Korean populace, since, as he argued, it need not interfere with their basic duty and deepest sentiment of ancestor veneration. With such views, and because of the considerable influence he exerted, Tasan served as an important bridge from traditionalism to modernity.

Inevitably, the bridging comprised a curious melange of incompatible old and new ideas and feelings. Neither Western modernity nor its first manifestation, Christianity, could come to Korea disassociated from traditionalism. People always adopt new beliefs from the perspective of their past. The sincerity of Korea's early converts is amply proved by the thousands who accepted martyrdom rather than renounce their faith. It is equally true that the nature of their beliefs included some parts of Taoism, of Confucianism, and of recurrent worry about the *mudangs* (teachers and priests) of Shamanism. The nature of this transition is interpreted in the following verses:

Through the night an eerie cry
And hard sharp clang of bells;
At midnight evil spirits fly
And must be fought with spells.

Evil, evil are the forms
That flit through darkest night,
And honest folk need strongest charms
To check their evil flight.

A blind man is the safest guard
(No spiteful forms can charm his eye);
So all night long he walks as ward
To safeguard homes where sleepers lie.

Some say there are no evil sprites—
That Christian faith has closed that door.
By day we trust, but through the nights
'Tis wise to trust in ancient lore.

On Sunday morns the farmer sits
And listens to the pastor pray;
But just the same, when daylight flits,
He still must charm the ghosts away.

Salvation is no easy gift;
Old ways may aid the newer faiths.
Trust God; but still 'tis safest thrift,
Meanwhile, to exorcise cruel wraiths.

So through the nights an eerie cry
(The Bible rests upon the shelves);
At midnight evil spirits fly
(Believers cross themselves).

Some say there are no evil sprites
(But Christian faith may falter);
By day we'll trust, but through the nights
Let's fortify the altar.

As in every country, in all times, among the churchgoers were many who were unquestioningly and wholeheartedly devout. There also were some who only half believed but who felt the odds favored those who steadfastly proclaimed their faith. Sill others "went along" with family members, friends, and neighbors. Some church members were "rice Christians," more intent upon earthly than eternal benefits. Variations of dedication were commonplace in Korea among Shamanists, Taoists, Buddhists, and Confucianists long before (and after) the coming in of Christianity. Government officials were accustomed to half-hearted believers and did not worry about them.

During the latter seventeenth and early-to-mid-eighteenth centuries, the society underwent many changes that were unrelated to the incoming of Christianity. It was a period of rapid growth. The census, maintained chiefly for tax purposes, indicated a national population of 2,290,083 in 1657—and

5,018,644 in 1769. Some 600,000 of these were slaves, 190,000 of them owned by the government and 400,000 or more privately owned. During the century the number of slaves steadily declined, as increasing opportunities for employment enabled slaves to earn their freedom and to rise into the *yangmin,* or peasant class. King Chongjo initiated many social reforms, including the liberation of the slaves. Under his grandson, King Sunjo, who reigned for thirty-three years, some of these reforms were discarded. The highest nobility, alarmed by the reduction of their privileges, revived the old State Council, which had become influential during the Hideyoshi invasions, to reshape it into a new governing council, the *Pibyonsa,* which actually ran the government, presumably as a service to the king. This system of cabinet authority, in which the king was little more than chief among equals, continued until the termination of Korean independence in the first years of the twentieth century. The *Pibyonsa* discussed all matters of government, with all members having an equal voice. If their discussion did not result in a consensus, a decision was postponed. Such a system was democratic but it proved to be both cumbersome and inefficient. Some of its democratic influence spread into the countryside.

In 1802, while some liberal and reform-minded officials left over from the prior reign were still in office, the magistrate of the county of Yongigun reported to the provincial governor how he dealt with the imposition of a new land tax.

> Both "big" and "small" people were called together [he reported] . . . to discuss the matter. Thus it was decided that by equitable levying, each land unit will be burdened with six extra *tu* [buckets of rice. Taxes were paid in goods, mainly rice and cotton cloth, in lieu of cash]. By this method, those who have large land holdings will be taxed considerably more, whereas those with small holdings will have a small tax. . . . By this method we are going to distribute the tax burden equitably and free those who have been bound from their long bondage.

The magistrate ended his report by forecasting that while the change would be beneficial to the poor, it would be resented by the rich. Such anticipated complaints did not deter him from putting the plan into effect—for, after all, it had been approved in a public meeting attended by all the county landowners. This was village democracy at its height.

Unfortunately for Korea, it did not last for long. It was destroyed partly by a new influence coming from the seas, posing dangers that resulted in a strengthening of centralized authority. Alien ships began appearing off the coasts. Some of these were from Vladivostock; some from the China Sea. The first European ship to be recorded in Korean annals was a Dutch vessel that was wrecked off the coast of Cheju Island (which Westerners called Quelpart) in 1628. Three survivors from the vessel reached shore and were taken to Seoul. They were well-treated but were not allowed to leave. They helped the Korean army to improve its weapons, and they participated in its maneuvers. Two of them were killed in fighting against the Manchurians. The third, Jan Janse Weltevree, lived out his life in Seoul, taking the name Pak Yon.

Another Dutch coastal shipwreck occurred in 1653. Again several survivors, among them Hendrick Hamel, were detained. They also were well-treated, and they, too, were forbidden to leave. After fifteen years, some of them, including Hamel, escaped to Japan and eventually got back to Holland. There Hamel wrote a book, *An Account of the Shipwreck of a Dutch Vessel Off the Coast of Quelpart, Together with a Description of the Kingdom of Corea*. Published in 1668, this book provided for Europeans their first introduction to Korea. It was quickly translated into English, German, and French. However, its description of life in Korea was too sketchy to arouse much interest, and the book, in its several languages, had a small sale and was soon virtually forgotten.

Inside Korea matters were not going well. The corruption of the government had reached appalling depths. Local magistrates acquired their offices by bribing provincial governors, who also won their positions by bribery, nepotism, or membership in powerful clans. Confucian examinations for office had become a mockery. Taxation pressed heavily on the peasantry. It took two forms—land taxes, and special levies to get exemption from army service. Farmers, who typically had large families, had accordingly especially heavy expenses from both types of taxation. National land taxes were levied at the tolerable rate of ten percent of assessed value. But at both the provincial and local levels officials added special taxes, often for reasons of their own invention, which tripled or quadrupled the total—and which they pocketed for themselves. The government also collected rice at harvest time, presumably as a loan, to be repaid in the spring when seeds and fertilizer were needed. But corrupt officials often overcollected the rice, stored it badly, and charged the spoilage against the farmers.

The deprivation of the people, severe though it had become, had small effect on government policies. From the perspective of the court, so long as reasonable harmony was maintained, the ways of their ancestors, the structure of traditional Confucianism, was the only tenable—indeed, the only imaginable—social and political system. It served the nobility, and those of the lower classes must continue to bear what ills they could not avoid. Peasant revolts occurred but they had little effect.

A new time was fast approaching, however, when Western modernism could no longer be ignored. Ships off the coast were sighted with increasing frequency. In early 1832, one of them, a British ship commanded by Lord Amherst, approached the Chungchong coast; Amherst asked permission to negotiate a trade treaty. The request was summarily refused and Lord Amherst departed empty-handed. But fourteen years later another English ship not only sought the right to trade but, ominously, began to survey and to make charts of the Korean coast. In that same year, 1847, two French vessels beached on a sandbar off the coast of southwestern Korea. The Koreans supplied the crew with food and water and offered to supply a ship to take them back to China. A British ship, meanwhile, passed by and took the crew members aboard. From that time on, foreign vessels requesting or demanding the right to land became frequent. Always they were turned away by port officials, with the warning that Korea was not open to foreigners. Overland, however, across the Yalu River, Western goods were seeping in from China.

Such goods were pouring into China in large quantities and many varieties. Canton's docks served ships from Portugal, Sweden, Denmark, Spain, Holland, England, and the United States. Along with trade, Western nations were steadily undermining China's independence. In 1839 Great Britain declared war against China, partly to force it to receive British exports of opium. This war ended in 1842, with Hong Kong leased to Great Britain and with five major Chinese ports opened to Western trade. In 1856 the British and French combined in an attack on China that led to the capture of Tientsin and the occupation of Peking. The imperial court was forced into ignominious flight from the capital, with dismay at the spectacle of its helplessness spreading across Asia. More trade opportunities were exacted by the victorious powers. As added insult and injury, extraterritorial and economic controls were assumed by Europeans over China's major ports. China was required also to reopen its territory to evangelization by Christian missionaries. News of these disasters intensified the determination of the Korean court to do all in its power to keep the foreign devils out.

Another influence came from the northeast, although its effects were long delayed. Russia expanded its empire at Chinese expense by annexing the eastern area of Manchuria, which, across the Tumen River, bordered Korea. Russian ships from Vladivostock began to appear often along Korea's northeast coast. No significant contacts were made, chiefly because Russian interest in securing an icefree port opening into the Pacific Ocean was, at that time, directed to the Kurile Islands, north of Japan. Even so, in 1865 several groups of Russians crossed the Tumen River and attempted to secure the right to establish trading posts. But they were turned back.

In 1864 King Cholchong, the last of the isolationist kings, died, leaving no direct heir to the throne. The Dowager Queen exercised sufficient power in the State Council to override the long dominant Andong Kim clan and to secure the succession of a twelve-year old boy, Kojong. To rule during the boy's minority, Queen Cho named the king's father, Tae Wongun, to have all the powers, though not the title, of regent. The queen's intentions went widely amiss, for the Grand Prince exercised his authority not for the queen's party but for himself. The Taewongun, as he is known in history, proved to be one of the most able and determined politicians of the five hundred year span of the Choson dynasty. He was a man of Machiavellian cunning, a master of intrigue, and in general an able administrator. He was also firmly committed to the conviction that Korea's salvation from the maladies of alien intrusion and unequal treaties that were extinguishing the old order in China and Japan required a prompt and full return to traditional Confucianism. And that, he well understood, could be preserved only by strict isolationism. This policy proved costly to Korea.

Despite his sternness, the Taewongun was personally attractive. He was uncompromisingly forthright in advocating and in acting upon his basic convictions. He also had a "softer" side, as illustrated by his skill in orchid painting and in his tact and sensitivity, which enabled him to develop and to maintain a devoted following. His beliefs were not new, but were the underlying foundation that had long held the society together, namely, that the principles of Confucianism, as they were manifested not only in Korean politics but in the psychology of the people, must be maintained. He well recognized that the threat to them was external. And he was determined to defend them.

What he did not rightly understand was that change, not stability, had become the regnant reality. He failed to realize the dynamic discontent that was manifested both in the recurrent peasant revolts and in the interest the yangban intellectuals were taking in the new learning. Neither was he aware of the full strength of the Western insistence upon breaking down the barriers, a determination that was fired both by missionary zeal and by the expectation of advantages to be won from exploitation of trade with the vast and undeveloped markets of the Far East.

One of the Taewongun's initial policies was to destroy the influence of the many private academies and discussion centers that were spread throughout the country. In these sowon schools, the local yangban and the peasantry both crystallized and expressed their resentments. The Taewongun recognized these schools as breeding places for revolution. Instead of dealing with the complaints that came from them, his solution was to close them down. Concurrently, he sought to strengthen and to dramatize the power of the court by rebuilding the Kyongbok palace in Seoul, which had lain in ruins ever since the Hideyoshi invasion in 1592. This undertaking was enormously expensive and to pay for it he had to levy additional taxes. To secure the needed revenue, he enforced payments by the provincial and local yangban officials, which, in turn, required them to exact additional payments from the peasantry. As another measure to restore traditionalism, he prohibited the import of British textiles and of all other Western goods.

In a more immediate and drastic blow against Westernism, the Taewongun in 1866 ordered the elimination of Catholicism from Korea. This policy resulted in the martyrdom of some eight thousand Korean converts, along with the execution of nine of the twelve French priests who were conducting an evangelistic movement in north Korea. This slaughter led the French government to dispatch a flotilla of seven war vessels, along with six hundred troopers, to effect a month-long blockade of the mouth of the Han River.

The Korean military, from its base on Kangwha Island, attacked these ships, and a decisive battle ensued. The French quickly captured and occupied the principal fort on the island. But in this and subsequent battles some eighty of the French soldiers were wounded, with the result that the fleet departed. To the Taewongun this was a notable victory, strengthening his conviction that he could ward off incursions from the West.

Another naval incident, in a different spirit, and conducted in a wholly different manner, occurred while the persecution of the Christians was reaching a frenzied climax. In early 1866 an American merchant vessel, the *Surprise,* accidentally went aground on the northwest coast. The captain and the crew, with due propriety, surrendered to the local authorities. They were courteously treated, and taken promptly to the Yalu River border, where they were turned over to Chinese officials to be escorted to Peking. Before parting from them, the Korean escorts tendered them an honorific farewell party.

Another shipping misadventure later in 1866 was of a much more serious, indeed a disastrous, character. This was the shipwreck of a steamer called the *General Sherman* in the Taedong River and the killing of its entire crew by an angered Korean mob. It was a climactic event, leading to circumstances that made the continued isolation of the Hermit Kingdom impossible.

The *General Sherman* was an American-chartered vessel under lease to a British firm, Meadow and Company. While the ship was based in Tientsin, the company recruited a crew of ruffians, who talked loosely about tombs of solid gold in which the kings of the ancient Koguryo dynasty, in northern Korea, were buried. At the worst, these crew members claimed, in their barroom gossip, if no treasure should be found, at least the bones of the kings could be carried away and sold or held for ransom. The ship sailed from Chefoo for an unannounced port in Korea, presumably to seek for trade, in defiance of Korean regulations barring foreigners. The ship sailed up the Taedong River, headed toward Pyongyang, but was beached on a sand bar. At first the heavily armed and surly crew was treated kindly by the local residents. But when the crew captured an official, a fight broke out and the entire crew was killed. The *General Sherman* was burned and its anchor chains were hung as trophies on the gates of Pyongyang.

The incident quickly became a cause célèbre. The French, returning from the battles on Kangwha Island, informed the American Embassy in Peking that an American vessel had been destroyed in the Taedong River. Anson Burlingame, the American minister to China, asked the Chinese to ascertain whether the ship was the missing *General Sherman.* The Taewongun's government replied brusquely that it was a British, not an American, ship. Moreover, the response continued, any further unauthorized incursion would also be repelled. During the following two years, two American vessels, the *Wachusett* and the *Shenandoah,* were sent up the Taedong River to search for clues. Both returned with no information.

The commander of the *Wachusett,* Captain Robert W. Schufeldt, asked through the Chinese Foreign Office for an explanation of what had happened. The reply from the Korean court, as Schufeldt reported to the U.S. Department of State, "was so statesmanlike in its character and bore such intrinsic evidence of the truth of its statements that both Captain Freiger [who commanded the *Shenandoah*] and I were convinced that the attack upon the *General Sherman* was made by an unauthorized mob under strong provocation."

This report, however, did not end the matter. Under prodding both from American missionary groups and from the French government—both deeply angered by the massacre of the Korean Catholics—the Department of State, in 1871, sent a flotilla of five war vessels, under command of Admiral John Rodgers, who took with him the newly appointed American minister to China, Frederick F. Low, to seek redress from the Koreans. On 6 June, as these ships approached Kangwha Island, the Korean official in charge warned the Americans against committing an "aggression." Admiral Rodgers's response was to dispatch a launch to survey the offshore waters. When the Koreans fired at the launch, the American naval guns silenced the fort's cannon and American troops landed. In the ensuing fight three Americans were killed, while all the Korean defenders died at their posts. As recorded in *Foreign Relations of the U.S., 1871–1872,* Minister Low reported to the Secretary of State Hamilton Fish, that "the Koreans fought with desperation, rarely equalled and never excelled by any people." An American Lt. Commander, Winfield Scott Schley, who participated in the battle, wrote in his memoirs, *Forty-Five Years under the Flag,* that the Korean troops "died at their posts of duty, heroically and without fear. The men of no nation could have done more for home and country." After the Korean defenders were exterminated, the American vessels withdrew; and once again, the Taewongun was confirmed in his belief that the policy of isolationism could be maintained.

The heroic death of the Kangwha Island garrison troops compares with the stand of the Greeks at the pass of Thermopalae and of the Texans slain in the Alamo. But the fighting had little effect. Factors far removed from the battlefront determined the future. Against the inexorable intrusion from the West, Korean isolationism could not prevail. This was a lesson the Taewongun had to learn again and again.

In 1868 a different kind of invasion occurred. A British ship, *China,* was chartered in Shanghai by a Prussian adventurer, Ernest Oppert, who was half-merchant, half-pirate. Oppert resolved to land in Korea and to raid the tomb of the Taewongun's father, which was believed to contain an impressive quantity of gold and jewels. He obtained the help of Father Féron, a French priest who was eager to revenge the slaughter of the Korean Catholics. Accompanied by several Koreans whom Father Féron recruited to serve as guides and interpreters, Oppert set sail with a crew of well-armed Malays. When the crew reached the tomb, they found it to be by far too massive to be despoiled with their picks and shovels. Oppert then sailed to Kangwha Island, where he informed the residents that his attempt to rob the tomb was in retaliation for the persecution of the Catholics. His demand for trading rights was repulsed, and he sailed the *China* back to Shanghai. Twelve years later, Putnam's published his book, *A Forbidden Land: Voyages to the Corea,* through which he sought fame as a fearless explorer. Oppert scathingly denounced the isolationist policies of the Taewongun; but he neglected to ascribe them to the border violations by himself and other foreigners.

The persecution of the Catholics, and the execution of thousands of them, meant to the peoples of the West that Koreans were unqualifiedly barbaric. Only a few recognized it as a response of desperation that was born of mingled fear and despair. Not only the Taewongun but also the great majority of the Korean people, and especially the yangban scholar-officials, dreaded what was happening in China and feared the worst for their own country. Moreover, they disliked even more the wave of Westernization that was being accepted and accelerated by the Meiji Restoration in Japan. Most of them shared the views of the traditionalist Japanese scholar, Aizawa Seshisai, who, in his influential book, *Shinron,* published in 1825, warned against destruction of Asia's ancient civilization by Western barbarism. Aizawa argued that "when those barbarians plan to subdue a country not their own, they start by opening commerce [as the Dutch had done at Nagasaki] and watch for a sign of weakness. If an opportunity is presented, they will preach their alien religion to captivate the people's hearts." To Koreans, this warning was highly relevant.

In Korean culture, religious toleration was deeply imbedded. The Confucian, Shamanist, Buddhist, and Taoist faiths existed not only side by side nationally but also concurrently for individuals. Individual Koreans commonly practiced two or more of these ancient faiths at the same time. Dynastic preferences for either Buddhism or Confucianism had, historically, resulted in sweeping measures of repression of one or the other. But so far as individuals were concerned, these faiths were compatible. Christianity was different. Its adherents insisted that it was unique. To accept it meant to renounce all others. Most objectionably to Koreans, Christians were flatly and strongly commanded by their priests to renounce ancestor worship.

Pyun Yung t'ae, later to be an ambassador and Foreign Minister, whose book, *My Attitude Toward Ancestor Worship,* was published much later, in 1926, long after the isolationism of Korea had ended, was a devout Christian. Nevertheless, he defended ancestor reverence or worship, which he said ought properly to be called "ancestor-commemoration." Through all history in Asia, as he says, "filial love is the seed of every virtue." Feelingly, he explained why.

> The family seems to them all in all, the only refuge against every manner of attack from outside. . . . A kind of hero-worship is mixed with and at the same time strengthens the natural reverence and affection due to their parents. At length old age steals upon the senior members of the little group and one day death suddenly claims one of them. What a grief! What a fear about the future! The most valiant of the community lies there, pallid and dead! They cannot brook the thought of parting even with the dead body. They detain it in their home as long as it has any semblance of their brave father. Then they bury it away, very close to their home. At every meal they cannot escape the sense of painful vacancy at the table. The spoon, the chopsticks, the largest bowl, used by the deceased when living, are still there, but alas! the man is no more. Their uncontrollable grief overcomes them. One of them bursts into crying, quickly followed by the others, all throwing themselves on the floor. Grief finding thus free vent, they feel themselves a little soothed. With the return of calm, in their untutored hearts, they feel that the tie of affection between the deceased and themselves is not broken and the spirit of the deceased seems to be with them, there at the very table in deep sympathy with them, and even partaking of the meal in some invisible manner, characteristic of a ghost of spirit.

Pyun went on to examine the Christian renunciation of ancestor reverence and declared how a true Korean reacted to this prohibition: "I would rather go to Hell than get into Paradise by turning my back to my ancestors."

Some Americans, sympathetic with Korea, defended their efforts to hold the West at bay. One of them, Homer B. Hulbert, the most effective of all the American advisors who came to Korea in the 1880s, justified the Korean reactions in an article in the March 1905 issue of *the Korean Review* by citing a hypothetical incident. "A stranger comes into my yard and acts in a queer way. I order him off the place, but he proceeds to climb in at the window. I forcibly resist his entrance. This is an insult to him which he resents." In the United States Senate, in a debate concerning the American attack on Kangwha Island, Senator A. A. Sargent said, as reported in the *Congressional Record,* 45th Congress, 2nd Session: "We may not allow any foreign vessel of a nation with which we even might have a treaty to come and survey our James or any other river, but here was a people peculiarly sensitive to these things, dreading aggression on one side from Russia and on the other side from China, maintaining a rugged independence, isolated from all the world by policy which it thought necessary in order to maintain itself as a nation."

Despite such isolated demurrers, the general Western policy was to push on into Korea, regardless of its protests. The nature of this intrusion was guided largely by two factors. The first and most basic was the imperialistic policies of the Great Powers, fueled by both Christian evangelism and the competition for the anticipated bonanza of the as-yet-unexploited trade with Asia's vast population. Since the Korean peninsula was the central point in which the interests of China, Russia, and Japan converged, the question of how to deal with Korea was crucial. The future of Northeast Asia depended on it. And the second factor evolved naturally out of this first one. It was the conundrum, mysterious to Western international politics, of the nature of Korean-Chinese relations. The Western definition of the nation-state was vastly different from the way it was defined in the Chinese sphere of interest.

Both nationalism and internationalism had different meanings for Westerners and for Asians. In Asia, China was the "middle kingdom." China was the nurturing founder of their culture. It was the center of their artistic and religio-philosophical loyalties. In effect, China was the elder brother in the East Asian family of nations. For Korea this elder brother relationship had been formalized in the Treaty of 1637. As it was understood by both Chinese and Korean authorities, in all domestic matters Korea was essentially independent. But both legally and morally it was expected to respect the guidance of China, even in domestic and especially in external affairs. What this meant in practice was that both Korea and China considered their nations to be wholly separate and sovereign when this view suited the immediate circumstances. But when it was convenient for Korea to accord with Chinese guidance, or when China felt a need to assert its overlordship, Korea was at least partially dependent. This interpretation was more mysterious to Westerners than it ought to have been—for it was closely akin to the initial concept of the British Commonwealth. In any event, confusion prevailed as Western nations sought to deal with Korea's isolationism. To what extent, and in what ways, should they—indeed must they—deal with Korea through the government of China?

The relationship was seldom troublesome to either Korea or China, for their leaders understood it. The behavior of each nation toward the other was carefully regulated ritualistically, as was most conduct under the Confucian code. Periodically, Korean officials visited the Chinese court, bearing great quantities of gifts and bowing before the Celestial Throne, as was requisite. In return, the Chinese also gave to the Koreans gifts of similar value and reaffirmed promises of dependable friendship. In one sense this exchange was a form of international trade. But it was also a mandatory manifestation of their family relationship.

As the West penetrated more and more deeply into the East, the contrast between the two hemispheric cultures became urgently evident and sometimes troublesome. Even before any Korean met any Euro-American, attitudes and feelings of the one toward the other began to crystallize. Koreans shared the general Asian view that the intruding and uninvited newcomers were unbelievably crude. These strangers knew nothing of the rituals of courtesy. Their loud assertiveness violated Eastern standards of propriety. They made outrageous demands and enforced them with guns. They blustered and bullied, while insisting that they represented a higher morality, the only true religion, and genuine civilization. The Western incomers, meanwhile, found much in the East that was basically objectionable—including peonage, concubinage, and slavery; the binding of women's feet (in China); the subordination of females to males and of youth to age; the prevalence of nepotism, favoritism, and bribery; and an apparent unfeeling cruelty in the enforcement of conformity in behavior and in thought. Most of these evils existed also in the West where they were taken for granted—but seemed "barbarous" in the exotic East.

If, for such reasons, Korea, like China, found the prospect of relations with the West to be troublesome, unwelcome, and threatening, there were even sharper difficulties in the dealings between Koreans and Japanese. For centuries there had been hostility between the two countries, highlighted by repeated Japanese raids and invasions. When, after 1854, Japan hastened to modernize (that is, to Westernize) its culture, the Korean yangbans resented what they considered to be betrayal of Asia's ancient civilization. Most specifically, Koreans feared and resented Japanese ambitions, which were openly avowed, to occupy Korea; and afterwards, as Hideyoshi had intended, to use it as a corridor through which to push on into the continent. As Japan built its own strength and studied the modes of European imperialism, the rallying cry to "Conquer Korea" signalled a policy of expansion that was hotly debated among its own political leaders. In 1873, when it appeared that an invasion was about to be launched, the principal Japanese political leader, Okubo Toshimichi, managed to avert it—not because it was wrong, but because the circumstances were not such as to guarantee success. Okubo argued that "Even if the campaign makes a favorable start, it is unlikely that the gains will ever pay for the losses incurred. What will happen should the campaign drag on for months or years? . . . I consider such a venture entirely beyond comprehension, as it completely disregards the safety of the nation and ignores the interests of the people. It will be an incident occasioned by the whims of individuals, without serious evaluation of eventualities or implications. These are the reasons why I cannot accept the arguments for the undertaking of this venture." For opposing the conquest of Korea, though he did support the seizure of Formosa, Okubo was assassinated. It became clear both in Japan and in Korea that expansion onto the continent had become the centerpiece of Japanese policy.

For centuries there had been limited trade between Japan and Korea, recognizing their brotherhood (though not in the sense of younger-to-elder) within the family of nations. Japanese ships were not uncommon visitors to Korea. However, the only port they were allowed to enter was Pusan, on the southern tip of the peninsula. Japan's efforts from time to time to establish diplomatic relations with Korea, patterned on the European model of internationalism, were summarily rejected.

The Taewongun had monuments erected throughout the peninsula, bearing this inscription: "Not to fight back when invaded by Western barbarians is to invite further attacks, and selling out the country in peace negotiations is the greatest danger to be guarded against." For ten years, from 1863 to 1873, the Taewongun ruled Korea with no effective opposition. Nevertheless, he made mistakes that led to his downfall. His foreign policy of strict isolationism had general support. However, on domestic issues, the old Korean nemesis of factionalism intensified. He became increasingly unpopular among the general populace because of the increase in taxation required to rebuild the Kyongbok palace and other projects. He lost favor with the yangban class when he required them to pay the levy to free sons from military duty. The clans continued their rivalry. The merciless persecution of the Catholics disturbed the moral feelings of many, for it violated the deeply implanted religious tolerance that had prevailed for centuries.

His chief mistakes were in his dealings with people outside his own circle. He infuriated the yangban scholar-officials (who in general strongly agreed with his emphasis on traditionalism and on isolationism) by reducing their influence and lowering their status. Much more damaging to him was his misjudgment in selecting a wife for the boy-king Kojong. In order to displace the members of the Queen-mother's clan, the Chos, the Taewongun selected as the lad's bride an orphaned girl from the Min clan, feeling confident that without adult supporters she would be unable to develop a court entourage of her own. His estimate of Queen Min was woefully amiss. She proved to have self-will equal to his own. She promptly rallied a Min clan faction that became dominant in the court. As Choe Ching Young makes clear in his definitive study, *The Rule of the Taewongun,* it was the quick ascendance to power of Queen Min that principally forced the Taewongun to surrender the ruling power, in 1873, to King Kojong—who had reached the age of twenty-three—and to retire to private life on his estate at Kwangju.

Korea's strict isolationism was under heavy challenges even before the Taewongun was forced to relinquish power. Between 1869 and 1873, the Japanese sent three successive missions to Korea in efforts to open treaty negotiations. Each in turn was repulsed, but the pressures steadily became stronger. The most decisive blow against Korean isolationism occurred in 1871, outside the peninsula. In that year the Japanese maneuvered successfully—utilizing the Europeanized political philosophy and methodology that had strongly influenced both Japan and China—to pressure China into a Western-style treaty that broke off the traditional elder-younger brother relationship between China and Korea and replaced it with the Western view of sovereign equality. The principal effect of this treaty was that China henceforth had to accept the right of Japan to deal directly with Korea, without going through the foreign office in Peking. Korea thereby lost its strongest barrier against Japanese intrusive diplomacy.

In August 1874, the Tsungli Yamen, serving as the Chinese foreign office, persuaded Emperor T'ung-chih to send a memorial to King Kojong "advising" him to enter into treaty arrangements with Japan, France, and the United States. The memorial pointed out that Japan had in the preceding year seized control over both Formosa and the Ryūkyū Islands and that it well might pursue the "Conquer Korea" policy that had wide favor in Japan. In order to prevent such a disaster, Emperor T'ung-chih urged, Korea could best protect itself by entering into treaties with Japan and with the major Western nations on the basis of the Westernized concept of sovereign equality. The "advice" was strengthened by the implicit warning that China no longer felt an "elder brother" duty to protect Korea from outside interference.

While the Taewongun remained in power, the Japanese overtures were rejected with brusque finality. After his enforced retirement, the Japanese government determined to force its way into Korea by gunboat pressure, somewhat as the American Commodore Matthew Perry had done in Japan. King Kojong, strongly influenced by the Korean delegates whom he sent to the Chinese court, inclined toward accepting the necessity and perhaps even the value of adjusting his international policies to accord with the Euro-American system of the sovereign equality of nations.

Japan rapidly strengthened its ability to deal with Korea on its own terms. In 1875 it signed the Treaty of St. Petersburg with Russia, which confirmed that Russia would not interfere if a Japanese-Korean war should break out. In early 1876 it sent a mission to Peking that successfully urged China to renew its counsel to King Kojong to accept a treaty with Japan. As a coup de grace, Japan then dispatched a gunboat, the *Unyo,* into Korean waters at the mouth of the Han River, thereby drawing fire from Korean defenders. With this *Unyo* incident as a pretext, Japan then sent a formidable naval force to stand off the coast of Kangwha Island, while its commander, Lt. General Kuroda Kiyotata, demanded that the Koreans enter into treaty negotiations. Under the joint pressure of advice from China and this show of force by Japan, King Kojong realized that the policy of strict isolationism had to be abandoned.

The Kangwha Treaty was signed in February 1876. Its first article, asserting Korea's independence, formally renounced the younger brother relationship of Korea with China. Other articles gave Japanese citizens the right of free passage throughout Korea and granted to Japan various extraterritorial privileges—including trade without import or export duties and the right of Japanese citizens in Korea to be tried by the Japanese judiciary. Such terms were more overtly unequal than were the ones imposed by Western powers on Japan, which the Japanese were urgently trying to revise on the ground that they violated the principle of equal sovereignty.

The first Japanese diplomatic mission, together with soldiers to protect it, opened offices in Seoul in 1879. In that same year Korea sent its first diplomats to Japan. Their reports to King Kojong were replete with accounts of Japan's adoption of Western weaponry, the telegraph, the railroad, and many more devices and methods from the West. In 1880 Japan requested a new treaty with Korea that granted "most favored nation" trading rights to Japan

—necessitated, the Japanese explained, by their perception that Korean treaties with Western nations were inevitable and imminent. Against this demand, protests to King Kojong poured in from all parts of the country.

Part of this reaction was the rise and rapid spread of a new and strictly native religion that arose as a product of renewed emphasis upon Tonghak, or Eastern learning. It was also in part a reaction to Christianity, aiming to hold at bay this threat from the West.

The founder of this new religion, born in 1824, was the orphaned son of an impoverished yangban scholar and a peddler widow, named Ch'oe Che-u, but remembered by his honorific name Taesinsa, meaning Great Godly Teacher. Highly intelligent, handsome, and ardently ambitious, he was frustrated by the impossibility, because of his parentage, of becoming a yangban scholar-official. In his natal city, Kyongju, the capital of the ancient kingdom of Silla, he grew to maturity with a lust for learning and for finding some means of self-assertion. At the age of twenty, he burned the Confucian books he had been studying and set out on a ten-year span of wandering from place to place, meditating and seeking understanding. He became keenly aware of the Westernizing influences spreading in China and Japan and was deeply alarmed by the threat of Westernism as it was seeping into Korea. At the age of thirty he returned to Kyongju and for several months lived in caves, seeking through prayer and meditation to "heavenly revelation" that he was to serve as surrogate for the Lord of Heaven. For yet another five years, he probed through his thoughts and feelings in search for inspiration. Then, in 1860, sitting in a meditative fast in the Yongdam Pavilion in the outskirts of Kyongju, he experienced divine approval for founding a new religion, Tonghak, based on the insight that "Man and Heaven are the same." Hanulnim, the one God who presides over the universe, enters into individuals as *Chi-gi,* or the Ultimate Force. Man's nature, Taesinsa taught, is *si ch'onju,* which translates as "bearing God," or "serving God."

Taesinsa's teachings, gathered in two volumes, became the bible of Tonghak. The first, written in Chinese for scholars, was *Tonggyong taejon,* or Great Eastern Classic. The other, written in the hangul alphabet, for the edification of women, children, and the unlettered peasantry, was *Yongdam yusa,* or Bequeathed Songs from the Yongdam Pavilion. Based on the convictions of these gospels, Taesinsa constructed an effective evangelistic organization. He devised an ecclesiastical structure calling for appointment of *chopchu,* or teacher-administrators, in all major centers, to win adherents. So successful was the movement that the government, fearing identification of Hanulnim with the Catholic God, and alarmed by Tonghak's teaching of equality, had him arrested in 1863 and executed the following year.

Successive leaders of Tonghak further interpreted and extended these teachings. The term *so ch'onju* was altered to *in naech'on,* meaning "Man is God." Between man and God there is no dichotomy, no "fall into sin," therefore no need for a Savior or Redeemer. In his original nature man is pure, and it is his duty to maintain this purity of thought and conduct throughout life. This was a notable alteration of the Confucian concept of *chun-tzu,* "the superior man." For, whereas Confucius believed that superiority is learned through study and from conforming to the virtues of ancient sages, the Tonghak doctrine was that virtue is man's natural state. It is his identification with the will of God. Sin and evil are departures from one's God-nature. Somewhat Confucian is the further teaching, that good conduct is selfless rather than selfish. Self-seeking, or individualism, the pursuit of one's own will, rather than that of Hanulnim, is wicked.

Within three years the new faith was established so thoroughly in Kyongsang Province, of which Kyongju is the capital, that an official report declared, "One can hardly pass a day without hearing about the Tonghak doctrine. Even women of village stores and children of mountain passes recite it." Taesinsa also incorporated in his religion many of the mystic rites of Shamanism, along with strict military training. Adherents were taught to dread the influence of alien customs and practices and to pledge themselves to the patriotic duty of maintaining the integrity of Old Korea. As a contrary and equally urgent aspect of Tonghak, Taesinsa taught that women should have equal rights, that slaves should be emancipated, that everyone was to be treated equally, that corrupt officials and social injustice should be rooted out of the government, and that strict isolationism was Korea's only safeguard from debilitating foreign influence. To give great urgency to acceptance of his views, Taesinsa warned that the world would end in 1884, so that the renovation of individuals and of the kingdom must be accomplished immediately. Foreseeing his arrest and martyrdom, Taesinsa handed over leadership to one of his most able followers, Ch'oe Si-hyong (1827–98), who proved to be so good an evangelist and administrator that Tonghak continued its rapid spread throughout central and southern Korea.

Choe Si-hyong was a pragmatist and spelled out Taesinsa's generalizations in very specific terms. As he wrote:

> The truth begins in meeting the people. Practice the principles of respecting people and things. Do not strike a child in the house of believers. If a guest comes in your house, think that God has arrived. The peaceful harmony of husband and wife is the heart of our religion. If a wife is disobedient, bow to her with all earnestness. If one bows once, twice, and repeatedly, even the wife who has the hardest of hearts will be reconciled. Treat all men like God. Do not strike a child, for striking a child is striking God. Do not judge others. Judging others is judging God.

These teachings reflect New Testament morality in some respects. In others they are strictly Confucian. Many are Tonghak innovations. Evil is regarded as a disease and salvation means being saved from that disease. Tonghak is humanistic in the sense that it does not promise an afterlife; it stresses the goal of life as self-improvement or self-cultivation. What people call death is simply the process of exchanging from one life-form to another within the totality of the universe—a return to union with all reality—akin to the teachings of Hinduism and Shamanism.

So far as such teachings led only to humane individual behavior, the government found them to be tolerable. However, the emphasis on equality and upon the duty of treating everyone with fairness, along with its military training of members, were threats to the socio-political system. Hence, in 1898, Choe Si-hyong, like his chief and mentor, was executed as an underminer of the state. In 1905, in an effort to emphasize the uniqueness of this religion, its leader, Son Pyon-hui changed its name to Chondogyo—by which it is now generally known.

Meanwhile, during the final years of isolationism, governmental abuses continued, not only unrestrained but intensified.[10] Thus, in a sad state, and with grave misgivings about both its own traditions and the unknown influences from abroad that were threatening to squeeze in, premodern Korea approached its inevitable end. Its prospects were not, and could not, be good.

Modernity entered Korea not by Korean invitation. It entered rudely, and it was resisted so far as Korean strength permitted. Naturally, it also entered only partially. Modern ways were not imposed upon Korea by force as fully or as drastically as in China, for the Western powers did not sense that they had much to gain from dealings with the impoverished and (in their view) the backward peninsular people. Neither was modernity propelled into a surging advance by governmental policy, as it was in Japan. On the contrary, it came into Korea falteringly, pushed by outside forces that, except for China, Japan, and Russia—which had vital interests of their own to serve—were at most half-hearted. Some Koreans understood the values of Western ways, and reached longingly for them. But these were a small minority. The best they could do was limited not only by the deeply implanted traditionalism but also by the self-seeking diversionary strategies of China, Russia, and especially Japan. Old Korea entered into the twentieth century world with its death throes already under way.

3

Caught in the Tangle of Imperialism

When young Kojong took up his duties as king in 1873 at the age of twenty-three, he was without special education, experience, or guidance for the challenging circumstances that confronted the nation. He did have good intentions and a flexible mind. He was much influenced by his self-willed wife, Queen Min, who was determined to replace the Taewongun's appointees on the State Council and in other influential positions with her own Min clan followers. King Kojong was becoming aware that the further maintenance of Korea's strict isolationism was as undesirable as it was impractical. Considerable information had filtered into court circles about Westernization from China and Japan. Some scholarly yangbans were thinking about innovative changes that might benefit Korea. Two of them, Kim Ok-kyun and Pak Yong-hyo, who were among the top aristocrats in the court circle, induced King Kojong to establish a Machinery Bureau that would explore the question of whether the import of Western machinery would be beneficial or hurtful. But the truly pressing issues were how to deal with the policies and ambitions of Russia, China, and Japan. Queen Min and her clan followers dreaded the continental ambitions of Japan and encouraged Kojong's pro-Chinese sentiments.

In Japan the clamor to "Conquer Korea!" was increasing. In China, Emperor T'sung-chih accepted the views of Viceroy Li Hung-chang and Prince Kung, who presided over the *Tsungli Yamen,* that China should once more assert its elder brother role of guiding Korea's foreign policies. They were alarmed by the rapid eastward advance of Russia and by Japan's obvious interest in expanding onto the continent. Already Russia had pulled back from its far northeastern expansionism by selling Alaska to the United States (to prevent its falling to Great Britain) and was pushing toward the all-year warm water seaports of the strategic Korean peninsula.

In August 1874, Emperor T'sung-chih sent to King Kojong a secret memorandum in which he urged that Korea protect itself from Russia and Japan by entering into treaty relations with France and the United States. This question was postponed by the successful maneuvering by Japan to secure its own treaty with Korea. Meanwhile, Kojong was developing sympathetic interest in shifting China's elder brother role to the United States.

The King's favorable attitude toward America was initiated by a memorandum that was written by Huang Tsun-haein, Counsellor to the Chinese legation in Tokyo, and sent to Kojong by his minister in Japan. In it Huang argued that the United States was a uniquely benevolent nation. Because of its commitment to Christianity and its devotion to democracy, Huang declared, the United States was inclined to help weaker nations. Hence, an alliance with it would well serve Korea's interests. This appeal by Huang helped to pave the way for the United States—which was by far less active in Asia than were Great Britain, France, Russia, Spain, Portugal, The Netherlands, or Germany—to become the first Western nation to enter into treaty relations with the Hermit Kingdom.

The United States was ready by this date to expand its interests in Asia. One reason was the strong urging by the very influential Protestant church bodies for support in their determination to evangelize the "benighted" Asian peoples. Another reason was the eagerness of America's post–Civil War industrialists to secure entry into what they envisioned as a potentially enormous mass market. Secretary of State William Henry Seward, purchaser of Alaska, strongly favored the strengthening of America's role in Asia, and so did his successors. Even so, the intitiative to seek the treaty was due to the exertions of one man, whose official position was relatively minor. Yur-Bok Lee, in his *Diplomatic Relations between the United States and Korea,* correctly pointed out: the treaty "was made possible largely because of the ambition, conviction, personality, and importunities of a single individual." His name was Robert F. Shufeldt—a naval officer with a flair for diplomacy.

Shufeldt was ruggedly ambitious not only for himself but for his country. He was unquestioningly convinced that Americanism was so superior that it was an act of selfless charity to extend its influence to alien peoples. From his early youth, Shufeldt was self-confident, socially attractive, and accustomed to success. Born in New York in 1822, the son of a well-to-do lawyer of Dutch ancestry, Shufeldt hastened toward the responsibilities of maturity. He spent just one year in the Philadelphia Naval School before enlisting in the Navy. For two decades, his career was dutiful but undistinguished. When the American Civil War broke out, Abraham Lincoln appointed him Consul General to Havana. During the next two years, Shufeldt educated himself in the processes of diplomacy. Then he returned to his naval duties and was assigned captain of a vessel sent to determine the circumstances of the destruction of the *General Sherman* in Korea.

Four years later, in 1881, when James G. Blaine, a friend of Shufeldt's family, became Secretary of State, Shufeldt persuaded him that the time was opportune for negotiating a treaty to end Korea's stubborn isolationism. Blaine sent Shufeldt to Peking, as naval attache to the American legation, with encouragement to explore means of negotating a treaty with Korea. Shufeldt quickly observed that the main impediment was the supervisory role of China. With which government could the United States negotiate?

Just before Blaine left office, to be succeeded by Frederick Freylinghysen, he wrote again to Shufeldt, instructing him to approach the Korean king to discover whether Korea "is willing to open its ports to our commerce," and to assure the king that the United States did not propose either "to use force or to entreat such action." King Kojong, pleased with this approach, appointed two diplomats to meet with Shufeldt in Peking to inform him that Korea was ready to sign a treaty. The remaining obstacle, as Shufeldt saw it, was Korea's subordination to China. However, he and the Korean Ambassador to China, Shin Hon, proceeded to Inchon (then called Chemulpo) where Shin gave Shufeldt a letter from King Kojong that read in part: "The King of Korea acknowledges that Korea is a tributary of China; but in regard to both internal administration and foreign intercourse, it enjoys complete independence." On this basis, Shufeldt and Shin Hon signed the treaty on 22 May 1882, in effect opening Korea to the world.

Korean conservatives, the vast majority of the people, were outraged. Army troops attempted to revolt. To restore order the Taewongun was brought back from his rural retreat and restored to power as regent. When a mob attack broke out against the royal palace and the Japanese legation, the Taewongun sought to get rid of his old enemy the queen. Queen Min barely escaped with her life, fleeing in disguise as an elderly peasant woman. The personnel of the Japanese legation fought their way to Chemulpo harbor, where they took refuge on an English vessel.

Neither was the American response to the treaty favorable. The U.S. Senate took the unusually long time of a year before it finally ratified the treaty. The delay resulted in large part because of strongly adverse public reaction to the entry into California of large numbers of Chinese laborers, which gave rise to fear of "the Yellow Peril." President Arthur, in his Third Annual Message to the Congress in 1883, after the ratification, commented that since the Koreans (whom he called the Chosenese) "in reaching for a higher civilization, have confided in this Republic, we cannot regard with indifference any encroachment on their rights." This appeared to be a reaffirmation of Article I of the treaty, which declared that if either party should become subject to unjust or oppressive treatment by a third nation, "the other party to the treaty would use its good offices to bring about an amicable arrangement, thus showing their friendly feelings."

Meanwhile, American public and official opinions about Korea were largely shaped by the publication in 1882 of William Elliot Griffis's *Corea, The Hermit Nation.* Griffis, who never was in Korea, served as a teacher in Japan in 1870–74, and thereafter throughout his long life wrote books and gave lectures extolling "the Mikado's Empire." In his *Hermit Nation* he argued that Korea was too small and weak to be considered a separate entity and that its people would best be served by its becoming a protectorate of Japan. By 1911 the book had gone through nine printings and was a major influence in the formation of Euro-American attitudes about Korea.

Korean society, after the signing of the 1876 and 1882 treaties, was deeply distraught. Incoming foreigners, mostly Japanese, were violating the Koreans' cherished customs and outraging their sense of propriety. Everything that was sacred to them was threatened. There was no means of mass communication through which to educate and reassure the people concerning the new dispensations. There was no adequate police force with which to maintain civil order. There was much reason for anxiety, fear, and resentment. The British diplomat G. N. Curzon, observing the situation, reported that "the race hatred between Koreans and Japanese is the most striking phenomenon in contemporary Chosan [*sic*]. Civil and obliging in their own country, the Japanese developed in Korea a faculty for bullying and bluster that is the result partly of national vanity, partly of memories of the past. Their lower orders ill-treat the Koreans on every possible opportunity, and are cordially detested in return." The Chinese in Korea similarly felt a strong sense of political superiority. After the rioting that led to restoration of the Taewongun, the Chinese government sent four thousand troops into Korea. Japan, in response, sent in a military contingent of seven hundred Japanese soldiers. A Chinese official, Ma Chien-ch'ang, who was sent to Korea to investigate conditions, captured the Taewongun and sent him into exile in China. Kojong resumed the royal authority. Kim Ok-kyun returned to Korea from Japan (to which he had gone to study the Meiji Westernization reforms) where he was reassured by Count Inoue's assertion that "Our armament programmes are not solely for our own defense, but also aim to assist your country to achieve full independence [from China]."

Japan and China hastened to take advantage of Korea's weakness. Japan sent to Korea one of its ablest diplomats, Hanabusa Yoshimoto, who negotiated a new treaty that opened to Japanese trade the key ports of Inchon and Wonsan. Hanabusa also courted the progressive elements in Seoul and promised them every available aid in modernizing Korea. He arranged for his military attaché to be hired by the court to train Korean soldiers to use modern weaponry. Li Hung-chang seized the opportunity to restore China's supervisory role over Korea. He named a strong-willed Chinese economics expert, Ch'en Shu-t'ang, as "Commissioner" in Korea. Then he persuaded King Kojong to accept the services of a remarkable and very able German, Paul Georg von Moellendorff, who had come to China as Consul General in Tientsin and remained to serve as an employee of the Customs Bureau.

Moellendorff arrived in Seoul in December 1882, along with several European assistants—the first Europeans King Kojong and the court officials had even seen. Moellendorff's bearing was both assertive and dignified. His abilities were impressive. He was fluent in Chinese and at once set about attaining a mastery of the Korean language. He adopted the Korean traditional dress and took the Korean name of Mok In-dok. For both Korea and him the appointment was momentous. In his diary Moellendorff wrote: "I will assume the most powerful position in East Asia. . . . It is like a dream."

King Kojong gave him his complete trust and control not only over the customs office but also over foreign affairs.

Moellendorff launched at once into a program he designed to renovate the whole of Korean society. He moved to curtail sharply the power of the parasitic yangban officials who were selfishly exploiting the masses. He projected the importation of milk cows, the reforestation of the denuded mountainsides, and measures to restore the fertility of the fields. He mapped plans for the building of railways, the import and implementation of modern machinery, and the establishment of an active import-export trade. He recommended the use in schools and in general publication of the simple hangul alphabet. In order to pay for this broad program, he urged reduction in court expenses, sweeping reform of the tax system, the export of ginseng, and the sale to foreigners of licenses for mining and forestry enterprises.

For two stormy years, his accomplishments proliferated. He negotiated a trade agreement with Japan and he guided to a conclusion treaties with Great Britain, Germany, France, and Russia. He initiated a survey of Korea's natural resources, implanted glass-making and other Western industries, revived the minting of coins, and, for Korea's defense, established an arsenal. Then, worried by Japan's continental ambitions, he started looking about for dependable Western allies. The United States, he concluded (contrary to King Kojong's expectations), had too little substantial interest in Asia to be depended on should Korea need military help. Great Britain and Russia were the principal European rivals for trade and power in Northwest Asia; and Britain showed a positive bias toward Japan. Russia, already sated with recent expansions of its Asian territory, with a clear record of enmity toward both China and Japan, and with strong naval and military bases in nearby Vladivostock and Port Arthur, seemed to Moellendorff by far the most promising of potential allies. He found Russia all too receptive of his proffers of Korean friendship, because of its rising interest in the ice-free port of Wonsan and other ports along Korea's northeast coast. Moellendorff persuaded King Kojong to "reject China and ally Korea with Russia." Li Hung-chang was outraged by the betrayal of the man he had delegated to Korea and sent in more Chinese troops, which built one fort beside the king's palace and two more along the Han River.

Moellendorff attempted to accomplish too much too quickly, and with too little political support. The Queen Min faction, which was strongly entrenched, was generally favorable toward China, Moellendorff's original sponsor, and clung stubbornly to conservative traditions that Moellendorff's reforms were undermining. The pro-Japanese liberals, led by Kim Ok-kyun, favored many of Moellendorff's initiatives but resented both his pro-Russianism and the strength of his alien domination. This liberal group organized a coup to place themselves in power.

On 4 December 1884, at a dinner party hosted by co-conspirator Postmaster General Hong yong-sik, the coup members attacked leaders of the Min faction and persuaded King Kojong to accept the protection of the Japanese embassy guards. They issued a memorandum of fourteen reform proposals, including the restoration of the Taewongun, along with adoption of quasi-democratic political measures. Chinese troops, along with two Korean battalions, quickly suppressed the revolt and brought the king back under Chinese protections. Moellendorff, who was present at the banquet, courageously carried Prince Min, who was seriously wounded, to safety on his own back.

This Kapsin Coup attempt, as it is known, was relatively inconsequential in itself, but it marked a historically significant turning point in the international politics of Northeast Asia. Its chief effect was to weaken the Chinese position in Korea and to strengthen the "conquer Korea" partisans in Japan. China was being weakened by the war waged against it by France, in the summer of 1884, to eliminate Chinese control over Indochina. Japan's emerging policies were well summarized by the nation's leading progressive, Fukuzawa Yukichi, when he wrote in an 1878 essay entitled *Popular Discourse on State Rights* that: "It is true that international law and friendship treaties have high-sounding names, but they are only external and nominal forms. . . . A few cannons are worth more than a hundred volumes of international law. . . . There are only two ways in international relations: to destroy or to be destroyed."

This frank avowal of imperialism was far from being unique at that time and in that region of the world. Great Britain, on 14 April 1885, without consultation with or notification to the Korean government, seized and occupied Port Hamilton—actually a group of three islands only a few miles off the southern Korean coast—which it promptly commenced to fortify as "the Gibraltar of the Pacific," intending the islands to serve as a cork in the bottle of the narrow Korean-Japan Straits, to control Russia's passage from Vladivostock into the Pacific. Moellendorff held secret talks with Russia's diplomat, Alexis de Speyer, leading to a private promise by Russia to protect Korea from attack by any foreign nation, in return for the "loan" of Port Lazareff (Songchorman) to Russia for use as a winter base. Japan's Count Itō met with Viceroy Li Hung-chang in April 1885 and bluntly informed him that Japan needed to have Korean rice, and needed to insure that excess Japanese labor could find employment in Korea. China's claim of fraternal suzerainty over Korea, Count Itō went on, was merely historical, with no present relevance. Thereupon, China and Japan agreed in the Treaty of Tientsin that each nation would have equal right to send its troops into Korea when there was an apparent need for them. The German vice-consul in Seoul suggested to King Kojong that he request the great powers to agree jointly to protect the independence of Korea. This suggestion was brushed aside without real consideration. Moellendorff preferred, instead, to seek unilateral Russian aid. As a result of these increasingly complex pressures, and because of the intense dislike Moellendorff aroused among the nobles he had displaced, taxed, and humiliated, in December 1885 Moellendorff was abruptly dismissed and left Korea, feeling like a "jilted lover." His supervisory functions were largely turned over to Yuan Shih-k'ai, China's chief agent in Seoul.

How this came about, and its enormous influence in stemming the modernization processes in Korea were summarized on 28 October 18855 in a letter from Li Hung-chang to the Chinese Emperor.[11] Concerning King Kojong's turn away from China and toward Russia, Viceroy Li reported:

> I have exerted my best efforts in tackling this recalcitrant monarch, but I am painfully aware that my exertions toward keeping this vassal kingdom under control have not availed so far. Much more needs to be done in this direction if we are to preserve this country. . . . Sub-prefect Yuan Shih-k'ai abounds in knowledge and stratagems. He has cultivated intimate friendships with native officials in the Korean foreign office and court over the past few years. It is therefore assumed that he is the kind of person well-suited to maintaining the local Korean situation to our advantage. . . .

The way in which Korean isolationism ended was full justification for its prior policy of being a Hermit Kingdom. Inundated in the floodtide of European imperialism, the Koreans were by no means masters in their own house. The United States did not play the role of Good Samaritan that King Kojong had hoped it would. Individual Americans did indeed rush into Korea and sought to be as helpful as they could be. Notable among them was Horace Allen, whose two decades (1884–1905) "of missionary activity, economic enterprise, and political intrigue" are dramatically depicted in Fred Harvey Harrington's book, *God, Mammon and the Japanese.*

Allen came to Korea as a medical missionary and quickly seized an opportunity to start an English language school in the king's palace. He soon became a favorite and confidant of King Kojong and a foe of Moellendorff, whom he found to be more "antimissionary than the Koreans themselves." Allen helped open the doors for such missionary giants as Horace Underwood, who walked the streets of Seoul distributing Bible tracts and selling kerosene; Homer B. Hulbert, whose influence became almost as significant as that of Moellendorff and Allen; and James Gale, whose love affair with Korea helped inspire the enthusiasm of American missionary bodies. "The gospel and the dollar are the keys to Horace Allen's life and to American diplomacy in Chosen [*sic*]," Harrington made clear. Both impelled an interest that was intense but limited in scope. In 1888, despite Allen's influence, King Kojong issued a decree that "forbid severely" the teaching of Christianity in Seoul. It was neither enforced nor obeyed and shortly Korea became, as the Presbyterian Church proclaimed, "the banner mission field in the world." On the economic front, aggressive American entrepreneurs secured mining concessions, lighted Seoul's streets with electricity, and built in Seoul Asia's first street railway system. By 1900 Allen could properly boast that "all the considerable financial undertakings in Korea are our own." But he was never able to interest the Department of State to take Korea seriously. President McKinley and Theodore Roosevelt both carefully avoided getting entangled in the international contest over Korea. Allen feared that Russia might come to dominate Korea, or that Korean independence might be obliterated if war broke out in the area. He came to the conclusion that "Japan will undoubtedly get this country soon."

King Kojong, well aware of the danger, desperately asked Allen in the spring of 1887 why the United States was so indifferent to Korea. When Allen told him it was because Korea had no legation in Washington, Kojong instantly promised to establish one, telling Allen that "everything depends on . . . interesting America in this country." The king appointed Pak Chong-yang as envoy extraordinary and minister plenipotentiary to the United States, with Allen to accompany him as the legation's foreign secretary. Then China intervened. Yuan Shih-k'ai informed the king brusquely that his soldiers would prevent the mission from leaving. King Kojong appealed to the Chinese Emperor. Viceroy Li Hung-chang "graciously" granted permission, on condition that Pak upon arrival in Washington would allow the Chinese minister to introduce him at the Department of State, and that Pak never would discuss "any important or serious question" with U.S. officials without first consulting the Chinese minister, who would then go with him for the discussion.[12] These conditions the Koreans kept secret from the American officials and also from Horace Allen. When the mission arrived in Washington, Allen was shocked to discover that the Chinese fully controlled the mission and that Pak accepted this dominance. Allen angrily refused to agree to Pak's subordination to the Chinese minister and threatened to resign unless Pak presented his credentials as a representative of a fully independent country. This Pak reluctantly did and Allen congratulated himself for "having been chiefly if not wholly responsible for securing for the country the independence she had long striven for." But the State Department saw the matter differently. On 11 March 1905 Secretary of State John Hay wrote to Allen: "I cannot imagine why Korea keeps a legation here. It is positively of no use to them."

These developments spanned two decades, during which much happened. The erosion of Korean independence amid the tangle of imperialism was a plot with many threads. An important one was Russian interest in the peninsula. In 1895 Czar Nicholas II instructed his foreign service that "Russia absolutely needs a port free and open throughout the whole year. This port must be located on the mainland [the east coast of Korea] and certainly, connected with our possessions by a strip of land." This was a policy that persisted even after the Bolshevik Revolution in 1917, leading in 1945 to the disastrous division of Korea along the 38th parallel.

Meanwhile, in reaction to the pro-Japanese Kapsin coup attempt, anti-Japanese politicians stirred up sentiment against Japanese residents in

Korea. These actions were tacitly encouraged by Yuan Shih-k'ai, who had been described to King Kojong by Viceroy Li Hung-chang as "loyal and intelligent." Then Li added, "Whenever you have important matters of internal and foreign affairs, implement them by consultation with him." To Yuan, Li gave strict injunctions to do everything he could to draw Korea back under Chinese control. In pursuance of these instructions, Yuan refused to stand when having an audience with King Kojong, but had himself carried in a palanquin into the throne room, where he remained seated, to indicate his equality or superiority of status. To Viceroy Li, Yuan wrote that the king and his anti-Chinese advisers seemed "to follow my advice to my face, but defy it behind my back."

King Kojong, furious at the insulting behavior of Yuan, determined to withdraw Korea from Chinese supervisory guidance. As a first step, he dismissed his pro-Chinese Foreign Minister, replacing him with pro-Russian So Sang-u. In July 1886, Kojong sent secret emissaries to Karl Waeber, the Russian Minister in Seoul, to discuss measures for bringing Korea under Russian protection. Yuan learned of this from Prince Min Yong-ik, who shifted alliances whenever it seemed desirable. In August, as Kojong sought assurances of support from Russia, Yuan Shih-k'ai asked Viceroy Li for permission to dethrone Kojong, to replace him with another member of the royal family, and to recall the Taewongun as Regent. Viceroy Li cautioned Yuan against any actions that might lead to war or other disastrous consequences but told him to deal directly with King Kojong on the matter. Yuan confronted Kojong and demanded that he dismiss his pro-Russian officials and return to obedient subservience to China. Yuan told him that "Korea is like a sinking ship" and that the king and his subjects, as passengers, could be safe only by following directions of himself as the "good captain." He presented to the king a series of essays he had composed, in one of which he said that Korea was "the world's poorest country, incapable of autonomy without the protection of a big country," and concluded that Korea's only safety was to depend upon China "absolutely." On 31 October and twice again in the next two years, King Kojong formally requested the Tsungli Yamen to recall Yuan and replace him. But this the Chinese refused to do.

Horace Allen, dismayed by these circumstances, tried again and again to arouse the U.S. Department of State to support Korean independence. The net result was indicated in a response sent by Thomas F. Bayard, President Cleveland's Secretary of State, to the American mission in Seoul, calling Korea "a centre of conflicting and almost hostile intrigues involving the interests of China, Japan, Russia, and England," and concluding that "it is clearly the interest of the United States to hold aloof from all this and do nothing nor be drawn into anything which would look like taking sides with any of the contestants or entering the lists of intrigue for our own benefit."

By 1888 it had become clear to both Koreans and the leaders of contiguous countries that China was dominant in Korea and meant to remain so. As Sir Robert Hart, the British head of the Chinese Customs Service, wrote: "China *will not only* fight anybody rather than give up her suzerainty, *but will* be forced to absorb Korea if troublesome scheming goes on there."

Christianity was once more becoming an important influence in moving Korea toward modernity, as it had been in the early years of the century. French Catholic priests were again actively and successfully seeking converts. Now various Protestant denominations were also active, most notably Presbyterians and Methodists.

Ewha University, which has become the largest women's university in the world, was started in Seoul in the spring of 1886 by Mrs. Mary F. Scranton, a Methodist missionary, with just one student, the concubine of an official, who wished to learn English so that she could become interpreter for Queen Min. Two years later eighteen girls were enrolled. Mrs. Scranton's purpose was "to develop them in such ways as to make them model housewives under the conditions in which they must pass their lives and to make them missionaries of the Cross among their relatives and associates."

A more immediately influential school, Paejae Haktang, or Hall for the Rearing of Useful Men, was started after King Kojong told the Reverend H. G. Appenzeller "if you can get pupils and start a school you are at liberty to do so." By 1887 Paejae had sixty-seven students and a renaissance-style hall containing a chapel, four classrooms, a library, an office for the principal, and a basement for teaching shop work. To insure that the school was not only for aristocrats, jobs were provided for students with the proviso that "everybody paid tuition and nobody was given money unless he earned it." The government showed its favor by appointing the advanced students to official posts.

Horace Underwood started a Presbyterian orphanage for boys with the aim of converting it into a school—which later developed as Chosen Christian College, now Yonsei University. From the beginning this orphanage, and also the missionary schools, had difficulties. The Koreans greatly valued education, and many of them were eager to learn English. However, to them and their parents, education meant mastery of the Chinese classics, for which the missionaries substituted Christian tracts. Chemistry, physics, and mathematics were learned gladly; many were also interested in Western history and social studies. But for all these it was necessary to learn English, which took time. Moreover, Western learning comprised many terms and concepts for which there were no Korean words. It was hard for the Koreans to believe in the unselfishness of the missionaries and rumors spread that the orphans and students would be sent as slaves to America—and even that they were being fattened up for the American table. The idea that girls should be, or could be, educated was strange to them. As Mrs. Scranton recorded, to get students it was necessary to visit the homes and persuade the parents who, far from being grateful, felt they were conferring a favor by allowing their daughters to attend.

Missionary evangelism was forbidden by King Kojong, but this edict was not enforced when the work was inconspicuous. Horace Underwood described the practice, as his wife recorded in *Underwood of Korea:*

> As soon as we had secured a little knowledge of the language, we regularly went out into the lanes and byways, and, sitting down under some tree, near a frequented highway, or beside some medical spring, to which the people were in the habit of flocking, we would take out a book and start reading, and when several gathered around us to ask questions we would attempt to explain to them the book, its truth, and what it meant. . . . Later this street work developed further, and gatherings were held on large streets, or in villages, and, in certain sections, street chapels were opened.

Finding that the circulation of Christian tracts was effective, in 1888 the Methodists established at Paejae the Trilingual Press. This press, at first intended for publication of evangelical materials, quickly became a major educational resource.

These promising educational influences were, unfortunately, limited to individuals in the small areas around Seoul and Pyongyang. Out in the countryside, living conditions were bad and getting worse. Japanese fishermen dominated waters that Koreans, much less well equipped, had used. Japan had by treaty won the right to export for its own use a large portion of Korea's annual rice harvest. Japanese products, freely imported into Korea, caused a debilitating increase in inflation. Meanwhile, ruinous exactions by corrupt Korean officials were taking from the people what little they had left. Severe droughts in 1876–77 and again in 1888–89 tragically reduced rice production, especially in the agriculturally crucial southwest. In desperation, thousands of farmers turned to banditry, often led by ruined yangban landlords, displaced government officials, or slaves.

In 1892 a new dimension of resistance to authority commenced, led by the Tonghak religious adherents. As foreign imperialism pressed ever harder upon Korea, this sect greatly expanded in numbers, particularly in southeastern Korea. Adherents developed a well-disciplined organization, and were zealous in their faith. Since Tonghak membership included many rebellious protestors and bandits, the new governor of Chungchong province used this as an excuse to confiscate the property of Tonghaks. In April 1893, forty Tonghak leaders went to Seoul to protest against these stern measures. Concurrently posters appeared all through Seoul demanding the expulsion of foreigners and the suppression of Catholicism. Foreign residents locked themselves in their houses, and foreign warships converged on Inchon to protect their constituents. King Kojong rejected the Tonghak petition and the forty leaders left the capital. In response, thousands of protestors gathered around government offices in Cholla and Chungchong provinces.

By February 1894, the disturbances had evolved into open warfare. In Cholla, Tonghaks led by Chon Pong-jun broke into rice warehouses and distributed the rice to impoverished families. They also stormed armories and seized the weapons. The government blamed the Tonghak religion for the disorders and began to arrest its followers, destroying their homes and confiscating their lands. Chon Pong-jun sent mobilization instructions to Tonghak leaders throughout the south. Revolution spread across the central and southern regions. In a series of battles in May, government troops were defeated in several encounters and the city of Chonju was occupied by Tonghak troops. To end the uprising, King Kojong promised to dismiss corrupt officials and to redress the peoples' wrongs. Accepting this assurance, the Tonghaks dispersed.

This Tonghak rebellion had two important effects. For one, the promised reforms were, at least in part, brought into fruition. "Correction Offices" were set up in the fifty-three districts of Cholla province and they were staffed by Tonghak members under Chon Pong-jun's direction. The Tonghaks then presented the government with a formal demand for suppression of official corruption, the burning of slave registers, the abolition of traditional hierarchical distinctions, the right of widows to remarry, equitable distribution of farmlands, and the punishment of all who had collaborated with the Japanese.

The second crucial effect was the outbreak of war between China and Japan. Chinese naval and military forces converged in Inchon and Seoul in response to King Kojong's appeal for help. The Japanese responded by sending to Inchon a naval squadron loaded with 8,000 soldiers. Both countries ignored King Kojong's protest that they were no longer needed since the revolt had been crushed. Tension between the two forces became so great than Yuan Shih-k'ai fled from Seoul in disguise. Japan announced that its troops would remain "to renovate Korean home affairs." King Kojong refused a Japanese demand that Korea end trade relations with China. During the night of 23 July Japanese troops occupied Kyongbok palace, drove out Queen Min, and arrested King Kojong.

What the occupation of Seoul meant to its inhabitants was vividly portrayed by an eyewitness, Mrs. Underwood, in her *Fifteen Years among the Top-knots.*

> The natives, high and low, were in a state of panic. The nobility fled from their homes in large numbers and in all sorts of disguizes, and sought refuge at the foreign legations or in the country; and to the country the common people started *en masse*. Every shop was closed, the city had the look of a plague-infested place. A solemn procession of men, women, chairs, pack-ponies, a continuous throng, in dead silence, with rapid steps, and set, terror-stricken faces, poured through the main thoroughfares and out of the gates. Many pathetic little groups were to be seen: little children, whose parents in wild fear had deserted or lost them in the crowd, trotting along with tear-stained faces, alone; women with babies on

> their backs and babies hanging at their skirts; men carrying all their worldly goods on their shoulders; here and there coolies with the chair of some frightened rich man or fine lady, shoving aside the crowd. High and low, rich and poor, hurrying away from the dreaded Japanese, the ancient enemy of their nation."

Another missionary stationed in Pyongyang wrote that "the decaying bodies of men, horses and cattle were so numerous, that no matter what direction we went we came across them constantly, so that the atmosphere was foul beyond expression." Meanwhile, Mrs. Underwood, among those who remained in Seoul, wrote that after the tragic exodus, "everything was quiet and orderly, and the Japanese deserve great credit for the fine discipline of the army."

Their occupation policies were equally disciplined and orderly and also deeply purposeful: they took full control. The Taewongun was recalled to head a pro-Japanese puppet government. Meanwhile, the Japanese disarmed Korean troops and began to string telegraph wires between Pusan and Seoul for their military communications. Through the agency of the Taewongun, Japan secured the right to build railways and a telegraph system, to have all the Cholla coastal ports opened to their ships, to have all Chinese residents of Korea deported, and to have the Korean military materiel turned over to the Japanese army.

In protest against this Japanization of their country, the Tonghak forces were again assembled, under the leadership of Chon Pong-jun. These forces attacked Japanese supply bases and cut communication lines. The main Japanese force in Korea was engaged in battles that were driving the Chinese out of Korea; but a seasoned battalion of troops was sent south against the Tonghaks. A desperate battle in November that lasted for seven days resulted in a complete Tonghak defeat. Chon Pong-jun and other Tonghak leaders were arrested and executed. All through December and January ill-equipped and untrained but desperately patriotic Tonghak bands continued to fight as best they could. Meanwhile, the Japanese troops swept through the countryside killing all the Tonghaks they could find.

In a great battle at Pyongyang, the Japanese defeated the last major body of Chinese troops in the peninsula. Japan's warships also defeated the Chinese naval forces. After the Japanese troops occupied Lushun, or Port Arthur, on the Liaotung peninsula, China surrendered in what was for Asia a momentous event. For many centuries China had been the Central Kingdom, the motherland of the whole region. Even though China's weakness in its dealings with Western powers had become evident, as had Japan's growing strength, this abject defeat was still viewed as the tragic end of the honored traditional past. The Treaty of Shimonoseki, signed on 17 April 1895, marked the end of Asia's ancient order.

For Korea it was even more decisively the end of its chance to enter into modernity as an independent sovereignty. The most notable of its reformist leaders in that transitional period, Kim Ok-kyun, was assassinated in Shanghai by an anti-Japanese Korean patriot. For Japan, momentous though its defeat of China was, its victory was only partial. Its fruits were snatched away by a European diplomatic coup. Japan was prevented from "surrounding" Korea by retaining the Liaotung peninsula by a tripartite warning issued by Russia, France, and Germany. The Taewongun, architect of Korean isolationism and defender of its old style traditionalism, was, ironically, enacting a new role as the tool of Japanese domination over Korea. King Kojong once more took up his place on the throne, but the foundation on which that throne rested had been cut away.

What, for Korea, was left?

4
The End of the Beginning

What was next for Korea was already becoming dismally evident. The country was too weak to protect itself from the ambitions of its much stronger neighbors. The mass of the patriotic population had no way of exerting a strength of its own. World public opinion was either indifferent or derogatory to Korea. The major Western powers saw no advantage to be gained by supporting Korean independence. Korea was by very far less known to the outside world than were China and Japan. The rapid Westernization (in externals) of Japan, which was sponsored and systematically developed by its government, contrasted sharply with Korean efforts to ward off foreign influences. Nor was there such an inpouring of Western power and commerce into Korea as was taking place in China. The feeble beginning of self-reliant modernization was ending before it gained momentum. Prior to the collapse of the country's independence, a few heroic individuals made a final desperate effort to rally both the popular and the governmental strength needed to preserve a culture and a national identity that had a notable history of some four thousand years. But no adequate foundation was left upon which they could build.

One such effort, led by a remarkable character, Pak Yong-hyo (1861–1939), well illustrates the mixed influences and the futilities of the time. Born into an obscure yangban family, he was fortuitously raised to high status by being adopted as the spouse of the aged princess Yonghye when he was just twelve years old. She died only three months after their marriage, but this impulsive union gave him lifelong status as Prince Kumnung. It also brought him into association with such notables as Kim Ok-kyun and So Chae-p'il, along with opportunity to study in Japan. During his three-month stay there he became enamored with ideas of modernistic reforms. In 1884 he joined in the Kapsin coup attempt, and after its failure he fled to Japan. There he remained for ten years (except for a three-month stay in San Francisco), as an enthusiast for the Meiji Reforms. He also became convinced that Korea's salvation lay in Japanese guidance over the peninsula. With Japanese support, Pak briefly attained power in Kojong's court in the latter half of 1894, while the Japanese military was in control. For a time he was a loyal supporter of King Kojong and Queen Min, while he sought to reform the police, to institute a system of universal elementary education, to hasten an array of administrative reforms, and to gather virtually dictatorial power into his own hands. During the spring of 1895 he succeeded in renovating the cabinet system but in the process won the enmity of the Russians and of Queen Min. At the end of June Pak attempted to consolidate his power by installing his own troops into the palace and plotted to assassinate the queen. By this time he had lost his political base and was surrounded by officials resentful of his ambitious plans. During the night of 6 July these officials conferred with King Kojong and declared Pak a traitor, to be executed for treason. Getting timely word of this decision, Pak fled and escaped to Japan.

During and after these eventful months, Pak composed a series of essays supporting what are known as the Kabo Reforms, sponsored by Japan while it was ending China's supervisory role in Korea. Many of them were of an advanced liberal character. In defense of these reforms, Pak insisted that the purpose of government was to serve the genuine needs of the people. The best resource of government, he declared, was the energy and initiative of individuals, who should be accorded maximum freedom to develop their own capacities and full opportunity to serve the state. Unfortunately, his personal ambition got in his way.

Thousands of Japanese, in search for land, markets, natural resources, and power, were pouring into the peninsula. So outrageously were they exploiting the Koreans, and so vigorous was the resentment their actions were arousing, that the enlightened Japanese Count Kaoru Inoue—who had left his post as Foreign Affairs Minister to accept the even more crucial position as chief of Japan's diplomatic mission in Korea—protested that "unless they reform themselves, my protection will not be of any use to them." The need for such reform was urgent.

Hulbert, in *The Passing of Korea,* described an incident on a railway platform that was not atypical:

> An aged Korean, leaning upon a staff, mounted the platform and looked about him with interest. It is likely that he had never before seen a railway train. A half-naked Japanese employee of the line seized the old man by the beard and threw him heavily upon the station platform. The Korean arose with difficulty and picked up his cane to go. The Japanese then threw him backwards off the platform onto the rails, and then stood back and laughed, as did all the other Japanese. Apparently there was not a single Japanese in all that company who saw anything but a good joke. . . . However good may have been the plans of the highest men in Japan, they have not a sufficient body of agents who are broad-minded enough to carry out the plans in the spirit in which they are given.[13]

Court politics were predominantly pro-Japanese, even while the Koreans were roiling with increasingly bitter hatred of them. The Taewongun, during his three years in China, modified greatly his isolationist-traditionalist views and became favorably inclined toward a triple alliance of Korea, China, and Japan as a means of stemming Western nations' advance in northeast Asia.

He and Pak, returning to Seoul at about the same time, sought to work together. But they and their clan followers were too ambitious to allow them to cooperate. Each tried to strengthen his own position with the dominant Japanese. Inoue sought to weaken them both by restoring the queen's Min clan to favor. The Taewongun was angered both by this move and by Japanese favor to Pak. He found the courage to refuse, however futilely, the court's approval for the Japanese attack against the Chinese in Korea. This was not only his last show of independence but it also was very nearly the last gesture of independence by Korea's shattered government.[14]

The Japanese cabinet in Tokyo decided that even sterner methods were required to insure their effective control over Korea. Count Inoue was recalled to Japan. Before leaving he assured Queen Min, as he reported to the Diet, that "it was the true and sincere desire of the Emperor and government of Japan to place the independence of Korea on a firm basis, and in the meantime to strengthen the royal house of Korea."

Both these promises were the precise opposite of what Japan promptly proceeded to bring about. The militants who controlled the Tokyo cabinet were dismayed by the depth of Koreans' resentment of their penetration into the political and commercial affairs of the peninsula. They also decided that swift action would be wise to strengthen their control before Russia and perhaps other European governments took effective steps to block it. Accordingly, to replace the conciliatory Inoue, they sent as the new minister the blunt and brutal General Gorō Miura. What Inoue had not accomplished by finesse, Miura would seek to win by force. He wasted no time.

Miura entered upon his duties in early September 1895. He assessed the situation in Seoul with ruthless shrewdness. It was Queen Min who was the effective center of resistance to Japanese control over the Korean government. The Queen's bitterest enemy, the Taewongun, still had a considerable following among the diehard conservatives. Miura called the Taewongun to his legation office and together they plotted the Queen's assassination.

After several preliminary meetings Viscount Miura and the Taewongun met again on 3 October 1895 in the Japanese legation, together with Okamoto Ryunosuke, who was the Japanese advisor not only to the Korean Department of War but also to the Imperial Household, and with Fukasi Sugimura, First Secretary of the legation, to conclude the details of their plot. Miura presented to the Taewongun a document pledging that the ex-regent would not exert his own authority in the actual administration of the government but would insure for the Japanese full economic and political control over Korean affairs. This treasonable document the Taewongun signed.

On 8 October at three o'clock in the morning the queen's apartment was forcibly entered by Japanese police dressed as civilians, by Korean soldiers trained and directed by Japan, and by a dozen *sōshi,* or Japanese gangsters, whom Miura had recruited. Another group of *sōshi* stormed into King Kojong's apartment and held him prisoner. The queen was stabbed by Okamoto, whom she had personally selected to be her advisor on household matters. Three of Queen Min's women attendants were shown the queen's still-living body, and identified it. Then they were killed and their bodies, along with Queen Min, were dragged into the courtyard, doused with kerosene, and burned. The Taewongun hastened to form a cabinet of his adherents and to arrest officials who had been of the queen's party.

On 10 October the *Court Gazette* carried an official announcement that the queen had interfered so gravely in governmental affairs as to endanger the dynasty. It said that she had "disappeared," and that, because of her guilt, she was deposed as queen and degraded to the lowest civil rank. On 26 November, however, this decree was rescinded.

Despite this official silence, a Colonel Cockerill, a correspondent for the *New York Herald* who was in Seoul, attempted to cable the story to his paper. The Japanese operating the cable refused to transmit it. Wives of missionaries, who were Queen Min's friends, were writing to their homes about the murder. When the deed could no longer be kept secret, Count Miura denied complicity, blaming the murder on Koreans.

To quiet the clamor of protests from around the world, the Japanese convened a court of inquiry in Hiroshima in January, and on 20 January issued its findings. These confirmed all the facts concerning the assassination. Nevertheless, the court reached the conclusion that "notwithstanding these facts there is no convincing evidence that any of the accused actually committed the crime originally meditated by them." King Kojong thereupon ordered his Minister of Law to conduct an independent investigation. This resulted in the arrest of thirteen Koreans, and a somewhat more detailed depiction of the events on 3 October. But, with the Supreme Court of Korea under Japanese control, the conclusion issued was precisely the same as that announced by the Hiroshima inquiry.

The exoneration of those who killed Queen Min aroused a storm of anger that swept across Korea. There was a violent but brief uprising of rebellious forces that called themselves the *Uibyong,* or Righteous Army, taking the name of the unofficial popular armed groups that opposed the Hideyoshi invasions in 1592–99. With no organization, no training, and only meager arms, these groups soon dissolved into banditry. But they left a nucleus and a sense of purpose that was to revive again, more effectively, after Japan made Korea its protectorate.

During December and January, Seoul was virtually paralyzed with fear. Koreans stayed in their homes. Shops were closed. King Kojong huddled in his apartment, refusing to eat until the food was tasted in his presence. Three American missionary men volunteered to take turns staying overnight with the king to protect him from assassination. As a blow against Korea's traditional order, the cabinet issued a decree requiring all Korean men to cut off their top-knots, which were their distinctive marks of adulthood, citizenship, and special distinction as Koreans. Clearly the Japanese were in control of the government and no one could know what would happen next.

During the early morning hours of 11 February, another mob, instigated by a pro-Russian, Yi Pom-jin, assailed the palace. King Kojung and his attendants, disguised as women, fled for safety to the Russian legation. There, by prior arrangement, they were welcomed and assigned the best quarters. In May Kojong sent Queen Min's brother to Moscow to ask Czar Nicholas to establish a protectorate over Korea. This request the Czar ignored, well understanding the strength of Japan's position on the peninsula and that its interest in staying there was paramount. In a futile effort to regain lost dignity, Kojong proclaimed himself Emperor of Taehan, the honorific name for Korea, hoping that this assertion of equality with the Emperors of China and Japan would favorably affect the policies of Western powers.

Of course it did not. The change of title had no visible effect. Far from enhancing Korea's international status, the futility of the linguistic juggling only exposed more clearly the nation's weakness. Lord Curzon, noted for his judicious judgment of Asian affairs, summed up his estimate of Korea's circumstances in his book *Problems of the Far East:* "The spectacle of a country boasting a separate, if not an independent national existence for centuries and yet devoid of all external symptoms of strength; inhabited by a people of physical vigor but moral inertness; well-endowed with resources, yet crippled by want of funds—such a spectacle is one to which I know no counterpart even in Asia, the continent of contrasts." There was, nevertheless, a foundation of strength in Korea's culture and in the character of the people that could not be denied, obscured though it was by the events of the decade.[15]

Weakness and strength are always intermingled in individuals and in nations. At this time in Korea it was weakness that prevailed, for there was a lack of leadership to rally the people. There was neither a clear-cut governmental policy line nor a widely-held body of political convictions from which the people could take direction.

For twenty years a small number of very active missionaries, and Western diplomats, businessmen, and teachers had intermingled with a larger number of Korean progressives and intellectuals. Nevertheless, the Koreans and the Westerners, beyond a very few in each group, did not know one another. Nor, sparing the few exceptions, did they want to. It was in the capital city of Seoul that the aliens and their influence were most visible. Yet as late as 1896 the Minister of Education, Sin Kison, wrote as guidance for the nation's school teachers a stern warning against accepting, let alone promulgating, ideas from Europe and America. "Europe and America," he pointed out, "are far removed from China, the center of civilization. It would not be too far from the truth to think of Europeans and Americans as more like animals than human beings. Their languages resemble the chirpings of birds more than human languages, so that one finds it hard to understand them. Their religion, called Christianity, is a paganism so full of vulgarities, fallacies, and superstitions that it is not worth our attention." For writing so foolish a book, Minister Sin was forced to relinquish his position and retire from public life.

The Westerners' view of Korea and its people, however, was equally disparaging and equally wrong. Captain Bostwick, commanding the U.S. warship *Palos,* with his sailor's-eye view of Koreans, expressed in rollicking verse his reaction to this

> . . . singular country far over the seas,
> Which is known to the world as Korea,
> Where there's nothing to charm and nothing to please,
> And of cleanliness not an idea.

The book in which many Western readers found their first introduction to Korea was *Korea and Her Neighbors,* by a very respected travel writer, Isabella Bird Bishop, published in London in 1898. She had written several travel books that were sufficiently authentic to win her honorary membership in both the Royal Scottish Geographical Society and the Oriental Society of Peking. Endorsing her book in its preface, Sir Walter C. Hillier, the British Consul General in Seoul, assured readers that "those who like myself, have known Korea from its first opening to foreign intercourse, will thoroughly appreciate the closeness of Mrs. Bishop's observation, the accuracy of her facts, and the correctness of her inferences." Her conclusions were not hastily formed but were the fruit of "long and intimate study," during four separate trips throughout Korea between January 1894 and March 1897. Hillier's own judgment about Korea was that "a condition of tutelage, in some form or another, is now absolutely necessary to her existence as a nation." With this, Mrs. Bishop agreed.

Her first impressions of Korea were mixed. She entered the peninsula through the southern port of Pusan—"A miserable place," similar, as she later found, to "the general run of Korean towns." When she arrived in Seoul, however, even though it was in the depths of winter cold, her reaction was much more favorable. She judged that its location, between North and South Mountains, was the most attractive setting of all the world's capitals. She admired the appearance of the typical Korean—"resembling neither the Chinese nor the Japanese, he is much better looking than either, and his physique is far finer than that of the latter." She also learned, in her more than three years of traversing the peninsula, that the climate was "as nearly perfect as it could be," neither too hot in the summer nor too cold in the winter, with nine months of clear blue skies and pleasantly crisp temperatures.

She was surprised to find that Seoul, the capital of the nation, had no buildings with even a second story. Aside from its palaces and shrines, most other structures were small huts, with only one or no windows, and with walls of clay plastered on willow or bamboo frames, under thatched roofs. These houses had no running water and no toilet. Sewage was disposed of (as had been true also in Europe a century or so earlier) by dumping it in shallow trenches that ran along the streets, washed only by the rains. The air was polluted by human excresence, causing the worst stench, Mrs. Bishop reported, that she ever had encountered except in Peking.

Cooking was done in a dirt-floored hut attached to the main room of the house where the men entertained their male friends, and where the family slept on the floor. The floor was covered with oiled paper above flues that warmed the floor while it carried the smoke and heat from the kitchen fire. In the rainy season (which fortunately came in the spring and summer while the rice was growing in paddies) the women washed the family clothing by pounding it on stones in the ditches—and during the rest of the year in streams. Womens' work was interminable, from early morning until late at night. Men dressed in white garb; and to launder it the women ripped the garments apart to insure thorough cleansing, and after each wash had to sew them together again. Heat for cooking and for winter warmth came from small braziers, which required the gathering by women and children of small twigs, leaves, and branches, which they searched out from surrounding hills.

The role of women in the society was a curious mixture. Within the home, women exercised authority in all matters domestic, even over their husbands and sons. A wife was known as "the inside master," just as her husband was "the outside master." The family finances were managed by the women and, however meager these resources might be, the women were expected to stretch them to meet the family's basic needs. Young girls typically lived happily, but they were married very young and without a choice of their own. Generally they did not even see the groom's face until after the wedding. Then they were taken to the home of the groom, where they came under the stern and normally harsh governance of his mother. Slavery, by then nearly extinct, was restricted to females, except for a few males who had to sell themselves to pay their debts. A slave girl would be married by her master to a free male, who would be paid for his subsequent services with food, clothing, and a place in which to live. Daughters born of a slave mother were retained in slavery, but sons were granted their freedom.

The streets in the daytime were crowded with small Mongolian ponies and oxen loaded with huge bundles of straw, along with carts often pulled by hand. Men strolled the streets aimlessly or on errands, with many squatting by the roadsides to play the Korean chess game, *go,* or to chat. Other men carried on their backs, in wooden frames called *chiqes,* loads weighing as much as two hundred pounds. Women were not allowed outside their homes except after dark, when men were forbidden to traverse the streets. To guard against occasional encounters the women wore shawls to cover their faces. Children rollicked in the streets or open fields, playing their many games with home-built toys, or flew kites, and young girls excelled in swinging on very high swings and in throwing one another into the air on teeter-totters. On street corners there often were story-tellers, groups of singers, fortune-tellers, or acrobats, surrounded by crowds of men and children. But Mrs. Bishop failed to note most of the fun and games. Seoul, she reported, "lacks every charm possessed by other cities. It has no ruins, no libraries, no literature, and lastly an indifference to religion that is without parallel." This was her first impression.

But like Horace Allen, the Underwoods, and other missionaries, she learned to love Seoul's easy relaxation and social friendliness. "I had known it for a year," she confessed, "before I appreciated it, or fully realized that it is entitled to be regarded as one of the great capitals of the world, with its supposed population of a quarter of a million, and that few capitals are more beautifully situated." Still later, she wrote that, "I must add that no city has environs so safe, and that ladies without a European escort can ride, as I have done, in every direction outside the walls without meeting with the slightest annoyance." She also learned that the hamlets out in the country were generally beautifully situated, surrounded by groves, often beside streams that purled down from mountainsides, making their presence known to approaching travellers by the sounds of happy laughter of children.

She often was received in private audiences by the royal family, which she liked and admired.

> The king is short and sallow, certainly a plain man, wearing a trim mustache and a tuft on his chin. He is nervous and twiches his hands, but his pose and manner are not without dignity. His face is pleasing and his kindliness of nature is well-known. In conversation, the queen prompted him a good deal. The crown prince is fat and flabby, and though unfortunately very near-sighted, etiquette forbids him to wear spectacles. . . . During much of the audience, mother and son sat with clasped hands.

What travellers can see, mostly superficialities, Mrs. Bishop saw and reported without reserve or prejudice. She portrayed the country as she saw it, especially the flaws and weaknesses that would be particularly noticed by a cultivated European woman, while Korea was resisting the incoming of Westerners and their ways. Her judgments in general were reasonably sound. "With a splendid climate, an abundant, but not superabundant rainfall, a fertile soil, a measure of freedom from civil war and robber bands," she wrote, "the Koreans ought to be a happy and fairly prosperous people." But she was also keenly aware of their problems.

The chief problem, she concluded, was the deep-seated corruption in their government.

> Every man in Korea knows that poverty is his best security, and that anything he possesses beyond that which provides himself and his family with food and cloth-

ing is certain to be taken from him by voracious and corrupt officials. . . . To such an extent are these demands carried, that in northern Korea, where the winters are fairly severe, the peasants, when the harvest has left them with a few thousand *cash,* put them in a hole in the ground, and pour water into it, the frozen mass which results then being earthed over, when it is fairly safe both from officials and thieves.

To this somber picture should be added the affirmation by the equally well-informed Arthur Judson Brown, in his *Mastery of the Far East,* that "Hunger does not go hand in hand with poverty as it does in China and India. The food is coarse, but such as it is there is enough." Brown went on:

The major vices, while common, are not so conspicuous as in many other countries. Gambling exists, but it is not a distinctive vice as in Siam and China. There is a good deal of immorality, particularly among the yangbans, who usually keep as many concubines and dancing-girls as they can afford. But before the Japanese occupation, outward signs of impurity were not nearly so much in evidence as in other Asiatic countries. Saloons are not numerous, save in the capital and the treaty ports, where they are largely patronized by foreigners. I saw very few intoxicated Koreans anywhere.

These foreign views of Korea were generally accurate, as far as they went. Without knowing the language, foreign visitors knew nothing of the literature, or the philosophy, and had little understanding of the customs. They were unaware of the printing of many books, including such new novels as Ho Kyun's *Tale of Hong Kil-tong,* Kim Man-jung's *Dream of Cloud Nine,* Pak Chi-won's *Tale of the Yangban* and *Tale of Hosaeng,* and the anonymous *Tale of Chunhyang*. If they had read these books, they would have learned that modernity of a wholly domestic character was slowly developing, led by the intellectuals. The novels depict individuals entangled in old-style problems, but confronting them with a keen awareness of social injustice, with humanitarian feelings, and with an urgent insistence upon civil and human rights. The writing of novels was a new development in Korea and, as in other countries, the novelists sought to portray social problems and to suggest solutions for them. But the solutions seldom went beyond being loyal, being filial, and trying harder. New ideas were only slowly taking concrete form.

The circumstances were not propitious for any organized reform movement, whether a popular uprising or a reversal of policies by the government. There was too much disorder within the country, too much pressure from outside interests, and too much entrenched inefficiency in the deeply corrupted bureaucracy. At the top the government was hopelessly split, with the followers of the murdered Queen Min and the traditionalist conservatives contending not only with one another but with the progressives, who, on their part, were divided into pro- and anti-Japanese and pro- and anti-Russian sympathizers. The general populace remained stubbornly traditionalist in their customs and beliefs. The people were rebellious against the corruption and injustice of the social and political systems but were aware of no better remedy than a cleansing and rehabilitating of the Confucian order.

King Kojong clung wistfully to his faith in Americans even while pursuing the pragmatic course of accepting Russian protection and guidance. Not a great man, he tried his best to be a good ruler. Somewhat mistily, he felt convinced that the welfare of Korea lay with adoption of Western modern ways and, bedevilled as he was by clannish cliquism and limitation of both his power and his resources, he did what he could to move the society in that direction. In the spring of 1897, he took the bold step of announcing plans for a national modern educational system and established in Seoul a teacher-training program to implement it. He also sought to restructure the cabinet and attain other reforms that would build public support.

An important factor, if not actually the key factor, in impelling the king to play an active reformist role was the founding of the Independence Club in the wake of Japan's defeat of China. The leaders in this movement were a remarkable group of men who believed that individual efforts can have a vital effect in shaping the destiny of the nation and who were strongly impelled to risk everything to make their influence effective. In the long view, what they accomplished did not even long delay the subjugation of Korea by Japan. Nevertheless, they implanted ideas of democracy and a belief in Korea's basic greatness that helped to keep the spirit of independence alive through a full generation of colonial exploitation.

The pioneer in this group was not even a Korean, but an American who was deeply and lastingly committed to selfless service and a love for Korea that persisted through his long life of eighty-six years. Homer Bezaleel Hulbert came from a New England family that on both sides was devoted to religion, education, and a sense of public duty. His father was a Congregational minister and president of Middlebury College. His mother was a descendent of the founder of Dartmouth College and the daughter of missionaries to India. Homer graduated from Dartmouth and spent two more years of study in the Union Theological Seminary. He was eager for service in the outer world, and when King Kojong sought for three Americans to teach English in the new royal palace school, young Hulbert eagerly seized the opportunity. He arrived in Seoul on 4 July 1886 and spent the next five years trying to teach the virtually unteachable sons of high nobles in the court. Despite this disappointing failure, Hulburt identified himself more closely with the Koreans than with the handful of Protestant and Catholic missionaries who were in the capital.

His zeal and his energy were remarkable. Within three years he not only mastered the Korean language but formed the solid conviction that restoring Korean society to its past glories could come not from a futile effort to reform the court bureaucracy but only from an enlightened and educated population. He set about writing, in the hangul phonetic alphabet (at a time when the scholars scorned any education except in the Chinese ideograms and classics), of an eclectic book grandly entitled *Saumin P'ilchi,* or *Knowledge Necessary for All,* in which he described world geography, world history, and the economic, social, and political systems of the West, along with its literature, art, and a smattering of science. He realized that the educational program he hoped for required a series of textbooks, and he was determined that they should be in the popularly available hangul script. At the end of December 1891, discouraged by the indolence and disinterest of his students, he resigned from the palace school and with his young wife, whom he had met at the Union Theological Seminary, he moved to Zanesville, Ohio, where he took a job in the Academy. Two years later, when he was offered the editorship of the Paejae Trilingual Press, he happily accepted and returned to Seoul in September 1893.

For the next four years he poured out articles and books—in *The Korean Repository,* which he edited, and in publications of the Trilingual Press. In the spring of 1897, as a start toward his projected national school system, King Kojong appointed Hulbert to convert the palace school into a teachers training school. Hulbert ardently pursued his own educational dream by also associating himself closely with the Paejae Middle School and by writing and publishing in swift succession the textbooks that were needed. He also engaged in research and in the writing of his two most enduring works, *The History of Korea* (in two volumes), and a voluminous account of Russian and Japanese peninsular intrigues under the title *The Passing of Korea.*

Another significant contribution was his sponsorship of the return to Korea in 1896 of Philip Jaisohn, to take the post as adviser to the Privy Council and to the king, who was living in the protection of the Russian Embassy. For the next several years Hulbert's endeavors, like those of Jaisohn and other leaders of the Independence Club, were devoted to trying to avert the fall of Korea. Then, for another full generation, from 1905 until his death in 1949, Hulbert conducted a one-man crusade of writings and lecturing to try to win for Korea the international respect and friendship of which it was sorely in need.

Homer Hulbert was an American who, next to his own country, loved Korea best. Philip Jaisohn, born So Chae-pil in a well-to-do upper level yangban family, was a Korean patriot who, next to Korea, loved the United States best. Next to the United States he admired Japan, which was setting the example for Asian conversion to Westernized modernity. Jaisohn was born in 1866 and died in 1951; for more than fifty of his eighty-five years, he lived in America as a naturalized United States citizen and prosperous medical doctor. Three times during his life he played a truly notable role as a democratic reformist liberal for his native country, and for a fourth time, his vitality almost spent, he returned home once more to seek succor for Korea under American sponsorship. His first biographer, Channing Liem, called him "America's Finest Gift to Korea." Koreans proudly claim him as their own, despite his American residence and citizenship.

While he was a youth of seventeen, because of his brilliant school record and the prominence of his family, he was selected as one of fourteen young Koreans to study in Japan at the Toyama Military School, from which he was graduated a year later in May 1884. Upon his return home he found his family zealously engaged in active reformist activities, along with Kim Ok-kyun and others who were plotting a palace coup. When the Kapsin Coup was undertaken in December, young So Chae-pil, because of his family connections and his military study, and even more because of his zeal, was chosen to lead the soliders who attempted to seize the royal quarters. For this exploit he came to be called "The Boy General." As the coup failed, young Chae-pil, along with others of the conspirators, fled to safety in Japan. His family was less fortunate. Several were slain and the family property was confiscated on the charge of treason, under the Confucian belief that families are responsible for whatever one or more of its members may do.

But Chae-pil had sufficient resources and connections to enable him to journey on to the United States. There he entered the prestigious Johns Hopkins University, where he proceeded on to an M.D. degree—the first Korean to win any kind of doctorate in America. After Japan's defeat of China, with pro-Japanese reformers heading the Korean government, Philip Jaisohn—the name he adopted and thereafter used—returned to help sweep his countrymen into modern civilization. One of Jaisohn's childhood friends and an associate in the 1884 plot, Yi Wan-yong, was a powerful individual in the court when Jaisohn arrived in Seoul in January 1896. Jaisohn naturally turned to him for help in establishing a pro-American liberal movement. Yi Wan-yong belonged to a yangban family of the highest rank, and he had the further advantage of close friendship with Horace Allen, whom he helped to secure business concessions for Americans.

With such connections and the support of the enormous prestige of his American doctorate, Jaisohn was offered the cabinet post of Minister of Foreign Affairs. He rejected the offer, preferring to maintain his political independence and American citizenship. Nevertheless, he did accept appointment as adviser to the Privy Council. Staying as clear as he could from involvement in the palace intrigues, he established a base for himself at the Paejae Academy, where he formed close ties with Homer Hulbert. Bursting with hopeful energy, Jaisohn launched into a lecture series at Paejae on Western politics and history. He also commenced a weekly bilingual newspaper, *The Independent,* in hangul and English, which Hulbert published at the Trilingual Press. Jaison edited the paper from its inception on 7 April 1896 until his precipitate departure from Korea in May 1898. Publication continued under the editorship of Yun Chi-ho through December of that year. Circulation reached over 3,000, which made it self-supporting.

Yun Chi-ho developed a strong attraction to Western ways during his long residence of the United States and in Shanghai. In the November 1985 issue of *the Korean Repository,* he answered his own question, "What Has Confucianism Done for Korea?": "With diffidence yet conviction I dare say that it has done very little, if anything, for Korea. What Korea may have been without Confucian teachings, nobody can tell. But what Korea is with them we too well know. Behold Korea, with her oppressed masses, her general poverty, treacherous and cruel officers, her dirt and filth, her degraded women, her blighted families—behold all this and judge for yourselves what Confucianism has done for Korea." It was this awareness, and determination to reform conditions, that inspired the Paejae refomers.

On 6 July 1896, while King Kojong was closeted in the Russian embassy, Philip Jaisohn, with the counsel and help of Homer Hulbert, announced formation of the Independence Club. For two years this club exercised the dominant political influence in Korea. The aim of the club was to animate citizens to support democratic reforms, much in the spirit of Japan's Meiji Reformation. Jaisohn was the guiding spirit of the club, but as a naturalized American citizen, he left its public leadership to others. The first president of the club, An Kyong-su, had served several terms as head of the national police, in which capacity he had escorted Kojong to the Russian legation. Secretary for the club was Yi Chae-yon, the mayor of Seoul. Among its initial members, the most widely known and highly respected were Yi Sang-jae, a pro-American Christian, and Chon Taek-pu, who afterwards in 1903 established the Y.M.C.A. in Korea and became its first president. Aside from conducting meetings, many of them attended by thousands, the next notable activity of the club was its replacement of the Gate of Welcome and Blessing, where for centuries Korea's kings had greeted newly arriving Chinese envoys, with a new Independence Arch, which was set in place on 21 November 1896.

The following month, Jaisohn took the more revolutionary step of sponsoring a debating society at Paejae. Its professed purpose was to guide its members in a study of parliamentary law, to give them practice in debating and in public speaking, and to accustom them to reach and to accept conclusions by majority vote. More broadly, the society taught the meaning and the practice of democracy.

The Paejae Debating Society held its first meeting on 28 December 1896. In *The Independent* Jaisohn gave it enthusiastic support. He wrote:

> The orderliness of the members, the earnestness of discussing the question before the meeting, the eagerness of taking part in the procedure by every member present, and the fearless manner in which they expressed their views were quite pleasing to the hearts of those who wish for Korea's welfare. We suggest that the members of the Council of State would better take a few lessons from these boys in parliamentary practice.

Lillian Underwood, who listened eagerly to many of the debates and heard many Korean pastors preach in their churches, exhort attendants at evangelical meetings, and speak persuasively in annual conferences, attested in her book that Koreans were not only better public speakers than Chinese and Japanese but that they ranked with the best speakers of the West. An Chang-ho, one of the leading champions of Korean independence, secured his first education in public speaking in the Paejae Debating Society, and attested later that Korean public speaking began in this cauldron of democratic debate.[16] Hulbert, in *The Passing of Korea,* wrote that the society "was composed of young men, many of whom doubtless were aroused for the time being to something like fervor," adding that "they were armed with nothing but a laudable enthusiasm."

Jaisohn was determined that the club would be "armed" with more than fervor and enthusiasm. On 20 February 1897, after King Kojong returned from the Russian legation to resume his own quarters, the Independence Club sent to him a memorial stating the purposes the nation should pursue:

> . . . first, it must not lean upon another nation nor tolerate foreign interference in the national administration. Secondly, it must help itself by adopting a wise policy and enforcing justice throughout the realm.

In this and other ways, Jaisohn sought to reassure the government that the club and the debating society were endeavoring to support, not to oppose, the government. At first the meetings were held on Sunday afternoons at the Paejae Academy. Afterwards, when larger quarters were needed, the meetings were held in the Hall of Independence, renamed by Jaisohn from its former title of The Hall of Adoration of China. Branches of the club were very soon established in Chonju, Pusan, Pyongyang, and other cities.

Throughout 1897 the Independence Club and the Debating Society grew in membership and in influence. In May the Crown Prince honored the Club by giving it a specimen of his own calligraphy to use as its emblem. Student speakers, members of the graduating class, celebrated the occasion with an hour-long debate on the resolution that "the time has come for the Orient to accept in the main the civilization of the Occident." To end the meeting, the newly composed National Anthem was sung in public for the first time, to the tune of "Auld Lang Syne." A little known national flag, Korea's first, which had been designed in 1882 by Pak Yong-hyo was also displayed. On 13 August the Club celebrated the 450th anniversary of the founding of the Choson dynasty, before a crowd of many thousands, with leading members of the cabinet and foreign dignitaries in attendance. Kojong's assumption of the title of Emperor was celebrated by the Club on 11 October. All through the year the exultant theme was "Korea for the Koreans."

After the meeting place for the debates was moved from the campus to downtown, relations with the government became increasingly tense. Students no longer predominated, for cabinet members and other prominent leaders attended and took part in the debates. Topics discussed included "improvements of streets in the cities as the first step toward improving public health"; "a nation's prosperity depends entirely upon the increase of commercial enterprises"; and "lighting the streets at night will check the increase of robberies." Assessing the importance of the debates to "the man in the street," Jaisohn pointed out that "since his opinion was asked he had the freedom of expressing it." All of this, he concluded, was teaching "the sovereign rights of the individual and the individual dignity of the human being which are the essentials of democracy."

Encouraged by the popularity of his newspaper and the debates, Jaisohn took the drastic step of launching a series of street meetings, in which he and other club leaders exhorted huge crowds that assembled to hear them. Jaisohn was a fiery and charismatic speaker. He pounded the podium, gestured vigorously, and his voice shook with indignation. His central theme was that "no government, however mighty, can take away these inalienable rights from you or me; any government which dares to ignore the wishes of the people, I tell you, is the enemy of the people." Unlike Homer Hulbert, he did not celebrate the virtues of Korean culture or its past glories. Instead, he argued stridently for a "completely new beginning." Instead of encouraging pride in what Korea had been, he pleaded for what it might become. "The questions that come up before the Council," he insisted, "will be debated by any member, and each will tell the world his own idea in the matter by his vote." Every citizen had his own responsibility and should learn how to exercise it. This required study, for "patriotism is in no small part a product of education."

These were revolutionary ideas. Their declaration in massive street meetings posed a danger; and, especially from conservatives, the Independence Club and its Debating Society came under a continuing barrage of criticism.

Some of his troubles Jaisohn brought upon himself. Although sympathetic and helpful to him, Homer Hulbert nonetheless noted in his *History of Korea* that "Dr. Jaisohn . . . was blunt and outspoken in his advice to His Majesty and it was apparent that the latter listened with growing impatience." Lillian Underwood, in her biography of her husband, observed that Jaisohn was not popular in the influential missionary circle. "Dr. Jaisohn was impatient, precipitate and lacking in diplomatic tact," she wrote, "and soon made many bitter enemies and did not succeed very well in gaining his ends and ere long returned to America." Factors other than his personality were more important. Pro-American liberalism was under heavy attack from many quarters—including conservative traditionalists and the major groups (pro-Chinese, pro-Japanese, and pro-Russian) that otherwise had very little in common. Jaisohn, always outspoken and challenging in his speeches and editorials, was the special target of abuse. His life and that of his family were threatened. De Speyer secured his dismissal as adviser to the Privy Council, thus ending the $3,000 annual salary and the many special privileges that enabled him to live in Seoul. Private individuals pledged to continue payment of his salary. But Jaisohn realized that his mission had failed and he took his family back to America. There he opened medical practice in Media, a suburb of Philadelphia, and for more than twenty years remained aloof from Korean ties.

After Jaisohn's departure, *The Independent* continued in publication and continued its advocacy of liberal democracy, under the editorship of Yun Chi-ho. Yun was the eldest son in a wealthy landholding family of the highest yangban rank. He might well have enjoyed a life of leisure, honor, and luxury with no effort or risk. Instead, in this time of danger he courageously and with great ability devoted himself to the cause of civil rights and equaliy.

Yun Chi-ho was just thirty-two when Jaisohn arrived in Korea. Already he had become, uniquely for a Korean of his time, worldly wise and multicultured. His family sent him for study to Shanghai, where he mastered English and associated closely with American diplomats and businessmen. In 1888 he went on to the United States, where he remained for five more years of observation and study. During these years he not only learned a great deal about democracy but came to admire its social and political effects. Unlike Jaisohn, however, he did not become Americanized. He had also a strong pride in Korea's heritage and a great faith in its moral, philosophical, and artistic accomplishments. What he sought was to improve Korea, not to Westernize it. And also unlike Jaisohn, Baron Yun (as he later became) was tactful, conciliatory, and prone to avoid arguments and to search for consensus. With such a background and such a personality, when the independence movement failed and Japan took over Korea, he adjusted himself to these new circumstances. In his latter years, in 1937–45, while Japan was trumpeting its policy of an "Asian Co-Prosperity Sphere," Baron Yun joined with some other prominent Koreans to become members of the Japanese House of Peers. This was the future; in 1896–98 he stood staunchly in the forefront of leadership that demanded basic reform of the society.

Another member of the Debating Society who was destined to play a central role in the history of modern Korea was a young man named Yi Seungman, later to become famous as Syngman Rhee. Syngman Rhee was born, as an only son, on 26 March 1875, in an impoverished yangban family living in a small house in Nung-an-gol, in the Pyongsan District.[17] When the boy was three years old, still further reduced circumstances led to the family's move to To-dong (Peach Village) in the southern outskirts of Seoul. There, in a small hut on a barren hillside, Syngman lived until once more the family moved back into Seoul in 1895. This move was significant, for it brought the young man, then twenty years of age, into association with Heung Woo (Hugh) Cynn, who was attending classes in Paejae Academy. Although Syngman's family was devoutly Buddhist, and his mother particularly was fearful of the influences of Western Christianity. Rhee commenced attendance in Paejae and quickly proved to be an apt student. He learned

English so quickly that he was hired, for the princely sum of twenty dollars a month, to teach Korean to newly arriving staff members. He joined the Independence Club and the Debating Society and became a frequent speaker. When Jaisohn initiated the holding of out-of-doors meetings, young Rhee proved to be adept as a "crowd-compeller." After Jaisohn's departure for America in the spring of 1898, Rhee became a leader in organizing citizen marches to the royal palace to demand democratic reforms. He also commenced printing and editing Korea's first daily newspaper, the *Maeil Shinmun,* or *Daily News,* which, like Jaisohn's weekly *Independent,* was written partly in Korean, partly in English. His theme, like Jaisohn's, was an ardent and repetitive demand for governmental and social reforms. He became an avid reader of books on American history and political science and of such magazines as *McClure's, The Nineteenth Century and After,* and *The Outlook,* which were supplied to him by the mssionaries.

One day Syngman took the family's ancestral tablets respectfully in his hands, bowed to his mother, and told her he was going to have his top-knot cut off. He found that his mother, sorrowful though she was, accepted that he would have to chart his own life. Neither the older nor the young generation was having an easy time adjusting to the transition toward modernism. The oldsters had to endure seeing their cherished traditions abandoned. The youngsters were entering into a new world without guidance and with feelings of guilt as they turned away from the standards of their forebears. Rhee, like other liberal members of his generation, was already feeling the contrasting influences of both the world's hemispheres and of both ancient traditions and modern ideas.

In the Debating Society, unlike Jaisohn who dealt with abstract principles, Rhee saw reform in intensely human and individual terms. The political society in Seoul was small and the infighting among factions was bitter and often vicious. Young Rhee learned early to value loyalty above almost all else. Those who were not for him, and for their common cause, he felt, were against him. Everything depended upon their standing dependably together. When he was marked for arrest, he fled to hide out briefly in Pyongsan. Then he returned, called a meeting of Independence Club members, and found them in agreement that Korea was near oblivion as a nation unless it could be saved by vigorous leadership. An Kyong-su, the club's president, however, fled to the safety of Japan. Yi Wan-yong, who replaced him, was bought off with appointment as a provincial governor and resigned from the club. Seventeen leading members of the club were arrested.

Rhee called for followers and started a march to police headquarters to demand release of the seventeen. A considerable crowd joined him and they remained there all that night, the next day, and the next night. A band of soldiers marched toward the crowd, but when it failed to disperse, the soldiers, under orders not to use force, withdrew. Then a sullen police officer informed the protesters that the seventeen prisoners were being released.

More gatherings continued however, day after day, persistently taking position before the royal palace. The crowd was set upon by members of the Peddler's Guild, who had been recruited by the government and who attacked the Independence Club members with clubs and tomahawk-like firefighters' hooks.

Emperor Kojong, fearing that a revolution was brewing, called the Independence Club leaders and other prominent liberals to a meeting in the open square before his palace, where an impromptu audience hall was erected. There, in the presence of his cabinet, foreign diplomats, and missionaries, he promised to reform the government and not to arrest any of the demonstrators. He also appointed a new Privy Council, with Yun Chi-ho as president and Syngham Rhee as a member. At the first meeting of the new Council, however, when Rhee proposed the pardon of all political dissenters who had fled to Japan, Kojong angrily dismissed the council and ordered the arrest of its Independence Club members.

For the next seven months Rhee was subjected to brutal tortures, then commonplace as a means of forcing confessions. The tortures were so severe that he prayed for death with passionate ardor. Daily he was beaten with split bamboo rods. His legs were tied together at the ankles and at the knees, and a pole inserted between his knees was rotated, causing him extreme agony. Bamboo slivers were inserted between his fingers, after which they were bound together so tightly that the flesh sheared away from the bones. Between torture sessions he was confined in a small cell with a heavy plank, fastened around his neck, so that he could neither stand nor lie down. During these sufferings he remembered the preaching he had heard in Paejae chapel. He felt a strange peacefulness even while he knew he was one of the most miserable wretches alive. One day a friend brought a hidden revolver into the prison, slipped it to Rhee, and led a dash to freedom. Rhee was quickly captured; because of this flight, when his trial ended, he was condemned to life imprisonment.

The cell in which the Independence Club members were to spend the next six and a half years was a converted rice storehouse with a wooden floor and a heavy tiled roof. The building was divided into four rooms, each about thirty feet square, with a narrow aisle in the middle. On the floor were thick ricestraw mats, and each prisoner had a roll of bedding. A single kerosene lamp hung in the aisle. Families were permitted to visit the prisoners at long intervals, to bring them extra food and other small comforts. Rhee was visited regularly by missionaries, who brought him books and magazines. He was converted and baptized. Daily he read to the other inmates from the New Testament, while someone turned its pages for him: his fingers were so mangled from his tortures that it was several years before he could use them without severe pain.

In the prison were seven other Independence Club members, including Hugh Cynn and Park Young-man, who were to mean much to him in later times. Together they organized a school, in which Rhee lectured on Western politics and history. He wrote editorials that were smuggled out and printed in the *Maeil Shinmun.* He wrote a poem that expressed feelings dominant in much of his life:

> Tied together in chains men develop new intimacies.
> Moving about in politics, one finds old friends estranged

He also wrote thirty-four chapters of a book, *The Spirit of Independence,* a completed version of which was later published by Koreans in Los Angeles. The general tone of the book may be illustrated by its key passages:

> The main reason why the people do not work together is that they do not know to whom the nation belongs. People often think that to work for their country is to work for others. They do not realize that what they do for others is most truly working for themselves. Hence, they wait for others to do what must be done. Will you not hasten to extinguish the fire in your own house, even if others ignore it? Isn't it much better to plunge into the fire to save what you can, whether others assist you or not? . . .
>
> If your own heart is without patriotism, your heart is your enemy. You must struggle against your own feelings if they urge you to forgo the struggle for the common cause. Let us examine our hearts now at this moment. If you find within yourself any single thought of abandoning the welfare of your country, take it out. Do not wait for others to lead or to do what must be done, but arouse yourself. If you do not do it, it will never be done.

This was guidance of which the Koreans had great need. But it came too late. There were no means by which the book could be published in Korea. Events there were hastening toward a climax—and they were controlled by aliens, not by Koreans themselves.

5

The Strangling of Independence

The twentieth century opened disastrously for Korea. With Emperor Kojong deprived of authority and confined to his palace under Japanese supervision, with Yun Chi-ho and Pak Yong-hyo remaining quiet, with Philip Jaisohn returned to America, and with Syngman Rhee in prison, as the twentieth century opened Korea was virtually without effective patriotic leadership. Its cabinet was as nearly without purpose as it was without power. Kojong's title of emperor was as empty as the mythical story of the founding of the nation 4,233 years earlier by the semi-divine Tangun. The shadow government was in effect controlled by Japan.

Throughout the country the prospects were gloomy. Ninety-five percent of the population consisted of peasants who felt themselves doomed to perpetual poverty. The five percent who were upper-level yangbans realized that the semi-luxury in which they lived was precarious. Large-scale manufacturing was nonexistent. Commerce, except for the outflow of rice and the inflow of Japanese goods, was limited to local exchanges. Education was scanty in both quantity and quality. Disease was endemic and medical service was sadly inadequate. The ill-trained and ill-equipped police provided little protection against banditry. Transport and communication facilities were minimal. The brave words of the Independence Club's call for democracy and civil rights were only misty memories.

Optimism was limited to missionary circles, which rejoiced that "the better class of the people" had been reached with the gospel light. In both the cities and the countryside, self-supporting churches and native evangelists were "multiplying the influence of the gospel everywhere," with the result that "saloons are closed, the Sabbath is kept holy, gambling and vice of every kind is suppressed and first of all idolatry is abolished." So read the missionaries' reports: Korea had become "the most Christian nation in the Orient."

In the whole population there were only seventy thousand Catholics, about ninety thousand Presbyterians, and some forty thousand Methodists. Christianity was far from dominant, but it provided the only pipeline Korea had to sympathetic understanding among the peoples of the West. The missions' reports to their headquarters were the only counters to the indifference of Western governments and the unfavorable depictions of Koreans by writers who drew most of their impressions from Japanese sources.

Mrs. Underwood, in her *Fifteen Years among the Top-knots,* accurately represented the value of this channel of communication. "The Koreans have been frequently spoken and written of," she said, "as a listless, dull, stupid, lazy, and inferior race; but I submit this has been said mainly by travellers who did not know them, or by those who are their enemies and had an object in making the world think them worthless." Then she presented her own estimate, written as "the conscientious opinion of one who has known them for twenty years, closely, in everyday contact, through all sorts of circumstances, in city and country." From this background, "to the writer it seems that there is a close parallel between the Irishman and the Korean. Both are happy-go-lucky, improvident, impulsive, warm-hearted, hospitable, generous. Take either in the midst of his native bogs, untutored, without incentive . . . he has apparently little ambition for anything better." But, "give him a chance to make a good living, and a certainty that he may keep his own earnings, and you will not find a better citizen, a more brillaint scholar. . . ." Her conclusion was that "they are not, perhaps, *par excellence,* fighters like the Japanese or merchants, like the Chinese. They have not the volatility and headstrong earnestness of the one or the stolid conservatism of the other, but they are the equals if not the superiors of either."

A transformation of Korea was proceeding gradually, much less rapidly or systematically than in Japan, and less widespread. Concessions granted to foreigners, including American, English, German, French, and Japanese companies, had resulted in the opening and operation of coal, iron, and gold mines, the construction of some six hundred miles of railroads, and a slowly expanding import and export trade. A postal service with international connections was established. A national education system was undertaken and a few students were sent to study abroad. On the darker side, whale fishing along Korea's northern coasts had been granted to Russians; and Japanese fisheries were squeezing out the ill-equipped Korean fishermen from the coastal waters. Competition by Koreans with such foreign enterprises was minimized by lack of both experience and investment capital. Initial efforts to establish a national currency and a banking system were similarly handicapped. Ominously, the Japanese arrogated the right to build military posts at fifteen-mile intervals along the railway lines they established.

As the century was opening, the blemishes were more apparent than the underlying quality of the people. Modernity and effective self-government were both diverted and delayed by the two factors of domestic corruption and foreign intrusiveness. Court officials, instead of rectifying conditions, sought to bolster their own positions by turning once again toward restoration of traditional patterns. In March 1899 the court appointed ten senior scholars to the faculty of the royal Confucian College, *Songgyungwan,* charging them to study methods for reestablishing the Confucian examination system. In the midst of untenable turmoil, the solution that was sought officially was to turn away from the future back toward the past. Outside the major cities, neither the psychology nor the living conditions of the people were much changed. Except for some surface appearances, the mass of the people lived, behaved, and thought much as had their ancestors during the long centuries of Old Korea. The details must be remembered, since they explained how independence slipped from Korea's grasp.

An Kyong-su and Kwon Yong-jin returned to Korea from Japan, where they had fled for refuge after an ill-judged effort they made in 1898 to force the abdication of Emperor Kojong and to enthrone the Crown Prince. To induce their return, they were promised a fair trial. Instead they were strangled to death in prison during the night of 27 May 1900. During this same year a reckless adventurer named Kim Yong-jun, who gained influence in the judiciary, enriched himself by haling wealthy men into court and torturing them until they paid him huge ransoms. In retaliation, in January of 1901 he was arrested, tortured severely in prison, and then strangled. Another equally unscrupulous official, Yi Yong-ik, cheated the ginseng farmers of Song-do (Kaesong) and also persecuted corrupt provincial officials to force them to pay him huge sums, which he pocketed. He connived, meanwhile, with first Japanese and then Russian agents, to grant them vital port concessions, upon payment of bribes to him. Then he saved himself from prosecution by the humanitarian act of buying large quantities of rice from Annam and selling it to the Korea public for reasonable prices during the drought in 1901.

Meanwhile, the attention of the world was diverted to China, which was victimized by a long process of European imperialism, leading to a massive uprising of patriotic young men who called themselves The Society of Harmonious Fists—leading Westerners to call them the Boxers. The Dowager Empress encouraged them by sending to all the Chinese viceroys a secret document, on 21 November 1899, which warned that "the various powers cast upon us looks of tiger-like voracity, hustling each other in their endeavors to be the first to seize upon our innermost territories." When at the end of May the Boxers, thus encouraged, fell ferociously upon foreign compounds, the major powers combined to crush them. Around the world, attention centered on what was called the barbaric and anti-Christian Yellow Peril. One result was worldwide derogation of Korea. Japan alone, because of its rapid Westernization, was exempt from this condemnation. England hastened to make a treaty with Japan, in 1902, in which the two governments promised to work together to pacify the Far East.

Both Russia and Japan intensified their efforts to establish strong positions in Korea. Russia connived with pliable Korean officials to secure grants of coal stations for their warships in the excellent ports of Pusan and Masan, but these efforts were rebuffed by Japanese domination of the Korean court. On 3 April 1901 Russia succeeded in obtaining a concession to exploit the timber resources in northern Korea and commenced at once to construct a network of military roads connected with their base across the frontier. During the next two years, hundreds of Russian soldiers in civilian dress directed large crews of Korean and Chinese laborers in construction of buildings they called "lumber warehouses," which in reality were military barracks and fortifications. At Antung, on the Yalu River, contingents of Russian troops were assembled.

Russia's Count Cassini had informed Li Hung-chang, after the signing of the Shimonoseki Treaty that ended the Sino-Japanese War, that "Japan will not be permitted, either now or in the future, to seize upon any part of Manchuria or the mainland." At the same time, as was later reported in *The Outlook* for 13 February 1904, a Japanese cabinet member (otherwise unidentified) told the American diplomat, Chester Holcombe, that "if we only had three battleships we would declare war against Russia within twenty-four hours." Japan hastened to buy warships and to build battleships, cruisers, and torpedo boats, while assigning some of its most brilliant young men to study the naval system of Great Britain and the military system of Germany. Adachi Kinnosuke, writing in *The World's Work,* April 1909, explained the dilemma his countrymen had had to solve: either Japan "must die a saintly death in righteous starvation, or expand into the neighbor's backyard."

The backyard upon which Japan had set its sights was Korea. Considerable and sustained progress toward this goal had been made. By 1904, there were some forty thousand Japanese in Korea, dominating its economy. Political control over the government was nearly complete. Military control over the population was assured. What remained to be done was to eliminate Russian interference and competition and to fend off interference by other powers.

France was actively pursuing its aim of taking over southeastern Asia. Spain was embroiled in a losing war with the United States. Germany was cautiously cultivating good relations with Russia while trying to avoid antagonizing England. China had been eliminated as a competitor by its decisive defeat in the 1894–95 war. England, which for several years had been seeking to contain Russia from advancing either in Europe or in Asia, was quite willing to accept advances by Japan. The United States, meanwhile, was flexing its muscles in a new emergence into Pacific imperialism. In 1898 it annexed the Hawaiian Islands, went to war with Spain, and hesitantly made the decision to extend its rule over the Philippines and Puerto Rico but not over Cuba. Theodore Roosevelt, when he was unexpectedly elevated to the presidency, was well acquainted with Europe but not with Asia. He was enthusiastic about the westward continental expansion of America into the largely unpeopled land beyond the Mississippi, which he celebrated with his book *The Winning of the West.* He was ambitious to expand American commerce and influence but was not clear as to how this could be accomplished in the well-populated countries of Asia. Like England, he decided that Japanese hegemony was probably inevitable and offered substantial benefits by holding Russia at bay and by policing, if not actually controlling, ineptly-governed China. As for Korea, what little Roosevelt had heard of it was its hapless inability to control its own destiny. He easily concluded that this was a natural role for the Japanese.

The Japanese government knew what it wanted and it felt both strong enough and secure enough to set about getting it. In June 1903 the cabinet drew up a series of demands, which were presented to Russia on 12 August. The third one was "to recognize the preferential interests of Japan in Korea." The fourth asked Russia "to recogonize the exclusive rights of Japan to give advice and support to any reforms in Korea." In October Russia indicated a willingness to accept a Japanese protectorate over Korea but rejected restrictions on its own role in Manchuria. On 21 December Japan again asked Russia to abstain from any restrictions on its right to make any use that it deemed necessary of Korean territory for its strategic purposes. Following further indeterminate exchanges during January, on 5 February Japan sent an ultimatum to Russia and, without waiting for an answer, on 6 February launched at attack on the Russian fleet based at Port Arthur.

The Russian historian Victor A. Yakhontoff, in *Russia and the Soviet Union in the Far East,* declared flatly that "the Anglo-Japanese Alliance and the friendly attitude of the United States were the deciding factors enabling Japan to risk a war." President Theodore Roosevelt wrote on 24 July 1905 to his English friend Cecil Spring Rice: "As soon as this war broke out, I notified Germany and France in the most polite and discreet fashion that in the event of a combination against Japan. . . . I should promptly side with Japan and proceed to whatever length was necessary on her behalf. Of course I know that your government would act in the same way."

The Korean government, anticipating the Russo-Japanese War, issued a manifesto of neutrality on 21 January 1904. Nevertheless, on the opening day of the war Japanese warships attacked Russian vessels at Inchon. Simultaneously, large numbers of Japanese troops were landed at both Pusan and Inchon. Once again, as in 1894–95, Korea was occupied by Japanese troops. On 23 February, Korea was induced to sign a Protocol of Alliance with Japan which (1) guaranteed Korean independence; and (2) accorded to Japan permission to take any steps necessary to combat either foreign or domestic threats to Korea. To effectuate this second provision, Korea was obliged to provide facilities for Japanese forces at "such places as may be necessary" anywhere in the peninsula. To effectuate article one, the Korean government was required to accept Japanese advice and assistance in its administration. This Protocol the Korean Foreign Minister did not sign until after the victory of the Japanese war fleet in Inchon, the entrance of four battalions of Japanese soldiers into Seoul, and the issuance of instructions to the Japanese minister in Seoul to "take appropriate measures" against any Korean officials who opposed the Japanese. In Tokyo the Council of Elder Statesmen declared that it was Japan's policy "to take possession of the real powers of protection in political and military matters of Korea and to promote the development of our economic rights and interests in Korea." As the next step, on 19 August the Korean government agreed to employ advisers on fiscal and foreign affairs who were recommended by Japan. An American, Durham W. Stevens, who was a loyal employee of Japan's Foreign Ministry, was appointed to take charge of Korea's foreign relations.

In July 1905 William Howard Taft, then Secretary of War, and shortly to assume the office of High Commissioner of the Philippines, stopped off in Tokyo for conversations with Prime Minister Katsura Tarō. Katsura presented Taft with a memorandum disavowing any intention of impeding United States control of the Philippines. Taft assured Katsura that "the establishment by Japanese troops of a suzerainty over Korea to the extent of requiring that Korea enter into no foreign treaties without the consent of Japan was the logical result of the present war and would directly contribute to permanent peace in the East." President Roosevelt cabled to Taft, "Wish you would state to Katsura that I confirm every word you have said."

The fall of Korea to Japan must be recognized as in part a result of racial discrimination. England was accustomed to high-handedness in dealing with its widely-scattered colored colonials. Americans were not only treating their own "emancipated" blacks with harsh injustice but were also fearful and resentful of the Chinese and other Orientals who were pouring into California and Hawaii as field and hand laborers. Theodore Roosevelt had clearly stated his own racism towards American Indians in his book on *The Winning of the West.* It was important, he wrote, that the American West had been won and it didn't matter how, for "it is indeed, a warped, perverse and silly morality which would forbid a course of conquest that has turned whole continents into the seats of mighty and flourishing civilized nations." Within a few years the Japanese were to be lumped with other Orientals as part of the Yellow Peril, and were, indeed, to become the chief villains. But as the twentith century commenced, Japan was enjoying the glow of Western admiration as the one Asian nation that was hastening to Westernize itself, while preserving, also, a special patina of beauty and delicacy as the apparent apex of oriental culture. In contrast, Korea's helplessness and lack of progressive modernity defined its people as unquestionably inferior. As in many other times and places, attitudes predominated over facts. It was "of incalcuable importance," Roosevelt wrote, that lands inhabited by "red, black, and yellow aboriginal owners" should "become the heritage of the dominant world races."

This general racism and specific derogation of Koreans had much to do with the acquisition of Korea by Japan. The contrary views of the missionaries were either wholly disregarded or dismissed as being merely reflections of their false sentimentality. Emperor Kojong, as his country was losing its independence, tried hard to find voices of support that would be heard. But the best Korea could do was of no avail.

One thing Kojong did do was to grant an amnesty to political prisoners following the outbreak of the Russo-Japanese War. During the spring and summer of 1904 many of the prisoners were released. Syngman Rhee, because of his attempt to escape from prison with a pistol in his hand, was not granted his freedom until 9 August 1904. The Korea into which he reemerged was far from joyful. In and around Seoul, fifteen thousand families had been dispossessed of their homes, which the Japanese claimed for their own use as a "military necessity." Japanese agents went through the peninsula, seizing properties on military authorization. Koreans were roughly treated and were denied access to any areas the Japanese declared "off limits." All Korean "waste lands" (including undeveloped mineral and timber resources) were granted to a Japanese corporation; and, although this grant was shortly rescinded, it was re-enacted after the annexation became official. As a further blow to Rhee's spirits, on 6 April 1904, while still in prison, he had received a letter from his mentor, Philip Jaisohn, that read in part: "So far Japan is on the side and waging war for the principle which every civilized being must uphold and support. . . . Japan or any other nation cannot help Korea unless Korea helps herself and is willing to be helped by others." Korea's situation appeared to be helpless, but there were a few patriots who did not give up easily.

Rhee talked with Prince Min Yong Hwan and Prime Minister Han Kyu-sol, both of whom had been supporters of the Independence Club and remained as the two most influential reformers in the court circle. He found them to be as disturbed as he was by the course of events. These three decided that little if anything could be accomplished inside Korea to check the trend of Japanization. They agreed that an appeal should be made to the President of the United States, based upon the Amity Treaty of 1882.

Prince Min and General Han (no longer recognized as Prime Minister) sent Rhee to Washington with one more plea on behalf of Korea's independence. After brief stops in Tokyo, Honolulu, and San Francisco, mostly to raise money from loyal Koreans for travel expenses, Rhee arrived in Washington on New Year's Eve. He presented letters from Prince Min and General Han to Senator Hugh A. Dinsmore, who had served briefly in the American legation in Seoul. Dinsmore was pleased to do what he could. Days and weeks passed fruitlessly, but in late February the senator took Rhee to meet with Secretary of State John Hay, author of the famed Open Door policy. Hay was a warm supporter of missionary activities in Korea and was concerned that the Boxer movement in China might spread to Korea. He assured Rhee, "as long as the Koreans do not start any anti-Christian movement, there will be no trouble." Hay concluded the interview by telling Rhee and Dinsmore that "I will do everything I can to fulfill our treaty obligations, either personally or representing this government, whenever, the opportunity presents itself."

On 10 June President Roosevelt formally invited Japan and Russia to conduct peace negotiations at Portsmouth, New Hampshire. Rhee and a friend, Reverend Yoon Pyung Koo, went to Oyster Bay, Long Island, where President Roosevelt was in his summer home, and on 6 July, dressed in formal diplomatic attire which they had rented, they were received informally by Roosevelt for a few moments of conversation in his hallway, following the departure of the chief Russian diplomat, Count Witte. Roosevelt assured them that he was always glad to be of help to any oppressed people and suggested they talk about the treaty obligation with the Secretary of State. Overjoyed, they rushed back to Washington. The friendly John Hay had died just two weeks earlier and the much sterner Elihu Root was the acting secretary. Rhee and Yoon went to the Korean legation, where Minister Kim Yun-jong was still living, although without authority. Kim informed them that he could not ask Root to see them unless he was so instructed from Seoul, which the Japanese would not allow. Rhee persisted in efforts to see Root, without effect. On 10 September he received a final letter from Prince Min, thanking him for his efforts and enclosing $300 for his expenses.

Then Prince Min committed suicide in a typical oriental form of protest against Japanese seizure of his country. A bamboo shoot grew up through the floor of the room in which he died—and all through the subsequent long generation of Japanese rule over Korea a favorite subject of Korean art was a spray of bamboo leaves, as a memorial to this brave and generous-minded patriot.

In October 1905 Kojong asked Homer Hulbert to go to America to present a letter from him to President Roosevelt. While Hulbert was on his way to Washington, Japan acted quickly. Hulbert, in *The Passing of Korea,* described what happened.

> Marquis Hirobumi Ito was sent to Seoul with definite instructions. Korea was to be induced to sign away her national existence voluntarily. Many conferences took place between the Japanese authorities and the Korean cabinet, but without result. . . . Not one of the Cabinet consented. It was quite clear that stronger measures would have to be used. . . . The Emperor and every one of his ministers stood firm. They would die sooner than acquiesce. . . . When this deadlock occurred, the scene shifted a little, and Japanese gendarmes and police suddenly appeared and surrounded the audience chamber and blocked every approach to the imperial presence. The Emperor, feeling sure that personal injury was determined upon, retired to a little anteroom. No sane person can doubt that he had sufficient reason to fear. . . . Hedged in by armed Japanese, their official chief spirited away and perhaps killed, there is little wonder that another turn of the screw resulted in the defection of several of the Cabinet, and at last a paper was signed by a majority of the ministers present, after a clause had been added to the effect that at some future day when Korea is strong enough and wealthy enough to resume her independence it will be given back to her.

This document was presented in Washington by the Japanese, and the Department of State accepted it as a voluntary Korean acceptance of a Japanese Protectorate. The American legation in Seoul was closed and the Korean legation in Washington was informed that henceforth the United States would conduct diplomatic matters regarding Korea through Tokyo. On 26 November Emperor Kojong cabled Hulbert that "I declare that the so-called treaty of protectorate recently concluded between Korea and Japan was extorted at the point of the sword and under duress and is therefore null and void. I never consented to it and never will." This cable the State Department declined to receive.

Patriots both inside and outside of Korea also took such measures as were available to them. During the 1905–10 period, some two thousand private schools (about one-third of them affiliated with protestant churches) were established throughout the peninsula with the principal aim of inspiring patriotism. Such journalist-historians as Chang Chi-yon, Pak Un-shik, and Sin Chae-ho hastened to compose and publish historical accounts with that same aim. A dozen or more scholar-officials followed the example of Prince Min Yong-hwan in committing suicide in protest against the 1905 protectorate declaration. Others fought back with violence. In Harbin, Manchuria, a young Korean nationalist, An Chung-gun, shot and killed Count Itō, who was en route to Moscow to discuss Japanese-Russian relations. In San Francisco, Chang In-hwan and Cho Myong-un killed Durham Stevens, who was assuring American lecture audiences that Japanese rule would be good for Korea. In Seoul, Yi Chae-myong attempted to assassinate Yi Wan-yong, who headed the pro-Japanese cabinet. Park Young-man, and Hugh Cynn, both former Independence Club members, rallied the Koreans in Hawaii and afterwards established military schools first in Nebraska, then in Hawaii to train Koreans as infiltrators. Rhee and P. K. Yoon organized an international conference held in Denver, Colorado, on 11–15 July 1908 to arouse support for Korea, with Korean attendants coming from around the continental United States and from Russia, China, England, and Hawaii. President David Starr Jordan of Stanford University addressed an open session attended by hundreds; and the 12 July issue of the Denver *Republican* reported "the purpose is the making of a nation, the throwing off of the yoke of subserviency. . . . They are going about it calmly, with quiet passion, and with no illusions."

Two more Korean patriots, Yi Chun, prosecutor of the Supreme Court and Yi Sang-sol, a former cabinet officer, persuaded Emperor Kojong to send them and Homer Hulbert as emissaries to the Second International Peace Conference at the Hague. At the end of June 1907, on Russia's motion, the Koreans were permitted to present their case to the conference. They argued that since the protectorate convention had been signed by Korean officials under severe coercion it was null and void. They asked that Korean independence be restored by the intervention of the powers assembled for the conference. The Japanese delegate replied that since Korea had granted all diplomatic functions to Japan, these spokesmen were without any authority. The Koream mission thereupon was ejected from the conference. Yi Chun, in protest, committed suicide.

The Japanese government, declaring that the dispatch of this mission to The Hague was in contravention to treaty agreements, decided that "to prevent further nuisance, Japan must control the internal administration of Korea as well as its foreign relations." To avert still further punitive measures against Korea, several cabinet members, led by the notoriously pro-Japanese Song Pyong-jun, demanded the abdication of Emperor Kojong on the ground that he and he alone was responsible for the Japan-baiting mission to The Hague. For several days Kojong angrily refused. Then the arrival from Tokyo of Japan's Foreign Minister Hayashi Gonsuke with grim news of further impositions on Korea obliged him to step aside. The date was 19 July 1907. Kojong was just fifty-six. He had endured one of the most troubled reigns in his country's history and, if not a great man, he had under severe circumstances done his best. His son, crowned as Emperor Sunjong, at the age of thirty-four, with little or no authority, assumed few burdens but endless humiliation. Song Pyong-jun was rewarded by appointment to the key ministry of Home Affairs, which directed the police.

The new regulations that Hayashi brought with him were brutally harsh. In essence, the Japanese Residency-General would henceforth exercise all authority over Korea's internal affairs. Every ministry would have a Japanese vice-minister who would run it. All judges and prosecutors as well as wardens and guards at the penitentiaries were to be Japanese. The Chief of the Police Bureau in the Home Ministry was to be a Japanese. So was the First Secretary of the cabinet. Japanese nationals were to hold the principal positions in the provinces.

In an enraged reaction, a large mass of citizens gathered in the streets of Seoul, calling for deliberations on the dangers facing the nation. Scores of Korean troops joined with the crowds in fighting Japanese policemen. In Seoul, and also in many outlying parts of Korea, Japanese were stoned and their houses were burned. On 1 August Japan disbanded the Korean army, which, at that time, consisted of some six thousand soldiers, all Japanese-trained and serving under Japanese control. Korean contingents rebelled against the orders to disband and sporadic fighting broke out in Seoul, in Wonju, in Kangwon province, and on Kangwha Island.

The Righteous Army, as these volunteers called themselves, consisted in part of disbanded Korean soldiers, in part of tiger hunters, all patriots who hated theJapanese and who fought fearlessly since they had little to lose. Their effectiveness was attested by an announcement issued in the fall of 1907 by General Baron Yoshimichi Hasegawa, Commander of the Army of Occupation. It charged that

> those who are ignorant of the march of events in the world and who fail to correctly distinguish loyalty from treason have by wild and baseless rumours instigated

> people's minds and caused the rowdies in various places to rise in insurrection. These insurgents commit all sorts of horrible crimes, such as murdering peaceful people, both native and foreign, robbing their property, burning official and private buildings, and destroying means of communication. Their offenses are such as are not tolerated by Heaven or earth. They affect to be loyal and patriotic and call themselves volunteers. . . . Unless they are promptly suppressed the trouble may assume really calamatous proportions. . . . Any of you who will seize insurgents or will give information concerning their whereabouts will be handsomely rewarded. In case of those who willfully join insurgents, or afford them refuge, or conceal weapons, they shall be severely punished. More than that, the villages to which such offenders belong shall be held collectively responsible and punished with rigour. I call upon each and every one of the people of Korea to understand clearly what I have herewith said to you and to avoid all reprehensible action.

According to Japanese Army reports, before the rebels were finally crushed in 1912, 141,815 Koreans fought, with 17,697 of them being killed and 3,706 wounded. The disproportionately large number of deaths over the wounded shows the ferocity with which the fighting was waged, both in the resolution of the Koreans and the ruthlessness of the Japanese. Japanese troops suffered just 136 deaths and 2,777 wounded.

The Korean public knew relatively little of the struggle by the Righteous Army, for the half dozen newspapers were strictly censored. The exceptions were the two newspapers, the *Taehan Maeil Ṣinbo* and its English-language sister publication, the *Korean Daily News*. Both were edited by an English citizen, E. T. Bethell. They carried general anti-Japanese news accounts, including stories on the Righteous Army rebellion. For the Japanese, Bethell was a difficult problem. His English citizenship for a time protected him, since Japan highly valued its alliance with Great Britain. Efforts were made to win Bethell over to support of Japan or to persuade him to discontinue publication of the papers. When these failed, Bethell and his Korean assistant editor Yang Ki-tak were arrested and imprisoned in September 1907. Further to counteract Bethell's influence, Japan established in Seoul its own newspapers, the English-language *Seoul Times* and the *Keijō nippō,* in both Japanese and Korean.

More difficult for the Japanese to control was the influence exercised by the Christian missionaries. During the five-year period of the protectorate, 1905–10, the number of foreign missionaries continued to increase. As that interim period ended, there were 205 missionaries in Korea, three-quarters of them protestant, most of these being Americans, with French and other European priests forming the majority of the Catholic evangelists. They maintained their position by exercising political caution. George Paik, in his history of the protestant church in Korea, reported that "as far as we can discover in the private letters of the missionaries, a large number favored and cooperated with the Japanese and made an effort to quiet the restlessness of the Christians." He also observed that "the problem of the missionaries was to win the confidence of the Japanese and at the same time to hold the faith and trust of the Koreans." When the Japanese forces landed in Korea in 1904, the missionaries welcomed them as the precursor of "better things." Marquis Itō, as the de facto ruler of Korea, actively sought the goodwill of the missionaries. As he told them, "In the early years of Japan's reformation, the senior statesmen were opposed to religious toleration, especially because of distrust of Christianity. But I fought vehemently for freedom of belief and religious propaganda, and finally triumphed. My reasoning was this: civilization depends on morality and the highest morality upon religion. Therefore religion must be tolerated and encouraged."

These declarations of mutual regard did not, however, govern behavior out in the country. As Koreans rose in wrath against the incoming Japanese, and as Japanese were systematically taking over Korean properties, clashes were inevitable. Church buildings and lands were often seized, on the ground of military necessity, with no compensation. And there was worse. Reverend Elmer M. Cable, in 1908, reported to the Methodist Board of Foreign Missions that "our church at Annai was burned to the ground by the Japanese soldiers, and at Sackhajhoe three of the Christians were seized and tied to a stake and ordered to be shot. Two of them were killed, but one escaped and his almost miraculous deliverance made a deep impression on the people." Korean students, including those in mission schools, harried the Japanese as best they could and in reprisal school buildings were burned.

During the Protectorate period the number of Christians in Korea increased by some forty percent. A Japanese editor of a newspaper in Seoul claimed that Koreans joined the Christian church for material gain. One of the missionaries, Reverend C. E. Sharp, writing on "Motives for Seeking Christ" in *Korean Mission Field* (August 1906) cited three motives: (1) to unite for mutual help; (2) to identify with Western learning and culture; and (3) to fulfill their faith. George Paik elaborated the reasons for conversion as being six-fold: (1) dissatisfaction with poverty, oppression, and corrupt government; (2) admiration for Western civilization; (3) the natural religiousness of Koreans; (4) escape from their powerlessness into the protection of the church; (5) the fellowship of the congregation; and (6) the influence of family, clan, and group—so that when an influential person was converted many followed suit. Whatever the reasons may have been, the conversion of even a small fraction of the population to Christianity proved to be important for the lifeline it established between Korea and foreign (especially American) centers of influence. This was particularly important since the colonial government had no reason to disclose Korean dissatisfactions. All during the period of Japanese rule Korea remained a "forgotten nation," with no diplomatic ties and with very few foreign news reporters interested in telling the peoples' story.

6

Korean Cultural Characteristics

The forceful termination of the sense of being special is the basest political blow against human dignity. It demands that the subjugated people renounce their feelings of "I am me" and "we are us" in order to accept the dominion of others and their new value system.

The question of what Koreanism means is central in the historical significance of the annexation of Korea by Japan. As Korea's independence was ending, the people were sobered by the great changes that were coming about in their lives. What would it mean to them? Would their lives be better, their society stronger, more prosperous, more rewarding in many ways—as the missionaries, the Japanese, and many private and public spokesmen from the West were telling them? They did know that under their own government, which was ending, they had suffered many injustices and irregularities. The little they knew about the world outside of their peninsula suggested that vast material improvements in their mode of living were available. Maybe the new order would be better than the old. But there were many reasons for them to dread the future with uncertainty and even with fear.

Before examining what Japan's annexation of Korea meant to the Koreans, it is appropriate to consider what their circumstances were as their independence was ending. Prior chapters have narrated the inadequacies of the government for the complex task of reshaping the entrenched political system, and the age-old customs and traditions that were challenged by modern knowledge and ideas. Imperialist ambitions of far stronger powers were jockeying with one another in a competitive effort to secure dominant positions in the peninsula; at the same time, the combination of internal and external pressures was a disruptive force that the government and the people were unprepared to deal with.

After the overthrow of the Taewongun, government was disrupted in a turmoil of contention among self-seeking clans and between conservatives and liberals. The decisions that had to be made were political. As is the rule everywhere, politicians contended against one another not only for their differing principles and policies but also for their individual and group advantages. Despite the valiant efforts of a few unselfish, able and ardent individuals, as described in chapters 4 and 5, the political and social systems were more weakened by deterioration than strenghtened by innovations.

It was unfortunate that the internal problems could not be dealt with by the Koreans without concurrent threats and interference from outside. Because of its strategic location and its plentitude of excellent ports, along with other valuable resources, the history of Korea has been likened to "a shrimp buffetted in the battles of whales." Foreign powers rushed to exploit the country much as birds of prey swoop upon a vulnerable victim. How Koreans might have responded to modernizing influences had they been free to make their own decisions is an unanswerable question, for such a condition did not exist.

But failure is by no means the complete verdict on this period of disintegration; nor is government the only basis for description. There were other qualities and factors that must be assessed in order to make possible a balanced historical judgment of the character and quality of Korean life before its independence was extinguished. What were the vital currents that were the driving forces for individuals and for the society? Some of these currents were the strong and steady value systems that were the traditional characteristics of the society. Others were new and variable crosscurrents of change.

A Korean proverb, derived from the country's geography, states, "Beyond the mountain are mountains." This is a succinct reflection of their lifelong (and centuries-long) experience. Whatever mountain is climbed, there are more mountains yet ahead. Also, however high and forbidding the mountains loom, between them are valleys. The meaning is deeply etched into their consciousness and illuminated in their behavior. There are challenges, there are difficulties, there are trials to be surmounted, by whatever effort, at whatever cost. And there are vales of comfort and of contentment to be enjoyed and treasured. Both are inevitable parts of life. This is their philosophy of the complementary nature of the *um* and the *yang*.

For Koreans this understanding is not fatalistic. There are many aspects of life that can be controlled by the individual, at least in part. There are differing ways of dealing with circumstances. The Korean temperament is well adjusted to the possibility, and indeed the necessity of making choices. True, the individual is heavily burdened by things beyond his control. But there is much that can be done to shape one's life. And what can be done should be done, even if sometimes at heavy cost. This belief undermines much of the disquiet that has persisted throughout Korean history and that is re-emphasized again in recurrent demonstrations and disorders.

The individualistic temperament, as well as the guiding ideas, that formed the structure of Korean culture are illuminated in the lives and in the writings of the country's greatest philosophers. Even in a history of Korea's modernization, these philosophers must not be neglected, for their ideas both affirm and represent characterizations that persist.

Among them was Chong Tojon (1342–98), who guided the constitutional character of the Choson dynasty away from Buddhism to Confucianism. *The Grand Rule of Laws,* which he propounded, interpreted Confucinism with a pragmatism that made it different from the Chinese model. Examinations to determine appointment of officials, Chong insisted, must not be based merely upon mastery of the literary classics but also upon administrative knowledge and skills. To separate ritualistic traditonalism from effective operations, under the nominal rule of the king, he argued, the duties of administration should be exercised by a prime minister, who could always be removed if his authority proved to be ineffectual. Laws were to be framed and executed not for punishment but as deterrents to crime.

Above all, Chong insisted that life must be lived according to a governing principle, which he proposed as being a devotion to righteousness. To allow selfish interests to determine conduct is to make man similar to beasts, he taught. There must be an inextinguishable light to keep individuals on a right path. The Taoist doctrine of self-fullfillment he dismissed as so individualistic as to be disruptive to social order; and he also disputed the Buddhist teaching that the mind of individuals is part of the ultimate essence of nature. Both Taoism and Buddhism, he claimed, were destructive of social responsibility—since both emphasized self-fulfillment—and therefore were a threat against humanity. Above all, he renounced the Buddhist view that the phenomenal world is an illusion. For Chong, reality consisted of the circumstances that must be dealt with.

His life ended in a political intrigue. King Taejo, the founder of the Choson dynasty, had eight sons, of whom the fifth, Yi Pangwon, was the ablest and most ambitious. Chong supported the Crown Prince and for this he was assassinated, dying in disgrace. Many of his reformist ideas were submerged after his death. But they did establish a Korean mode of Confucianism that was long studied in Asia as a realistic pattern for government. In modern Korea they have come alive again in renewed study of his works.

Kwon Kun (1352–1409), who became the chief adviser of King Yi Pang-won, sought to reconcile Neo-Confucianism with Buddhism. He represented King Pang-won, who took the dynastic name Taejong, as lamenting: "Now as I presume with my unworthiness to govern the people, my anxiety is as one who attempts to control a horse with rotten ropes." Kwon Kun's effort was to strengthen government so the harness would no longer be rotten. Rule goes amiss, Kwon assured the king, when "your reverence does not seek the way in the principle within your mind and the mandate of your nature, or in the proper human relationships." What should be avoided is to be "a traveller with no destination." There must be governing principles. Kwon belonged to a devout Buddhist family and was himself sympathetic with Buddhism, but he fully endorsed and developed Chong's insistence upon practicality in the pragmatic assessment of conditions and in searching for remedies for problems. The Buddhist Way, he concluded "is like empty space, without difference between the self and others." Reconciling this interpretation with Chong's Neo-Confucianism, Kwon concluded that "the mind is not separate from material forms; it is not a matter of stillness and trance." Instead, "it is manifested in things and affairs." Again, the emphasis is upon practicality.

Another thorough-going pragmatist, Yi I (1536–84), known also by his pen name of Yulgok, founded the "Ki School" of Neo-Confucianism, which may be said to combine essentials of the two very different Chinese philosophers, Chu-Hsi and Wang Yang-ming, who are generally considered to hold opposing views. Yulgok undertook to reconcile their divergent philosophies. According to his "theory of enlightenment,"— *what exists* and *what is thought to exist* both vitally affect human conduct. Recognition of the importance of both is necessary if society is to be rightly organized. What the right nature of society meant to him was, in modern terms, a veritable welfare state. Everyone should receive a proper reward for his work. Everyone should enjoy normal human rights. To accomplish such results, both the facts of nature (the Buddhist and Taoist emphasis) and the guiding principles of moral behavior (the Confucian emphasis) must be brought into accord. The reforms he called for were (1) to reshape the government towards the goal of insuring an acceptable standard of living for everyone; (2) to revise the tax collection to prevent corruption, to increase government revenues, and to protect the people from illegal over-collection of taxes; (3) to regulate the local loan, insurance, and savings systems and institutions to insure fairness; (4) to reform the recruitment for military service, to make it apply equally to all social classes and all localities; (5) to insure equality of opportunity for education to all social classes; (6) to create jobs for everyone who is willing and able to work and insure adequate support for the aged, the handicapped, and orphans; and (7) to allow widows to remarry (a right that was long denied them on the ground that they must remain loyal to their first husband). Such reforms were not, in fact, adopted; but they received widespread recognition as a special Korean interpretation of Confucian ethics.

A century later, the teachings of Yulgok's "theory of enlightenment" inspired the School of Practical Learning, or *Silhak,* led by Yi Ik (1681–1763), which called for such agricultural reforms as (1) redistribution of land to self-employed farming families; (2) reduction of costs of both farm-tenancy and agricultural loans; and (3) expansion of land under cultivation. Like Yulgok, Yi Ik believed that institutions should aim primarily to serve the real needs of the people. This, again, was a further development of Korean-Confucianism.

Toegye, whose family name was Yi Hwang (1501–70) was another of the greatest of Korean philosophers, along with Chong Tojon, Yulgok, and Tasan. Toegye's chief concern was to reconcile "what is so" with "what should be so." Human nature is what it is, and we see the result in a mixture of good and bad. Morality consists of our ideals as to what should be. The purpose of government, indeed the purpose of human endeavor, is to bring behavior as nearly as may be into conformity with the moral ideal. Toegye insisted upon the discipline of self-control. As he wrote, "wrath can easily be aroused and is the least controllable of human feelings. However, the fact that we can easily calm our wrath and judge right and wrong according to reason proves that the temptations of our external surroundings themselves are not a sufficient cause for stimulating evil." As the Korean proverb avers, "Blame yourself, not the river, if you fall into the water." To explain the relationship of principle to conduct, he used the metaphor of a ship. A ship moves over water because it is the nature of a ship to do so. If the ship is driven upon rocks by a typhoon, the ship behaves contrary to its nature, for it no longer can sail. This accident denies neither "what should be" nor "what is." Our aim in life is to act so that we are not driven to wreckage. In his major work, *Diagram of the Supreme Ultimate,* Toegye points out that "what should be" and "what is" are inseparably linked, but that the distinction between them must not be blurred. In short, matters do not always go as we wish, but this should not lead us to conclude that what happens is either inevitable or necessarily right. We may not be "master of our fate, "but we should try to be as best we can.

These abstractions were converted into explicit practicality when Toegye fell ill and an older associate, Yi Hyon-bo (1457–1555) explicated his teachings by presenting a three-part listing of "violations of rites and mores that do harm to local customs." The first set, to be most severely punished, consisted of these offences:

I

Disobeying parents.
Quarrelling with brothers.
Disrupting the peace and order of the family.
Interfering with official business and meddling in village affairs.
Arrogating the power to usurp public functions and pursue private gain.
Insulting village elders.
Seducing, threatening, defiling, or corrupting virtuous widows.

The next order of violations, to be somewhat less severely dealt with, were:

II

Impairing good relations among relatives.
Displacing legal wives.
Causing disharmony among neighbors.
Beating or reviling fellow workers.
Shamelessly corrupting the mores of gentlemen.
Relying on coercion to intimidate, or cheat, or blackmail the weak.
Ganging up with vagabonds to commit wicked or violent acts.

Criticizing in public assemblies those who govern.
Fabricating evidence to slander or incriminate others.
Idly refusing assistance to the unfortunate, when able to help them.
Taking advantage of the absence of officials to commit evil deeds.
For no good reason, failing to attend marriages, funerals, and sacrifices.
Failing to respect village ordinances.
Resisting, resenting, or failing to submit to village consensus.
Engaging in village activities for selfish gain.
Failing, for no good reason, to attend farewell feasts for departing officials.

Finally, a yet lesser order of moral failings was listed as:

III

Arriving late for public meetings
Sitting in a disorderly fashion and violating decorum.
Being noisy and argumentative in public meetings.
Leaving one's seat at will during meetings.
Leaving early for no good reason.

Obviously to Toegye moral behavior primarily meant harmonious behavior; the greatest departure from "what should be" was to disrupt or destroy family harmony. In addition, acts harmful to others were immoral. This theme was continued by Yulgok, with more emphasis upon "what should be," in his 1571 book, *The Community Compact of Sowon,* written as guidance for local officials. Evil deeds to be discouraged and punished included: "Indulging in drinking and gambling, delighting in dispute and taking pleasure in fighting, and fabricating rumors falsely to revile others." Good conduct that the officials should encourage and reward Yulgok described as follows: "Effectively showing filiality toward parents, effectively showing affection for siblings, effectively showing friendliness to relatives and acquaintances, effectively instructing the sons and daughters of the family that they may be guided to righteousness, effectively maintaining one's honesty and integrity, extending charity, guiding others to become good, disentangling people from quarrels and combat, and helping those who are in difficulty and misfortune."

These were moral strictures that were handed down, from generation to generation, with emphasis upon behaving rightly rather than merely ritualistically or being satisfied just to understand right principles. Proper family relationships were stressed in Korea much as they were in China. The Korean codes, however, emphasized much more strongly the need for and the modes of neighborliness than did those in either China or Japan. Moreover, the Korean portrayals of "what should be" represented horizontal flows of behavior, in terms of mutuality. As was true throughout Asia, hierarchical relationships—those of subordinates to superiors—were important for Koreans. But as the cited codes clearly show, by far the commonest factor in ordinary human relations was the equality of responsibility for upholding morality and maintaining harmony. As the centuries passed, "what is" by no means always corresponded with "what should be." Nevertheless, Koreans were taught to know what is right and to judge themselves and others by what is done rather than by what is professed.

How well did this teaching work in practice? Better than might be expected —remembering the pressures of poverty, the cynicism engendered by the corruption of officials, and the guilefullness that had to be exercised to counter the exactions to which the people were exposed. The all-encompassing guilds were an important factor in policing and enforcing standards of fair and helpful behavior. Outside of officialdom, virtually everyone was a member of not one but of several guilds—one vocational, the other cooperative, for serving the ritualistic needs of weddings, funerals, birthdays, and holidays. In many and vital ways, the individuals in communities were interlocked and interdependent. There was no avoiding the principle that what is good for one must not conflict with what is good for all, or from its corollary, that what is good for all is ultimately good for one.

What Koreans are like is determined not only by their nationalistic ideals but inevitably in part by their geography. The people are bound together as a nation first of all by the fact that their country is a peninsula. The top end attaches to Manchuria and Siberia, much as an extended thumb from a closed fist. The mountainous mass called the Everwhite Mountain, and the tumultuous Yalu and Tumen Rivers provide a northern border that is definitive, though not as decisive as the seas surrounding and forming the other three sides. In its early history, Korea's northern kingdoms reached far into Manchuria; and in more recent times several hundred thousand Koreans have migrated across their northern border to settle in Manchuria and in Siberia. Nevertheless, Koreans are a peninsular people, united by their geography, much as Italians are.

They also are a mountain people, again like the Italians, but even more so. There are twenty-six peaks in Korea that are above 6,000 feet in height. Moreover, the peaks and ridges are composed of relatively new upthrusts, so that they are very precipitous. This mountainous terrain has consequences that are as determinate as is the peninsular shape of the country. As is true around the world, mountainous peoples tend to be self-reliant, sturdy, and individualistic. They value their freedom and in their mountain fastnesses have means for local defense of it. They are provincial, with their attachments strong to their local, and therefore readily accessible communities. The corollary is that, historically, they have proved to be geographically disunited—group-centered but between groups competitive and quarrelsome—within the encompassing national unity. Transportation and even communication within the peninsula has always, until recent years, been sparse and difficult. Governmental authority, as is true everywhere, extends outward from the capital, much like the tenacles of an octopus. Officials in the various provinces receive their appointments and their authority from the capital and give to it, not to the locals whom they govern, their fundamental loyalty. Since they are relatively remote from central control, it has been easy for them to take advantage of their authority to coerce and to exploit the local peoples. Hence, from early times the communities that have been all too often abused and robbed and repressed have tended to resent and rebel against the center from which these injustices flowed.

The most basic factor that has united all Koreans, despite their geographic or clan-induced divisiveness, is their language. Linguistically, Koreans are unusually homogeneous. There are some dialectical differences, reflective of localities, but these are by far less marked than is true of most other peoples. Koreans are not separated from one another as are the peoples of India, who speak in some five hundred different languages, fifteen of them being so distinct as to be mutually unintelligible; or the people of China, who share a written language in common but from province to province talk differently; or the people of England, the United States, Germany, Japan, the Philippines, and, indeed, most nations, all of whom have strong dialectical distinctions, if not actually differing languages. In Korea, natives of Pyongyang, Seoul, Kwangju, Pusan, and other major centers do speak with sufficient dialectical characteristics to distinguish their locality. But Koreans everywhere, speaking their own common language, readily understands one another.

The importance of language can scarcely be overemphasized. Language and culture are inextricably intertwined. People who talk alike not only understand one another, they also feel a strong kinship. Language is more than vocabulary, more than grammar, more than syntax, more indeed than words. The way a people talk includes such factors as their inflections, their intonation, their typical rate of speech, their gestures, their fluency, their readiness to talk freely or not, to argue or not, to talk or not to talk with strangers, to value formality or informality as typical modes of discourse. Every special groups, such as lawyers, farmers, doctors, or construction workers, has its own "language" by which it identifies itself as a group. Outsiders are dismissed as being those who "don't speak our language." Language is an essential mark of identity.

Well recognizing the importance of linguistic identity, Korea's leading linguistic scholar Chu Si-gyong, who was a member of the Independence Club, realized that dependence upon Chinese ideograms for writing was a form of "cultural slavery." He devoted himself to the study of the hangul alphabet and undertook to modernize it so that it could suitably represent the new knowledge and the ideas and attitudes of the liberal reformists. With the changes Chu introduced, Philip Jaisohn was able to use the hangul script in *The Independent,* and Syngman Rhee in the *Maiel Shinmun.* This strictly Korean alphabet, they urged, was fully adequate as a medium of communication to serve all the needs of discourse, for both "the high and the low, the noble and the despised." Chi Sok-yong, a young scholar in his twenties, who was to live and to work until 1935, joined them in the campaign to rescue hangul from the stigma of being fit only for writings directed to women and children, and for such subjects as riddles and folk tales. They rejected the term *onmun,* meaning "vulgar script" and substituted for it the terms *kugo,* meaning national language, *kungmun,* or national script, and hangul, the name that was used for this phonetic alphabet when it was introduced during the reign of King Sejong in the fifteenth century. They called it "the best alphabet in the world," because of its phonetic character, and demonstrated that it had "scholarly merit" in being able to represent general meanings accurately. Moreover, they pointed out, this alphabet was so simple that it would save the "precious and urgent time" required to master the cumbersome Chinese ideograms and, instead, would spread literacy broadly, thereby helping the nation to gain "enlightenment, prosperity, and power."

The enormous range of influence exerted by language is difficult to comprehend. It is a common and serious mistake to conceive that languages are fully translatable. The complete meaning of any linguistic form is ineffable. A word that is confidently defined is nevertheless partially undefinable, because it has in its use a vast range of meanings that are dependent on who is speaking to whom, under what circumstances, on what subject, at what time, with what intent, in what mood; and also on the nature of the relationships between speaker and hearer—both in general and specifically at the moment of the communicative interchange. Translation depends on identification tags that cannot accurately reproduce these exceedingly variable factors.[18]

The annexation of Korea by Japan meant, basically, that the Korean language no longer was "primary" for Koreans. They could not be prevented from speaking it, but henceforth, as subjects of Japan, it was Japanese that was to be their primary tongue. The Japanese government, well understanding the importance of language, made sustained efforts to replace the Korean language with its own or, at the least, to stress the inseparable relationship between usage of Japanese and acceptable status.

The grammar and vocabulary of Korean and of Japanese are more similar than either language is to Chinese. But this does not mean that they are in any true sense related (although many Koreans, including some linguistic specialists, like to think that Japanese is really a derivative of Korean). Linguistic specialists can only speculate as to how languages have developed. All languages, no matter how different they seem, somewhat resemble one another. The science of historical linguistics is said to have originated in a lecture given by thirty-year-old Sir William Jones, before the Asiatic Society of Bengal in 1786, in which he posited that all languages have "sprung from some common source, which, perhaps, no longer exists." From this hypothesis, linguistic scholars have decided that Indo-European was the parental source for the languages of the broad area from India on throughout Europe. Since then, other long-lost "source" languages have been identified, such as the "Malaya-Polynesian," the "Proto-Algonquian," and the "Tibeto-Burman." Yet another source language was the "Ural-Altaic," which fathered the languages of northeast Asia. Linguistic specialists study both the similarities and the differences found in language groups. Korean and Japanese "somewhat" resemble one another, as do Sanskrit and Greek and Latin; nevertheless they have had wholly disparate development. Efforts that have been made to derive Japanese from Tamil or from Korean have been abandoned.

Every language is imbedded in its own cultural matrix. To require a people to change their language is to tear them apart from the vast network of intricacies that comprise their own culture. For them to think, to feel, and to communicate in a language foreign to their own culture is to mutilate their personalities. The effect is very different from the voluntary learning of a foreign tongue as an individual's secondary language. Neither is it denied that some individuals successfully become "socially marginal," so that they are equally at home in, say, Korean and English, or German and Swedish. Such individuals become truly acculturated in two different cultures as well as in the two languages. This is by their own choice, and it is a feat that only a few can achieve. But for the great mass of the people, to force them to surrender their own primary language and to accept another as their own is to challenge their group identity. And this, in effect, was the fundamental transformation that the annexation of Korea by Japan imposed on the Koreans.

Changes were coming in abundance. Among them, the independence of Korea was laid away. But like Banquo's ghost, it would not stay down. The sovereignty of Korea was drugged. Its death was announced. But as the next decades would show, it would not stay dead.

7

Patterns of Colonialism

Defeat and conquest are so commonplace in human history that it is easy for them to be taken for granted—except by their victims. In the histories of modern Asia, the annexation of Korea by Japan is generally treated as an incident in the large pattern of imperialism. It was essential for Japan's movement onto the continent. It invites attention not to Korea but to Japan. What it meant to Koreans has a poignancy not easily felt except by those who lived through it.

One of them was Younghill Kang, who provided vivid insights into that period in his autobiography *The Grass Roof.*[19] He portrayed the Kang family as being relatively prosperous farmers, living in a remote village named Song-Dune-Chi (The Village of the Pine Trees), in north Korea, just below the Tumen River. Some of the soil was rocky and sandy, some fertile. The mountain streams that converged in the river that ran beside the village insured water for irrigation in times of drought. For upwards of a thousand years the Kang family had lived in this same village, whose inhabitants were all in some degree related. They were accustomed to sparse living. The exactions of moneylenders and of corrupted tax-collectors were not more onerous than they were able to bear. The disruptive influences that were tearing Korean society apart around the turn of the century scarcely penetrated into the remote countryside in which they lived. But then, in late August 1910, news more devastating than an epidemic of cholera reached them. Korea was annexed by Japan.

"My father," Kang wrote, "turned a dark red and would not even open his mouth. My uncle *pak-sa* became suddenly very old, and he shrivelled and fainted in his own room. My crazy-poet uncle sat staring straight ahead of him until far into the night."

> There was no supper that night. My grandmother sat up by candlelight, in the same dress she had worn in the morning. Again and again she took a cup of rice tea to my father, but he lay heavily on the mats, and he would not accept it.
>
> In the morning, it was found that several of the young men who had been among those drunk the night before had committed suicide. Their bodies lay along the banks of the stream where the women usually did washing on this day.
>
> A Japanese policeman came to our village, at the head of a band of pale-blue-

coated Japanese, each armed with a long sword. Of course they knocked at our gate, and asked why we did not have the sun flag of Japan instead of the red and white flag of Korea betokening the male and female realm, and in accordance with the Confucian philosophy of the Book of Changes, sun and moon, and all the elements used in geomancy. My father shrugged his shoulders and pretended not to understand. The small Jap policeman then flew at my father, kicking and striking him, with menace of the sword. My grandmother saw from the window, and ran out, without even stopping to put her coat over her head and screen her face from vulgar eyes.

"Don't you touch my son!" she screamed, stepping between, "because he had nothing to eat for these two days and doesn't know what he is doing."

As soon as she came between them the policeman knocked her down. He kicked her fiercely with his Western boot. Her sons seeing it, gasped. In the eyes of Koreans to touch an old woman, the mother of sons, was a crime punishable by death. Even criminals were safe behind her skirts. My father would have strangled him, but he saw that my grandmother had fainted with pain. He at once lifted her on his back and started off towards the marketplace where there was a fairly good doctor. But her ankle was broken and she was sick for many weeks.

That night I went into my crazy-poet uncle's studio and lay down on the mat, crying miserably. By and by I heard the crazy-poet walking around and muttering in the next room. With my wet finger I made a hole in the paper wall and looked through. He stood at the outer door and just shook his fist in the face of the sky.

. . . Was Korea ended then?

In a way, it was. Korea was renamed Chōsen. Korea as such disappeared from world maps. Foreigners soon forgot it, for its circumstances were largely unknown and very little discussed. What Korea became was never clearly or legally defined. Its status was vaguely ambiguous. Technically, it was not a colony; but it was treated as one. The Japanese term *Nikkan heigō,* meaning "amalgamation of Japan and Korea," was not really intended and never took place. Essentially, Chōsen was treated as a colony—that is, as a territory foreign and external to Japan, to be ruled in a distinctive way, quite differently from the governing of the island empire that had annexed it.

According to the annexation proclamation, the Japanese constitution did not apply to Korea or to Koreans and would not for a period of ten years. In 1919 the Japanese premier Hara Kei, after the *manse* uprising, promised that "it is the ultimate purpose of the Japanese Government in due course to treat Korea as in all respects on the same footing as Japan proper." Actually, Koreans never did become full or equal citizens of Japan. Even yet, Koreans who have been residents in Japan for two or even three generations are not granted citizenship.

The governmental structure for Chōsen was different from that in Japan. A Japanese explanation has been that the population was unready to exercise the full responsibilities of citizenship and therefore could not, until after a period of tutelage, have all the customary civic rights. As for Koreans still resident in Japan, they are victims partly of prejudice against their race and partly of Japan's strict policy of protecting the "purity" of its own population. On the peninsula, Koreans were governed in a manner that served the purposes that brought Japan there. Whether Chōsen should be called a colony, a special province, or something else, its status was unique.

The governance of the peninsula was militaristic. Of the eight Governors-General who successively administered Chōsen seven were army generals and the other was an admiral. Garrison forces were established at key points throughout the peninsula. In June, preceding the annexation, the 10,000 Japanese gendarmes and police in Korea were placed under the direct command of a major-general. Transport and communication facilities were under military control, and the military developed plans for their expansion—primarily to meet its own needs. As the Japanese historian Shakuo Shunjo frankly avowed (in his *History of Korean Annexation,* published in Tokyo in 1926) the "entire Korean peninsula was turned into a military camp." Japanese historians typically describe Terauchi's administration as "military dictatorial government."

The whole governmental structure under which Chōsen was administered was outside of, as well as different from, Japan's political system. Under the Governor-General, reporting to him and subject to his orders, were the thirteen provinces of Chōsen with 11 prefectures, 317 districts, and 4,322 towns. Seoul, renamed Keijō, was classified as a special prefecture. The thirteen Korean provincial governors were replaced by Japanese. All top administrative offices in the Government-General and in the provinces were filled by Japanese. Between 1910 and 1943, there were 87 bureau chiefs in the central bureaucracy, only two of whom were Koreans. In 1943, of the 4,562 higher officials in the Government-General, 86 percent were Japanese. An announcement on 1 January 1945 that ten Koreans would be elected to the House of Lords of the Diet and sixteen to the Assembly was not brought into effect. Even minor Korean bureaucrats were dismissed, except for the few who were fluent in the Japanese language and compliant with their superiors. Korean factions, or special interest groups, were well-established, but there were no political parties, nor were any allowed to form. Security was a principal concern. Both informal political discussions and public assemblies for discussion of affairs were banned. Individuals who were even suspected of fostering anti-Japanese sentiments were arrested. Newspapers that carried or earlier had editorials or news stories critical of Japan were suspended.

With all these measures either in place or prepared for implementation, on 29 August 1910 the Japanese Emperor proclaimed the annexation. It had become necessary, he explained, "to maintain public order and security and to advance the happiness and well-being of the Korean people." As a conciliatory gesture to foreigners, the proclamation also promised that those in Korea would be assured the same rights as those resident in Japan. Export and import duties and regulations governing the tonnage of shipments would be the same for foreigners as for Japanese. All treaties with Korea were henceforth to be null and void. There was no Korea anymore.

General Masatake Terauchi, who had been Resident General since May, arrived in Seoul in July, a month before the annexation, with the city already resembling an armed camp. In his inaugural address as Governor General he promised to the Korean people "the benefit of a judicious and benevolent rule"—for as long as they remained careful "not to go astray." He also gave assurance that the royal family, the yangban class, and all others who were "dutiful" and "virtuous" would be treated honorably. To the great mass of the population, the farmers, he announced that their unpaid taxes from prior years and unpaid loans from the government, used for the repurchase of their own rice harvests, would not be collected. He also pardoned local officials who might have withheld portions of the taxes they collected. And he granted a limited amnesty to "deserving" political prisoners.

In the cities, tightly patrolled by soldiers, there was little public reaction. Out in the countryside, where fighting between Japanese troops and the Righteous Army was continuing in bitterly contested local actions, the government troops were under orders to take no prisoners. Control over the country had been imposed not suddenly but progressively, over a period of years. The climax of annexation found the people with little or no means of resistance.

Emperor Sunjong justified the acceptance of annexation as a necessity "in order to maintain public order and security and to advance the happiness and well-being of the people." He must, he told the people, "entrust Our great task to abler hands than Ours" in view of "the long-standing weakness and deep-seated evils" that had undermined Korea's independence. In a final token of helpless humility, Sunjong sent a note to Terauchi pleading that the money grant for the royal expenses would not be decreased. Graciously, Terauchi promised that it would be continued. He also sought the favor of the nobility by offering to some seventy-five of them, most of whom had been high officials, titles of nobility, ranging from marquis to baron, together with annual stipends appropriate to the titles. Sixty-seven of these Koreans accepted his offer. This array of bribes offered to the broad range of Koreans, and their acceptance of them, was less generous on the part of the Government-General, and less advantageous to the recipients, than they seemed; for the new government proceeded promptly and efficiently, mostly through tighter tax collection, to more than regain what these offerings cost.

The effects of what Japan did in Korea during the 1910–45 period have been and probably always will be hotly debated. Japanese and Korean historians, quite naturally, reach very different conclusions about it. The period has not been exhaustively studied.[20] Korean historians have not found satisfaction in examination of this period of humiliation and futility. Japanese historians have felt even less pleasure in unveiling what they recognize as a chapter in militant imperialism that led on into grievous misfortunes both for Japan and for the countries it invaded. Much remains to be discovered about the conditions of life in the peninsula during that period before a final judgment is feasible.

Enough is known, however, to justify a conclusion that the colonial period was not for either Korea or Japan a fortunate transition from their ancient traditionalism into modernity. Both gained some, and both lost even more. *Modern history would have been quite different if the Japanese had remained at home, on their own islands.*

Japanese policies for governing Chōsen divide into three fairly distinct stages. From 1910 through 1919 the emphasis was strictly upon subjugation of the population by military dictatorship. Koreans were denied political participation. Newspapers critical of Japan were abruptly suspended. Punishment of dissidents was swift and severe. Under Terauchi, his successor General Yoshimichi Hasegawa, and their chief subordinate, Lt.-General Akashi Totojiro, the Koreans were subjected to what even Japanese hstorians describe as "unscrupulous and brutal oppressions" under "authoritarian despots." The Governor-General had more unchecked authority than the Prime Minister had in Japan. He was answerable only to the Emperor and the Emperor remained aloof from administrative problems and programs. The tone was set by Terauchi, with his warning that if he met with resistance, "I will whip you with scorpions."

After the popular uprising of March 1919 brought conditions in the peninsula under worldwide scrutiny and criticism, Japan revised the Government-General policies in an alleged attempt to win the people by conciliation (which, however, proved to be strictly limited), with Admiral Minoru Saitō as the new Governor-General. Saitō's concern was not with basic policy but with methods for implementing it. The question was not whether Japan would retain Korea but how its rule could be rendered more effective. One policy guide given to Saitō concluded that: "Study of Korean history shows that Korean people . . . if they are oppressed cannot be obedient to their rulers. . . . If they are treated with kindness they are a docile race." A Tokyo "hard-line" political leader, however, thought that even General Yoshimichi Hasegawa had been too "soft" and warned Saitō, "if the Koreans are handled gently they immediately rise up and revolt; if you give them one thing, they demand two; if you give them two, they ask for four."

Saitō promised that his long-range goal should be to elevate Koreans to the same level as were the Japanese. Saitō's biographer summarized the goals that Saitō set as his guidelines as follows: to apply, so far as feasible, all Japanese legislation to Korea; to establish in Korea a local government system similar to that in Japan; to abolish the gendarmerie and substitute for it a civilian police force; to reform the legal system; to provide "equal" education for Koreans; to end segregation of Japanese in Korea and to permit intermarriage; to recruit and to promote talented Koreans in the Government-General; to end the uniform-wearing and sword-carrying by Government-General officials; to abolish flogging of offenders; and to expand the budget for Korea.[21]

Conciliation, however, was only superficial and partial. Almost none of the goals proclaimed by Saitō was attained. Only thirteen percent of elementary-school-age Korean children were enrolled in school ten years later in 1930. What little schooling they got was only "to make them economically useful." In 1945 only twenty-two percent of Koreans were literate, and even this literacy was in the Japanese language. Meanwhile, the number of police increased from 7,700 in 1910 to 19,000 by 1930. Korea's separate form of government was not much changed. Local provincial councils were created but the members were appointed by the Governor-General.

The third period commenced around 1935–36 and extended to the defeat of Japan in 1945. Japan's military, in full control of its home government, was mobilizing all available resources, including those in Korea and Manchuria (renamed Manchukuo), for the 1937 launching of war against China. Japanese publicists were turning from defensive to offensive tactics in responding to Western criticisms of Japan's policies of expansion. Koreans were subjected to increased totalitarian government. Freedom of speech and the press was abrogated. "Patriotic neighborhood groups" were organized to enforce adherence to a broad range of new regulations. Christianity came under heavy pressures and State Shintoism was decreed as the official religion of the peninsula. Workers of all ages and both sexes were forced into labor gangs to do whatever work the government decided was needed—both in Chōsen and in Japan, to which impressed workers were taken. Industrialization was speeded, especially in the north, to convert the peninsula into a support base for the war in China, and this led to the enforced dislocation of large numbers of individuals and families.

Naturally, in all three of these periods, the ruling Japanese interpreted their policies and programs in affirmative, not negative, terms. Even in the first period, while the controls were most stringent, the Government-General encouraged continuation of the study of Confucianism, though with a new and different emphasis. In its *Annual Report* for 1911–12, for example, the government declared that Koreans "should be encouraged to pursue their old Confucian ethical teachings, under which not only have they lived for centuries, but upon which they have also founded their social considerations." Among the awards granted by Terauchi at his inauguration, 9,811 went to Confucian yangban scholars "whose behavior was esteemed a model for good subjects"; others were given to "filial sons" and "virtuous wives" who manifested Confucian respect for parents and husbands. The 1914 report added that "all officials and lectures in [Confucian] service should not be contented with merely reading Chinese classics and holding religious services for Chinese sages, but should endeavor to aid in the promotion of the moral culture of the people at large by making themselves models of good behaviour to their neighbors as well as by remedying their bad customs and promoting their good usages." Of course "model behavior" meant acceptance of and obedience to the new laws and regulations.

In 1911 the Government-General brought into effect "The Chōsen Educational Ordinance," which contained the following provisions. First, and basically, the purpose of education was to make "loyal and good subjects." To enforce this aim, a commission was appointed to rewrite all the textbooks. Second, educational opportunities would be adapted to the needs of the people—which, as interpreted, meant that Koreans were restricted to elementary and vocational training, with the higher schools and classes in liberal and humane arts restricted largely to Japanese residents in Korea. The functions of all the schools were four-fold: (1) to root out so far as possible Korean culture and patriotism; (2) to provide vocational training; (3) to discourage liberal reformist thinking; and (4) to discriminate in educational goals and opportunities between Japanese and Koreans. By the end of this first period, in 1919, there were in the peninsula, for Korean attendance, 482 elementary schools, five middle schools, and two girls' high scools. For the one-ninth of the population that were Japanese, there were 380 elementary schools, five middle schools, and eleven girls' high schools.[22] In all the schools, public, private, and missionary, teaching was in the Japanese language, except in Korean language classes. The study of Korean history became a subsidiary part of Japanese history. The school day was opened by singing the Japanese national anthem. The Japanese teachers all bore swords as a mark of respect for militarism.

In 1920, as part of the new liberalization policies, a new Educational Ordinance declared that education should interpret culture in accord with the desires of the people. But this did not happen. Keijō Imperial University was established in Seoul. Its faculty was almost entirely Japanese, its student body was predominantly Japanese, and entrance requirements weeded out most applicants who were not pro-Japanese. One normal school was established in Keijō (Seoul) and one in each of the thirteen provinces. These for the first time offered extensive teacher-training facilities in the peninsula.

In 1925, the Government-General created a Society for Compiling Korean History, explaining that it wanted to rectify the "scandalous" neglect by Koreans of their own traditions. By 1913, this Society completed publication of thirty-one volumes, all of which developed the theme that Koreans had been hapless and disorderly until, finally, Japan had graciously assumed the role of their protector and benefactor. On 20 April 1937 the Government-General issued instructions to the governors of the provinces, telling them that "to mold our national character, to form our national morals, to cultivate a firm and fiery national faith—these are the first principles in our national education."

After Japan's 1931–32 seizure and occupation of Manchuria (which they then reshaped into Manchukuo) and the 1937 attack on China, the Government-General in 1938 once again revised its educational policies to support three principles: (1) to inculcate acceptance of Japan's enlarged role of creating and directing the "Great East Asia Co-Prosperity Sphere"; (2) to stress Japanese-Korean unity; and (3) to induce in students a devotion to labor. To accomplish all three objectives, all schools were reorganized as semi-military institutions. Students were to devote part of each day to work on programs and in factories devoted to serving the war needs. Male students were formed into work units under the orders of Japanese soldiers. Girl students were placed in groups that sewed uniforms for Japanese troops or prepared gift packages to be sent to front line soldiers. After the oubreak of war with Britain and the United States, the eighth day of every month was designated for re-emphasizing loyalty to the Emperor, for lectures on the war, for collection of donations of money, food, or labor to support the war, and for visits to Shinto shrines. As an instrument for tightening "thought control," the Government-General organized "The Society for the Encouragement of Learning." By various measures, students were virtually forced to volunteer for the army.

In accord with these policies for control of education, sustained efforts of other kinds were also made to limit access of Koreans to knowledge about the world beyond their borders. These efforts, varying in severity through each of the three periods, had only limited success—partly because modern means of communication make the diffusion of information hard to control, and partly because of the missionary ties between Korea and the West. Despite restrictions, vital information continued to flow both into and out from the peninsula. So did misinformation.

The relations of religion and politics in colonized Korea were a tangled skein of contradictions. Religion deals with what individuals live for and politics with how they live. Efforts to keep them in separate categories are always difficult. Christian missionaries wanted, above all, to continue their evangelism—and in this they had such success that between 1900 and 1910 the number of converts increased by more than thirty percent. This accomplishment was possible only by kowtowing to Japanese authority. Arthur J. Brown, Secretary of the Board of Foreign Missions of the Presybterian Church, speaking on behalf of the general missionary body in Korea, attested, in a letter to a Japanese official on 16 February 1912, that "Japanese administration is far better than Korea would otherwise have had and far better than Korea under its own rule." The Federal Council of Churches of Christ in America in 1919 published its conclusion that "Prior to the annexation the administrative system was chaotic. By stern enforcement the Japanese have introduced quiet and order." These judgements were just, as far as they went. But "quiet" and "order" are distinct from "freedom" and "justice."

The distinction was clarified by Dr. Rentara Midyuro, who had served as Superintendent of Schools in Korea, in speaking to a Missionary conference in Pyongyang, in the spring of 1920. Many Japanese, he warned the audience, were dubious about the loyalty of the Christians. "Critics even go so far as to say that some missionaries in Korea do not in reality consider Korea as an internal part of Japan and Koreans as Japanese subjects," he said, "and under the pretext of neutrality in politics, ignore the Japanese sovereignty over Korea." Japanese sensitivity was so keen that a Tract Society pamphlet in which Korean Christians were urged to "expel the devil within them," was suppressed because, as the censor indignantly told the editor, "When you say devil you are referring to Japan, you are urging Koreans to rise in rebellion!" The Government-General thereupon issued instructions forbidding use of the term "devil" in any missionary publications thereafter.

As previously noted, Japan actively supported Confucianism and thereby won sufferance if not actual support from the considerable body of influential Confucians. It also gave verbal support to Buddhism. The 1914–15 *Annual Report* on the Administration of Chōsen affirmed that "Buddhism is the only religion in Chōsen existing from olden times that can be regarded today as worthy of the name." Instead of cultivating good relations with the Buddhists, however, Japan sought to control them. In 1911 the Government-General promulgated a "Temple Law" that placed all Buddhist temple properties under government control and that granted the Governor-General authority to appoint all abbots in the headquarters temples. When applied to Korea, Japanese Buddhist practices (such as authorizing the marriage of abbots and giving them virtual dictatorial powers) so enraged Korean Buddhists that they became active political opponents of the colonizers. As for Chondogyo, the Government-General attempted to suppress it because of its strong advocacy of democratic equality and national independence.

In Japan, religion and politics were closely related. Shinto was the legitimization of state authority. From its inception, the Government-General of Chōsen sought to impose Shinto religious values upon all segments of Korean life. Shinto shrines were erected in practically every Korean city, town, and village, and in every school. In the third period of colonial rule, in 1935 the government ordered the obeissance of all teachers and students, including those in Christian schools, in observance of Shinto shrine daily ceremonies. When Christian missionaries protested, the government described these ceremonies as being not religious but patriotic. This position caused some furor among Japanese Shinto leaders, who felt constrained to protest that "the ceremonies that are performed therein have a full religious character." The Catholic missionaries received instructions from Rome to accept the Shinto shrine ceremonies as "mere expressions of patriotic love." Since the Protestant missionaries could not justify obeisance "dedicated to other spirits," they decided to retire from conducting secular education. However, in order to reopen their schools, the Methodists in 1937 and the Presbyterians in 1938 accepted "the official assurance that Shrine attendance is a patriotic rather than a religious rite."

A climactic action on the Shrine issue took place on 30 September 1938 in Pyongyang, in a meeting of the Korean General Assembly. With three uniformed Japanese police officials on the platform, with plainclothes policemen scattered throughout the audience, and with all known opponents of Shrine ceremonies excluded from the meeting, a resolution was introduced asserting that "the Shrine service is not religious; it is not in conflict with Christianity; it is a national patriotic ceremony. The Shrines should be encouraged, and in such an unusual time as this [the ceremonies are] an aid to the mobilization of the national spirit and should be observed by the officials and people who are behind the guns." No discussion was allowed. The call for an affirmative vote brought only a few ayes; no negative vote was taken. By such means, the Shrine policy was affirmed. After the outbreak of World War II, Shrine attendance was strictly enforced. Every Korean family was ordered to erect a Shinto shrine in its home. Some two thousand Christians who refrained were imprisoned and fifty of them, whose opposition was public as well as persistent, were executed.

Japanese Christians in general took the position that Christianity in Korea had best be promulgated by Japanese missionaries rather than Western. One of their spokesmen, Ebina Lansei, wrote in 1907 that "if Japan wishes to assimilate the Koreans, she must not only reach them politically and economically, but also in the depths of their hearts. The true religion of Christianity must be preached in Korea by Japanese people in order effectively to save the people." Another, resenting the pro-Koreanism of many American missionaries, protested that "I feel deeply angered and insulted that these missionaries not only block our government's policy but also foster ugly irreligious attitudes that agitate Koreans against us." In such ways, the Japanese practically forced the Korean missionary group to oppose the annexation and the colonial government of Korea, despite the initial tendency for them to welcome and support it. The dilemma faced by the missionaries was not easily solved. If they pleased the Japanese, they offended the Koreans, and vice versa. Hard as they tried to walk a tightrope mid-position, they could not avoid slipping off on one side or the other.

However soul-searing spiritual problems were for the Koreans, for the Japanese the major problems in Korea concerned its development as a market, as a source of supplies, as an outlet for its surplus population, and as a transportation route to Manchukuo. These goals, taken separately and cumulatively, required substantial modernization of Korea. These processes provide the principal supports for the view that Japan's colonial policies were beneficial to the Korean people. Modernization was, indeed, hastened.

What was of the utmost consequence was that the Japanese enterprise regarding the peninsula after 1910 was not directed toward a foreign country, Korea, but, rather was administered within a newly integrated part of Japan—Chōsen, whose population was to be recast from Korean to Japanese. Under the Protectorate, the avowed purport of Japanese control was to guard, to guide, and to sponsor the well-being of the people of Korea. After annexation, the declared aim was to advance the well-being of the people and the government of Japan. What was intended and what was done thereafter could not be for the advantage of Korea or of Koreans—for, in both legal and realistic terms, so far as Japan and the global diplomatic community was concerned, there no longer was any Korea or Koreans. Instead, there was an expanded Japan and an addition of thirteen million to the total population of the Mikado's empire. Whatever consoling words the Governor-General might utter from time to time assuring the peninsular people of his care for them, his authority stemmed from Tokyo. To it he made his reports; to it he owned his loyalty and his best efforts; by it he was judged; and it was the government in Tokyo whose interests he served.

Some have compared the inrush of Japanese immigrants into Korea with the rising tide of newcomers in nineteenth-century America. The Japanese who rushed into Korea by the thousands, and then the tens of thousands, and then the hundreds of thousands, came in to dominate the Korean population, even though the newcomers were mostly poor landless farmers without education, coming to make their fortune at the expense of inhabitants whom they contemptuously treated as inferiors. They were demanding, they were pushy, and they used their advantageous political status to dispossess the resident population and to seize properties for themselves. In Korea they started as small farmers, small businessmen, and small traders, and through the competitive advantages assured them by the colonial administration they became bigger, richer, and more powerful. Comparison with American immigrants is misleading. The Japanese immigrants forced their way into communities that were already overcrowded and asserted the mastery of conquerors.

From 42,460 Japanese residents in Korea in 1905 the numbers increased to 708,448 by 1940. These immigrants included farmers, businessmen, soldiers, construction workers, and bureaucrats. In 1945, 41 percent of them were, in one manner or another, government employees. They established the Oriental Development Company and the Fuji Industrial Company, which were empowered to expropriate land and to develop it in order to institute veritable agricultural and industrial revolutions. Farm plots were enlarged, dry lands were irrigated, new systems of cultivation and new varieties of seeds and fertilizers were introduced, and an agricultural extension service was established to deal with plant diseases and to guide educational and marketing practices. In 1910 Japanese owned about three percent of the arable land in Korea; by 1930 about sixty percent. Royal properties, unused land, and land for which ownership was not properly attested by valid documentation were all nationalized and then bought and administered by large Japanese firms. Land ownership in traditional Korea had been informal, linked closely to the social hierarchical system. A report published in the *Korean Repository* in August 1896 describes the "land ownership" circumstances as follows: "All land primarily belongs to the king. Subjects acquire it in two ways: (a) by purchasing from previous owners, who may have acquired it originally through inheritance, by building on it, or by cultivating it; and (b) by 'squatting' until the fourth crop is gathered." Tenants who cultivated land for yangban landlords occupied hereditary plots and shared in the produce.

They did not hold documentary rights to the land, and neither, in many cases, did the yangban overlords. Yet there was no question of their "rights" of occupancy and use of the land.

After annexation, conditions changed drastically. By 1930 four-fifths of the Korean farmers were tenants or partial tenants. Productivity of rice paddies increased by some fifty percent during 1915 and 1935—but the question is, for whose benefit? During that period, a "Rice Increase Plan," instituted in 1920, increased the export of rice to Japan from fifteen percent of the annual crop to thirty-seven percent. Between 1915 and 1935, the average consumption of rice by individual Koreans was reduced by almost fifty percent; and by the mid-thirties individual Koreans were consuming only about one-third as much rice as were individual Japanese. Such were the principal policies that marked the agricultural revolution.

The industrial revolution proceeded concurrently. The rapid industrialization led to drastic changes for the Koreans. Japanese comprised only five percent of the work force, but they held a large proportion of high-level nonagricultural jobs. In both the 1930 and 1940 censuses, fully eighty percent of the gainfully employed Japanese in Korea were in manufacturing, commerce, transportation, civil service, and other professions. Japanese firms owned some 92 percent of the working mines in Korea in 1933. The working conditions of the Korean labor force in the mines was described by a contemporary visitor from China: "There was no eight-hour day there, we learned, but two twelve-hour shifts. The workers . . . looked pale and seedy. They seemed to live in single-room houses, where the families swarmed together like rabbits. And always the price of coal increased, and the wages decreased."

Industrial growth in Korea was largely for the benefit of Japan and of Japanese. As late as 1938, the production from Korean industrial plants amounted to only 4.4 percent of production from plants in Japan. In Korea, women workers in textile plants were paid less than half the wages that were paid to their Japanese supervisors. The chemical industries, which were Korea's most important manufactures, were partly in small household plants (producing fish oil, fish fertilizers, vergetable oils, and so forth) that were Korean-owned. But almost all were in huge plants, owned by Japanese. After 1937 their production was shifted from peacetime to wartime products, with the result that fertilizer for agriculture became scarce; by the war's end the fields were badly depleted. Industrialization proceeded rapidly after the commencement of war against China. In 1938 there were 608 textile factories in Korea, employing 47,384 workers; in 1944 the numbers were 2,082 textile plants, with 81,441 workers. The number of metal working plants increased from 296 with 13,612 workmen to 619, employing 61,523; machinery and tool factories increased from 613 employing 24,745 to 1,226 with 64,048 employees. On the Yalu River the largest hydroelectric plant in the world was erected. In northern Korea, supplied with abundant fuels and electricity, old cities were industrialized and expanded and new industrial centers were established. The infrastructure was dramatically improved—but not the welfare of the Koreans.

Koreans who worked in the government were restricted to low-level positions. Those in the professions were mostly nurses, orderlies, clerks, and secretaries. Families that had together worked their small plots of land moved into cities in search of jobs, leaving behind their deeply rooted relationships. In the cities, too, family solidarity was threatened as fathers, mothers, and children aged fifteen and older worked at different jobs, in different locations. In 1919 there were thirteen incorporated cities in the peninsula, with a total population of 583,602. By 1940 the twenty incorporated contained 2,818,440 inhabitants. This urbanization not only changed many traditional social customs but also intensified feelings of separateness between residents of major cities and also between the urban and rural dwellers.

The militaristic sternness of the social control systems, along with the loss of special Korean identity (and, for many, the loss of their homes), led also to the emigration of Koreans. Between 1910 and 1920, some thirty thousand Koreans emigrated to Japan—seeking better jobs, better educational opportunities, and relief from the oppressive rigidity imposed on their homeland. After 1922, the worldwide postwar economic depression increased the numbers. By 1925 there were 187,000 Koreans living in Japan; by 1945 the number was around two million. Between 1939 and 1945, some 800,000 Korean youths were drafted into Japan's imperial armed forces.

Manchuria and Korea had many cultural ties and by 1910 an estimated 200,000 Koreans were living in Manchuria. During the next decades the numbers increased to 530,000 in 1925 and 1,400,000 in 1940. After the seizure of Manchuria by Japan in 1932, the colonial government encouraged and assisted the migration of Korean farmers and factory workers to hasten the development of the area. As heavy industries were developed in north Korea, more labor was also needed there.

Some of the severely disruptive changes were those common everywhere throughout the rapidly industrializing world. But changes of many kinds were occurring at a speed seldom matched in any other developing country. Railways and highways were constructed from the dozen port cities to Keijō, and throughout the length of the peninsula. Establishment of many newspapers and, during the twenties, the rise of radio, along with growth of elementary schools, combined to inform farmers of alternative ways of living and weakened their generations-long ties with their localities. As population flowed increasingly into the cities, unemployment became a problem, especially for the young, the old, and women. All such problems are typical of rapidly industrializing societies. They were intensified in Korea simply because the pace of change was imposed, was particularly rapid, and was focused particularly to benefit Japan.

Money is the lifeblood of economic development. Koreans had established five Western-style banks by 1903; these were superceded by Japanese banks. At the time of Japan's defeat in 1945 the Bank of Chōsen had thirteen branches; the Japanese Industrial Bank had sixty-seven branches, besides operating the all-important Oriental Development Corporation. Besides several savings banks, trust banks, and ordinary banks owned by Japanese in Korea, three large Tokyo banks maintained branches on the peninsula. These gave Japanese a virtual monopoly of banking business, with consequent vital benefits to Japanese entrepreneurs. Further control over the economy derived from the issuance of paper money, along with debentures and bills of credit, by the banks. The interest rates charged for the lending of money by the banks varied in practice by a wide range, with the highest rates charged to Koreans. The lowest rates were charged for loans used for purposes approved by the government. Farmers were particularly victimized by this system. Much of their essential borrowing was from loan sharks, who secured their money from banks at rates far below those they charged to farmers. A Japanese economist, Shirusi Sadanao, in his study entitled *Korea's Agricultural Regions,* estimated that in 1940 fully 60 percent of Korea's farm families lacked sufficient food and in order to survive had to borrow heavily in the early spring, when they also needed to buy seeds and fertilizer.

An American economist, Harold G. Moulton, in 1931 produced a study for the Brookings Institution, *Japan, An Economic and Financial Appraisal,* in which he concluded that the governing of Korea cost Japan more than it gained. "The contributions from the Central Government for the support of the colonies," he noted, "have shown a steady increase since pre-war [World War I] days. . . . From a fiscal point of view, the colonies as a whole [including Formosa and the Ryūkyūs] have thus far clearly been a liability rather than an asset." He reached this conclusion by the peculiar rationalization that the military and naval installations developed by Japan were for the protection and benefit of the colonials, rather than to serve Japan's imperial policies. Grajdanzev reached a more realistic conclusion, writing that "in one year, 1940, the Government took more in taxes than it had spent on agriculture in Korea since the annexation."

Whether, or to what extent, Japan profited from its governing of Korea, it appears to be evident that the Koreans did not. Some Korean industrial companies were started, but not successfully. In 1920 a *Tong-A Ilbo* editorial charged with some justice that "the most frequent cause of unsuccessful business enterprise can be found in lack of cooperation among Koreans. Because they seek prestige more than solid accomplishment, they fight viciously for the presidency and other high executive positions. Smooth operation of an enterprise requires the cooperation of everyone concerned. That is why we urge all Korean businessmen to unite for the good of their country." By no means should Japan be blamed for all of Korea's ills.

The essential basis for crediting Japan with improving and modernizing Korea during the colonial period is that it accomplished major material advances. Undoubtedly, it did. But in the process Korean industrialization and its whole economy was unbalanced. It was shaped to serve Japan's imperial needs. It was kept subordinate to Japanese industry—so that parts of products (for example, the filaments used in electric light bulbs) could be produced only in Japan. Bicycles were made in Korea, except that the ball-bearings they needed were manufactured in Japan. Few Korean plants were wholly self-contained. Agriculture was controlled to increase Japan's food supply. Indubitably, during the colonial rule, Korea was transformed. Businessmen instead of the yangban became symbolic of status and success. Many Koreans were destitute when the annexation was proclaimed; many were when it ended. There can be no final answer as to the whole effects of Japan's rule. But one conclusion is significant. When Japanese controls ended, Korea's economy simply collapsed. A major reason was the division of the country along the 38th parallel, which occurred when the war ended. But another reason was that it had been so closely integrated into that of Japan that it could not stand alone. Its reconstruction, on an independent basis, proved to be a stupendous task that attained success only after some thirty years. This was part of the cost that Koreans paid.

Balancing the books on Japan's governance of Korea is no easier than judging the eventual worth of England's rule over India, America's over the Philippines, Holland's over Indonesia, or that of various European nations over their many colonies in Africa. Naturally, material advancements were made. Inevitably, colonized peoples and their colonizers continue to disagree over the nature and the extent of benefits and of disabilities that were received. Termination of colonial rule did not, anywhere, result immediately in vastly improved conditions. Perhaps a final judgment on the worth of colonialism is implicit in the fact of its termination. If it had been truly satisfactory, for the rulers and for the ruled, it would have not been ended. In the long view of history, colonialism failed. The extent and the nature of its failure are difficult or impossible to measure precisely. What is certain is that the Koreans did not like being colonized and they adamantly refused to be Japanized. It seems equally clear that the seizure of Korea by Japan, which opened a corridor into increased and intensified Japanese imperialism, proved to be disastrous for Japan itself. Obviously, there were short-term gains for both Korea and Japan. Equally obviously, for both peoples colonization was not a relationship that could or should last.

8

Efforts to Regain Independence

Some historians, both Korean and foreign, have contended that the self-reliance of the Korean people was weakened by the fact that the nation's independence was not regained by their efforts but by the allied victory over Japan. If this assessment were true it would apply with equal pertinence to most of Europe, China, and the whole panoply of countries in South Asia and in the Pacific Ocean. Japan was defeated not by Asian peoples but by an American-led alliance, because its ambition overreached its capacities. Generalissimo Chiang Kai-shek made the point very well when he assured Chinese troops who were about to go into another losing battle that "so long as Japan is unable to conquer the world, she cannot destroy China or dominate Asia. . . . No matter how strong Japan is militarily, she is already placed in isolation."[23]

The Korean people were submerged but not really subjugated. They won a victory that should not be underestimated. This victory was their refusal to surrender. Despite all the varied and powerful pressures exerted upon them, they remained devoted to their own Koreanism. Nor was this merely a passive victory. All through the years of Korea's colonial status, Korean patriots continued their efforts to renew their country's independence. In view of the severity of the police surveillance, the difficulties of communication, the continued clannish, regional, and ideological divisiveness, and the increasing impoverishment of the great majority of the people, what they accomplished is impressive. Why they did not accomplish more is of equal historical importance.

Their method, like the parallel movement in India, was largely nonviolent, except among the Koreans in China and Manchuria who were led and financed by Communist militants. Korean resistance, however, lacked the coherence, the unity, and the sustained continuity of the Indian independence movement. The reasons were both external and internal. For one thing, Japan was not England. Nothing like the All-India Congress Party was possible in colonized Korea. Even so, in many respects the Korean and the Indian independence movements were similar, especially in their appeal to conscience as the ultimate arbitrator. In both, the resort was less to force than to the humane sense of what is right and just. This was vital, and also admirable; but it meant that their salvation was not in their own hands.

In the Korean movement there was no single strategic plan, such as civil disobedience, nor was there any leader or coterie of leaders, comparable to India's Gandhi and Nehru, who were able to dominate and guide the resistance. The succesive individual efforts, however, were sufficient to make evident the reality of the spirit of *Manse,* "May Korea live for ten thousand years!" Some of the leaders who organized protests were inside Korea, risking and suffering imprisonment and other punishments that were anything but benign. Some were elsewhere in Asia, outside of Korea's borders. Some were in the United States. The leadership was bold and often brilliant; but it was also divisive and competitive, as leadership among Koreans, and among exiled nationalists of all countries, has tended to be. It reflected regional and clan divisions that were of long-standing. Inevitably, it also reflected personal ambitions and animosities, as well as significant ideological differences.

The Korean independence movements were strongly influenced by World War I and the Russian Revolution. Inspiration was provided by the calls for "self-determination of peoples" by Woodrow Wilson and by Lenin and Trotsky, in a new era that presumably was to be marked by brotherhood, justice, and peace. Both the Fourteen Points that were supposed to be the agenda for the Versailles Peace Conference and the founding of the Asian and the Korean Communist Parties offered encouraging but vague hope for global support for the renewal of independence.

There appeared to be nothing vague, however, about Wilson's speeches supporting his "self-determination" theme. On 22 January 1917, for instance, he asserted that "no peace can last, or ought to last, which does not recognize that governments derive their just powers from consent of the governed, and that no right anywhere exists to hand people about from sovereignty to sovereignity as if they were property." Wilson sent a mission to Russia, headed by Elihu Root, to convey to Tsar Nicholas Wilson's determination that "no people must be forced under sovereignty under which it does not wish to live." In Article IV of his Fourteen Points, Wilson promised a "free, open-minded, and absolutely impartial adjustment of all colonial claims." On 11 February 1918 Wilson clarified his war aims in notes to the German and Austrian Foreign Ministries, in which he said: "National aspirations must be respected; peoples may now be dominated and governed only by their consent." Such language seemed to be clear and precise. What was left unsaid, however, was that the promised liberation was intended only for people who had been victimized by the Germans. Japan, however late and however ineffectively, was among the victorious Allies. This was the fatal flaw in the otherwise reasonable expectation of Korean patriots that their country's independence was to be restored.

An earlier serious effort to create a nationwide movement was the founding of the *Sinmin-hoe* (New People's Association) in 1907, by An Chang-ho and a few associates, including Yi Tong-whi, Yi Kap, and Yang Ki-tak. These men were Christians and educators. As a youth of eighteen, An had gone to Seoul from his home in Pyongyang in 1896 to take part in the Independence Club movement. After the Club was disbanded by the government, An went to Los Angeles and tried to organize the Korean students who were studying there. Later in that year he returned to Pyongyang and established the Taesong School to educate Korean youth for leadership. This was what An's "fight for independence" largely amounted to—to educate Korean youth so that they would be ready for leadership when Korean sovereignty was regained.

An was an eloquent speaker, with a charming personality, and he quickly won widespread support. Prince Itō, Japan's first Resident-General during the protectorate, tried to persuade An to support Japan's plan for a united Asia, to resist Western imperialism. An agreed that this was an attractive idea, and confessed to Itō that in his opinion "Asia is like one human body, Japan its head, Korea its neck, and China its body. The parts of this body, however, are not well connected together but all are separated with suspicions of one another." When Itō again urged that An seek Korean support to unite the parts, An replied, "As the Japanese people modernized Japan, let Korea be modernized and reformed by the Korean people. Would you have kept silent if the United States made Japan a protectorate to help your Meiji Restoration?"

An's program of trying to save Korea by educating the people continued to animate him. He gave many hundreds, maybe thousands, of speeches in Korea and among Korean expatriates in China and America, always combining appeals for self-improvement with demands that Japan allow Korea to shape its own future. In 1932 he was arrested in the French quarter in Shanghai and imprisoned for three years. Back in Seoul on 7 July 1937, when Japan attacked China in the Marco Polo bridge episode, An Chang-ho courageously denounced this as an act of outrageous imperialism. He was again arrested and in prison suffered severe tortures. Released in mid-December with his health broken, he was taken to the Seoul Medical College Hospital, where he died on 10 March 1938 at the age of sixty. He is still highly respected by the Korean people. His most lasting memorial is the Heungsadan Society, a divisive political group more regional than ideological, headquartered in Pyongyang, which long retained a large following of expatriates and of south-dwelling North Koreans.

A much more militant convert to the *Sinmin-hoe* was a young firebrand named Kim Chang-am (Kim Ku), who was born in 1876 in Hwanghae Province in north-central Korea. Kim was rebellious as a child, resenting his family's poverty, his father's excessive drinking, and his mother's youthful incompetence and neglect. He proved to be a brilliant student. But when at the age of sixteen he took the government's Confucian examination for appointment to office, he was enraged to find that the examinations were corruptly conducted. In his anger, he joined the Tonghak movement, and his leadership abilities promptly won for him command of a four hundred-member cavalry troop in the *Uibyong* anti-Japanese army. When this armed group was dispersed, he decided to go to China. On his way, he encountered Captain Tsuchida, who was alleged to have helped murder Queen Min, and killed him. He publicly and proudly proclaimed this deed and was arrested for it and condemned to death. Emperor Kojong commuted his sentence to a brief period of imprisonment. While in prison, young Kim read widely, including Yu Kil-chun's popular *Soyu Kyonmun* (Story of Western Travel). After escaping from jail in 1898, Kim went to a Buddhist Temple and planned to become a monk. His reading of Western books, however, led to his conversion to Christianity. In 1907 he changed his name to Kim Ku and launched into a career of patriotic activism.

In November 1910, some three months after Japan's annexation of Korea, Kim went to Seoul to attend meetings of the *Sinmin-hoe.* In January 1912, the Japanese authorities arrested the *Sinmin-hoe* leaders, including Kim Ku, and the movement collapsed. Kim Ku emerged from prison in 1913 and engaged in desultory activities until, in March 1919, he went to Shanghai, where he became an enforcement officer in the security forces of the exile Provisional Government. In 1925 he was elected its premier.

The *Sinmin-hoe* meeting in which Kim Ku participated led to the world-famous "Christian Conspiracy Case" in 1912. The Japanese tried the Christians on the charge of treason and sought to discredit the entire Christian enterprise in Korea. Three of those who were arrested died under torture while being interrogated. Nine were exiled, and six, including Yun Chi-ho, were imprisoned for terms of five to ten years. The case was widely reported in the world press. The defense argued that the Christians met not to plan revolution but only to discuss Korean wrongs and aspirations.

A much more militant movement against Japan was taking root in Manchuria, where soldiers from the *Uibyong,* or Righteous Army, found refuge after being defeated by superior Japanese forces inside Korea. Between 1912 and 1918 three separate groups, the Righteous Army for Korean Independence, The Restoration Association, and The Society for Korean National Sovereignty, were organized in Manchuria with different and competing leadership, all aiming to restore Korean independence by force of arms. In Shanghai in 1915, Pak Un-sik, Yi Sang-sol, and Sin Kyu-sik organized the New Korean Revolutionary Party, which sought to unite the militant groups in Manchuria and Siberia. These leaders favored German victory in the world war, expecting that afterwards there would be a combined German and Chinese attack on Japan.

On 4 July 1917 fourteen of these leaders drew up a Declaration of Common Cause, pledging to work together in harmony. This was followed in November of 1918 by another memorial, the *Muo* declaration, in a militant spirit well portrayed in its opening words: "Rise up, independence fighters! . . . There is no one who can be exempted from mortality, and who indeed wishes to live like dogs or pigs. . . . To establish our country's freedom from evil and to regain our independence we must engage in a heroic armed struggle." The aims affirmed in the declaration were "to distribute wealth and power equally in our society, create harmony between men and women, the rich and the poor, introduce equal opportunities for the educated and the illiterate, and the young and the old, among all classes of society." Chang Tok-su and Cho So-ang carried news of these activities to the Korean students in Japan and to patriots in Korea. In both places, the support for independence was taking a different, nonviolent cast.

The independence movement taking form in Japan actually had some Japanese assistance. Since the early 1880's a small number of Korean youths had gone to Japan to study. During 1910–15 they were encouraged by a "mass awakening" movement, the Taishō Reforms, that reacted against the militarization of the government. Along with seeking domestic democratic reforms in Japan, leaders of this movement opposed the annexation of Korea and the broader policy of imperialist penetration into Asia, which they rightly interpreted as an overextension of national ambition that would lead, eventually, to defeat. In 1892 Korean University students in Japan organized debate clubs and in October 1912, they united them as The Korean Student Fraternity, with five branches in Tokyo universities, and one each in Kyoto and Osaka. The debates resembled those of the Paejae Debating Society that had been sponsored twenty years earlier by the Independence Club. Japanese police recorded student speeches that celebrated Korean traditional culture and advocated the restoration of Korean independence. However, such youthful exuberance was not considered to be dangerous. Shortly, the students began to support the democratization of politics in Japan. They happily joined with Japanese student groups led by liberal professors, and dedicated themselves to education for revitalizing Korean society through democratic reforms, economic justice, and eradication of the yangban hierarchical social system. In March 1915 the student groups attracted more police attention when speakers forecast assassination of Governor-General Terauchi.

The Korean students most active in this movement included Paek Kwan-su, Kim To-you, Choe Pal-young, So Chun, Song Kye-baek, and Yi Kwang-su. Yi Kwang-su won notoriety with his 1917 novel, *Mujong* (Heartlessness), on a theme that had become popular in Korean literature—asking people to pay less attention to politics and more to the reconstruction of their own lives. There was much good, he stressed, in Japan. In December of that year he published an article in the Korean Fraternity Society journal, entitled "Our Ideology," in which he urged Koreans to imitate rather than oppose

Japan. "Recently," he wrote, "having succeeded in importing Occidental culture, Japan has attained the role of instructor of the entire culture of Asia, and is striving to create a unique blend of East and West, so as to become the Greece of the future. Whatever Japanese youths one meets, they invariably say that they are seeking Japan's new ideal through the 'merger of Eastern and Western cultures.'" What Yi Kwang-su intended was to encourage Koreans to "out-do" Japan by adopting Christianity and Western ways so thoroughly that they would become the dominant leaders of the new Asia. His example inspired and encouraged other writers.

Literary movements are important because they help to shape the sentiments of the people and, even more, because they reflect what the people are feeling. Such writers as Yi Kwang-su and Choe Nam-son regarded themselves as "renewers of life, makers of a new and better age." They were less interested in "renewing" than in "making." Yi Kwang-su, for example, regarded their function as "to create everything anew as if on a clean-swept vacant lot." Their colonial status, however, denied them such an opportunity. Thus, Professor Peter H. Lee, a leading historian of Korean literature, pointed out that "in the shadow of Japanese colonialism . . . the new literature in Korea became one of sorrow, reflecting a grief-stricken and despondent outlook."

An influential poet, Kim Ok, seeking to rally Korea's poets, founded a bimonthly magazine *Pyeho* (The Ruin), taking as its motto a quotation from one of Schiller's poems: "The old style has been destroyed and times have changed. My life comes from the ruins." Kim Ok's favorite poet, Kim Sowol, wrote a typical lament, ending with the lines

> Though I die, suppressing grief,
> Never will I weep.

Another leading poet, Pak Yong-chol, founded a "pure poetry group" and published a magazine named *Shimunhak* (New Literature), in which he editorialized: "As men, as well as poets, the most important thing for us is to have a vigorous flame in our minds. The flame may burn in secret, like the sacred fire in a Roman Temple, or burn down everything with its smoke and blaze. . . . A poet can move forward when he is able to kindle the flame gradually but permanently." Kim Hae-gyong (Yi Sang), who died in 1937 at the age of twenty-seven, deliberately developed an obscure style that concealed more than it revealed. Defending it, he wrote, "I do not know why they say that I am mad. . . . 'Iron'—this is a symbol of my new method; I will never belong to anybody." A well-practiced translator of Korean poetry, William Rozycki, notes that "translating poetry is like transferring a spider web from one location to another." Nevertheless, he believes he properly preserves the meaning of Kang Un-gyo, another prominent poet, in this revealing translation:

We are all
Stones thrown by someone.
Stones licking our wounds,
lying quietly in the grass.
Stones fragmented, broken, scattered about;
We embrace together and form a cliff.

Andrew C. Nahm, in his study of the literature of the period, concluded that its dominant theme was "an undeniable and profound sorrow." Professor of literature Kim U-chang similarly characterized the feelings of the writer of the time as having "a profound sense of futility that gnaws at his heart and makes him turn to a futile mill of sorrowful brooding." Even those poets who were hopeful were not dynamic. Typical of this genre was Han Yong-un's "A Ferry Boat and a Passenger," which affirms: "I am a ferryboat, you are a passenger. . . . If you do not come, I will wait for you from night to day." Professor Sung-Il Lee, in his 1990 volume *The Wind and the Waves,* presents his translations of four poets who lived through this time of sorrow and who expressed their grief, as did Yi Yook-Sa (1904–44): "Whenever I see the distant stars or the blossoming flowers, I long for the days we have long lost." Under highly restrictive censorship, the writers presented their patriotic views allegorically, rather than directly. A typical lyric, "Song of Blue Birds," pleads that the birds (Japanese) refrain from damaging fields of green beans (Korea). Another mourns that "When coal burns smoke rises, but when my heart burns neither smoke nor flames rise." Meanwhile, such Western songs as "Auld Lang Syne" and "Onward Christian Soldiers" became popular. An old song, *Arirang,* mourning for a lover who has gone away, was popularly revived. Andrew Nahm judged that "the singing of those songs and reciting of those poems of the colonial period were almost ritual with a religious reverence, and it was a logical way to cope with the harsh realities of that period."

Yi Kwang-su, reversing his admonition to follow the example of Japan, as the Tasishō Reforms faded, wrote a Declaration of Independence, which on 8 February 1919 was read to a wildly cheering audience of four hundred Korean students in the Korean Y.M.C.A. in Tokyo. Police arrested the leaders, dispersed the audience, and the movement subsided. Its contents record the sentiments of Korean intellectuals, in their response to Wilsonian idealism and the Allied victory in World War I. With youthful exuberance, the declaration opened: "As representatives of the twenty million Korean people, the Korean Youth Independence Association declares before those nations of the world which have secured victory for Freedom and Justice, the realization of our independence." What Yi Kwang-su called for, however, was not violence but a reasoned appeal. Korea's claim for world support to restore its sovereignty he defined as follows:

1) Korea's history and culture are ancient.

2) The independence of Korea was recognized in treaties with Japan, the United States, Russia, and Great Britain; and the 1905 protectorate proclaimed by Japan also asserted that Korean independence would be restored.
3) Koreans had proved their devotion to independence by resisting Japanese rule as best they could.
4) Japan had delayed Korea's modernization by suppressing all Korean efforts for self-betterment.
5) The peace of Asia depends on Korea's sovereign independence, since Japan's "sinister intent" is to use the peninsula as a corridor for conquest of Asia.
6) Once Korean independence is restored, the people would proceed to reconstruct their country to make it a contributor to Asian peace.

The Koreanization efforts by students in Japan were akin to the educational emphasis of An Chang-ho. Their views were that nobody would "grant" independence to Korea, and that Korea was not strong enough to gain it by force. Instead, through education and enlightenment, the people must become worthy of self-government. This view was most clearly affirmed by So Chun, in one of the Korean Fraternity debates, when he said: "The annexation of the weak by the strong is an inescapable principle of life. As individuals we must surely demand, on an equal footing, Justice, Liberty, and Equality. But unless as a nation, as a body, we have actual power and ability, what profit can possibly result [from agitating for independence]?" This view, however, was far from universal. Countering it, some, particularly leftists living in exile in Manchuria and in Siberia, tried to arouse a new feeling of hope: "The curtain of darkness has opened, the Sun with new ray rises over the Eastern hills." Yi Kwang-su joined the militants, writing: "Advance, advance, our Army of Independence, the War of Independence has come."

The March–April 1919 movement, known at first as the "Manse" and later as the "Samil" March First movement, was different. It was another and stronger expression of the independence sentiments manifested in the earlier declarations. But it was much more significant than these prototypes and its inspiration owed little or nothing to them. The effective organizers of the movement were leaders of Chondogyo (formerly Tonghak), Korean Protestant Christians, some Buddhist monks, and a few non-religious Korean activists. The missionaries apparently had no advance information concerning the plans, but once the movement was launched some of them gave it sympathetic support. Expatriate Koreans also helped prepare a new drive for independence. Lyuh Woon-heung (Yo Un-hyong), in Shanghai, sent a message to Woodrow Wilson, who was already at the peace conference in Paris, declaring that "we are not conquered, but merely only cheated and destroyed by the Japanese falsehood. . . . Korea must be redeemed." Sonu Hyok hastened from Shanghai to his home area, in and around Pyongyang, where he earnestly besought Christian leaders to give some overt sign to the peace conference of Korean independence determination. In America, An Ch'ang-ho's Korea National Association made plans to send Syngman Rhee and Henry Chung to Paris, which it was unable to do; and for Park Young-man to take part in conferences of the League of Small Nations, which was meeting in New York City,

In November 1918 a Chondogyo leader, Kwon Tong-jin, read in Japanese newspapers of the "wild ravings" of Wilson about the "self-determination of peoples." He sought out two other Chondogyo associates, O Se-chang and Choe Rin, and together they decided that something must be done, and soon. On 22 January, former Emperor Kojong died suddenly of a stroke, and rumors spread in Korea that he was poisoned by the Japanese for opposing the marriage of his grandson to a Japanese princess. Meanwhile, reports of independence declarations from many European groups (perhaps as many as a hundred in all) seeped into Seoul.

On 28 January the three Chondogyo friends met at the home of Son Pyong-hui, their superior in the order. They reported to him that they heard rumors the Christians were planning a massive protest movement. Despite the religious rivalry of the two faiths, political considerations demanded that they cooperate. The Chondogyo group decided that Choe Rin should make plans for the event and that he should seek the cooperation of Christian leaders. Choe Rin began immediately to hold daily meetings with Choe Nam-son and with Song Chin-u, who was principal of the Chungang Middle School.

They decided that to win mass support they must recruit prominent figures from the prior Korean government. When they approached Pak Yong-hyo, Han Kyu-sol, and Yun Chi-ho, whose credentials as patriots were outstanding, all three refused to participate. Yun recorded in his diary the reasons he gave for his refusal:

> 1. The contrast between Korean misgovernment and the efficient Japanese administration was so striking and well-known that it would be practically impossible to convince the [Peace] Conference that Koreans were worse off now than before. 2. Korea being a life and death problem for Japan, the latter would not let the former go unless absolutely compelled to by force of arms. Then, is America or England going to war with Japan just to make dear little Korea independent—Inconceivable! 3. History gives no instance of a race or nation gaining its political independence without fighting for it. As long as Korea can't fight, it's no use talking about independence. Since we don't know how to be strong, let us learn how to be weak.

Yun later explained, further, that he mistrusted the Chondogyo leaders, suspecting them of raising money for the "movement" but actually putting it into their own pockets. Despite such discouragement, the planners went ahead.

Choe Rin contacted two prominent Christians, Yi Sung-hun and Song

Chin-u, who at once set about actively organizing support by pastors in Seoul and Pyongyang. Somewhat reluctantly, because of their religious differences, the Christian pastors agreed to cooperate with Chondogyo. Since the Japanese planned to hold Kojong's state funeral on 3 March, the planners knew that police security on that day would be very strong. They decided the best date for their demonstrations would be March 1. Choe Nam-son, a scholar publisher just twenty-nine years old, drafted a Declaration of Independence, which the group approved. Fifteen Chondogyo leaders and sixteen prominent Christians agreed to sign the document. Han Yong-un, a Buddhist priest, was invited to sign it also, to make it more representative, and he gladly did so.

On the evening of 27 February, the Declaration was printed in a Chondogyo printshop, with twenty-one thousand copies produced by eleven p.m. Half a dozen Christians, as many Chondogyo members, and the Buddhist priest, Han Yong-un, each took about three thousand copies and set off on dangerous missions to deliver them to key points throughout the peninsula.

A meeting to lauch the demonstrations was scheduled for Pagoda Park, in Seoul, for two p.m. on March first. However, since it was anticipated that Japanese police would be on hand to monitor the meeting, and would break it up, the signers agreed to meet quietly that morning in the Myongwolgwan (Bright Moon House) restaurant, where they listened to a reading of the document. After this, they called in the Japanese police and quietly gave themselves up. Choe Rin, on behalf of all the signers, explained to the police what they intended:

> I joined the independence movement for the following reasons. First to insure the right of the Korean race to survive. Second, to force the Japanese government to repent of its policies toward Korea. Third, at the present time world peace is being advocated at the Peace Conference and I hope to create sympathy for the Korean people among the Powers.

The planners were clear in their own minds that the movement must be completely nonviolent. To the students who gathered in Pagoda Park were given a message that also was relayed around the country with copies of the Declaration:

> Whatever you do
> Do not insult the Japanese
> Do not throw stones
> Do not hit with your fists
> For these are the acts of barbarians.

The declaration itself was stated in peaceful terms. After the opening, "We hereby declare that Korea is an independent state and that Koreans are a self-governing people," the declaration continued in conciliatory terms:

> We do not intend to accuse Japan of infidelity for its violation of various solemn treaty obligations since the Treaty of Amity of 1876. Japan's scholars and officials, indulging in a conqueror's exuberance, have denigrated the accomplishments of our ancestors and treated our civilized people like barbarians. Despite their disregard for the ancient origin of our society and for the brilliance of the spirit of our people, we shall not blame Japan; we must first blame ourselves before finding fault with others. Because of the urgent need for remedies for the problems of today, we cannot afford the time for recrimination over past wrongs.
>
> Our task today is to build up our own strength, not to destroy others. We must chart a new destiny for ourselves in accord with the solemn dictate of conscience and not malign and reject others for reasons of past enmity or momentary passion. In order to restore natural and just conditions, we must remedy the unnatural and unjust conditions brought about by the leaders of Japan, who are chained to old ideas and old forces and are victimized by their obsession with glory.

The Declaration ended on a hopeful note: "All of us, men and women, young and old have firmly left behind the old nest of darkness and gloom and head for joyful resurrection [the Christian theme] together with myriad living things [the Buddhist theme]. The spirits of thousands of generations of our ancestors protect us [the Confucian theme], and the rising tide of world consciousness assists us. Once started, we shall surely succeed. We march forward with hope." This Declaration was read, in whole or in part, until the reading was interrupted by police intervention, not only in Pagoda Park in Seoul but in scores of other cities, towns, and villages, mostly in the north and a few in the south.

The Japanese police first learned of the declaration shortly after midnight in the first hour of 1 March. They had no information on what was to be done with it. Some leaflets passed out along with copies of the declaration seemed ominously threatening. One, for example, concluded: "Rise up as one and help carry out the great deed." But what deed? When? And where? and How? The leaflets gave no answers and the police were perplexed. Later in the morning, they learned that students were not reporting to their schools. By two o'clock in the afternoon, some four or five thousand students were mingled with the crowd that customarily gathered in Pagoda Park. From a nearby substation, Japanese police quietly watched the apparently aimless gathering. Then a handbill entitled "The Independence Newspaper" was handed around. It announced the reading of the declaration and the arrest of twenty-nine signers in the Bright Moon House restaurant. The handbill included a warning to avoid destructive acts, because "even one act of violence would ruin Korea's chances for independence forever." A student grabbed a copy of the declaration and bravely stood on a platform reading it through, loudly and slowly.

The crowd broke into cheers and started, singing and laughing, through Seoul's city streets. With no assembly point in mind, different crowds of three or four thousand went in various directions. The police summoned army help and three infantry companies and a mounted platoon responded.

As evening settled in, the police began making arrests. Individuals seeking to escape surged into police lines and people were knocked down and trampled. Japanese civilians attacked the crowds, launching a brutal assault against the unarmed and terrified Koreans. Gradually the police restored order. Stories of the brutality, with exaggerated accounts of Koreans maimed and killed, spread from Seoul out into the countryside. Telegraphic reports to General Utsunomiya, commander of Japan's military force in Korea, confirmed that the demonstrations against Japanese rule were spread throughout the five provinces of north Korea.

The second day of March, a Sunday, was relatively quiet; but on 3 March the Korean hatred of their Japanese oppressors led to outbreaks of violent attacks on police stations and on homes and shops of Japanese. The next day small armed bands of Koreans attacked Japanese gendarmes and killed several. Demonstrations continued and increased. Almost all of them were peaceful expressions of desire for independence and neither the crowds nor the police engaged in unrestrained violence. By 6 March the movement spread into the south. The protests eventually turned into attacks on Japanese civilians and police as the hatred of their exploiters flared and hope grew that this might be the time to regain Korea's sovereignty. Korean shops were closed and crowds armed with stones and clubs stormed through the streets. By the end of March the demonstrations were turning into revolution. Fighting broke out all through the country, but the rebels were neither armed nor organized. On 11 April, General Yoshimichi Hasegawa announced that his troops had the situation under control and that participants in the demonstrations and attacks would be sought out, arrested, and summarily punished.

Thus began a period of brutal suppression that, by the end of April, crushed the movement with such inhumane severity that Japan was condemned around the world. In the town of Suwon, police ordered twenty-nine Christians into their church, then set fire to it and burned them all to death. Brutalities were committed by both sides; but since the Japanese had by far the superior force, theirs were the greatest and most numerous. An unpublished manuscript, *The Unquenchable Fire,* by the famous Canadian missionary Frank W. Schofield, who witnessed the events of 1919, quotes a Japanese Army Major, T. K. Kodama, as reporting to the Japanese War Office: "The way to put down Korean rioters is to beat them and kill them." The most authoritative examination of the March First movement, the Columbia University doctoral dissertation presented by Frank Prentiss Baldwin, Jr. in 1972, found that "the successive waves of reckless patriotism, brutal Japanese repression and bitter Korean resistance touched all strata of the Korean people and every region of the country." The authorities estimated that a million Koreans participated in the demonstrations; Koreans estimated the number at two million. The Japanese placed Korean casualties at 553 killed in March; as the struggle intensified and continued, the official count was 7,645 Koreans killed, and 45,562 wounded. Another 49,811 were arrested and imprisoned. The Chondogyo organization was a major casualty, for the order never again regained its strength. Christian evangelism also was subjected to increased curbs.

The Government-General conducted an investigation, reported in its 1921 annual report, to determine what organizations were responsible for the uprising. Of demonstrators who were subjected to the brutal interrogation (called "questioning") by the police, 14.89 percent admitted to being members of the Chondogyo; 14.80 percent to being Presbyterians; 3.40 percent to being Methodists; and 6.09 percent confessed membership in various other Christian churches. Doubtless all these figures were understated, as loyal church members sought to protect their denominations from blame. No figures were cited for Buddhists or Confucianists; and 60.70 percent of those queried denied any religious affiliation.

What the March First movement accomplished has since been hotly debated. By some historians it is regarded as the crucial turning point that demonstrated decisively the failure of Japan to Japanize the Korean people. Others point out that it sputtered out quickly and left few visible effects. One of its student leaders, Hyon Sang-yun, later recalled that "at this time we did not believe that Korean independence would be immediately realized. . . . But we seriously felt that we must express the desires of the people before the world, as a beginning stage of the independence movement."

Serious efforts were made to accomplish this objective. Kimm Kyu-sic, carrying an appeal to the Peace Conference, arrived in Paris on 13 March, unaware that President Wilson had already decided that "self-determination" would be offered only to peoples whose countries had been directly involved in the war. Colonel House, Wilson's very influential aide, sent to Kimm what he meant to be a consolatory refusal: "If we deal out justice in Europe and punish the criminals here it may prove a leaven of righteousness in other fields. Perhaps the League will be able to curb Japan when it has less pressing matters nearer at hand to deal with."

The movement entered into a new stage as leaders of diverse types undertook to keep it vital and to render it effective. These new activities were based in Shanghai, Manchuria, and the United States. The most manifest specific effect on the independence movement from the Samil demonstrations was an effort to legitimize the Provisional Government that was operating in Shanghai.

So much confused controversity still persists concerning what led to failure of the Samil and Provisional Government movements that the circumstances need to be reconsidered with attention to the whole tangled skein of circumstances. Syngman Rhee was designated by the groups in Seoul, Manchuria, and Shanghai as chief executive of this Shanghai-based Republic of Korea in exile. His credentials were impressive and were well-known to the Korean people. His choice by the Korean groups to head the exile republic was the consensus choice, although Son Pyong-hui and Yi Tong-whi were also considered.

Unanimity either of sentiments or of unified action was not a Korean characteristic. Rhee became embroiled in quarrels with An Chang-ho, who wanted to avoid political programs and to concentrate on education for citizenship; and with Park Young-man, who felt his mission was to recruit Korean youth and to train them for military opposition to Japan. An Chang-ho did not master the English language, so had little opportunity to familiarize himself with the principles of American democracy. Park Young-man was devoted to his own program and had close ties with the armed forces in Manchuria. Rhee sought to end the rift between them, writing to Park that "there is no better friend for you than your old prison mate," and urged him "not to throw yourself into the hands of these men." None of these three was willing to sacrifice his own view of what should be done in the hope to satisfy the others.

An Chang-ho sent a radiogram to Dr. Rhee in August 1919, instructing him to use the title "Chief Executive" rather than "President," concluding: "Please do not act as President." Rhee replied, "I cannot alter it now. If the news of conflict among ourselves is known to the world, it will create a great obstacle to the independence movement." In America Kim Yeungjeun, publisher of a periodical he grandly named *The Voice of Korea,* and Han Kilsoo, claiming wide support by Koreans in Japan and in California, were both actively advancing their own claims to primary leadership of the independence movement. Another separatist group, headed by An Tae-guk (who died shortly thereafter on 5 February 1920) set up a Communication Center in Antung, purporting to "unite" all groups in and out of Korea. Within the cabinet and the Assembly disharmony also prevailed. An immediate cause of dissention was whether or not to endorse restoration of the monarchy. They debated also the question of whether the "Chief Executive" should be termed "President" or "Premier." On this issue the division was roughly fifty-fifty. Some of the Shanghai group complained that undue honor was given to both Dr. Rhee and Yi Tong-whi, who was leader of the Communist faction. The Provisional National Assembly nevertheless confirmed Rhee as President and Yi Tong-whi as premier.

The Shanghai group also differed hotly about tactics. One group strongly favored a campaign of propaganda to win friendly support by Western governments, which was the position of the leaders in America—Rhee, Kimm Kyu-sic, and Philip Jaisohn. Rhee insisted that the primary effort must be to win diplomatic support by the United States, for which purpose he asked for special funding for his activities—which, he insisted must be centered in America, rather than in Shanghai. Other groups, led by Yi Tong-whi and Kim Won-Bong, wanted to mount a military attack upon Japanese forces in Korea, from bases in Manchuria. These men wanted to shift the Ministry of Military Affairs to Chientao and the Russian Maritime Province, there to organize "at least ten regiments in readiness for combat before the end of the year." Still another group, led by An Chang-ho, was convinced that only a generation-long program of preparatory education for reclaiming Korea was feasible. Dr. Rhee warned that military action in Manchuria and threats to assassinate Japanese officials had no effect except to incense the Japanese and to antagonize world opinion. He again urged that the only hope for success was to seek diplomatic support. Exercising such authority as his election to the presidency provided, Dr. Rhee appealed to the Department of State. Stanley Hornbeck, in the Far Eastern Division, responded by sending a radiogram to Joseph Grew, Secretary to the American Commission at the Peace Conference, asking that the Korean delegate should be heard. This request was rejected with the following comment: "In view of the fact that the U.S. has recognized the annexation of Korea, the representative ought not to be received."

In a final desperate effort Kimm Kyu-sic, on 10 May 1919, sent a carefully prepared appeal to Wilson, Clemenceau, and Lloyd George, arguing that "the fact that the outbreak of the war did not find Japan an ally of the Central Powers—a political combination that had always been envisioned by the German-trained advisers of the Mikado—is no reason why the Korean people should be suffered by the Peace Conference to continue to live under a system of military government which is a denial of every principle for which men have lately died on the soil of France." When this document received no reply, Rhee sent another message, supported by a plea from Stanley Hornbeck, asking whether "the American government will be able to do anything in regard to giving the Koreans a hearing?" Again, there was no reply.

Syngman Rhee and Philip Jaisohn, who were holding daily conferences on strategy, set up a meeting of the First Korean Congress, on 14–16 April 1919, held in Independence Hall in Philadelphia, to remind Americans of their own struggle from colonization to independence. Some seventy Koreans from around the mainland attended. With Jaisohn chairing the meeting, the Congress adopted an appeal to the American people, declaring that "our aim is freedom from militaristic autocracy; our object is democracy for Asia; our hope is universal Christianity." To explain Rhee's presence in America, Jaisohn issued an explanatory statement: "It does not make any difference whether the President of the Provisional Government is in prison or whether he is in France; he may be in America; that does not make any difference. . . . It is the will of the people that makes the government."

The Congress set up a Korean Information Bureau, headed by Jaisohn, which started publication of a monthly *Korean Review.* It also published two books: Frederick A. McKenzie's *Korea's Fight for Freedom* and Henry Chung's *The Case of Korea,* with the necessary money supplied by Dr. Rhee's society, the *Tongji-hoe.*

Rhee engaged in a campaign to win the support of the American Congress.

On 30 June Senator Selden P. Spender of Missouri introduced a resolution asking that the Secretary of State advise the Senate whether the American-Korean treaty of 1882 obliged the United States to assist in restoring Korea's independence. Six weeks later Senator George W. Norris of Nebraska raised the same question in the debate on the Versailles Treaty. On 19 September Senator Spender read into the *Congressional Record* "Briefs for Korea," prepared by Kimm Kyu-sic and Rhee. Resolutions expressing sympathy with Korea's aspirations were introduced into both the Senate and the House, but remained buried in committees. The American ambassador in Tokyo informed Japan's Army Minister that "the wretched conditions in Korea should be reformed." A League of Friends of Korea was formed in England and a magazine, *La Coree Libre,* was published in France. Speeches favoring Korean independence were given in both the British parliament and the French national assembly. By such means, the Korean cause was at last brought to world attention even if, in Yun Chi-ho's words, no nation was about to go to war to "liberate dear little Korea." Rhee established in Washington the Korean Commission, a quasi-diplomatic office to represent the unrecognized Republic-of-Korea-in-Exile, as Rhee called the Shanghai government. Kimm Kyu-sic went to Washington from Paris, and Rhee appointed him chairman of the Korean Commission.

The Provisional Government in Shanghai was similarly active. Yi Tong-whi organized the Korean Peoples Socialist Party and appealed to the Bolshevik regime in Moscow to send funds and military supplies for use by Korean armed groups in Manchuria and Siberia. To the cabinet of the provisional Government, Yi argued that "to join with the Russian Bolsheviks is the only short cut" to Korea's freedom. An Chang-ho and Lyuh Woon-heung joined with Yi Tong-whi to secure agreement on sending a mission to Russia to seek financial help for the Provisional Government. Han Hyong-gwon was dispatched to Moscow, where he was given 600,000 rubles, with a promise of a total of two million.

These were the circumstances when Syngman Rhee arrived in Shanghai, on 8 December 1920. He was greeted sullenly by the cabinet, which attacked him for having sent a proposal to President Wilson that the Korean question might be solved by having the peninsula placed under a mandate by the League of Nations, pending an election. Complaints were voiced that Rhee's policy of seeking American aid had failed. He was also attacked for using for his own diplomatic efforts the money collected by *Tongji-hoe,* rather than sending it to Shanghai. In December 1920, 400,000 rubles from the Bolsheviks were received in Shanghai. Yi Tong-whi withheld them from the government, on the ground that it was in disarray and that the money should be diverted for use by the militant groups in Manchuria.

In the continuing conflict of views, over a period of months of increasing animosity, prominent members of the cabinet, including Yi Tong-whi, Kimm Kyu-sic, Nam Hyong-u and, An Chang-ho, resigned. A group of Koreans in

Peking, headed by Park Young-man, demanded that the Provisional Government be dissolved. A majority of the Assembly announced their support for the government and for Rhee as its President. Hugh Cynn commented that there was fault on all sides but that Rhee's lack of the "sense of compromise" was the principal reason why the Provisional Government was distraught. Another outstanding nationalist, Paek Chol, explained that the failure of the March First demonstrations "meant the bankruptcy of the nation," adding that because of this failure "an era of despair and pessimism dawned upon the entire people." Yi Tong-whi established the Koryo Communist Party and gave to it the money sent from Moscow to aid the Provisional Government.

Chong-sik Lee, the principal historian of the movement, concluded that the difficulties were largely caused by shortage of funds and by quarrels as to how the scanty resources should be used. Rhee abruptly returned to Washington, where, he said, the principal work had to be done. There he made a fruitless effort to have the Korean claims reviewed by the Disarmament Conference that was held in Washington in 1921–22.

The Provisional Government continued its desultory existence but with little effect. In 1925 President Rhee was "impeached," on a charge of neglecting his presidential duties, and Kim Ku, who had gained the support of Chiang Kai-shek, was named "premier" in his stead. Conditions in China were so unsettled that material help from the Nationalist government was impossible. Japan's conquest of Manchuria brought an abrupt end to the organized recruitment and training of Korean troops. Help from the Bolsheviks led to Siberia becoming a base area for the Greater Korean Independence Army. However, the Communist faction disarmed and dispersed the troops that were loyal to the Shanghai group. In America, efforts to win support for Korea dwindled, partly from lack of funds, but also from American disinterest, and from factional quarrels, with Han Kilsoo and Kim Yeungjeun continuing to dispute Syngman Rhee's claim to leadership. In 1933 Rhee made yet another effort for Korea's redemption, by going to Geneva to appeal to the League of Nations, after Japan's invasion of Manchuria. He won favorable publicity; but the League was already powerless to act on any critical issue,

One last major effort to stimulate a peninsula-wide resistance was made by the Korean Communist Party, which was implanted in Seoul in 1925. In the spring of 1926, Kang Tal-yong, secretary of the party, undertook to create a united front. On 10 March he met with Kwon Tong-jin, a Chondogyo leader, and with other prominent nationalists, to discuss formation of a Korean National Party, "of which we plan to become the core," as he disingenuously confessed. An opportunity was seemingly offered by the death of the deposed Emperor Sunjong, who died on 25 April. His funeral was scheduled for 10 June, and it appeared to be a time when the Communists and the Chondogyo could unite to organize a nationwide demonstration modelled on that of March 1919. The police, however, fearing just such a plan, made mass arrests of suspected dissidents and confiscated some fifty thousand copies of a printed leaflet headed: "Twenty million compatriots—Drive out the enemy! The price of freedom is blood—Long live Korea!" The hoped-for mass demonstrations did not occur.

One further result of the Communist-Chondogyo cooperation was establishment of a coalitionist organization called *Shinganhoe,* which between 1927 and 1931 was remarkably successful in winning converts. President of the organization was Yi Sang-jae, publisher of the *Choson Ilbo* newspaper. Yi was a highly respected Christian nationalist who had been an active reformist advocate ever since his youthful membership in the Independence Club. The Shinganhoe organized student strikes and protests that culminated in a Kwangju uprising, that agitated Korea during the winter of 1929–30 and eventually involved 194 schools and some 54,000 students. Their purpose was not to gain independence but to secure fairer educational opportunities for Koreans. The movement faded and the Communists withdrew from the Shinganhoe, bringing it to a finally futile end.

The breakup of the Shanghai and American independence efforts has been blamed by many Korean historians as resulting from Rhee's stubborn insistence upon having his own way. This is an over-simplified explanation. The disease of factionalism was deeply and widely implanted. An Chang-ho, Kim Ku, and Yi Tong-whi were also stubbornly uncompromising in insistence upon their own ideologies and methods. So were virtually all the other chief participants. Compromise was not an available solution. An Chang-ho proposed what he called a "compromise plan" that was really an affirmation of his own policy. Let us agree, he said in effect, that all of us are right; but meanwhile, let us postpone any kind of action while we concentrate upon education to develop a new generation of capable Koreans. Too little money and quarrels as to how that little should be used was surely a basic problem. But to it should be added the facts of historically deeply implanted factionalism, of very crucial ideological differences, and of the typical Korean individualism and insistence upon personal status. A further explanation for the futility of the March First and Provisional Government movements (and of the others as well) is that the world at large accepted without protest Japan's rise to dominance in Korea and that the subjugated Korean populace had neither resources nor any opportunity to build an effective organization. Under all the adverse circumstances, what matters is not the failure but the basic success—the maintenance of the spirit of Koreanism and of the refusal to surrender.

9

The Closing Years of Colonialism

Koreans growing into adulthood in the 1930s and 1940s were vastly different, in their outward behavior and appearance, and also in their inner thoughts and feelings, from their parents who reached maturity around the turn of the century. Korea was the same country geographically—almost the size of the United Kingdom and with a population in 1945 of some thirty million, that ranked it among the large nations of the world—but it was a far different country industrially, politically, socially, and psychologically. Questions that are difficult to answer, and that are generally answered differently by Japanese, Korean, and foreign historians and commentators, concern what happened to them in the meantime. In what ways did the Japanese colonial rule benefit Koreans and to what degree and in what respects did it harm them?

The factors that must be considered in order to answer such a question rationally are broad-based. In basic respects, simply by definition, the imposed colonization was unquestionably and deeply harmful. The Koreans were deprived of their national sovereignty, of their right of self-determination as a distinct people. During their long history they were often invaded, pillaged, and despoiled. But this was different. Japan denied them their right to be Koreans. This claim to be different is a basic right which many peoples (Slovaks, Serbians, Czechs, Poles, Greeks, et cetera) have continued to demand even after generations, even centuries, of subjection. This is the right that Japan first of all, and most obviously of all, took away from the people of Korea.

Koreans were Korean even in their early history, when they lived under several different governments within their own peninsula and in Manchuria. Koreans often remain Korean, perhaps for two or three generations, after they voluntarily expatriate themselves as immigrants, whether in America, Europe, China, Siberia, Southeastern Asia, the Middle East, South America, or Japan. To be Korean is to be a special kind of person, with proud traditions, and with unique customs, and manners, and traits, and attitudes. Such factors are important for the self-identification of individuals, of groups, and of whole societies. Universally, people cherish their own inheritance, and seek to preserve and to transmit it. As Rupert Brooke wrote in a poignant poem about dying as a soldier "on some foreign strand," wherever there is an Englishman or an English grave, "there is forever England." Wherever there are Koreans, there is forever Korea. But this is, precisely, what Japan sought deliberately and inclusively to destroy, Koreanism was to be replaced by Japanism.

The transformation was not accomplished. It was a failure. But the effort to accomplish it was inclusive and penetrated into every aspect of Korean social and individual life. Instead of knowing their own Korean history, Koreans were to know it as a subsidiary segment of Japanese history. Instead of having pride in being Korean, they were told to take pride in being Japanese. This was the kind of inner transformation that even overmatched the loss of self-government. What it demanded was the demeaning denial of self-identification. The fact that the effort did not succeed does not diminish the humiliation, and the resentment, and the burning anger of having to endure the many pressures of many kinds that were exerted in trying to accomplish it.

Somewhat akin, but different from traditional culture, are matters of the spirit, such as religious beliefs, aesthetic values, artistic creativity, even athletic competition, in which individuals express their own individual ideals and abilities and their pride in their own ethnic and nationalistic loyalties. One significant instance in this category illustrates both the importance and the sensitivity of such matters. In the eleventh Summer Olympic Games, held in Berlin in 1933, the first and the third finishers in the marathon were two Korean runners, Son Ki-jong and Nam Sung-yong, who were graduates of Korean high schools but had to be members of the Japanese team. These victories were celebrated in Japan as nationalistic triumphs. In Korea they were hailed as deeply felt proof of the superior prowess of the Korean people. In posters advertising motion pictures of the race, and in front-page photographs appearing in *Tong-A Ilbo* and *Choson Chungang Ilbo,* the Japanese flag pictured on the breasts of the runners was blocked out. For this offense, the one newspaper was suspended, with some of its staff members subjected to forty days of "interrogation" in prison and then debarred from ever practicing their profession, and the other newspaper quickly suspended itself. Such severity of punishment did not deter Koreans from rejoicing in their very own examples of their ethnic accomplishment, nor did it lessen the angry resentment they felt in being denied the right to celebrate openly.

The religious sentiments of sincere believers are most especially important, since they involve beliefs concerning what life means and of eternal salvation. After the "Christian Conspiracy Case" of 1911–12, again after the 1919 March First movement, and even more stringently in the 1930s, while world exposure of Japan's imperialist advances in Manchuria and China were making the Japanese hypersensitive to foreign criticism, Christian missionary activities and the conduct of Christian services were restricted and scrutinized by the police. The erection of Shinto shrines and of required obeisance before them was not only humiliating but also sacreligious for

Koreans who nurtured faiths of their own. Particularly in the 1930s, with militarism dominant in Japan and with its wars in Manchuria and in China marked by upsurges of patriotic fervor, Koreans who were found guilty or were just suspected of even minor offences were punished in addition to other ways by being required to apologize before Shinto shrines erected in Seoul on South Mountain, and in other areas. Korean Buddhists were deeply angered by imposed Japanese rule over their monasteries and abbots, and by the mandatory imposition in Korea of Japanese forms of Buddhism—all the more resented by Koreans since Buddhism and its modes of worship had initially been introduced into Japan from Korea. Actually, Korean Buddhist beliefs were significantly different from those in Japan. Confucianism, too, had different emphasis in Japan than in Korea, and it was the Japanese modes to which Koreans were required henceforth to conform.

Matters of the spirit is an inclusive phrase not readily encompassed. Korean food, Korean folk tales, Korean proverbs, Korean games, the Korean dress, Korean songs, Korean dances, the basic concept of the Korean theatre, all differed greatly from their Japanese counterparts. Because of the differences, the Japanese sought sedulously to submerge or forbid the Korean modes, or at minimum, to ridicule and belittle them. Anything markedly Korean that could not be forbidden or replaced was disparaged and derided. The very term "Korean" became a derisive tag, much as "nigger" was in the jargon of many American whites at the time. The Japanese view of themselves as a superior race was generally inclusive, not in itself specifically a derogation of Koreans. A typical Japanese view has been stated often by its writers in such terms as "our country, as a special mark of favor from the heavenly gods, was begotten by them, and there is so immense a difference between Japan and all other countries as to defy comparison." Koreans living under Japan's arbitrary rule felt especially keenly the multiplied expressions of Japanese assumed superiority.

Korean painting differs markedly from the typical Japanese styles. The tea ceremony, highly regarded in Japan, is foreign to Koreans. The Japanese cosmetic practice of whitening the bride's face for wedding ceremonies is very different from the brightness of costumes and the freshness of complexion of Korean brides. Japanese music differs in its tonality from Korean. The highly stylized theatrical No and Bakuki performances in Japan contrast with the more realistic, if melodramatic, presentations in Korea. Sumo wrestling, highly esteemed in Japan, is very different from the distinctive Korean mode. The theme of revenge, which is central in Japanese literature, is very unlike the theme of sorrowful suffering that may or may not be finally relieved that marks Korean literature. Horticultural and architectural distinctions between the two countries are equally marked. Korean place-names were altered, as in these examples: Chongjin changed to Seisin; Hamhung to Kanko; Wonsan to Genzan; Pyongyang to Heizyo; Kaesong to Kaizyo; Inchon to Zinsen; Chongju to Sesyu; Kwangju to Kosyu; Pusan to Busan;

and Ulsan to Urusan. Korean family names, such as Kim, Cho, Han, Lee, and Kang, could not be translitereated into a Japanese equivalent; instead, after February 1940, they were recast as something entirely different—such as Miyahara, Watanabe, Hasegawa, Komatzu—which seemed to Koreans an especially demeaning betrayal of their ancestry. The list of differences goes on and on, including many that are trivial along with others of serious substance. But all of them are significant expressions of two cultures that are widely divergent. These, too, are matters of the spirit that made the attempted Japanizing of Korea psychically traumatic.

In the broad array of matters psychological, sociological, and aesthetic, there is no question that Koreans suffered grieviously from Japan's rule. For Japan it was a necessity that on such matters Koreans must be Japanized, whether the changes required one generation or several, in order to transform Korea into a province of Japan. But the cost, even for the failed attempt, for the Koreans was bitter. Nor did it, finally, bring any benefits to Japan. On the contrary, it left the need for the present and future generations of Japanese to struggle to reshape their own attitudes in order to live, as now they must, with the Koreans as neighbors and, in time, as friends.

There were curbs on the freedom of information, for schools were strictly regulated as to what they could teach, writers as to what they could write, and publishers as to what they could print. Freedom of speech was sacrificed. Newspapers and magazines were censored as to what news they could report, as well as for what editorial opinions they might express. Public assemblies were limited and supervised. Even complaints uttered in casual conversation might lead to floggings or imprisonment. Restricted also was the freedom of choice as to where to live, what work to do, and whom they might marry.

Provisions for education are an especially vital test of the quality of colonial rule, since they indicate what the government intended for the colonized people to be like. The educational policies of Japan in Korea followed a consistent pattern, from 1910 through 1945. The guiding principle was to insure a little education (enough to produce a low-skill, low-paid work force) but to discourage and restrict the development of a well-educated intelligensia that might breed rebellion. What this meant in practice was that beyond elementary schooling, all in the Japanese language, there were very few educational opportunities for Koreans at higher levels. In the closing years of the colonial period, after Japan went to war with China, the schools were even more tightly controlled and restricted. In 1939, only 5.52 percent of Koreans were attending primary schools, 0.13 percent in secondary schools, and 0.12 percent in vocational schools. Only twenty-seven Koreans per one hundred thousand were in tertiary level schools, including teachers colleges, and less than one Korean per one hundred thousand gained admission to a university.

After 1938, and until Japan's defeat in 1945, not only were the schools forbidden at all levels to use the Korean language, but also any teaching of Korean literature was banned. Hence, at liberation, the whole youthful population of Korea was uneducated in the cultural traditions of their own country. Fully seventy percent of all Koreans were illiterate in their own language, and a 1942 Japanese study reported that only twenty percent were "competent in the Japanese language." The few Koreans who attended college-level Japanese schools, whether in Japan or in Korea, came from well-to-do families that, for one reason or another, secured favorable treatment by the Japanese. Such special favors, branding these individuals as "pro-Japanese," also constituted a barrier between them and the bulk of the Koreans.

Another significant measure of the effects of the colonial government was the nature of the judicial system. The legal code that was instituted in Korea after 1910 was identical to that of Japan. As Chin Kim and Craig M. Lawson demonstrate in their article, "The Law of the Subtle Mind: The Traditional Japanese Conception of Law," what laws mean and how they are to be applied is left to a high degree to the interpretation of judges. The basis for their interpretation is that the regnant sociopolitical system must be preserved. "Disputes arise only when persons have stepped outside the community of thought. . . . And the non-individualistic emphasis on the group in Japanese society has been reflected in the historical fact that the law rarely ever functions to protect individual rights." Koreans who sought protection in the courts from unjust treatment or seizure of their properties were guilty per se of rejecting their colonial status. The legal profession was virtually entirely Japanese, consisting of lawyers who were educated either in Keijō Imperial University or in Japan. Nominally, the purpose of any judicial system is to enforce justice and thereby to protect and to serve the people. In practice, however, the police and the courts were employed primarily as mechanisms through which the authorities controlled the population. To the people it appeared that the laws and their enforcement were intended and operated to serve the interests of the elites—that is, of the Japanese and of those Koreans who collaborated with them. This widespread feeling led to lack of respect for the laws and to evasion of them so far as was feasible without undue risk. Disrespect for the court system led to avoidance of civil litigation and the settlement of disputes outside the law. Even though this accorded an unfair advantage to the well educated and those who had advantageous social, economic, or political positions, voluntary legal actions tended to be regarded as derogatory to family honor and hence were avoided. The legal system itself, the judges, and the police were regarded by the Koreans not as friends of the people and defenders of social order but as persecutors and enemies. This attitude was not basically different than it had been under the monarchy, but it became intensified during the colonial period, partly because of the increased enforcement efficiency, and, more importantly, because the entire enforcement personnel, including police, lawyers, judges, and prison wardens, were Japanese. Whatever its origin, disrespect for law and guileful efforts to subvert it became so deeply entrenched that it persisted well after the colonial period ended.

Similar sentiments, for similar reasons, marked the labor-management relations that developed during the colonial period, strongly in its latter years. In simple terms, the labor force was Korean, the management group was Japanese. Neither admired, respected, or sought to be cooperative with the other. The more the laborers defied, harassed, or avoided compliance with their management, the more patriotic they felt and the more they were esteemed by the public. The lower pay, the more menial jobs, and the worse working conditions of Korean workers in comparison with the Japanese who were resident in Korea, contributed to feelings of hostility. In sum, laborers had little confidence in their ability to secure just treatment and instead of striving for the usual goals of improved reward for their work, they pursued political anticolonial goals and methods. An ingrained attitude developed that the only real relationship between labor and management was that of enmity; this led to cynicism concerning the bargaining process and to noncompliance with rules, carelessness in handling tools and machinery, absenteeism, malingering, and violence. In short, the lack of confidence in equitable treatment led to attitudes and habits that caused inefficiency and that became too entrenched to be quickly eradicated. This was another legacy of the colonialism, whatever the degree of fault for it may have been Japanese or Korean.

One of the major casualties of Japan's colonization policies was the Korean family. It is impossible to overemphasize the importance of family in Korea's culture. Marriage was universal, from an early age. Married and unmarried individuals were differentiated by their external appearance, including hair styles, head-covering, and clothing. To remain unmarried or to postpone marriage resulted in ridicule and other forms of social punishment. Marriage was the keystone of the whole social structure. Parents selected the marriage partners for their sons and daughters. The bride went to live with her new husband's family. The birth of children was eagerly anticipated and happily celebrated. The ideal family was to have three or four sons and two or three daughters. The entire family lavished care on infants and children. Babies were carried about, wrapped in shawls, on the backs of grandmothers, of older sisters, or of other family members. Divorce was almost nonexistent. The separation of family members was a grievous circumstance. But this separation is precisely one of the detrimental effects of the colonial policies.

Contrasting with Japan's derogation of Koreans, who have consistently been charged by Japanese with lacking decent standards of morality, during World War II thousands of Korean women were forced into prostitution to serve Japanese soldiers. After years of denying this charge the government of Japan officially admitted and apologized for it on 13 January 1992. Aside from the suffering of the women themselves, this undermining of sexual morality had effects upon the Koreans' consciousness of their own self-worth which contributed to additional promiscuous sexuality during the Korean War. Along with the other factors cited, the immediate acts (damaging as they were in themselves) had widespread and lasting debilitating effects. The very concept of the cohesive Confucian family suffered from this and the other disruptive blows.

Part of the disruption resulted from migration from rural villages to cities, which lowered the rural population from 95 percent in 1906 to around 75 percent in 1945. Outward migration was also striking. The number of Koreans resident in Japan in 1905 was 907; by 1920 it was 40,755; by 1940, 1,241,615; by 1944, 1,911,307. Between 1910 and 1944, some million and a half Koreans emigrated to Manchuria and another 300,000 to Siberia. The number of "slash and burn" farmers (dispossessed and seeking new land, however poor) amounted to 246,000 in 1916 and 700,000 in 1947. The chief reason for the major population shifts was governmental pressure to secure cheap labor for the wartime industries. The patrilineal extended family structure was broken up as sons necessarily left their parents and, at least equally distressing, left their ancestors' graves unattended. Marriages were disrupted as husbands left wives and children behind. Census figures for the period are scanty but the general picture is clear. The Neo-Confucian family, based on ancestor reverence, patrilineal continuity, and filial devotion and responsibility, was broken up. Even for those families that remained undisrupted at home, the traditional values were challenged as they observed the broken homes of relatives, friends, and neighbors.

Industrialism also had other effects. Mining became important in Korea during the colonized period. Coal and iron mines employed tens of thousands of workers. Gold mining, by the early forties, amounted to seventy-five tons annually. Other important mineral extraction included tungsten, magnesite, zinc, molybdenum, lead, barytes, graphite, lithium, mica, and fluorspar—all important industrially and several of them absent in Japan. It is questionable whether Japan could have waged war effectively for so many years, continuously from 1937, if it had not been for the essential supplies of Korean minerals that are scarce in Japan.

Landowners with mineral deposits to exploit unexpectedly and suddenly became rich. A few of these were pro-Japanese Korean. Under the Unused Land law, and through expropriation of lands that were determined to be needed by the armed forces, as well as by transfers of ownership of land from Koreans whose land titles were lacking or incorrectly or incompletely registered, much of the mineral lands came into Japanese possession. Even when Koreans owned mineral-rich lands, they seldom were able to develop them, since to do so they needed permits from Japanese authorities and loans from Japanese banks. Not only Koreans were squeezed out of mining operations; so were Europeans and Americans. In 1910 there were forty-one Euro-American mining enterprises in Korea. The number decreased to eleven in 1921 and to none in 1941. A 1916 mining law forbade new foreign investments in Korean mines. At the end of December 1938 there were 121 Japanese mining corporations in Korea and only 29 Korean ones. But the comparison goes well beyond these figures, for the Korean operations were small, the Japanese large. Such huge Japanese firms as Mitsubishi and Sumitomo virtually controlled the Korean mining industry.

Young-iob Chung, in his study "Korean Investment under Japanese Rule" published in 1977, found that

> In comparison to Japanese activity in Korea, Korean investment was very small. The number of Korean "companies" represented 25–30 percent of Japanese "companies" headquartered in Korea during 1910–1929, while the amount of Korean investment in these companies on the whole was even smaller, making up approximately 10 percent to 13 percent of the Japanese. Furthermore, the Korean share of their capital decreased from about 55 percent in 1910 to 10 percent in 1929, and most likely it continued to decrease until the end of Japan's rule.

Concerning the lasting effects of Japan's industrial dominance, Chung concluded that "Koreans were unable to take over the entire productive enterprises in operation for some time after the Japanese left the country, and without modern technology, management experience and adequate inflow of foreign capital, Koreans could not expand investment and continue economic development."

Concerning the overall modernization of Korea during the colonial period, the conclusion reached by Sang-Chul Suh, in his 1978 book *Growth and Structural Changes in the Korean Economy, 1910–1940* seems to be justified. "The similarity of the growth pattern in Korea to that of modern economic growth elsewhere is only superficial," Suh wrote, "because of the 'imposed' nature of the growth in the Korean experience." What this "imposed" pattern meant was two-fold. First, "the institutional reforms placed the privileged group [Japanese residents in Korea and some "pro-Japanese" Korean landlords] in a strategic position to achieve their policy objectives." Second, "the major objectives of economic development policy in Korea were derived from Japan's overall economic circumstances: her growing food shortage, the need for foreign markets for her expanding industrial production, and her factor endowment [The government-enterprise partnership]. Policies were carried out with much more vigor and force in Korea than in Japan for the simple reason that colonies could be readily coerced by power. Accordingly, the individual incentive of an average inhabitant was seriously impeded because the colonial rule did not provide any real connection between his efforts and rewards during the process of rapid development, as shown in the striking contrast between domestic production and consumption."

In short, the Japanese modernization program served the needs of Japan rather than of Korea; furthermore, it taught Koreans the undesirable lesson that their best labors and efforts did not and could not serve their own needs. The only way Korean laborers could "fight back" against their exploitative employers was by laziness, by careless mishandling of their tools and machines, and by general misbehavior and irresponsibility. Such habits, once developed, were not thereafter easily or quickly dislodged. Thus, while modernization advanced by some measurements, it was impeded in vital respects.

Such behavioral characteristics persisted to some degree during the years after establishment of the republic, for two reasons. One is that habitual behavior tends to persist, especially when it is supported by attitudes that are readily transmitted from parents to children and from neighbor to neighbor. The second reason is that the successive Korean administrations have been overwhelmed by severe problems—including the hostile division of the nation, the disasters of the destructive war, the continuing high rate of inflation and of unemployment, and the economic inequalities characteristic of "quick growth" economic policies—that nurtured rather than corrected such attitudes and behavior. The real remedy could come only with economic, political, and social improvements spread widely throughout the population. These were necessarily of slow growth. As Koreans have amply demonstrated, their more recent successes economically have brought many benefits, just as continuing political restraints have resulted in a continuance of resentments and disorderliness.

The most striking flaw of the colonial developmental pattern was its dualism. This was evidenced in several ways. What it means primarily is that it advantaged the Japanese, while disadvantaging the Koreans. It profited absentee landlords of farmlands, at the heavy expense of the tenant and part-tenant small plot farmers. Also, as previously noted, the educational program served the Japanese residents while actually degrading the Koreans (linguistically, culturally, vocationally, and psychologically). The dualistic development placed transportation routes and facilities where they would serve the north-south needs of Japan, rather than the unifying needs of the Koreans. Dualistic regional development established hydroelectric power plants, heavy and chemical industries, and mining operations in the north, while leaving the south with agriculture, light fabrication plants, and in-home small manufacturing. Another kind of dualism was payment of much higher wages and overall income to Japanese residents than to Koreans. One more was subordination of Korean industry to the needs of Japanese manufacturing. Yet another effect was downgrading of Korean abilities by restricting employment of Koreans to low-level positions in all private and public vocations. For all such reasons, the transition of Korea to modern economic development had to be postponed until well after the renewal of independence.

Japan's wartime needs increasingly dominated its governance of Korea after the 1931–32 conquest of Manchuria, then the initiation of war with

China in 1937, and finally the Pacific War that began with the 7 December 1941 attack on Hawaii's Pearl Harbor. In the 1931–1941 decade, the share of manufactured goods in Korea's total production rose from 21 to 40 percent, geared to satisfy Japan's urgent needs. In Japan proper and in Korea the first priority became refocused efforts and enforced sacrifices to help win the wars. These bore more heavily upon Koreans than on Japanese, if only because the wars were not waged by Korea for Korean benefits. Quite to the contrary, Korea would have been better off if none of these wars had been undertaken or if the Japanese defeat had occurred far sooner than it did. The entire Korean population was required to work, to sacrifice, and to rechannel their lives at the behest of their rulers to serve not their needs but Japan's.

After Japan withdrew from the League of Nations in 1933, it became increasingly isolated internationally. But, paradoxically, its imperialistic program appeared all the more unchallengeable. The League of Nations had proved incapable of preventing Japan's seizure of Manchuria. It did not even try to prevent or to stop the war against China. No Western nation or combination of nations was willing to stand in Japan's way, except the United States, in protests and threats preceding the attack on Pearl Harbor. To most Koreans, resistance appeared futile. This was a theme that dominated the writings of Korea's short-story writers during the latter colonial period. One of them, Hyon Chin-gon, in his 1926 story "A Society that Drives to Drink" expressed typical feelings: "I mean, what can you do in a society like this? The man who tries to do anything is a fool. . . . The only thing to do in this kind of society is become a drunkard." Korean nationalists, or at least those who were in Korea, instead of trying to combat Japan's aggressive imperialism, could do little but play the role of mere spectators. In America, Syngman Rhee commenced work on his 1941 book *Japan Inside Out,* warning that Japan's ambitions threatened the United States as well as all Asia. But in America, in England and in France, isolationism and pacifism were ascendant. There was no support for any crusade to enforce international justice.

Japan's attack on China in mid-1937 intensified government controls in Korea. The peninsula became the primary vital supply base for Japan. All labor, materials, funds, and prices were brought under strict government control. The general array of middle-sized and small industries, which were largely owned by Koreans, and which produced mainly consumer goods for domestic consumption, were closed or ruined. Lack of consumer goods forced the closure of many small stores and businesses. Unemployment sharply increased. Prices rose in a surge of rapid inflation. The situation was exacerbated by a ruinous drought in 1938. Japan's need for food led to demands that more Korean rice be exported to Japan, just when less was being produced. An inclusive "Movement for the General Mobilization of the National Spirit" was promulgated in Japan and in July 1938 it was transplanted into Korea. A neighborhood "patriotic group" system was established to insure full compliance with the tightened regulations. As war casualties mounted, Koreans were conscripted both for the Japanese military and for basic labor in Japanese mines, transportation, and industries. In the words of Chong-Sik Lee, "Korea went into another 'dark age' after 1937." Police controls became even more severe. A police report on Kyonggi Province in 1939 explained why: "There are those who assert that the government policy is merely to uproot the traditional Korean civilization and that Korean youths do not have any relation to the war". Korean students, it added, "with the slightest excuses . . . promote opposition between Japanese and Koreans." The report claimed that Japan's rapid victories in China caused "the general public" in Korea to be "pleased with the government policy." However, with contrary effect, "The lack of rice and staples gave an extraordinary shock to public opinion, and society is in a precarious condition, easily manipulatable by the recalcitrants."

The generation of rule by Japan, and the added stringencies of the long wartime period (from 1931 to 1945) left Koreans without internal leadership and fragmented the persisting activist independence movement. Consequently, in 1945 there was no effective nationalist base in the peninsula. Hatred for Japan was strong but such negativism did not provide a foundation for constructive action. As one of the student leaders of that time, Young Hoon Kang, related later, in 1972: "We, the nationalists on the home front, failed in providing the nation with realistic guidance for action and were ill-prepared for new and rapid developments that were to follow. . . . We were a peculiar breed of idealists—not prudent realists. . . . And certainly we lacked experience in a pluralistic approach to accommodation." The people had little to which to cling except a faith that leadership would come back to them from long-exiled patriots. The redemption they could not find within themselves would, they hoped, be brought back to them from outside.

Then, in August 1945, with the dropping of atomic bombs on Nagasaki and Hiroshima, the war unexpectedly came to an abrupt end. For Korea, "liberation" brought into quick and unprepared focus an urgent demand for drastic transformations: politically, socially, and culturally. Overnight, the "closing years of colonialism" became the "opening years of renewal." But, as it turned out, neither from within Korea nor from the return of exiled leaders, nor from the foreign powers that accomplished Korea's liberation was there the requisite "realistic guidance" that was so urgently needed. The new challenges had to be confronted with little or no advance preparation. It was not surprising that the opportunities were beset by disappointments and failures. For this failure, the people of Korea were to have a staggering price to pay.

10

A Policy-making Dilemma: What to Do About Korea?

The defeat of Japan was followed by division of the Korean peninsula into two zones, each of them under the rule of a foreign military force. In some respects the years 1942–48 were, for Koreans, similar to the years 1894–1905. In both periods the status of Korea was subject to decisions by major outside powers. In the first period the powers were China, Japan, and Russia. In the latter period, the dominant power was the United States, with China being a futile partner, and with Russia emerging from the sidelines as a surprise winner. In neither period did Koreans have significant influence over their own destiny.

The fifteenth of August 1945 was for the Korean people a time for deeply felt and long-delayed celebration. But along with relief and hope, it brought shock and disappointment. Their ancient nation, their homeland, was torn apart. This was a disaster with depths that only gradually became fully apparent.

The effects were both better (the liberation) and worse (the division) than had been the 1905–10 loss of Korea's independence to Japanese colonialism. This time Koreans had not one foreign master, but two. In this latter period the people were less exploited but even more impaired. The division of the peninsula was ruinous for the economy and shattering for the society and the age-long traditions of Koreanism. Families were separated, with husbands and wives, parents and children, and other relatives in many cases never to see one another again. For many people, birthplaces and family graves could never be visited again. The future existence of Korea as a nation was ominously threatened by inimical ideological differences that developed between the two sections and even more by the Cold War enmity of the two occupying powers. Seldom in all its long history had the well-being of the people been more bleak. This was what the world press and the allied government spokesmen called "liberation" and "victory." There was indeed a consolatory promise of eventual freedom. But so had there been when Korea was placed under a protectorate in 1905.

The decisions that determined the postwar status of Korea began to take form shortly after Japan's attack upon Pearl Harbor. The first public revelation of what allied victory would mean for Korea (although it was not named) came in President Franklin D. Roosevelt's radio address on 15 November 1942. Describing policy guidelines for dealing with "liberated" peoples, Roosevelt drew two conclusions from American experience with the Philippines. "The first is that there be a period of preparation," he said. "The second is that there be a period of training for ultimate independent sovereignty."

Roosevelt's idea that there was an essential similarity between the Philippines and Korea blinded him to the vital differences between the two. He was convinced that the American-controlled period of tutelage over the Philippines was a success (true only in partial degree) and that this success could be duplicated in Korea (an impossibility under the Cold War conditions). He ignored such vital facts as the vast differences in the history of the two countries, and that there had been no significant international rivalry for control of the Philippines, in sharp contrast to the millenia of self-government in Korea and to the international contention for control of Korea. Neither did he show awareness of the even more vital difference between unilateral colonial control, such as that exercised by the United States over the Philippines, and trusteeship exercised by four uncooperative powers with widely differing degrees and kinds of interest. What he did clearly understand was that Japan must be debarred from Korea to prevent any recurrence of its ambition to penetrate onto the Asian continent. Neither is there doubt about his feelings concerning Russia's interest in the peninsula. Some historians assert that Roosevelt undertook to avert Soviet seizure of Korea by getting Stalin's agreement for a multipower trusteeship. But the best way to have averted that would have been to grant American recognition to the exiled Republic of Korea (with perhaps such qualifications concerning elections and reforms as seemed proper). The evidence is clear that Roosevelt planned to induce Soviet entrance into the war against Japan by promising it satisfaction of its desire for a position in the Korean peninsula. This was in accord with his policy (which Churchill strongly opposed) of agreeing to Soviet preponderance in Eastern Europe. Neither decision amounted to "surrender to Communism," as has been charged by Roosevelt's severest critics. Roosevelt felt strongly his two-fold responsibilities—first, to win the war, second to win the peace. Both demanded the cooperation of the Soviet Union. It was this realization that underlay Roosevelt's Eastern European policies, his plans for the United Nations, and his plan for Korea. Not all nations and not all peoples could be pleased, or treated justly, but the twin objectives of victory and lasting peace were well worth the sacrifices that had to be demanded. So he believed. Whatever the costs, this was the course he felt constrained to pursue.

Shortly after Roosevelt's 1942 radio speech, the Institute of World Affairs suggested that trusteeship for Korea would be a reasonable bridge from colonization to independence. Speaking from China, as premier of the Korean Provisional Government, Kim Ku responded with a demand for Korea's "absolute independence"; and Cho So-ang, heading the Korean Independence Party in Shanghai, warned that unless Korean sovereignty was restored, the rivalry for control of the peninsula would endanger the future peace of Asia.

In the United States, Syngman Rhee secured an appointment with Alger Hiss and Stanley Hornbeck at the Department of State on 18 December, in which he argued that prompt American recognition of the exiled Republic of Korea would be the only way to thwart Soviet entrance into the peninsula. Hiss angrily retorted that he would not listen to pleas to subvert the aims of America's most powerful wartime ally and showed Rhee out of his office. Stanley Hornbeck, in a memordanum on the meeting, stated his view that recognition of any exile group "might involve responsibilities which in the light of later events it might have been better for this government not to have assumed."

On 28 February 1942 Rhee and his associates opened a three-day "Liberty Conference," affirming Korea's independent nationality. This event received favorable publicity and on 2 March Under-Secretary of State, Sumner Welles, announced that the State Department did indeed have the Korean question under consideration. In July Secretary Cordell Hull endorsed the efforts of any exile group that might fight for its country's independence. Army Chief of Staff George C. Marshall advised that it would be "doubtful policy to blindly pick some group . . . thus antagonizing other groups."

In August Arthur B. Emmons III, the American vice-consul in Korea, returned from captivity in Japan on the *Gripsholm* and warned that Korea would become a dangerous focus of rivalry among China, the Soviet Union, and Japan "unless such pressure could be neutralized by some effective form of international agreement to which the Far Eastern Countries concerned would give their sincere effective support." During the autumn of 1942, John Carter Vincent, head of the State Department's Division of Far Eastern Affairs, proposed creation of a joint U.S.–China–New Zealand committee to "cooperate with the Korean people . . . in forming a temporary trusteeship under which there would be given advice and technical assistance." This recommendation was ignored. Clarence Gauss, the American ambassador to China, warned the State Department that Generalissimo Chiang Kai-shek was inclined to grant Chinese recognition to the Korean Provisional Government, which would have interfered with Roosevelt's trusteeship plan. In April China's Foreign Minister, T. V. Soong, proposed in a letter to President Roosevelt that the Allies should promise postwar independence to Korea and meanwhile should train and equip a "Korean Irregular Army" to conduct espionage and sabotage inside Korea. This suggestion was not adopted. Owen Lattimore, Roosevelt's special advisor on dealings with Chiang Kai-shek, wrote to the Generalissimo to warn him that "it would be undesirable to exclude Russia from such problems as the independence of Korea." All these developments were part of the reasons for Roosevelt's decision that postwar Korea should be placed under a multipower trusteeship.

Great Britain, for its own reasons, was determined on continuance of postwar colonization. Lord Halifax, British ambassador in Washington, in February 1943 sent a memorandum to the Department of State noting his government's conclusion that some colonized peoples would require a period of supervision before being set free. On 22 March Anthony Eden, Britain's Foreign Secretary, met with Hull, who agreed with him that before any colony could be granted independence the allies must have positive assurance of its ability for self-rule. In his *Memoirs* (II:1238) Hull said the policy was "to offer them *at some time* when they could *prove* they were capable of independence, the *possibility* of so conducting their political development that they *might be able to hope* for this achievement" [emphasis added]. In short, the prospects for even "eventual" independence were viewed as being dim.

All this was background for President Roosevelt when he met with Eden on 27 March and proposed to him that "Korea might be placed under an international trusteeship, with China, the United States and one or two other countries participating." From this point, America's Korean policy began quickly to take firm shape. In April the State Department worked out a proposal for an international trusteeship program, in which it noted specifically that Korea was a suitable territory to be "temporarily administered . . . anticipating independence." On 4 October Hornbeck wrote to Secretary Hull that "the future of Korea" would be of "paramount importance" to the Soviet Union, which should be expected to exert efforts to assure that the future government of Korea would be favorably disposed and "ideologically sympathetic" to the Soviet Union.

Syngman Rhee wrote to Roosevelt in January 1943 that failure to recognize the Korean exile government would "inevitably result in the creation of a communist state." He wrote again to Roosevelt on 15 May, saying that "the danger of Russian expansion, so feared and dreaded by the United States forty years ago, has not entirely disappeared." He urged Kim Ku to discontinue having Communists in the Provisional Government cabinet. Rhee's conviction that compromise or collaboration with Communists was impossible was capsulized in his frequent reiteration that "you can't cooperate with cholera."

In October Hull won Molotov's agreement that trusteeship for colonies was worthy of studied consideration. With this groundwork accomplished, Roosevelt, Churchill, and Chiang Kai-shek met in Cairo, Egypt, in late November to work out plans for postwar settlements in Asia. Chiang urged issuance of a promise of independence for Korea. Instead, just before adjournment of the conference, the three leaders issued an ambiguous assurance that "mindful of the enslavement of the people of Korea," the three allied nations "are determined that in due course Korea shall become free and independent." Roosevelt's suggested wording had read "at the proper moment." It was Churchill who suggested "in due course" as being vague enough to leave the question of timing entirely free. In view of the record of Roosevelt's policies regarding Korea, the phrase foreshadowed a "holding action" for his plan to engage the cooperation of the Soviet Union, both in war-making and in peacekeeping, by acceding to its ambition for a foothold in "the strategic heartland of Asia."

From Cairo, Roosevelt proceeded to Teheran, where he was pleased to win Stalin's agreement that "the Koreans are not yet capable of exercising and maintaining independent government and that they should be placed under a *40-year tutelage*" [emphasis added]. Korean spokesmen responded in outrage to both the Cairo and the Teheran declarations. Kim Ku called the Cairo statement "insulting" and asked what "in due course" meant. Syngman Rhee was shocked by the Rooseveltian assurance that he had secured for Koreans and other Asians the opportunity "to build up their own forms of self-government without molestation," which was so instantly contradicted by the claim that a multipower "tutelage" would last for forty years—the precise length of Japan's rule over Korea. He wrote to both Roosevelt and Hull that the projected tutelage blotted out the essential meaning of the allied "charter of freedom," for which the war presumably was being fought. Sumner Welles, who had been booted out from the Department of State because of personality differences with Cordell Hull, leaped to the defense of Koreans by writing a syndicated column in which he sought to divert the emphasis from trusteeship to independence, concluding that "with the restoration of Korean independence, one of the great crimes of the twentieth century will have been rectified, and another stabilizing factor will have been added to the new international system which must be constructed in the Pacific."

America's top officials were not unmindful of what their policies were leading to. Alger Hiss and O. Edmund Clubb prepared a paper for the State Department pointing out that since the largest organized Korean exiled group in Asia was the thirty-five thousand Siberian Korean Communists who were equipped and trained by the Soviet Union, it was inevitable that if the war ended with Russia as a participant, the Soviets would take over a large portion of the Korean peninsula. A second paper argued that multipower control over Korea was the only way to prevent one power (Russia or China) from dominating it. A third paper proposed that since there was no pool of trained and experienced Korean technicians or industrial managers, Japanese who were holding such positions in Korea should be retained and utilized there. State Department experts on China told their Washington superiors that Chiang Kai-shek was threatening to undermine plans for postwar American-Soviet cooperation by trying to force Kim Ku to affront Russia by eliminating Communists from the Korean Provisional Government. The U.S. War Department warned Roosevelt that undesirable complications would develop when the Soviet Union attained, as it would, a dominant position in Manchuria and Korea. Roosevelt saw no reason to change his plans.

In October 1944 Stalin assured Averell Harriman, the American ambassador in Moscow, that the Soviet Union would enter the war against Japan within three months after the defeat of Germany. A few months later Roosevelt went to Yalta to hold a week-long meeting, 3–11 February, with Churchill and Stalin. Roosevelt took with him a State Department briefing paper which read in part: "It is desirable that an understanding be reached with the British and Chinese Governments and, depending on developments, with the Soviet Government, on the question of what countries should participate (1) in the military occupation of Korea and (2) in the interim international administration or trusteeship for Korea if it is decided such an administration should be established." This discussion guide also read: "The position of the Soviet Union in the Far East is such that it would seem advisable to have Soviet representation on an interim international administration [of Korea] regardless of whether or not the Soviet Union enters the war in the Pacific."

While these passages were advising Roosevelt to invite the Soviets into Korea, another warned against permitting it to have a dominant position there: "It is possible that the Soviet Union will make strong demands that it have a leading part in the control of Korean affairs." This warning echoed an earlier (March 1944) State Department study that anticipated Soviet "occupation of considerable portions of Korea" and advised that the postwar occupation by Russian and American troops should not be "zonal."

Strangely, there was no American preparation for governing Korea. Nor was there any coordinated planning among the Allied leaders for the respective roles of their nations within the structure of the projected trusteeship. One possible explanation is that the American officials expected that postwar government of Korea (under the trusteeship) would be by the Soviets. The only other available explanation is sheer inadvertance or neglect. Whatever the reason, the fact of "no American preparation whatsoever" is clear. There was a full understanding of Soviet interest in Korea and also knowledge of Soviet control over "35,000 Communist-trained Korean exiles in Siberia" as was stated in the study paper by Hiss and Clubb. The connection between these facts was apparently ignored.

When President Roosevelt died on 15 April, Harry Truman suddenly became president without having definitive information as to what either the United States or its major allies were committed to do regarding Korea.

When Truman went to Potsdam in July to hold his first meeting with Churchill and Stalin, his leadership was untested, his personal prestige was by far less than theirs, and he lacked their knowledge of the details and the nuances of prior agreements. As he wrote to his wife, "I wish I didn't have to go, but I do and it can't be stopped now." Neither, he felt, could there be any stoppage of policies and plans that had been set before he was projected into the presidency. Two factors bolstered his position. One was his knowledge of the successful development of the atomic bomb; the other was his blunt and confrontational personality. He did not pursue the Rooseveltian policy of seeking to build lasting peace by submitting to Russian demands or by mollifying Stalin's feelings. But Truman fully realized that what had been agreed upon was what had to be done.

Actually, at Potsdam the political discussions were virtually confined to Europe. In the State Department's *Potsdam Papers* (I:313) is a study paper that advises, "it might be advisable to designate Korea as a trust area and to place it under the authority of the Untied Nations organization itself." But the question was not discussed. Truman, Stalin, and Churchill met together only briefly, for on 28 July Clement Attlee, having displaced Churchill as Prime Minister, arrived to replace him at the conference. As their talks began, Truman received word that the atomic bomb was ready to be used. Even so, entrance of Russia into the war against Japan was taken for granted. The only action taken regarding Korea, without discussion, was agreement to reaffirm the Cairo declaration that "in due course" Korea would become "free and independent." Discussion of Korea was held only by the military planners. There should be joint planning, they agreed, for attacks on Japanese forces in Manchuria, Korea, and Japan. To prevent confusion after Russia's participation commenced, they agreed that an air-sea operational line should be drawn roughly along the 45th parallel, with Soviet planes and ships to operate north of that line, American to the south of it. General Marshall answered concerns expressed by the Russians by assuring them that the United States did not expect to conduct either any amphibious landings or any land operations in Korea. General John E. Hull, Chief of the Operations Division of the United States Army, suggested that the 38th parallel would be a suitable boundary between Russian and American land forces when they went into Korea; but the question was not discussed. The American side took it for granted that Soviet troops would be rushed into Korea, but they left for the political leaders the question of how to get them out afterwards. General Marshall did caution the Soviet military contingent that it would be "politically inadvisable for any of the interested parties alone to invade Korea." But no agreement was sought on this point. After two weeks of inconclusive discussions, the Potsdam conference adjourned. Truman, confirming his forebodings about going there, wrote to his mother and sister as he was returning home: "You never saw such pigheaded people as are the Russians. I hope I never have to hold another conference with them—but of course I will."

Harry Hopkins, in Moscow, reminded Stalin of the Yalta agreement for a four-power trusteeship over Korca and suggested that it might last for *twenty-*

five years. Stalin made no reply. On 23 July, Ambassador Harriman visited Secretary of War Henry Stimson and warned him that the Soviet Union was intending "to branch in all directions." T. V. Soong also reminded the State Department of the 35,000 Koreans in Siberia that had been specifically trained to move into Korea and to establish control. Stimson added his own warning that these Siberian Korean divisions "will probably gain control, and influence the setting up of a Soviet dominated local government." Such warnings were submerged under the exhilarating expectation of a quick end of the war.

As events were rushing toward their climax, a State Department study paper was completed on 22 June that is revelatory of the degree to which the minds of the officials charged to chart policy lagged behind the facts and the recommendations that were pouring in upon them. As to what should be done after the defeat of Japan, "it is not certain," the paper read, "to what extent, if at all, the United States and Soviet objectives in the Far East are in conflict. The future Soviet course of action can only be surmised."

On 6 August the first atomic bomb was dropped on Hiroshima. Two days later Russia declared war on Japan, which was already making efforts to surrender. The bomb was dropped on Nagasaki on 9 August, while Soviet forces were racing toward the Korean border. By 14 August, the Russian forces were already deep in Korea. The only fighting they had to do was on the east coast, where Japanese troops opposed their landing. Japan surrendered on the following day, recognizing, in the words of Naotake Satō, the Japanese ambassador to Moscow, that "we are at the mercy of the enemy and committed to whatever the enemy should will." Even then, no plans for the governing of Korea were initiated.

In Korea the Japanese Government-General asked Song Chin-u, former editor of *Tong-A Ilbo,* to form an interim government to prevent Korean attacks upon the resident Japanese and to maintain order. When he refused to accept the responsibility, the offer was extended to Lyuh Woon-heung, a long-time left wing and coalitionist-minded patriot who had suffered arrests for his participation in the Shanghai-based Provisional Government. Lyuh countered by demanding release of political prisoners, workers, and peasants. Then he announced creation of the Committee for the Establishment of Korean Independence. By the end of August Lyuh had 145 People's Committees serving throughout south Korea. The Committees were predominantly but by no means wholly Communist. They won wide popular support because of Lyuh's attractive record and personality; because Communism was widely held in Korea to be the most dependably anti-Japanese force; because they offered the only immediately available means of self-government; and because their promise of equal distribution of land was strongly appealing to the peasantry.

The surrender of Japan galvanized activities of many kinds. President Truman and his advisors realized full well that quick and decisive action was required if the Soviets were to be prevented from occupying all of Korea. General Douglas MacArthur issued General Order Number one, which established the 38th parallel as a barrier to stop the rapidly advancing Soviet troops. Lt. General John R. Hodge was ordered to take his Twenty-Fourth Corps from Okinawa, where it had been fighting bravely and doggedly, to Korea to become the occupation force. The first units arrived at Inchon on 6 September, with Hodge so ill-informed and so undiplomatic that he publicly informed the Koreans that he considered them "the same breed of cats as the Japanese." He further enraged the Koreans by declaring that he would retain the Japanese police and bureaucrats in their duties—a plan the State Department quickly ordered him to drop. The People's Republic, proclaimed by Lyuh on the very day of the American landing, was refused recognition by the American command and was promptly dissolved. But the local Communist committees and labor unions it had initiated long continued to serve as centers for dissent from first the American and afterwards the Republic of Korea government.

How was the division of Korea converted from a temporary line intended solely as a convenience for the disarming of Japanese troops into a permanently fixed political division? A Korean historian, Kim Se-jin, charged that the fault was not Russo-American but Korean, in a compilation entitled *Korean Unification* published in 1976. "Although the division of Korea was decided by the major powers," Dr. Kim wrote, "the Koreans themselves could have prevented the division of Korea particularly in the last months of 1945 when the Russo-American relations were not so deteriorated as in 1946–48, had they been firmly united in the struggle to achieve the goal of unification." This conclusion is at variance with the whole course of affairs after August, 1945. What Kim might better have said was: *had they been willing to accept Communist domination of the entire nation.* It was not flawed leadership by Koreans that solidified the division of Korea. It was the Soviet Union.

The United States, realistically, might have prevented it by recognition, after the Pearl Harbor attack, of the Republic-of-Korea-in-Exile. It might have given lend-lease funds and support to utilize the strongly anti-Japanese population of the vital Korean peninsula to cut the supply line for the Japanese forces in China and to establish a base for an attack on Japan itself. Even before Pearl Harbor, in July 1941 President Roosevelt appointed Colonel William J. Donovan to be in charge of intelligence operations preparatory to the defeat of the Berlin-Tokyo Axis. Donovan chose as his special adviser on Asian affairs Dr. Esson M. Gale, who was well acquainted with both China and Korea. Donovan and Gale met almost daily with Colonel Preston Goodfellow and a few others to plan how to use Chinese and particularly Korean civilians to sabotage and obstruct the Japanese military forces. In meetings with Navy, War, and State representatives, Dr. Gale urged that the Koreans "represented a tremendous potentiality for subversive action." He also argued that "a recognition of Korean national aspirations by the Allies would be accepted by other subjugated Asian nations as a signal of Allied liberality towards Asiatic peoples. This would serve to counteract Japanese Pan-Asian propaganda." Dr. Gale's arguments impressed Colonel Goodfellow and some of the others. But, as Dr. Clarence Weems concluded from his study of these meetings, "in failing to adopt the Korean strategy from the beginning, official Washington was unconsciously influenced by Theodore Roosevelt's conclusion in 1905 that the Korean people did not deserve help because they could not help themselves. This concept was kept alive in the World War II period by the partly incorrect, partly questionable, and totally unimaginative downgrading of Korean potentialities by prejudiced and poorly-informed Old Asian Hands in Washington and Chungking." The most that these conferees would agree to was that Syngman Rhee be asked to recruit one hundred suitable Korean-American young men who would be trained by Colonel Goodfellow for underground sabotage leadership in Korea. Even this limited plan was shortly afterwards disapproved by State and War Department officials who considered it so small-scale as to be futile. Also ignored was Gale's further recommendation that the exile Korean government be recognized, "as a wartime measure," and be granted lend-lease aid for developing an effective force.

If it was considered by the State Department to be unwise to ensure the presidency to Syngman Rhee, as it was, or to Kim Ku, or to any other individual, the recognition could have been qualified by the insistence upon holding an American or a United Nations supervised election after Japan's defeat. Perhaps Russian troops might have invaded Korea in any event despite such recognition, but this is by no means a certainty, and probably not likely. Russian insistence on sharing the post-war rule of Japan was successfully resisted by the United States. Maybe an effort to insure Korea's undivided independence by an American preclusive recognition might not have worked. At any rate, it was not tried.

After Russian troops, along with an accommpanying body of repatriated Korean Communists, were actually within north Korea, down to the 38th parallel line, it is clear from the record that the Soviet Union would accept nothing less than a Communist government in Korea. The Soviet Union tried to win American concurrence for reuniting Korea under a coalition that, assuredly, would have been controlled by Communists. This kind of solution the south Korean leadership and people refused to accept, as did the United States. Had they agreed to it, Kim Il-sung would not only have become the dictator ruling north Korea, but the south as well. Bruce Cumings, for one, in his essay on "American Policy and Korean Liberation," argued that the preservation of south Korea from Communist control was no benefit. "In American eyes," he wrote, "it would be a bulwark against Communism. Instead, it became a bulwark of discredited privilege against the Korean people." This represents the persistent leftist contention that the people of south Korea would be better off under Communism. Against this view, the record speaks for itself.

General Hodge and his staff were stunned by the enormous burden placed upon them of governing south Korea without any plan, with very limited resources, and with no special knowledge of the Korean people, their needs, their capabilities, or their attitude toward the occupation. The AMG officers' perplexity and their apprehensions were clearly revealed in a series of reports sent back to the State Department by H. Merrell Benninghoff, General Hodge's political advisor. His first report, dated 15 September 1945, estimates, probably accurately, the feelings of the Korean people:

> Southern Korea can best be described as a powder keg ready to explode at the application of a spark.
>
> There is great disappointment that immediate independence and sweeping out of the Japanese did not eventuate.
>
> Korea is completely ripe for agitators.

By 29 September Benninghoff had a bit more confidence that the American Military Government had at least a tentative grasp of the situation. "There is the so-called democratic or conservative group," he reported, including "many of the professional and educated leaders who were educated in the U.S. or in American missionary institutions in Korea . . . they demonstrate a desire to follow the Western democracies, and they almost unanimously desire the early return of Dr. Syngman Rhee and the 'Provisional Government' at Chungking." Again, on 10 October, he urged the prompt return to Korea of Rhee and others of the exiles and warned against permitting the entrance into south Korea of the Koreans who were serving under Mao Tse-tung in Yenan.

William Langdon, another of Hodge's State Department advisors, answered charges that the AMG was being unduly influenced by conservative interpreters by explaining: "For practical reasons we had to hire persons who spoke English, and it so happened that these persons and their friends came largely from moneyed classes because English had been a luxury among Koreans."

On 5 October the Military Government announced appointment of a Korean Advisory Committee chaired by Kim Song-su, organizer of the conservative Korean Democratic Party, and (in view of his large textile mills and land-holdings) a presumed collaborator with the Japanese. Eight of the remaining ten members of the Committee were also members of the Democratic Party. Major-General Archibald V. Arnold, serving as Military Governor under Hodge, described them as "men greater than politics and men above any groupings or outside interest." This committee was set up as a measure for countering the influence of Lyuh's network of 145 local committees, which were seen by the Military Government as agents of the Soviet Union. After a few months of further experience in trying to deal with north Korean authorities, Hodge reported to the State Department his conviction that Korea never would be reunited "until the Russians are sure that the whole will be soundly communistic."

Japan's surrender aroused a renewed burst of determined activity by all Korean nationalists. The exiled leaders—notably Kim Ku and Kimm Kyu-sic in Chungking and Syngman Rhee in America—sought immediately to return home. Dr. Rhee arrived first, on 16 October. His reception was honorific.

General Hodge first offered to house him in an apartment in the Kyongbok Palace. When Rhee refused, he was given a suite on the third floor of the Choson hotel. General Hodge introduced him to a huge crowd in front of the Government-General building, which Rhee addressed in both English and Korean. He announced plans to bring back from China the Provisional Government leaders, except the Communists, and before the end of the month Kim Ku and Kimm Kyu-sic were back in Seoul. Lyuh Woon-heung offered Rhee the presidency of The Korean People's Republic, which he declined. On 23 October Rhee presided over a meeting attended by a wide spectrum of political leaders, representing the Committee for the Preparation of Korean Independence.

Not only the American Military Government but also the Korean Communist Party hoped that Rhee would serve their purposes. On 25 October the *Haebang Ilbo,* published in Pyongyang, editorialized:

> Dr. Syngman Rhee has come. The revolutionary Dr. Syngman Rhee, who has traversed the world for the sole purpose of obtaining the liberation of the Korean people in his lifetime, has come. The Korean people, who are at a historic turning point today, earnestly demand a great leader. Therefore, the return of Dr. Syngman Rhee has great significance, and the expectations of the people are very great. The duty of the leader is to perceive accurately the world situation, perceive correctly the conditions in Korea, and provide direction to the masses.

The 23 October meeting marked the end of Rhee's "honeymoon" association with the American Military Government almost before it began. One reason was that the meeting adopted a resolution denouncing as "a great insult" a statement President Truman had issued in September declaring that "immediate independence" for Korea was not contemplated. The underlying reason for the split between Rhee and Hodge was that Rhee refused to play the role of "front man" for the American policy for Korea. The State Department, MacArthur, and Hodge had all taken it for granted that in view of Rhee's age (which was seventy) he would accept honorific treatment and would help them to implement their own Korean program. Instead, Rhee launched his own "Society for the Rapid Realization of Independence" and began building a strong organization to support it.

The next several weeks were a time of efforts, beset by disagreements, to create a "united front" of independence advocates. Lyuh Woon-heung abandoned his claim for the sovereignty of the People's Republic and in its stead organized a new People's Party. Pak Hon-yong, head of the Communist Party, declared that expatriate Koreans had done nothing to win Korean freedom from Japan and promised to support the military government in order to establish "a bourgeois democracy as a necessary step toward full freedom of all classes." Syngman Rhee insisted that until Korea was reunified and secured its full independence, no one, neither the Communists nor the pro-Japanese collaborators, should be excluded from the shared effort. The Communists rejected these overtures. Lyuh Woon-heung issued a pamphlet that pointedly distinguished between "Traitors" and "Patriots." Pak Hon-yong denounced Rhee's appeal to the Allied Powers to end the partition of Korea and rejected cooperation with "pro-Japanese" or with Kim Ku and his associates who had returned from Chungking. Among them all, in the words of the major historians of the period, Scalapino and Lee, Rhee "was emerging as the purest, most strident nationalist." Others charged that he was allowing his personal ambition to overshadow his concern for the well-being of the Korean people.

A group of wealthy Koreans, who were lustily denounced by leftwing critics as "Jap collaborators," bought a house for Rhee and he promptly moved into it, to terminate the ambiguity of being a "guest" of the American Military Government. He commenced a series of weekly radio talks in which he hammered away at the theme that Communists were the enemies, rather than the supporters, of the Korean people. This was a crucially important campaign, for among the Korean people there was widespread appreciation of Communists, for the reason that the Soviet Union and the Communist Party had been their sole effective supporters during their long oppression by Japan. Scalapino and Lee, in their epochal study of *Communism in Korea* (I:240) point out that "It was easy to portray them as heroes in the struggle against Japanese oppression, and to bestow upon them all the attributes of Robin Hood." Rhee's theme, in his speeches and in his talks with leaders of all types, was that Communists aimed not to help Koreans but to impose upon them a Moscow-directed Communist government.

The issue came to a head swiftly. On 26 December 1945 the Foreign Ministers of the Soviet Union, Great Britain, China, and the United States, meeting in Moscow, announced their plan for a trusteeship for Korea, to last for not more than five years, and to be administered jointly by four powers—Russia, the U.S., Great Britain, and China.

In both north and south Korea massed crowds took to the streets, carrying signs that read "Down with Trusteeship!" At first the Communists joined in denouncing the Declaration, but shortly they received orders to support it and on their signs crossed off "Down" and substituted "Up." Kim Ku called a general strike of all Koreans employed by the Military Government and for three days (until he called it off) the government buildings were without heat and without services, while garbage piled up and the AMG officers felt the strong tide of Korean resentment. The American government regretted the trusteeship agreement almost as soon as it was announced. Hodge immediately appealed to Washington to "kill the trusteeship idea." In a 5 January letter to Secretary of State Byrnes, Truman charged Bynres with having lost his nerve in the Moscow conference and said he ought to have demanded creation of a strong government encompassing all of Korea. The letter ended with the defiant exclamation, "I'm tired of babying the Soviets."

General John R. Hilldring, newly appointed Assistant Secretary of State for Occupied Countries, wrote of his reactions:

> You and I both know that it wasn't many weeks after the Moscow Conference before nearly everyone who had anything to do with the Korean Declaration deeply and honestly regretted it. But it is one thing to regret a mistake and quite another to come forward and recommend that an international agreement be renounced in order to correct the mistake. The cold war was already on, which further tightened the conviction of most officials, particularly the career diplomats, that any abrogation by us of an agreement with Russia would have disastrous consequences. In any case this was the dilemma of the U.S. Government.[24]

What the American Military Government could do to mitigate the blow to Koreans was limited. What it did do was to establish an Emergency National Assembly appointed by General Hodge to initiate measures for expediting Korean independence. This Assembly was convened in February 1946. Its first resolution was to request creation of a Representative Democratic Council of South Korea, to advise the Military Government of the sentiments and demands of the Korean people. Its purpose, as the AMG explained, was to give General Hodge continuing political advice, to represent Korean public opinion, and to help "educate" the Koreans about the necessity of compliance with the Moscow trusteeship declaration. All the principal political leaders in south Korea were appointed as members. They elected Syngman Rhee as chairman, with Kim Ku and Kimm Kyu-sic as vice-chairmen. Lyuh Woon-heung accepted membership on the Council but resigned after he was twice kidnapped by Communists and "persuaded" to withdraw from it. In one of those "educational sessions" he was held out over a cliff on South Mountain while his captors "reasoned" with him.

Despite the charge they were given, none of the Council members intended to accept trusteeship. The Council became an organ through which the members could express their opposition to postponement of Korean independence, and within which they could thrash out differences among themselves. State Department spokesmen at first sought to reconcile Koreans to trusteeship by explaining to them that it did not mean colonization and that it was a positive step forward toward independence; meanwhile, it would provide them with much-needed material help and education for self-government. The Koreans, however, understood that "trusteeship" was a form of foreign government that was to be imposed upon them against their will. As for its promise that within five years it would be succeeded by independence, Koreans remembered only too well that Japan's proclamation of the protectorate had also promised that it was simply a step toward independence. They also believed that the "four power" trusteeship would eventuate quickly in unilateral control by the Soviet Union—for Great Britain had little interest in Korea and had insurmountable problems of its own to deal with; Nationalist China was too weak even to maintain its own independence; and the United States was manifestly determined to withdraw from Korea as fully and as soon as possible. In contrast, the Soviet Union had a determination to remain in Korea and to establish there a government sympathetic with its own idealogy and subject to its will.

Of course anti-trusteeship sentiment among the Korean people was not unanimous. Countering it was the realization that the immediate establishment of an independent government would be beset by enormous difficulties. One was the lack of administrative experience after a generation of colonial rule. Another was lack of funds to pay for even the barest essentials of government. Most damaging of all was the collosal fact of the foreign-imposed division of the nation, which could only be ended by the decision of those powers. There was no constitution and no apparatus for determining what the form of self-government would be—whether monarchical, a presidential democracy like that of the United States, a cabinet system headed by a prime minister like that of Great Britain, or something else. What taxes should be imposed, and how should they be collected and spent? What could a weak and resourceless government do to increase productivity, curb inflation, and solve the prevalent illiteracy, unemployment, and poverty? If a five-year trusteeship could serve as a bridge strongly supported by the powers administering it, and leading promptly to a well-prepared and adequately supported independent government of the reunited peninsula, would that not, by all means, be Korea's best solution?

Such doubts and such questions were real. So were the fears that a four-power trusteeship would not and could not produce the hoped-for results. This was the dilemma the Korean people had to confront, just as the controlling powers had their own dilemma of what policies should be brought into effect.

11

Military Government American-Style

The quickness of Japan's surrender following the dropping of the atomic bombs was not without disastrous effects. The Soviets celebrated their entry into Korea with Orwellian black-is-white language, as their troop commander General Shtikov proclaimed: "You the people of Korea! You have become a free nation. The military forces of the Soviet Union have provided all conditions for the people of Korea to start creative efforts freely." General Douglas MacArthur, pursuant to the sometimes undiplomatic tendency of the United States to "tell it as it is" announced in his General Order Number One that "the administrative control of the area south of the 38th parallel rests with me and all residents in this area should obey orders bearing my signature." General John R. Hodge, unexpectedly propelled into commanding the military government of the south, nervously cabled the Pentagon: "Under the existing situation and policies the U.S. occupation of Korea faces no success and is being pushed both politically and economically into a state of absurdly great difficulty." He concluded by recommending: "Let the Korean people take care of things in Korea as they please and settle their problems after going through a civil war which would inevitably ensue." The Koreans were equally clear in their conviction that they should be governing themselves.

The American Military Government (hereafter, AMG) in south Korea was marked by goodwill and good intentions but also by futility and ineffectiveness. Very evident was the determination of the United States to end the AMG as soon as possible and to withdraw from the peninsula, and from involvement in Korean affairs, as completely as it could. The policies governing the operations of the AMG were unclear, even to itself. The feelings and attitudes of its personnel were strangely mixed, ranging from "We like you and want to help you" to "We dislike being here and we want to leave you as soon as we can." The result was confusion and uncertainty. The Koreans did not really know what to expect from the Americans. The Americans did not really know what it was that they were supposed to accomplish.

This additional three-year period of alien rule contrasted sharply both with the Japanese colonial rule and with the American Occupation of Japan, as well as with the Soviet rule of the north. The AMG maintained the general structure of the Japanese Government-General of Chōsen, for it had neither the intention nor the ability to devise and impose a different political system. But its operations were by far more relaxed than the rigidity and sternness that marked the colonial period. They were also less purposive and less efficient than the rule exercised by General Douglas MacArthur over Japan. The AMG was set up and was conducted under conditions that gave it no possibility of success. The reasons stand out with startling clarity.

First, and fundamentally, there was no preparation for it. Neither of the two responsible departments, State and War, did any kind of advance planning. It was as though the need for a military government of south Korea emerged suddenly and unexpectedly out of the void. In sharpest contrast to the extensive and detailed planning for the occupation of Japan, the responsible authorities did not set up study groups to determine what problems would be encountered in Korea and to evaluate alternative ways for dealing with them. No personnel were selected to receive training. No Korean language-study program was initiated. Until near the end of July 1945 there was no decision as to what troops or what commanding general and staff would be assigned for the occupation and administration of Korea. No guiding policy directives had been prepared. Although a multipower trusteeship over Korea was gradually formulated as American policy, no liaison was established with the other governments to work out agreements on how it should operate. Edwin O. Reischauer, in his 1955 book *Wanted: An Asian Policy*, accurately summed up the situation: "It is a strange irony of history that our preoccupation with the defeat of Japan so blinded us to our other Asian problems that we prepared on the whole wisely for the postwar needs of our defeated enemies, but ignored those of our victorious or liberated friends."

Second, the decision concerning personnel to be used was inappropriate and unwise. Lt. General John R. Hodge, the second choice to command the occupation (after Chiang Kai-shek opposed bringing in General Joseph Stilwell and his troops from China), was selected simply because he and his troops were close at hand in Okinawa, from which transport could most easily be arranged into Korea. General Hodge was an admirable leader of troops in battle. The Twenty-Fourth Corps serving under him was battle-hardened and had acquitted itself heroically in hard and bloody fighting in Okinawa. He was conscientious and wanted very much to do well whatever duty was assigned to him. But Hodge was a battlefield commander, not a civil administrator. He was completely ignorant about Korea. He lacked the education, the training, and the experience required for the governing of a foreign, civilian, and resentful population. He never had been sensitized to the nature of crosscultural differences. He had no knowledge of Korean culture or of how in many respects it differed from American ways. He had neither the temperament, the tact, nor the sensitivity suited for political management. He didn't want the job and, as he said to a friend, he wouldn't stay with it for a million dollars, if he had a choice. The soldiers under his command were both as shocked and as resentful as were the Koreans when, instead of being sent home at war's end, they were sent into Korea. They had already amply fulfilled every duty that could be expected of them. They had more than earned the right to be sent back to the United States, to be demobilized and sent to rejoin their families, to take up again their normal civilian pursuits. It was especially galling to them to know that this return to civilian home life was accorded to millions of other soldiers, many of whom had suffered less or no travail of battle. They were asked to undertake duties for which they had had no training and for which they had neither taste nor capability. For many reasons, their adjustment to new and different service in Korea was unwelcome and difficult.

Third, the American government had no clear policy for dealing with communism, which was a basically disruptive factor is south Korea. A network of People's Committees was established throughout the south. Pro-Communist feelings were widespread, as we have seen, because of the history of Russian support to anti-Japanese independence fighters. In the United States, there remained strong sentiments of admiration for the Soviets who had withstood the sieges of Stalingrad, Leningrad, and Moscow. The trusteeship plan pointed toward close Soviet-American coordination in Korea. Although Russian behavior in Eastern Europe very soon initiated a strong revulsion against communism in the United States, and although a primary interest of the United States in Korea was to make of it "a bastion against communism," and despite the quick discovery by the American Military Government that Communists in the south were destructively uncooperative and actively hostile, even so, the eleventh decree issued by the AMG, on 9 October 1945, prohibited "discrimination on account of race, nationality, belief and ideologies"—thereby guaranteeing for the Communists freedom to organize, to evangelize, and to infiltrate into every branch of government and into all aspects of the society.

Fourth, the Americans and the Koreans were unknown to one another and were very different in their respective cultures, in their expectations, and in their behavioral patterns. Inevitably, both disliked the diverse roles of rulers and ruled that they were required to play. They had no common language in which to communicate. Misunderstandings between them were inevitable and serious. To the incoming troops, the peninsula was a part of Japan and the Koreans had been part of the enemy with whom they had fought ferociously and with hatred right up to their assignment to Korea. The Koreans, meanwhile, expected independence and instead got more alien rule—plus the division of their nation.

Would immediate independence have been practicable? Some American participants in the occupation thought so. William Langdon, in his role as a State Department advisor on Hodge's staff, cabled to Washington his own assessment in December 1945: "The old native regime internally was feudal and corrupt, but the record shows that it was the best disposed towards foreign interests of the three Far Eastern nations, protecting foreign lives and property and enterprises and respecting treaties and franchises. I am sure that we count on at least as much from a native government evolved as above." Koreans, with four thousand years of self-governing history, had no doubt that they could rule themselves. But the trusteeship plan precluded that solution.

Feelings on both sides were basically, and sometimes actively, antagonistic and did not fundamentally change much during the three years of the occupation. The American soldiers called the Koreans "Gooks," which was partly affectionate but largely condescending. They accused the Koreans of stealing from them—which surely happened, though only by individuals, not involving the general populace. Meanwhile, the Americans indirectly and institutionally stole from the Koreans—by placing many treasured artifacts (taken from the repatriated Japanese, who had taken them from Koreans) for sale at the ludicrously low price of 75 cents per item in the Post-Exchanges, to which only Americans had access. Many soldiers sent home up to a dozen or twenty footlockers of handicrafts and antiques, which they got as "gifts" or by "liberating them," as GI jargon phrased it.

An overall estimate of the period of U.S. Military Government was published in 1978 as "Investigation of Korean-American Relations," a report of the House of Representatives subcommittee on International Organizations. In summarizing the postwar years the subcommittee commented: "Economically, the immediate postwar years in the southern region of Korea were harsh. Its economy, long dependent on Japan, and dismembered by the division of the country, was in shambles. Liberation had resulted in an influx of millions of Koreans from China, Japan, and the U.S.S.R., who had been dislocated during the 36 years of colonial rule. Most returned to their hometowns in southern Korea, the area traditionally most densely populated and from which most Koreans had emigrated in prewar years."

Then the report pinpointed reasons for the failure. "The economic depression was exacerbated by the failure of the U.S. military government to effect meaningful nationwide land reform, control the extremely high rate of inflation, or stimulate agricultural and industrial production. U.S. economic assistance took the form of relief, consisting principally of goods and basic necessities. Further, because the military government failed to settle disputes over formerly Japanese-owned commercial, industrial, and agricultural assets, much of the preexisting economic base was underused."

Korean reactions to the occupation were various. Not all Koreans shared the same feelings. Some, including some of the best educated (mostly in the cities), sought to work with the Americans and to share in the government. Another few looked for opportunities to enrich themselves by securing properties that the AMG expropriated from the repatriated Japanese. The vast majority, mostly rice-paddy farmers, were little affected by the shift from Japanese to American rule. Among the articulate dissidents, Professor Pyun

Young-tae expressed, in a series of articles in the English-language *Seoul Times,* the reasons for their discontent. In the 19 February issue, he complained bitterly: "To us Koreans, the subdued, the down-trodden submission is a weakness, and revolt seems the only virtue." In the 9 January 1946 issue he wrote: "What have we done, after all, to earn this mean, creeping, crocodillian form of slavery called trusteeship?" On 14 March, he was trying to be conciliatory: "With the first landing of American troops, we implicitly believed that the good-neighbor policy of Uncle Sam had been extended to the land of Morning Calm. . . . For the sake of both Korea and America, it is a pity to see things happen that are likely, if continued, to discredit and eventually undermine that trust." A year later, on 7 February 1947 he viewed the occupation in the best light he could: "America's utmost concern, incidentally that of China, too, is not to allow Korea to fall into the hands of another potential aggressor dreaming of world conquest."

What Koreans resented most deeply of all was the partition of their nation, and the prospect that under the Cold War conditions there was no remedy for it. None, that is, except to accept reunification under Communist rule. If that was the only way to accomplish reunification, many Koreans were willing to accept even that. Typical of the sentiments of many was a bitter letter written on 18 June 1947 by Colonel Ben. C. Limb, (Im Pyong-jik) Chairman of the Korean Commission in Washington, in which he proffered this unwelcome advice to Syngman Rhee:

> Looking realistically at the present situation in Korea, what should the Korean people do? Americans berate them for their dislike of Communism, and tell them that they must learn to live happily with the Russians. In the final analysis, perhaps this is correct. If America will not stand by its commitments of honest Korean independence—if the United States treats Korea primarily as a bargaining item that may perhaps be profitably traded off for advantages elsewhere—then the proper course for Korea becomes clear. We shall be forced to shift horses in the middle of the stream. We shall be forced, though much against our will, to work out our destinies as a people within the Soviet sphere.[25]

A fifth reason why the AMG could not succeed was that the Koreans were virtually ungovernable by unwanted foreign military power.[26] A full generation of Japanese rule had taught them to hate an imposed foreign government and to resist it by all available means.

Now again, under the Americans, they were ruled by foreigners, who spoke a language that very few Koreans understood. Only a very few AMG advisors, mostly missionaries who returned after the war's end, were able to speak, understand, read, or write the Korean language. Few of the governing personnel had any even introductory understanding of Korean ways. In the necessarily continuous and detailed relations between the AMG and the population, neither side could comprehend the psychology or the customs of the other. The Korean people were required to obey rules that could not be explained to them and they had few opportunities and even fewer means for making known to the authorities their own wants, needs, and objections. Across the gulf of strangeness, resentment and misunderstanding flowed both ways.

Along with rioting or rebellion, the means of protest that were available to Koreans were deceit, concealment, guile, disobedience, and malingering. Since the AMG exercised its authority through the basic political structure that had been maintained by the Government-General of Chōsen, the Koreans were well experienced in evading or avoiding or disrupting its operations. When the American army officers who served as administrators treated resistance and law-breaking with leniency, many Koreans combined their dislike for any alien governance with disdain for what appeared to be weakness and surely was inefficiency in administering the political system. Some GI's committed thefts, rapes, seductions and personal abuse. These attitudes and behaviors made even the best-intentioned American efforts more difficult and less productive, thereby strengthening the conviction of the homesick occupation troops that they were saddled with care for feckless and incapable Gooks. "Good people," they said, "but not our kind."

A sixth factor made the rule by the AMG inevitably difficult. Communist and populist cells were widespread all through the south. They increased both in numbers and in their popular appeal as weeks, and months, and then years passed without a solution for Koreans' material needs or of the 38th parallel impasse. They did what they could to impede the AMG (and, later, their own government, ROK) as the soundest means for serving the cause of global Communism, while also increasing their own prestige and enlarging their membership. Especially after the climactic success of the Communists in China, in September of 1949, the Soviet Union undertook a fresh assessment of its relations with the various national Communist parties in Asia and enhanced its efforts to encourage and instigate the disruptive activities in South Korea.

Throughout the south, but most markedly in South Kyongsang and North Cholla provinces, in the rice-paddy areas south of Seoul, the AMG officers met with violent resistance. These were areas with a very high percentage of farm tenantry. Local People's Committees seized control of civil and police functions. Violent outbreaks of resistance to AMG efforts to take control of local government resulted in imprisonment of Communists and other dissidents. Resentment and resistance were widespread. The People's Committees raided county offices, where land records were kept, and destroyed the records. Ownership of many rice paddies became a cause for riotous disputes. An AMG team sent to assess public opinion reported that "civil war will develop along the entire east coast as soon as MG leaves." As events proved, this was a perceptive prophecy.

In late September 1946 a railway strike in Pusan spread rapidly and immobilized rail transport throughout south Korea. The strike soon turned into violence. In Taegu thirty-eight policemen were seized by Communist rebels, tortured brutally, and murdered. Homes of government officials were sacked. People's Committees distributed handbills, reading: "It is not that we hate the police, but that we are ready to die for the independence of the fatherland. . . . Let us build an independent country with our own hands. Transfer all power to the people. Distribute the land among the people equally. Let us oppose the collection of all grains." Chough Pyoung-ok, a leader in Kim Song-su's Democratic Party and also in An Chang-ho's Heungsadan, in September 1946 told the Americans: "It has been an open secret what the Commies have been planning since last May, to stage a nation-wide opposition to the Military Government." Lyuh Woon-heung, after a visit down through the southeast, on 29 November reported to General Hodge that communism was not the only problem. "The cause of dissatisfaction is much more deep-rooted. The embers are there, it was only fanned to a conflagration. . . . There is almost no authority. It is a case of everyone for himself." Within a few months more than two hundred policemen and around one thousand civilians were killed. Some twenty-five thousand or more people were arrested before the disorders were brought under control.

Seventh—an equal or even greater problem that was never successfully solved—was identification by the Korean public of all those of their fellows who were "successful" economically or educationally as being "pro-Japanese" collaborators. It was with this group that the Americans necessarily had their closest association. These were the Koreans who spoke English. These were the ones with experience and training in middle and low-level management of factories or in holding subordinate governmental positions. These also were the Koreans who were the best dressed, the best housed, the most urbane, and consequently, were by the Americans the best liked and most companionable. To the mass of the Koreans, however, this preference by the AMG made it appear that the new rulers were essentially like the Japanese.

Finally, as an eighth factor, there was deep-seated jealousy and resentment over the far greater speed and thoroughness of the rehabilitation of Japan under the rule by General Douglas MacArthur. American policy guidance, American supplies, and American interest went first of all, and most of all, to Japan, while Korea remained in every respect "at the end of the line."

The AMG dealt as best it could with the tragically distressed economic conditions of the south Koreans. Since it was without adequate policy guidance from Washington, and its staff was largely ignorant of Korean economic needs, it inevitably made serious mistakes. Fortunately the rice harvest of 1945 was unusually large. Under Japanese government, at least a third of it would have been diverted to Japan. To accomplish this, an elaborate system of "rice collection" was in place, and price controls were established to maintain some stability in the domestic market. Both of these systems were summarily abolished by the AMG. With similar intention of insuring justice within a free enterprise economy, the AMG set a ceiling of one-third the annual crop as rental payment for the land. The problem was that no workable provisions for grain distribution and for supervision over prices and rentals were brought into effect.

The resulting market confusion was deeply aggravated by massive population movements. The more than 700,000 Japanese residents in Korea, who were promptly repatriated to Japan included government officials, key transportation and communication employees, and all the supervisors of the rice collection, price controls, and distribution of grains to the markets. A different kind of population movement—the return from Japan of some million Koreans and the incoming of between two and three million refugees from China, Manchuria, and the Communist-controlled north—created an enormous demand for housing, clothing, food, medical and educational services, and employment. Competition, misunderstandings, and resentment among these groups, and between them and the resident population, were inevitable. Inflation mounted rapidly and a black market in currency and commodities competed with the legitimate market structure.

How much American financial aid was provided to deal with these urgent problems cannot be determined. What is certain is that it was not enough. Unpriceable military surpluses, left behind on Pacific islands at war's end, were shipped into Korea, after the most usable portions were taken to MacArthur's Japan. The cost of the military occupation, including salaries paid to American experts who were either brought into south Korea or who worked on Korean affairs in Washington, or Tokyo, or elsewhere were categorized as American "aid to Korea." The American Congress was under heavy pressures to reduce the war-inflated U.S. government budget, including foreign aid, as quickly and as greatly as possible. Some of the money it did appropriate for Korea was never, for various reasons, actually allocated. Some parts of supplies that were dispatched to south Korea never arrived; others were partially spoiled, or were unusable on arrival, or were unsuited to the needs. These problems were inevitable and are typical of general aid programs, especially those of an emergency nature.

The dollar amount of American aid to south Korea cannot be reliably determined. Andrew Grajdanzev, reporting to the Institute for Pacific Affairs, estimated it at $285 million for the three-years plus three months from 15 August 1945 to 31 December 1948. He broke the amount down by years, as follows: $6 million in 1945–46; $93 million in 1946–47; $113 million in 1947–48; and $75 million from 1 July 1948 through 31 December 1948. The Nathan Report, which was commissioned by the U.S. Congress, estimated the total amount of aid as amounting during the AMG period to $300 million. Ninety percent of this was in grants; the remaining ten percent was in loans, in the form of surplus U.S. military supplies, to be paid for later by the Republic of Korea government. Statistics compiled by the Bank of Korea estimated the total dollar worth of the aid from August 1945 through the end of 1948 at $400 million, allocated by years as: $4,934,000 in 1945; $49,496,000 in 1946; $175,371,000 in 1947; and $179,593,000 in 1948. Inaccurate though the figures are, the amounts were generous. They also, inevitably, were inadequate for the needs.

After the Moscow declaration that trusteeship was to be imposed upon Korea, 1946 became a year of trial and error to search for ways of reuniting the peninsula and of setting up a new trusteeship government. Three divergent points of view made this goal an impossibility. The Soviets wanted trusteeship because it was the means by which to insure that Korea would become their satellite. The United States, which had proposed the trusteeship plan, quickly came to realize that the result would be, as in Eastern Europe, Soviet control; nevertheless, the Americans were committed to trying to accomplish it. Most Koreans, fearing and mistrusting trusteeship, opposed it with fierce determination. Naturally, members of the Democratic Party, which represented the more conservative property-owning, best-educated, and most Westernized Koreans, were the most effective opponents of trusteeship. These three policy positions proved to be irreconcilable. The rapid, if unprogrammed, course of events made Korea the principal arena in which the Rooseveltian hope for world peace was converted into the Cold War.

Korea was the single area in the world in which the United States and the Soviet Union confronted one another directly without the meaningful intervention of any third power. No division of the country was planned, but it developed inexorably. At Yalta, Stalin urged adoption of the 38th parallel dividing line because this accorded with long-standing Russian policy. In military staff talks held there it was agreed that Russia should engage the Japanese in north Korea and American troops would operate in south Korea. After the military staffs agreed in Potsdam that a line should be drawn to separate their operations in the peninsula, confirmed in General MacArthur's General Order Number One, Secretary of State James Byrnes explained that "for purposes of military operations the occupation of Korea was divided north and south." Assistant Secretary of State John R. Hilldring added that "in no sense was this agreement more than a military expedient between two friendly powers. The line of demarcation was intended to be temporary and only . . . for carrying out the Japanese surrender." Hugh Borton, Chief of the Japanese Division in the U.S. Department of State, added his clarification: "It was made to assist us and our Allies, the Russians, in fighting the Japanese in Korea. But they surrendered before we got there and the military division stuck and became a political one." In the Moscow Conference in December 1945, the American delegates declared their belief that Korea consisted of "an economic and administrative whole"; but nevertheless the diplomats accepted the zonal division without demur. When General Hodge discovered that the Soviets would not accept a unified administration of the peninsula, he reported that "no aspect of military government can escape the effects of an arbitrary division of Korea into two zones of occupation."

The swift and complete domination of Eastern Europe by the Soviets persuaded the American Government to maintain south Korea as an obstacle to further Soviet advance. General Christ, heading MacArthur's G-5 division in Japan, defined the function of the AMG as being, "to form a bulwark against Communism." In that same conference, held on 12 October 1945, a spokesman explained that "it was not the intention to give the impression that the U.S. Military Government intends to compete with the Soviet Union." But the report on the meeting confirmed that a major duty of the AMG was "to see that the southern area is democratized." Paul Hoffman, Administrator of the Economic Aid Administration, later confirmed that the American aim was to develop south Korea as "a bastion of democracy." In part this meant that Communism, however much disliked, must not be suppressed. It, too, was to be insured of democratic freedom to operate and expand.

On 16 January 1946 General Hodge and Colonel General Ivan Chistiakov, who commanded the Soviet Military Occupation of north Korea, convened a meeting in Seoul to discuss means of cooperation between the two zones. After fifteen sessions these talks were discontinued without any concrete result. The Soviets were willing to agree only to a very limited exchange of goods between the two zones. This was a promise only slightly carried out, and in May of 1949 all exchanges of goods between the two zones ended completely. The Americans sought establishment of a Representative Democratic Council for all Korea, as a "newly organized Korean government," consisting of "a coalition group of all important parties," to serve as a liaison between the Korean people and the trusteeship administrators. A State Department memorandum, prepared on 20 March, declared the "primary American objective" was to prevent Soviet domination of all Korea; and the secondary objective was "to form a Korean government which could be granted complete independence within the next few years."

On 20 March, a second session of the U.S.-U.S.S.R. Joint Commission convened in Seoul and continued in stormy disagreement for six weeks. The Russians insisted that no Koreans could be consulted except those who pledged to support trusteeship; the Americans equally firmly insisted that "all Korean parties," regardless of ideology, would have to be represented. The Soviet spokesman flatly declared the aim of its delegation was establishment of a Korean government "friendly to the Soviet Union."

Syngman Rhee, in weekly radio speeches, warned that a government representing a coalition with Communists meant surrender of independence to Soviet control. In response, William Langdon reported to the State Department that General Hodge "does not necessarily feel that Rhee is essential or even desirable in a future provisional government, but so long as he is one of the few nationally known leaders among democratic elements, his cooperation can hardly be dispensed with." In June General Hodge privately adjudged that "Rhee is so much the greatest of Korean statesmen that he may be said to be the only one, but so long as he refuses to cooperate with Communists, he can have no part in a Korean government." The impasse between north and south Korea, and also between the south Korean left-wing and the south Korean conservative (i.e., anti-Communist) parties had become virtually irreconcilable.

On 22 July General Hodge sought to solve the problem of disunity by creating a Coalition Committee, in which Kimm Kyu-sic and An Chae-hong headed a group of rightists, and Lyuh Woon-heung and Ho Hon led a group of leftists. This group was charged to meet twice weekly to find means of uniting the pro- and anti-Communists in South Korea. Lyuh's chief rival for control of South Korean Communists, Pak Hon-yong, returned from a visit to Pyongyang to urge the Coalition Committee to support trusteeship, to unite with north Korean parties, to exclude all rightists, and to insist on transfer of power to the local "People's Committees." Kimm Kyu-sic and An Chae-hong rejected these demands and the Coalition Committee broke up. Ho Hon was found to be operating a currency counterfeiting printing press in the basement of the Communist Party in Seoul and fled to the north to escape arrest.

After the failure of the Joint Commission talks and the break-up of the Coalition Committee, the AMG sought for means of ameliorating south Koreans' resentments of the division of their country and of the continuing uncertainty of the future by two partial steps toward self-government. It first created a South Korean Directorate, headed by An Chae-hong, to conduct administrative functions under AMG supervision. Then, on 1 July 1946, General Archer L. Lerch, newly appointed Chief of Civil Administration, announced plans for establishing an Interim Assembly—which he carefully explained would not have any governmental authority but would be merely advisory. Forty-five members would be elected, and another forty-five would be appointed.

In November the elections were held in four successive stages: in villages, in towns, in counties, and in provinces, with the voting restricted to taxpayers and property owners. The voting was supervised by observers of the AMG. Thirty-one seats were won by so-called conservatives—members of Kim Song-su's Democratic Party, Kim Ku's Independence Party, and Syngman Rhee's Society for the Rapid Realization of Independence. Twelve more were rightist independents. Two leftists were elected in Cheju Island. Kimm Kyu-sic complained that the elections were not fairly conducted, and as a result the AMG invalidated the results in Seoul and in one province. When these elections were reheld under close supervision, the same candidates were again elected. The AMG then invalidated the election of three members, including Kim Song-su, who were stigmatized as collaborators with the Japanese.

Dr. Rhee rejected plans to elect him as chairman of the Assembly, saying "I do not wish to get into the Government, because I will be more help if I remain behind and support it. If I get into it, my hands are tied and it will be hard on me, and who else is there to do the talking. I can do much more as long as I remain a private citizen."[27]

The organization of the Interim Assembly resulted in a complete break between General Hodge and Dr. Rhee. In a bitter conference between them, Rhee objected to appointment of forty-five anti-Rhee members; and Hodge angrily replied that he had no intention of allowing Rhee to "seize" power. Then he appointed forty-five more members to the Assembly. Rhee thereupon stated that he would have to oppose the AMG openly and Hodge retorted that he would not be bullied or cowed by threats. He told Rhee that he would either have to cooperate with the AMG or be destroyed. On 2 December the Assembly convened and elected Kimm Kyu-sic as its Chairman. Another bitter confrontation occurred when Dr. Rhee asked General Hodge to arrange transportation so that he might go to Washington to protest the way the Assembly was chosen. Hodge said he was "hurt" by Rhee's plan to "go over his head," and pointed out that he was acting fully in accord with State Department policy. Anything Rhee wanted to say to authorities in Washington, Hodge added, could be said directly to him in Seoul.

Seoul newspapers on 23 November announced that Dr. Rhee was leaving for Washington. The Representative Democratic Council raised $10,000 for his expenses and, on an AMG military plane, he flew to Tokyo. General MacArthur granted him passage on a military plane and on 7 December Rhee arrived in Washington.

The atmosphere there was far more friendly to Rhee than it had been in his relations with General Hodge. Plans were already in process to shift control over the American zone in Korea from the Pentagon to the Department of State. Many officials, and much of the news media, agreed that Hodge's nullification of the election results was undemocratic, unwise, and unfair. Moreover, by this time, Cold War conditions had dismayed and angered the American public and government over Soviet global aims. A change of policy for dealing with the Soviet Union was overdue. General John R. Hilldring, the newly appointed Assistant Secretary of State for Occupied Countries (Germany and Korea), was well-disposed to deal with Rhee as a legitimate representative of the Korean people. America's policies for dealing with the problems, however, were still unformulated and Dr. Rhee got no assurances as to when or how Korean independence would be restored.

Accordingly, Rhee formulated a six-point program which he presented to the Department of State. These were its provisions:

1. An interim government should be elected for southern Korea, to serve until the two halves of Korea can be reunited and a general election held immediately thereafter;

2. Without disturbing general Russian-American consultations on Korea, this interim government should be admitted to the United Nations [in which the United States then held an "automatic majority"] and be allowed to negotiate directly with Russia and the United States concerning the occupation of Korea and other outstanding questions;
3. Korean claims for reparations from Japan should be given early consideration, to aid in the rehabilitation of the Korean economy;
4. Full commercial rights should be given to Korea, on a basis of equality with other nations, and with no favoritism accorded to any nation;
5. Korean currency should be stabilized and established on the international exchange;
6. United States security troops should remain in southern Korea until the two armies of occupation simultaneously withdraw.

While these discussions were proceeding, Dr. Rhee's wife Francesca wrote a letter, dated 11 December describing conditions in Korea:

> Since Dr. Rhee left, a cold north wind is sweeping the country and the people are suffering more than they tell. The Koreans are a proud race—they will not tell how cold they have it in their homes. Their clothing is so poor. There are no gloves on the market, only a few American-made gloves on the black market, selling for 500 Won [$5] a pair. For a ten-day supply of firewood we pay 8,000 Won and this does not include the cost of the steam heating system. Coal is nearly impossible to get, although the miners are not on strike. We are always lucky to get it, but the price is so high that I have the house heated in the morning, with no heat from noon on. I depend on a little electric stove when there is electric current. There has been no current for the last three evenings from 5:00 p.m. on. I eat my lonely dinners by candlelight—not because I want to be fashionable. Later there is nothing to do but to go to bed and look at my poor candles.

Mrs. Rhee's letter was a potent reminder of how much needed to be done—on the economic as well as the political front. Problems multiplied. On 30 December, Song Chin-u, who best represented the views of conservative Koreans, was assassinated. His assailant was unknown but was widely considered to be a follower of Kim Ku. The problems were monumental. For one, the 38th parallel division of the peninsula was ruinous to the economy. In the north, from Yalu River hydroelectric power plants there was more electricity produced than in all of France. In the north there were coal reserves sufficient to last all Korea for eight hundred years, including 1,340,000 tons of anthracite and 410 million tons of bituminous coal; but none of it was available to the south. North Korea had at least twenty million tons of high grade iron ore, along with several billion tons of low-grade but usable iron ore. These minerals more than served to sustain north Korean metal fabrication and fertilizer plants. In contrast, in south Korea by midsummer of 1947 industrial production amounted to only 20 percent of its prewar level. Moreover, the AMG lacked policies, plans, and resources for maintaining even such mining and manufacturing as would otherwise have been possible. So long as the United States continued to seek agreement with Russia on how to implement the trusteeship plan, its only long-range goal in Korea was to get out as soon and as completely as it could. Instead of progressive improvements, there was only stagnation.

On 2 March Kim Ku convened in Seoul a meeting of the Korean People's Representative Assembly with 1,500 delegates from all parts of Korea, north as well as south, and asked them to announce the establishment of the Provisional Republic of Korea—a move Dr. Rhee, from Washington, vigorously urged him not to take. As Robinson declares in his book *Betrayal of a Nation* (a study of the AMG), AMG officials suspected that Syngman Rhee was actually encouraging Kim Ku to take this action.[28] The contrary is true. I was with Rhee while he was warning Kim Ku by radiogram that such an action would be a fatal blow to Korean independence. The falsity of this charge is also indicated by what happened in Seoul, at the Assembly meeting, and after its conclusion. After several hours of sharp debate, the delegates refused to approve this proposal. Kim Ku resigned as chairman of the exiled Provisional Government and Dr. Rhee was elected to replace him. Rhee sent orders for the People's Assembly to revert peacefully to the role of a political party. This proceeding ended any further accord between Kim Ku and Rhee. Meanwhile, in the Interim Assembly, Kimm Kyu-sic, with the cooperation of Lyuh Woon-heung, bottled up a motion to establish a committee to write a constitution for an independent and sovereign government of Korea. Rhee sent from Washington a radiogram outlining his views, which read in part as follows: "Independence for South Korea will soon be an accomplished fact. . . . The essential elements for a new program have already been agreed upon in substance. This new program is intended to provide a solid basis for Korean-American cooperation during the interim period until the Russians can be induced to keep their promise to withdraw from north Korea and thus make possible the unification and complete independence of the whole country."

Dr. Rhee arrived back in Seoul on 21 April after General Hodge made an unsuccessful attempt to prevent his return. On 22 May the American-Soviet Joint Commission again convened in Seoul. General Hodge issued a statement telling the Korean people that the Moscow Agreement to establish a trusteeship was "immutable law" and must be obeyed. Rhee, for his opposition to this "law," was placed under virtual house arrest, which continued through the spring and summer. His telephone was removed, MPs guarded his home day and night, his mail was channelled through the AMG, and visitors who sought to see him were turned away. His weekly radio talks were suspended. The Joint Commission ended its discussions in deadlocked disagreement. General Lerch announced on 11 September that Koreans had made "remarkable progress in learning how to handle Korean affairs" and that all departments of the AMG would be turned over to administration by the Korean Directorate, with Americans functioning only as advisors.

General Hodge invited Philip Jaisohn, then eighty-five years old, to return to Korea to oppose Dr. Rhee's leadership. On 11 July Jaisohn was welcomed at Inchon by a large crowd led by Kimm Kyu-sic and Lyuh Woon-heung. In a news conference, Dr. Jaisohn declared that Koreans were not ready for self-government: "They do not even know how to make a cake of soap." The next day Lyuh was assassinated as he rode in the back seat of his automobile. General Lerch, back in Washington for consultations, urged Rhee to cease opposition to the AMG. On 21 July Rhee sent a radiogram to Lerch, reading: "We stand now as we always have for Korean-American cooperation in ending division of Korea and establishment of an elected government." General Wedemeyer returned to Washington after an assigned mission to China and Korea, recommending changes in American policy.

American policy was indeed changing. On 11 August Secretary of State George Marshall proposed to Molotov a meeting to find a replacement for the Moscow agreement on trusteeship. On 26 August this proposal was formalized as a call for a Four-Power Conference by the Soviet Union, the United States, Britain, and China, to set up plans for reunifying Korea and to hold supervised elections in all Korea to establish a Korean government. This proposal was rejected by the Soviet Union. On 17 September Secretary Marshall proposed that "The Problem of the Independence of Korea" should be placed on the agenda of the General Assembly of the United Nations.

Trusteeship for Korea no longer was "immutable law."

12

The Communization of North Korea

The circumstances in north and south Korea after Japan's surrender were strikingly different. The Russians arrived a month earlier than the Americans, and they came vastly better prepared. The Soviet troop commander, Colonel General Ivan Chistiakov, had been selected well in advance. There was no detailed Soviet plan for its occupation of the north; but General Chistiakov was authorized to deal with problems as they arose according to his own judgment. He, his staff, and his troops were experienced in dealing with Asians, and specifically with Koreans. They had some understanding of Korean culture and of the wants and needs of the people. Moreover, they brought with them from Siberia 35,000 Korean Communists, who had been recruited, indoctrinated, supplied, and trained by Soviet officials. Consequently, there was no significant language barrier between the incoming forces and the population. And there was a racial bridge across the ideological differences.

For Chistiakov's general guidance, there was an established and well-tested methodology for Communist takeover of foreign populations. It had both "good cop" and "bad cop" features. One aspect of it was a system of substantial rewards for those who submitted and cooperated. The other was utter ruthlessness toward protestors and dissidents. The Soviets were clear about the distinction between *good* Koreans who were to be rewarded and *bad* ones who were to be targeted for punishment. All those who accepted and supported the occupation goals and methods were "democratic" and "progressive." Critics and opponents of the occupation were "reactionaries," "pro-Japanese," and "anti-democratic." The Soviets also well understood that large segments of the population, including the peasants and urban workers, were in effect neutral, watching to see how they would be dealt with. For them the immediate need, as the Soviets saw it, was for indoctrination concerning the vast superiority of communism's classless, peace-loving, and proletarian principles over imperialistic, profit-greedy, exploitative capitalism. Another group, including such intellectuals as teachers, journalists, doctors, lawyers, and writers, was to be carefully watched; individuals were to be bribed, frightened, or coaxed to support the Communist program. For the rest—such as landlords, capitalistic owners of mines or factories, collaborators with the Japanese, and identifiable anti-Communists—there were approved methods of punishment, including execution, imprisonment, dismissal from jobs, and expropriation of their properties.

In the early months of the occupation, before rigid enforcement systems could be made operative, the Soviet occupation problems were eased by a swift exodus of malcontents. Many Koreans who had fled into Manchuria and China to escape from the Japanese rule rushed back into north Korea where, as non-Communists, they were not welcomed, and proceeded on southward across the 38th parallel. So did north Koreans who knew about, disliked, and feared communism. There are no dependable statistics on the numbers, but responsible estimates of the total from China, Manchuria, and north Korea are upwards of three million. These were Koreans who "voted their preference with their feet." Their choice had to be based on a great depth of feeling, for it meant leaving some relatives and friends behind, as well as loss of their property. Equally or more traumatic, it meant leaving ancestral graves and familiar scenes in which their ancestors had dwelt for many generations. It required them to endure severe hardships and to risk harsh punishment as they eluded guards and travelled at least partly by foot on backroads or through unsettled land, carrying small children, elderly parents, and such possessions as they could on their backs. From the Soviet point of view, this mass exodus—amounting to more than a fifth of the north Korean population as well as the returning emigres who went south—had dual advantages. For one thing, it quickly and easily relieved the occupation of having to deal with them as dissidents and malcontents. It also greatly increased the difficulties of the American Military Government, which had to find as best it could food, shelter, and jobs—not only for these propertyless refugees but also for an additional million more Koreans who rushed home from Japan, where they had served as impressed laborers or soldiers during the war.

Because of its general and specific preparation, the lack of a language barrier, and an incoming force of Korean Communists to help out, the Soviet occupation acted to create an operative government much faster and much more efficiently than the Americans were able to in the south. All through north Korea, as in the south, People's Committees were already in existence or were quickly created. In the north, unlike the south, they were promptly brought under the occupation's control. They provided reliable channels by which the Soviet authorities could keep in close touch with the people, both to inform themselves of public opinion and to inform the people of what they should or must do. Committee members, knowing their neighbors and their neighborhoods, could report on the behavior, even on the thoughts, of the people. The people were left in no doubt as to the choice they must make: to submit and be rewarded, or to dissent and be punished. Again in contrast with the southern zone, both the occupation authorities and the people knew clearly what to expect from one another.

In accordance with their established practice in dealing with "liberated" peoples, the Soviet authorities lost no time in setting up the appearance of north Korean authority. Neither, however, did they leave any doubt that theirs was the power and that they intended to exercise it. On 24 August 1945, for example, the Soviet commanding officer, upon entering the port city of Hamhung, issued the guiding announcement: "Until the political course for Korea is determined, the Soviet Army will administer through the existing Japanese government and military apparatus. . . . Those who harm or destroy public peace will be severely punished or given the death sentence." Another announcement read: "What we must do is establish a completely independent country embracing all strata of the population," with its contradictory conclusion: "Evil, pro-Japanese elements will be thoroughly swept out; a strict purge of all impure elements within and without camp is needed."

Discipline among the Russian troops was far less stringent than it was for the Korean population. The war, including the hard fighting against the German invasion, had drained Russian resources to the bottom. As a result, many of the incoming Soviet soldiers were shoeless and poorly dressed; for their food and other supplies they were expected to live off the country. They took what they needed or desired, without any payment for it. As in Eastern Europe, they were allowed to seize and to ship back to their homes such booty as they could find. The young and uncultured Russian peasants who composed the occupation army looted and raped with impunity. It was January 1946 before the Soviets brought their military police into the zone to restore order. Before that, for a period of some five months, the Russian soldiers were as poorly fed and dressed as were refugees from China and in the words of a Benedictine monk, they "gave themselves to rapine and pillage on an extensive scale." The closure of mines and factories after the departure of the Japanese, and the disabling of many of them as the Japanese left, resulted in immediate unemployment and in hardships for both the troops who had to live off the land and for the Koreans. Somewhat ameliorating the situation was the fact that the Russians expressed very little of the racial prejudice with which Americans denigrated the "Gooks" in the south.

As the Japanese were retreating, a highly respected Korean nationalist, Cho Man-sik, headed the Japanese-appointed Committee for the Preparation of Korean Independence in the province of Pyongyang. Cho was a Presbyterian educator who had pursued a course of moderate opposition to Japan, along with Kim Song-su and Song Chin-u in the south. Like Lyuh Woon-heung, he had cooperated with both leftist and rightist indepdendence advocates. Korean political prisoners, released from prison by the Japanese defeat, joined with Cho Man-sik. By the end of August this group was organized as the People's Political Committee, with Cho appointed by the

Russians as its chairman. The Soviet occupation authorities enlarged the committee by adding to it their own appointees.

Other Communist Korean leaders who were prominent, or quickly won prominence, included Pak Hon-yong, Secretary-General of the Korean Communist Party, and three who came back into north Korea with the advancing Soviet troops—Kim Tu-bong, Mu-Jong (Wu Ting), and Kim Il-sung. Kim Tu-bong, an intellectual who had served under Mao Tse-tung in Yenan, sought favor of the occupation by writing in support of trusteeship, which he described as an American idea to which the Soviet Union had agreed only as a means of hastening Korean independence. Kim Tu-bong organized the New People's Party, composed primarily of intellectuals; but it was soon integrated into Kim Il-sung's much larger North Korean Labor Party. Mu-Jong was an officer in the Chinese Eighth Route Army, in charge of artillery, and had been with Mao Tse-tung on the celebrated "Long March" in 1934–35. He was an eloquent speaker with strong personal charm. He travelled around north Korea making stirringly patriotic speeches that urged cooperation with the occupation as the surest and quickest route to independence. The Chinese Communist Party favored Mu-Jong for north Korean leadership, but it was the Soviet Union that had the power of choice.

Korean initiative was far from lacking. Along with the Communist Party, there also quickly emerged the Democratic Party, and the League of Independence (which was recast by Kim Tu-bong as the New People's Party). The urgency to win reforms led also to a proliferation of large social organizations that represented workers, peasants, intellectuals, and other special segments of the population. The most influential of these were the Federation of Labor, the Peasant's Union, the Women's Federation, the League of Democratic Youth, and the Chondogyo religio-political organization. Each of these was potentially powerful. But the Soviet occupation authorities moved swiftly to eliminate "reactionary" influence within them, after which they were amalgamated to make possible, as a Soviet spokesman declared, "a people's self-government based on a strong bloc of all the anti-japanese, democratic parties and organizations." What form this "self-government" would take, and which among the claimants for leadership would head it, was for the Russians to decide.

The choice by General Chistiakov settled upon Kim Il-sung. Outwardly, he did not apear to be a likely candidate for Soviet favor. He was unattractive personally, both in appearance and in personality. Born in a small village near Pyongyang on 15 April 1912, he was taken by his family to Manchuria after the collapse of the March 1919 movement. At that time his name was Kim Song-ju. In his maturity he fought with Korean guerrillas against the Japanese and took for himself the name of a legendary Korean independence warrior, Kim Il-sung. As written in Chinese characters, this name meant "Lone Star," meaning, as Kim intimated, that he would be "a bright morning star leading the Korean people out of the darkness into the dawn." Probably the crucial reasons for Kim's choice were that he had lived in Siberia since 1941, was a major in the Soviet army, was well versed in the Russian language, and had proved himself amenable to Soviet control.

On 14 October 1945, a huge rally was held in Pyongyang to welcome exiled Korean leaders who had come home with the Soviet "Army of Liberation." Cho Man-sik was the principal speaker, after which a Russian general introduced Kim Il-sung. When the huge audience heard the name of the venerated freedom fighter, they broke into tremendous applause. The Russians were impressed by what seemed to them proof of the thirty-three-year-old Kim's great popularity. As described by Cho Man-sik's secretary, Kim Il-sung made a short and rambling speech, in which "he particularly praised and offered the most extravagant words of gratitude and glory to the Soviet Union and Marshall Stalin, that close friend of the oppressed peoples of the world."

Four days later, *Haebong Ilbo,* the Communist newspaper newly established in Pyongyang, editorialized about the goals that should be pursued in a 1 March 1946 conference (actually delayed until April) that would accomplish the transition "in the shortest time possible" to a People's Government. Along with exposing "anti-democratic intrigues and deceptions," the editorial urged that "the conference must obtain unlimited freedom of speech, publication, and assembly, and it must stand on broad democratic principles. It must be based on equal suffrage and the right to be elected for those over eighteen years of age without regard to sex, occupation, or property." After this promising vista was portrayed, the editorial continued to state what really was planned: "On the other hand, we must severely search out political collaborators with Japanese imperialism and national traitors, deprive them of suffrage and the right to be elected, and prevent their infiltration into the conference."

In dealing with Cho Man-sik, General Chistiakov misread his man, just as General Hodge misjudged Syngman Rhee. Both were selected to serve as mere frontmen by the respective commands, and both instead insisted upon being independent leaders. The significant subsequent differences in their careers resulted from the contrast between Russia's ruthless domination of the north and America's much more permissive governance of the south. At the first administrative meeting of the People's Political Committee, General Chistiakov brusquely ordered Cho Man-sik to take guidance from the Communists for government of the provinces and counties. Cho angrily refused, whereupon Chistiakov changed the order to "cooperate with the Communist Party." In order to insure that Cho adhered to the party line, Chistiakov appointed Kim Il-sung to be vice-chairman of the Committee. Kim used this position not only to supervise Cho but also to undermine rivals, including Pak Hon-yong, Mu-Jong, and Kim Tu-bong. When the Northern Bureau of the Communist Party was organized, General Chistiakov named Kim Il-sung as its Secretary-General. After the 26 December nnouncement of trusteeship, Cho Man-sik denounced it and resigned from he People's Political Committee. He was placed under house arrest, and ater the Soviets offered to trade him for Communists who were arrested in he south. After this was refused, nothing further was heard of Cho.

In a 17 December 1945 speech, Kim Il-sung told his audience, largely nembers of the People's Committees, what to expect for the future, using s his text this quotation from Lenin: "The Communist Party will be able o perform its duty only if it is organized in the most centralized manner, if on discipline bordering on military discipline prevails in it, and its Party Centre is a powerful and authoritative organ." Two months later, in February, the Russians gave him the opportunity to put this political philosophy nto effect. The essence of his philosophy Kim summarized in two statenents. The first was the basic Leninist-Marxist doctrine: "Uniting the broad nasses is a decisive guarantee for the victory of the revolution." The second e made the central theme of his continuing program: "At present we are uilding our country in an extremely complicated situation. In south Korea ow, unlike in North Korea, pro-Japanese elements, traitors to the nation, nd other reactionary forces are gathered up under the wing of U.S. imperialsm, and they are running amuck to stand in the way of our people who have isen to build a new, democratic Korea." General Chistiakov named him Chairman of the North Korean Interim People's Committee—in effect, the dministrative government of the north.

In comparison with the military government in the south, the Soviet operation was more efficient and was accepted with less open protest. In some espects, it actually did better satisfy the desires and the hopes of the people. The well-to-do collaborators with the Japanese were not granted favorable ositions but were stigmatized and punished as "enemies of the people." In March 1946 the Soviets put into effect a major land reform program. It xpropriated, without compensation, some two million four hundred thouand acres of lands formerly held by Japanese, by collaborators with them, y large landholders, and by the Christian church and Buddhist temples. Use of this land was distributed at no cost to farmers who had to prove to he People's Committees that they were loyal to the regime. Members of the ocal committees, well knowing their neighbors, were able to distinguish ccurately those whose support could be depended upon from those who arbored open or hidden resentments and reservations. This land distribuon, or "reform," was a powerful means of controlling the population. The ollowing June, Kim Il-sung's interim government nationalized all large-scale ndustries, mines, transportation and communication facilities, and banks. Thereby he was able to insure full employment. He also reduced the workay to eight hours and proclaimed equality for men and women, both in the workplace and in voting.

For a few months, the Communist regime permitted private ownership of and and limited free enterprise, in the form of household handicraft and small plant shops. A principal motive for this deviation from strict Communism probably was to maintain a system which south Koreans could be induced to join. But this promised liberalism did not last for long. Between 1946 and 1949 public ownership of industry increased from 72.4 percent in 1946 to 90.7 percent in 1949, while private ownership of industry decreased from 29.6 percent in 1946 to 9.3 percent in 1949. Along with the premise of economic liberalism, the north Koreans were also enjoying a distinctly higher living standard than that of the impoverished south. The Soviets inherited from the Japanese an impressive industrial development, supported by hydroelectric power equal to that of all of France, from the Yalu River power plants and its extensive and developed coal mines. North Korea possessed ample coal, iron, and eighty-five percent of Korea's chemical production facilities, including the vital fertilizer plants. All of this, which had served all of Korea and much of Japan's needs, was available to the one third of Koreans (roughly ten million) who lived in the northern zone. Everything needful was available in abundance—except food, for the high mountain valleys of north Korea were suited for dry field, not paddy, rice production. But the Japanese had filled their warehouses with grain and other foods, and these the Russians appropriated for their troops and for shipment back home. What was left was distributed to the people. At least in 1946 the circumstances in north Korea looked comparatively rosy.

The slogan for the occupation was not "Build Socialism," but "Create a Democratic Revolutionary Base." The reality was quite different from the propaganda. From the start of the occupation, north Korea's economic activities were oriented toward the Soviet Union. Russian advisors and technicians brought the mines and factories back into operation. The Soviets replaced Japan as the principal trading partner. In contrast with the American aid program in the south, the north Koreans were required to pay for the services of the Soviet specialists. The whole product of north Korean gold mines, which amounted in 1950 to nine tons annually, went to Russia in payment for "services and supplies." In basic respects the Russian economic policies were like those of Japan. Instead of developing a balanced and rational economy, the emphasis was upon serving the needs of the Soviet Union.

Since the Soviets realized the importance of cultural reorientation, one of their major efforts during the occupation was to replace the Japanese cultural influence with their own Russian brand. At the same time, in accord with their practice in dealing with satellite countries, they also helped to restore, as well as to alter, the submerged Korean culture. They at once made Korean the national language. They outlawed use of Chinese ideograms in the news media in June 1949, and replaced them with the hangul alphabet. In offering satisfaction for the Korean hunger for education, they imported Russian books and journals on Soviet science, technology, language, litera ture, and the arts, as well as on Marxian politics, many of them translated quickly into Korean. Russian history and Communist ideology were also basic in the curriculum. At the time of Japan's defeat, north Korea had only 50 middle schools, and only 35 per cent of primary-age children were in school. Three years later, the Soviet authorities were claiming that adult illiteracy had been eliminated and that 5,000 middle schools, 69 technical schools, and 15 colleges were in operation. A Korean-Russian cultural agreement signed in 1949 provided that some 150 Korean students would be sent each year to schools in the U.S.S.R.—at Korean expense.

By 1948 the study of Russian was compulsory at the middle school level, beginning in the fifth grade. Reminiscent of the Japanization policies, all upper level officials were required to be fluent in Russian. The Russification program, however, was much better designed and was conducted with much more skill than Japan had exhibited. In accord with its practice in Europe and elsewhere, the Soviet Union sought to integrate nationalistic cultural pride and loyalty into a broad-based acceptance of communist universalism and adherence to the Soviet Union. In effect its message to the Korean people—in the south, so far as it could reach them, as well as in the north—was: Be Korean, but in the Russified communist way.

The Russian purpose was not to destroy Koreanism but to reshape it—not to remake north Korea into a part of Russia but rather into a satellite state that would insure for the Soviet Union a friendly bastion on its southwestern flank between two of its traditional enemies, Japan and China. To accomplish this as an enduring fact, the Soviets would have to convince the Koreans that the Communist ideology was indeed superior to that of the Western peoples and that the Communist sociopolitical system would indeed serve the genuine well-being of the Korean people.

In pursuit of these aims, the regime sought to accomplish three revolutions—ideological, technical, and cultural. All three demanded strict controls over education. The stated educational goal was to produce "builders of socialist society" and "a new breed of communists." To accomplish these goals, an extensive educational system was developed. At its bottom were pre-kindergarten and kindergarten schools, then four years of primary schools, another four of middle schools, topped by two-year technical and vocational schools "for the masses" and colleges and universities (of which Kim Il-Sung University was the apex) for "exceptional" students. This system was not only free for all, but all were required to attend. At all levels, some 60–70 percent of the time was spent studying Kim Il-sung's thought, the history of the Korean "revolution," and the processes of the socialization of north Korea. In the Kim Il-sung University, 65 percent of the 1,300 class hours (in the four-year course) were devoted to the study of the Great Leader's life, teachings, and achievements. Very few of the teachers (including university professors) were educated abroad. They had little knowledge of or interest in the histories of other countries. Historical facts were distorted to fit their educational goals. The students united each morning in singing patriotic songs, of which "The Song of a Paradise" is a fair sample:

> The proud voices of students ring across this country
> Of learning, where everyone is studying free.
> Everywhere there is a hospital neat, bright and clean,
> Everyone is healthy and evergreen.
> We are free from exploitation, even from any tax or levy,
> Free entirely from worries about food or clothing.
> Oh, how blessed we are all in the grateful embrace
> That treasures man more than anything else.
> Oh, ours is a socialist nation, best in the world,
> The Great Leader has built.

That leadership was less singular than many believe. As much or more than Stalin and Mao Tse-tung, Kim Il-sung so well cultivated the personality cult of The Great Leader that many outside observers, as well as the North Koreans, believe it is real. There was, however, in North Korea fundamental (however well controlled) opposition as well as adulation for Kim. Actually, there were three distinctly different Communist groups (not to be confused as political parties) in the northern zone. One of these consisted of domestic Koreans, another of Yenan-Koreans, and the third of Siberian-Koreans. The differences among them are real and important.

When the Korean Communist Party was organized in 1925, those to whom it chiefly appealed were the nationalists. The theme of global universalism was not dominant in the ideology of early Korean Communism. It was, however, relatively strong among the Yenan Communists (Korean and Chinese) and even stronger for the Siberian group. All three of the Communist groups entertained significant beliefs that created a widening gulf between them and the true nationalists. The nationalists aimed to preserve and strengthen the Korean culture and to regain Korean sovereignty; the Communists aimed to destroy the private property system and to align Koreans with the worldwide class struggle. Both the cultural-oriented nationalists and the ideological Communists found common cause in their aim to drive out the Japanese and to restore Korean sovereignty. But they differed greatly in their social beliefs and aims. When the Communists were placed in power in north Korea by the Soviet occupation, the nationalists led by Cho Man-sik were given short shrift by the Communists.

On 28 August 1947, by which time Kim Il-sung's predominance was well established and the three-group categories lost significance, he clarified the role of the NKCP as being largely ideological:

1. Our party must carry out propaganda and educational works in people's councils in order to achieve ideological and political unity among the members of the people's councils.

2. Our party must further strengthen social organizations, must educate masses through these organizations and rally them firmly around our party.

Undoubtedly, Communism has etched deep changes in the population of north Korea, subject as it has been for a full generation to intensive and extensive propaganda and the reshaping of its economy and social structure. The result has been a Sovietized cultural renaissance. Theatrical troupes were organized and theatres were built. Some forty newspapers and half a dozen journals were established. By the summer of 1946 six radio broadcasting stations were operating. The Korean language was used, but Communist ideals predominated. Strict censorship greatly restricted any inflow of information from outside and limited what could be disseminated. The basic theme in the schools and the media for the first several years was glorification of the Soviet way of life and of the Soviets' key role in the defeat of Japan and the consequent liberation and rehabilitation of the Korean people—along with the lament that half the peninsula and two-thirds of the people were still being "shamelessly exploited by the greed of capitalistic and imperialistic America." A concurrent theme has been that the south Korean regime, and specifically the "corrupt and dictatorial" Syngman Rhee, were puppets of the United States, manipulated to the detriment of the Korean people. Because of Soviet virtues and American vices, the "captive" population of south Korea "longed for liberation and reunion with their brethren in the north." This is what the northern people were told, again and again, and in all manner of ways.

Andrew Nahm, making an extensive visit in North Korea in 1977 reported in his book *North Korea,* found a "monolithic culture." Academicians and others with whom he talked derided the "outmoded Culture of the past," which had "corroded the minds of the people." He attended six operatic performances in Pyongyang's National Theater. All were on the same theme: the glorification of the "national struggle" under the leadership of Kim Il-sung. One of them, "The Fate of a Self-Defense Corps Member," which was named as the revolutionary opera of 1974, was purportedly written by Kim Il-sung himself. Another, "Sea of Blood," was credited to his son, Kim Chong-il. The actors performed "extremely well," and the costumes, stage lighting, and settings "were superb," Nahm attests. When the operas ended, "the suppressed emotions of the audience exploded in joy at the final stage when the victorious revolutionary heroes appeared on the stage waving the red flags, accompanied by the liberated villagers." Then the performers and the audience joined in singing a song with its chorus: "We wish Marshall Kim Il-sung a long life and good health."

This propaganda line has had real but only limited success. When refugees from the north were interviewed in the summers of 1949 and 1953, they were virtually unanimous in their responses. Yes, they said, they did believe what they were told about the puppetry of the leadership in the south, for they had no information to the contrary. But no, they did not believe the constantly reiterated claims of the superior virtues of Communist rule, for the evidence against it was all about them. What they experienced was sufficiently bad to induce them to flee into the south, even though they did not know what to expect when they got there.

A literary revival in north Korea adhered closely to the Sovietized propaganda line. Korean works were beginning to be translated into Russian and Russian literature and sociopolitical treatises into Korean. Literary associations were formed to promote the integrative study of Korean and Russian history, of the Russian language, and of the foundation works of Lenin, Stalin, and Marx. A new school of writers, of whom Li Gi En (Yi Ki-yong) and Han Sul Yan (Han Sul-ya) were most prominent, wrote novels extolling communism, the Soviet Union, and the "enriching influences" of Russia upon the Korean society, along with portraying the personalities of individual Koreans. By such means, they said, were the new Koreans rescued from the stagnant rottenness of ancient traditions and from the soul-destroying self-centeredness and greed of Western capitalism. This cultural renaissance was bolstered by exchanges of cultural missions between north Korea and Russia and by the grant of medals and other awards to intellectuals who truly represented the approved ideology.

Along with this cultural transformation, the chief emphasis was always on building military strength. The main outlines of the militarization of north Korea are clear, though many specific details are still unknown. The first Korean troops to cross the Yalu River were two units of the Korean Volunteer Army, that had operated in Manchuria and China, one under the command of Kim Il-sung, the other led by Mu-Jong, Kim Tu-bong, and others. Another 2,000 or 2,500 Korean guerilla fighters commanded by two young Korean officers, Kim Kang and Kim Ho, were stopped at the Yalu River border town of Antung by Russian security forces. Those who were willing to surrender their arms were then admitted into north Korea; the others were turned back into Manchuria. Both the Russians and Kim Il-sung were reluctant to allow the Yenan-affiliated Korean soldiers into Korea, from fear that they might not be completely amenable to the Sovietized regime. Those Koreans who returned to rejoin the Chinese Eighth Route Army became the nucleus of a force that grew into the tens of thousands of well-trained, battle-experienced Korean troops that in late 1949 became the key shock troops of the North Korean Democratic People's Republic, as it prepared for the invasion of the south.

In December 1945 the Pyongyang Military Institute opened to commence the training of officers for the armed forces. Even earlier, in October, a military academy began to train low-rank officers. More officer-training centers went into operation in July and August 1946. Formation of the Korean People's Army took place in September 1946, based on graduates of these training centers and on Korean troops returning from China. The KPA commenced training manuevers in Manchuria. Meanwhile, Kim Il-sung was clarifying his own purposes.

In June 1946, announcing the formation of the North Korean Democratic National People's United Front, Kim declared that "we must fight with our utmost to maintain the Party's purity, unity, and iron discipline. If we were to fight against the enemy without meeting these conditions within our ranks, it would be nothing less than folly." The propaganda ministry began issuance of pamphlets designed to create an image of Kim Il-sung as the source of all wisdom, as well as of all power. Two typical passages illustrate their nature:

> The Great Leader Comrade Kim Kil-sung is the Legendary Hero who Led the Anti-Japanese Armed Struggle to Victory.

> When General Kim Il-sung came here, a new bright star appeared in the Galaxy at midnight. . . . With his magical power and skills, General Kim Il-sung attacks the enemy on both sides of the mountains and in the west and in the east simultaneously, and wipes them out.

It was under these conditions, and with these attitudes prevailing in north Korea, that the United Nations, in the fall of 1947, undertook to find a solution of its own for its General Assembly agenda item: "The Problem of Korea."

13

The United Nations Achieves a Partial Solution

The United Nations, like its ill-fated predecessor the League of Nations, aimed to make "international law" something more than an empty phrase. The forty-five nations that composed its first membership agreed to pursue their own national interests within a constrained new context. They agreed that no nation henceforth should or could be allowed to ignore the commonality of global needs and problems. They recognized that war anywhere threatens peace everywhere, that economic effects are not confined by national boundaries, and that there is a standard of human decency to which all peoples are entitled. What the United Nations lacked was not proper goals but power to achieve them.

The Korean problem confronted the member nations with the first real test of whether such professions were, somehow, by some means, and to some degree, enforceable. The prospects were dubious because by that time the United States and the Soviet Union were engaged in their bitterly divisive Cold War. The test came when, on 17 September 1947, the United States requested that the problem of what to do about Korea be placed on the agenda of the General Assembly of the United Nations. In response to Russian objection, Secretary of State George Marshall declared that "further attempts to solve the Korean problem by means of bilateral negotiations will only serve to delay the establishment of an independent, united Korea." It was a momentous move for the United States to make for three significant reasons. For one, it showed the seriousness of the American determination to rectify what Sumner Welles had called "one of the most serious crimes of the twentieth century." Second, it marked the abandonment by the United States of the plan for trusteeship over Korea. And third, it was a dramatic and concrete confrontation of the two major powers in the developing Cold War.

Acceptance of the proposal by the United Nations was no less momentous, for this was the first initiative taken by that organization to settle a divisive issue between its two most powerful members. Korea was not asked for its opinion. It could not be, for there was no government empowered to speak for the Korean people.

These factors predetermined the course that eventuated in the creation of two separate and hostile states in the bifurcated Korean nation. The whole process was conducted amid controversies of the most serious nature that were both unavoidable and insoluble. Historians argue, and will continue to do so, in their evaluation of the proceedings. All agree that the outcome was unsatisfactory. But could it have been better? Did the Koreans themselves impede the establishment of a free and united nation? Did Syngman Rhee, Kim Ku, and Kimm Kyu-sic pursue helpful or hurtful policies? Did Kim Il-sung? Basic facts may readily be traced. But strident arguments continue as to what facts were of greatest relevance or of most decisive significance.

The central question at issue is what, or who, was primarily responsible for the kind of solution that led to the 10 May 1948 election that established the Republic of Korea. Was it the intransigence of the Soviet Union that prevented an all-Korea election and left the south Koreans only the one choice—that half a loaf was better than none? Was it the United Nations, which accepted a responsibility it could not carry out? Was it the United States, which abrogated the Moscow Decision of 26 December 1945? In order to answer such questions, it is necessary to pursue apparently trivial events (such as who invited whom to dinner). The relevance of the details will be apparent as they are seen in relationship with one another. The inquiry must be broad-based.

In attempting to untangle these deeply and bitterly implanted controversies, it is helpful to recall the counsel of the justly-admired diplomat George F. Kennan, included in his book *American Diplomacy, 1900–1950*.[29] Actions and decisions are not to be judged individually by themselves, he warned, for inevitably they are parts of a large fabric consisting of prior events and of worldwide factors. In his words, "every mistake is in a sense the product of all the mistakes that have gone before it, from which fact it derives a sort of cosmic forgiveness; and at the same time, every mistake is in a sense the determinant of all the mistakes of the future, from which it derives a sort of cosmic unforgiveableness." The question of who or what was responsible for the continuation of the division of Korea involves the history of modern Korea, and also of imperialism in Asia. Post–Pearl Harbor events are particularly relevant. The factors were both complex and numerous.

In 1942 the United States might have joined with China to divert Soviet ambitions to control Korea by recognizing the Korean Republic-in-Exile. It did not do so largely because (by midsummer) Russia was bearing the brunt of the German attack and had to be treated gently. During the succeeding years, international political planning for postwar Korea was preempted by the urgency of military considerations. Moreover, since the United States was determined to deny Russia any role in the postwar military occupation of Japan, its policymakers deemed it unwise to be similarly intractable concerning Korea. The absence of any recognized Korean government made it easy to avoid consideration of Korean claims and interests. Generally speaking, major nations are well accustomed to avoid complicating their own policies by considerations of the wishes and feelings of small and weak countries. These were among the factors that influenced the treatment of Korea.

When the United Nations undertook to solve the Russo-American impasse over Korea, it was constrained by its own character and limitations. It was organized as an aggregation of sovereign nations that would act in unity only insofar as they consented to do so. As long as national sovereignty continued to be the rule, this was as far as its organizers could go. Despite the very wide differences among its members in terms of size, population, economic strength, and military power, every member of the General Assembly was unrealistically but necessarily accorded an equal vote. In the Security Council, five major nations—the United States, the Soviet Union, Great Britain, France, and China—were granted the power of veto, with which to block any action of which even one of them might disapprove. Except for this veto, during the first decade or so of the United Nations, the United States enjoyed a virtual "automatic majority." In part this was because what it wanted the U.N. to do accorded generally with what the great majority agreed should be done. Other reasons were the preponderance of power held by the U.S. through its burgeoning economy and its monopoly of the atomic bomb; the American generosity toward needy nations, exemplified by the Marshall Act; the record of commitment by the United States to the purposes and principles of the U.N. Charter; the preponderant financial support to the U.N. organization given by the United States; and the location of the U.N. headquarters in New York, thereby subjecting its operations to the penetrating inquiries of the mass media and the globally significant influence of American public opinion. The left-wing interpretation, as Jon Halliday stated it in Frank Baldwin's *Without Parallel,* was that the American-led coalition in the General Assembly "was a veritable gang of reactionaries and lackeys, including the United Kingdom, France, South Africa, Greece, and Turkey." Whatever the reasons, when the United States requested that the U.N. take on the Korean problem, acceptance of the request was inevitable; and in large degree, the problem was dealt with thereafter much as the United States believed it had to be.

From the point of view of the Koreans, the chief merit of the role of the United Nations was that it moved the question of Korean independence off its dead center immobility onto a course leading to action. Andrei Gromyko, heading the Soviet delegation, objected to U.N. consideration of the question as being an "illegal" repudiation of the Moscow Decision. Nevertheless, he announced that the Soviet Union would participate to the extent of submitting its own proposals. The Soviets proposed that all foreign troops be withdrawn from Korea by the beginning of 1948. The American delegation countered that "all occupying forces" should be withdrawn "at the earliest possible date" *after* the national independence of Korea was re-established.

With these proposals in hand, the First (Political) Committee of the U.N. commenced its consideration on 28 October. To effect a prompt solution, the U.S. asked that elections should be held under the sponsorship of the occupation forces, with observation by a United Nations Commission, not later than 31 March 1948. It asked further that the U.N. Commission have the power to travel and observe throughout Korea; that it offer its good offices in the establishment of a National Government and a National Assembly, and that representation in the National Assembly would be proportionate to the population, which meant assuring to south Korea two-thirds of the Assembly membership. The Soviet delegation proposed that U.N. consideration be suspended until "elected representatives" of north and south Korea could participate. This partially appealing idea was opposed by the United States (and rejected by the Assembly) on the grounds that it would unduly delay establishment of a Korean Government and, further, that the question of what kinds of Koreans were eligible to be consulted was precisely the disagreement that blocked any decision in the U.S.-U.S.S.R. Joint Commission, thereby rendering its continuance futile and making referral to the U.N. necessary. To have inserted this same insoluble disagreement into the U.N. process would have insured interminable delay and a final impasse. After the committee voted 35 to 6 to proceed to hold elections in Korea, Andrei Gromyko announced that "the U.S.S.R. would not be able to take part in the work of the commission." Despite this warning that no contemplated action could apply to north Korea, the General Assembly, on 14 November, voted to establish a Temporary Commission on Korea (UNTCOK) to oversee elections and to establish a national Government in Korea.

The reactions of Koreans were a mingling of rejoicing that the long delay in re-establishment of their independence was ending and of concern that the transitional stage was shrouded in uncertainties and ambiguities. To what extent and by what means were Koreans to be consulted concerning unsettled questions of the utmost importance? If the Soviet Union refused to permit elections in the north, would they nevertheless take place in the south, or would the whole plan be jettisoned? This central question was neither settled in the U.N. resolution nor even mentioned in the preceding debate. Who would decide it? What powers the UNTCOK would have were not indicated. In expectation that an impasse was inevitable, the General Assembly created an Interim Committee, promptly termed the Little Assembly, to remain in session to receive reports from UNTCOK and to authorize such specific measures as might prove to be needed. The 14 November resolution did, in fact, affirm that such problems were "primarily a matter for the Korean people itself," and accordingly resolved that "elected representatives of the Korean people be invited to take part in the consideration of the question." It failed to specify how. In the North there was already established a "People's Committee," headed by Kim Il-sung, that presumably spoke for the whole population of the northern zone and claimed to represent the entire peninsula. The policy position of the northern regime was formulated in a speech by Kim Il-sung after the breakup of the May 1946 Joint U.S.-U.S.S.R. Commission, in which he said that "North Korea, which is advancing toward true democracy, and South Korea, which is being dragged back toward a reactionary, antidemocratic and anti-national course under the despotism of reactionary elements, [were] moving in opposite directions." There was no such apparatus through which UNTCOK could listen to the voice of the people in the south. Should a temporary southern regime be elected to speak with the U.N.? If not, how could the Koreans take part in the consideration of the question? How could their real views be clarified?

The membership of UNTCOK consisted of representatives of Australia, Canada, China, El Salvador, France, India, the Philippines, and Syria (after membership was refused by the Ukranian Republic). The three leading Koreans in the south, Syngman Rhee, Kim Ku, and Kimm Kyu-sik, were all deeply disturbed by the failure of the U.N. to invite into its deliberations any spokesmen for the Korean people. When it was explained to them (unofficially) that this could not be done because south Korea had no designated spokesmen, Kim Ku and Kimm Kyu-sic reacted by suggesting that Kim Il-sung invite representative south Koreans to Pyongyang to formulate an all-Korea proposal. Syngman Rhee, pointing out that north Korea did have a quasi-government, urged that an immediate election should be held in the south, to insure for it an equal voice. This, he urged, was required by the 14 November resolution specifying that "elected representatives of the Korean people be invited." On the grounds that such an election would result in more delay and would solidify the north-south division, this provision of the U.N. resolution was being ignored.

In early January members of UNTCOK straggled into Seoul, organized under the chairmanship of Kenara P. S. Menon of India, where on 12 January they were greeted by an assemblage of some 75,000 in Seoul Stadium. The AMG-appointed Police Chief, Chough Pyung-Ok, serving as chairman, opened the meeting with an abrupt warning to the UNTCOK that "Korea is on the verge of a breakdown, political, social, and economic, because the flower of liberty has not yet borne fruit." Chairman Menon, in response, said that north Korea, too, had patriotic leaders and concluded his brief speech by saying, "Independence is not enough. There must be unity." Kim Ku and Dr. Rhee thereupon walked off the platform and left, because, as they said, "the weather was too cold."

The weather was miserably cold and housing arrangements for the UNTCOK members were very inadequate. The AMG Colonels who were billetted in the Choson Hotel declined to be moved out and UNTCOK was quartered in two very shabby and poorly heated hotels with broken and dirty floor mats, army cots in the small rooms, and only common toilet facilities down the hall. The circumstances were not conducive to deliberation. The French delegate showed his opinion by leaving Seoul for a hunting jaunt out in the country. Dr. Rhee wrote to Oliver that "the Commission members go around and any English speaking Korean is trying to get hold of them. They are already so confused that people get discouraged." The Canadian delegate secluded himself for two weeks, presumably awaiting instructions from his government. Dr. and Mrs. Rhee gave dinner parties on 22 and 27 January for different members of UNTCOK because "they do not wish to be invited together with the others." General Hodge appointed followers of Kimm Kyu-sic to be translators and advisors for the UNTCOK members, thereby lending further support to a 3 February report in the *Christian Science Monitor,* written by the very able and well-informed reporter Gordon Walker, that Kimm Kyu-sic had been "slated by the American Military Government" to be the president of the new government.

The mandate to hold elections not later than 31 March was manifestly impossible to fulfill. On 9 February Menon and Assistant Secretary-General Wellington Koo of China were requested by the U.N. to return to New York to receive instructions concerning whether to hold a separate general election in south Korea or a series of local elections to choose Koreans with whom UNTCOK might consult. It the Interim Assembly debate Philip Jessup, speaking for the United States, said that with two-thirds of Koreans in the south, an election there would result in a truly national government, which the north could be invited to join. Lester Pearson of Canada argued that such an election would be both illegal and unwise, since it would formalize the division of Korea. Mr. Evatt of Australia warned that an election would establish two rival governmnents in Korea and that if war should break out between them, "the United Nations might be placed in the difficult position of having either actively to support or else to renounce all responsibility for the government it had established."

On 26 February, by a vote of 31 to 2 with eleven abstentions, the Interim Assembly authorized the holding of elections "in such parts of Korea as are accessible to the Commission." Australia and Canada cast the two negative votes. The Communist bloc abstained. By this vote the United Nations dealt with the division of Korea in the best way it could—that is, by recognizing that it already was divided and that the division could be ended only with Soviet consent.

While these discussions were continuing in New York, in Seoul political maneuvering was active.[30] Kim Ku and Kimm Kyu-sic met for a long and secret discussion. According to what Korean news reporters could learn, they agreed to tell UNTCOK that free elections in the south were impossible, that all political prisoners held by the AMG should be released, and that

Kim Ku, at the risk of his life, should be allowed to go to north Korea to discuss the situation with Kim Il-sung. UNTCOK wrote to the Soviet commander to request permission to pay a courtesy visit; but he refused to accept the letter. Mr. Liu, the Chinese Counsul General in Seoul, suggested to Dr. Rhee that he invite Kim Ku and Kimm Kyu-sic for lunch, to end talk that the three were in conflict with one another. Kimm responded that instead of meeting at Dr. Rhee's house, the three go to the Chinese Consulate. They met there socially with their wives on Chinese New Year's Day, along with the Liu family. That afternoon, the three met again by themselves to explore a policy on which they could agree. The next day, 12 February, Rhee described the result:

> They said that since the Soviet has turned down the election proposition, we all agree to the general election in the South. But before we do that we must try to discuss the problems with the leaders in the North, and that is where opinions differ. I said the joint conference idea has been brought up more than once and the Korean people are opposed to it because that will delay the general election. However, if the joint conference should not delay the election, I will have no objection to it. We all said, then, that we had reached a general agreement—that Kimm Kyu-sic and Kim Ku agreed to a general election in the South and that Rhee agreed to a joint conference between leaders of North and South. . . . Dr. Kimm said that Dr. Rhee should not openly advocate the joint conference, because if he does the Communists in the North might not be willing to join with us. To this we all agreed.

The same afternoon, General Hodge called in Dr. Rhee, Kim Ku, and Kimm Kyu-sic, urging that they must end all disagreements in order not to discourage the U.N. from holding an election. Dr. Rhee reported on the agreement the three had just reached. Both Kim Ku and Kimm Kyu-sic responded that they did not oppose a general election in the south but wanted to talk over the matter with the northern leader before hand. Kimm Kyu-sic said that there were worrisome problems still unsolved. "If we support the general election in the south without exhausting every means to see whether we can get the North and South united, we will be called in history traitors who perpetuated the division of the country." Then he added that he had two more objections: "First, will this government be recognized by the U.N.? Second, how much aid will we get from the United States to help us along? Without knowing these things, we cannot plunge into it." To this Dr. Rhee replied, "Kyu-sic, if we Koreans do not know what we can do for ourselves, how can we ask foreign nations how much they can do for us?" The conference broke up, with Kim Ku stating that, "The Soviet plan for a meeting in the North is only a draft and we do not yet know what it means."[31]

On 20 February, Kim Ku gave a dinner for Korean news reporters and told them that he was opposed to a separate election in the south. Two days later Kimm Kyu-sic issued a similar statement. The Representative Peoples

Assembly adopted a resolution approving the election, with forty-three favorable and ten unfavorable votes.[32] On 28 February, responding to the approval by the U.N. Little Assembly, the UNTCOK members still in Seoul agreed to hold the election on 9 May (changed later to 10 May).

Kimm Kyu-sic wrote to Kim Il-sung suggesting that United Nations intervention in Korea might be bypassed by the holding of an all-Korea conference in Pyongyang. Kim Il-sung responded that he would host such a conference, provided that "reactionary politicians" be excluded. Thereupon, he issued invitations to some forty south Koreans, pointedly excluding Syngman Rhee. When Kim Ku, Kimm Kyu-sic, and the others arrived in Pyongyang, they found that the agenda for the conference and the resolutions to be approved had already been prepared. The meeting was held from 19 April to the 25th, with unanimous adoption of resolutions renouncing U.N. intervention and opposing any separate south Korean elections. After the return to Seoul of the southern delegation, Kimm Kyu-sic announced that he had lost faith in the possibility of agreement with the Communists and that he was resigning from public life. Kim Ku declared that he intended to continue to seek an all-Korea coalition.

The continuing political turmoil encouraged reports that the Indian, Syrian, Canadian, and Australian delegates on UNTCOK were all either dubious or opposed to the 10 May election. Questions multiplied as to how the election should be conducted. Should the refugees from north Korea, most of them with no settled residence, be allowed to vote? Their leaders formed a North Korean political party and demanded separate elections through which they could elect forty-five of the one hundred Assembly Members whose seats would be reserved for the northern population.

The situation was further complicated by the State Department deciding that all the land formerly owned by Japanese and being held in trust by the AMG would be sold, prior to the election, to its tenant operators. Rhee objected that this plan would forestall his own land reform plans. As he said, "a considerable portion of this land was confiscated from its Korean owners; and we have all the records and papers to prove these things. Therefore, we can prove that this is not *enemy* property, this is property legally belonging to the Korean people, and the AMG has no right to dispose of it without an authorization by the Korean Assembly."

A report spread that Kim Ku planned to have Dr. Rhee, Chough Pyung-Ok, and Chang Taik-Sang, the Seoul police chief, assassinated. Kim Ku and Kimm Kyu-sic joined with leftist groups in promising to boycott the election on the ground that it was divisive. All these charges and disagreements were given emphasis in global news discussion of the Korean situation. American congressmen indicated reluctance to vote aid funds for the projected new government.

Meanwhile voter registration throughout south Korea was so heavy as to make absurd the claims that substantial numbers were boycotting the election. Political campaigning was roiled by rumors, charges, and counter-charges. An American, Abell Sturgess, who had served with the AMG, was circulating in America a lengthy statement containing "evidence" that Koreans were incapable of self-government. Kimm Kyu-sic declared that "independence" would be curbed by appointment of an American High Commissioner, who would rule south Korea much as the United States had for a generation ruled the Philippines. By this time, voter registration had topped eight and a half million, over eighty-six percent of all who were eligible.

Campaigning was not only vigorous but sometimes vicious. All shades of political opinion were represented. Communists published many small newspapers, and also owned a large proportion of motion picture theaters, through which they denied the validity of the election. They also erected billboards bearing threats against any "traitors" who tried to vote in "the imperial election planned by the United States through its puppet the United Nations." General Hodge responded to UNTCOK's request that he free all "political prisoners" by declaring that there were none. Nevertheless, he had 669 law-violators turned free "to restore full political liberty." In February a Communist-organized railway strike erupted in violence which the AMG subdued only after bitter fighting around Taeju, in which forty eight were killed and fifteen hundred were arrested. On Cheju Island, Communist guerrillas, from their shelters in the high central mountains, terrorized the villagers.

Amid all the turmoil, with charges and counter-charges confusing the public, the south Koreans who had attended the Pyongyang conference were expressing contrary opinions as to what should be done. UNTCOK sought to restore clarity by announcing on 28 April that its field teams had reported from various key districts that there existed a free atmosphere, in which the democratic rights of free speech, press, and assembly were all observed and that consequently, there was no reason not to hold the election.

On 10 May the first free election to establish an independent government ever held in the long history of Korea brought 92.5 percent of all registered voters to the polls. United Nations teams observed the conduct of the election as best they could. Polling places were guarded by AMG soldiers and police. AMG off-duty personnel were curious unofficial additional observers. The election was assuredly among the freest held anywhere—keeping in mind that the United States, by contrast, was still excluding *latinos* and blacks from the electoral process, and that only in American-governed Japan and in parts of Western Europe were there serious efforts to conduct elections fairly. UNTCOK, after studying all available information reported on 25 June that there had been "a reasonable degree of free atmosphere," including "the democratic rights of freedom of speech, press, and assembly" and that the election was "a valid expression of the free will of the electorate in those parts of Korea which were accessible to the Commission and in which the inhabitants constituted approximately two-thirds of the people of all Korea."

From among two thousand candidates for the Assembly, the two hundred members were elected. To their 27 May organizational session, General Hodge maladroitly sent a message suggesting that instead of electing a chairman they accord that position to their oldest member, a man named Sur, aged seventy-eight. An uproar of dissent arose, partly in disagreement with the suggestion and partly to renounce American interference in the formation of the new government. Dr. Rhee then quieted the disturbance by escorting General Hodge into the hall and introducing him by saying: "If there is any one person who deserves more credit than any other single individual, it is General Hodge." Then, turning to the entourage accompanying Hodge, Rhee went on: "We are happy to see so many Americans here. You have been with us in most difficult times. You were perhaps misunderstood and unjustly criticized, but all these unpleasant experiences will soon be forgotten forever. One great fact will remain and stand out in history: you have come here to help us to restore our independence and you have accomplished it. Our people will remember this for generations to come with a high sense of profound gratitude and appreciation."

The elected Assemblymen were broadly representative. Eighty-five had run as independents, forty-eight as followers of Rhee, thirty as members of the Democratic Party (led by Kim Sung-su), with the remaining thirty-seven belonging to various splinter groups. On 31 May, by a vote of 189 to 8, they elected Syngman Rhee as Chairman of the Assembly. During the next six weeks, the Assembly drafted, debated, and adopted a constitution.[33] In the Assembly, one hundred of the three hundred seats were reserved for an election to be held in the north. The Republic of Korea was declared to be the government of the whole peninsula. After adoption of the constitution, on 19 July, the Assembly elected Syngman Rhee president of the Republic by a vote of 180, with sixteen members voting for Kim Ku. On 3 August President Rhee's nominee for prime minister, Lee Bum Suk, was confirmed by a vote of 110 to 84. It was evident that President Rhee would have a sound working majority in the Assembly and that there was a strong minority to serve a "watchdog" function.

On 15 August President Rhee was inaugurated in ceremonies attended by General Douglas MacArthur (the first time he set foot in Korea), who placed his arm around Rhee's shoulders and remarked into the open microphone, "If Korea should ever be attacked by the Communists, I will defend it as I would California." The day was heavily overcast, with rain predicted, but as Rhee stepped forward to deliver his inaugural address, the clouds parted and strong beams of sunlight illuminated his white hair and crinkled face. Many hoped this would be prophetic of good times ahead.

Taking up his presidential responsibilities at the age of seventy-three, Rhee called for "the active support of every citizen, whatever his former beliefs may have been." Then he plunged into his text:

> As we receive, in the name of the whole people of Korea, our sovereign government once more into our own hands, our national independence—there are certain strong foundations upon which we must build anew the structure of our life: (1) we should place full trust and faith in democracy; (2) we must protect civil rights and fundamental freedom; (3) generosity and cooperation should be the keystones of our new government; (4) liberalism must be understood, respected and protected; (5) we must strive to unite our divided nation; (6) our foreign policy is devoted to world peace—our relations with the United States of America are especially cordial. We are proud of the close ties maintained with our neighboring government of China for milleniums. . .
>
> We await with hope and determination the missing third of our representatives from the north. The 38th parallel division is no part of our choice and is wholly foreign to our destiny. Nothing must be neglected to keep wide open the door to reunion of the whole nation. The Everwhite Mountains are as surely our boundary to the north as are the Straits of Korea to the south. No temporary international situation can obscure what has been established through the centuries as a historic fact.

How this ultimate re-unification and the solution of other pressing problems were to be brought about, he indicated in his conclusion:

> We realize that without the goodwill and assistance of free nations, the many problems before us might be insuperable. But we know that we have their goodwill and feel we can count on their assistance. Above all, we need and we count upon the loyalty, the devotion to duty, and the determination of all Korean citizens. With hopeful hearts and minds alert we take into our own hands today a sovereign republican government that will long endure.

In North Korea, a sharply contrasting process was unfolding. There was no United Nations observation, no international press reporters, nor any other means for discovering the will of the people. On 1 May, the existing Korean People's Committee published its own constitution for what it called The Democratic People's Republic of Korea. In early June it set 25 August as the date for convening the Supreme People's Assembly. It was to consist of 572 members, who were to represent all Korea. There was no political campaigning. There was no freedom of speech, or of press, or of assembly. There was no alternative slate of candidates.

Kim Il-sung conducted an elaborate program, in which the South Korean Peoples Committees were utilized to conduct an extensive campaign to gather signatures on petitions of support for candidates who would presumably represent a "united Korea." As John Merrill reports in his *Korea: The Peninsular Origins of the War,* U.S. intelligence agents estimated that names representing as many as a quarter of the adult population were on these petitions. Only five per cent of the real petition signers, however, "knowingly" were supporting the North Korean government. General Hodge concluded that "vote manufacturers" swelled the total of signatures by forging the names of rightist politicians, fishermen who were out at sea, people who had died, more who never lived, and, in Merrill's words, "common last names followed by the Chinese characters for spring, summer, autumn, and fall, or near, far, and distant." From the names on these fabricated petitions, so-called South Korean representatives were selected by a Communist convention, held in Haeju, just to the north of the 38th parallel, on 22–24 August. On 3 September, without debate, the new Supreme People's Assembly ratified the new constitution. Four days later it inaugurated Kim Il-sung as president of what they proclaimed to be an all-Korea government.

In a series of speches, Kim Il-sung explained to the people what these actions meant. Speaking on 13 November, to the Democratic Youth League, he said:

> If we, who are in the most stern period of the history of our nation, fail to work out the destinies of the country and nation in the right way, we shall bring about great misfortunes not only for our own generation, but also for our posterity and commit a crime indelible for all time. If we carve out the destinies of the country and nation correctly, at this solemn juncture, we shall provide happiness to all generations to come and our exploits will shine forever in the history of the country.

Then he explained what had been accomplished and what it meant:

> According to the general will of the people in north and south Korea, the Supreme People's Assembly of Korea has been elected as our highest organ of state power, the Democratic People's Republic of Korea proclaimed, and the central government of the Republic set up. The Soviet Government, which always respects the rights of the peoples of other countries, has decided, at the request of the Supreme People's Assembly of Korea, to withdraw its troops from our country by the end of this year. . . .
>
> The U.S. imperialists say in their propaganda that they are "worried" about a "civil war" and "disorder," as if they were concerned for the Koreans. But the fact that the absolute majority of the north and south Korean people [sic] took part in the general elections of August 25 and established their central government, has positively proved that there will be no disorder or confusion even when the foreign troops withdraw from our land.

On 21 September the United Nations convened in Paris, and the General Assembly had to decide what to do about the two rival Korean governments. The Republic of Korea was invited to participate in the General Assembly discussion on Korea and, for this purpose, sent a delegation headed by a mild-mannered principal of a Catholic high school, John Myun Chang. The UNTCOK submitted its report, declaring that the Republic of Korea was "a lawful government," that it represented "the great majority of the people of Korea," that it was "based on elections which were a valid expression of the free will of the electorate," and that it was "the only such government in

Korea." Mr. Menon questioned whether adoption of such a resolution would not imply U.N. designation of the Republic of Korea as, in fact, the government of all Korea. John Foster Dulles, speaking for the United States, responded that the resolution "had been carefully worded" so as "not to deny that another regime existed in certain parts of Korea." Chang Myun, in his turn, declared that it was the view of the Republic of Korea Government that it did, in fact, represent all Korea and that it would regard U.N. adoption of the resolution as agreement with that claim. Again Mr. Dulles spoke, asserting that the ROK should be recognized, "so that, stamped with the seal of legitimacy, it could maintain its prestige and authority in Korea and throughout the rest of the world." On 12 December the General Assembly approved ROK as "the only lawful government in Korea," and established the U.N. Commission on Korea (UNCOK) to "travel, consult and observe throughout Korea." It also called upon all member nations of the U.N. to "establish relations" with ROK and to "refrain from acts derogatory" to "bringing about the complete independence and unity of Korea."

Thus, in some respects ambiguously, the U.N. encouraged the Republic of Korea to go ahead, with U.N. support, as the only sovereign government in Korea.

14

Implanting the Two Governments

The "two governments" so diversely established in divided Korea posed two fundamental questions. Both had to do with the quality of life available to the Korean people. The first question is: What were the characteristics of the two new governments? The second follows closely: How did the people fare under each of them? The answers derive from the nature of the two regimes, from how they were established, from U.N. observation in the south and lack of it in the north, and from the nature of U.S. versus U.S.S.R. sponsorship.

In their basic nature, the governments and the societies that confronted one another across the 38th parallel were fundamentally different. Kim Il-sung commanded his Soviet-built monolithic dictatorship through a tightly-organized apparatus that was partly governmentally bureaucratic and even more pervasively a non-governmental network of Communist Party cells. Syngman Rhee, by contrast, was elected by the National Assembly because he was the only Korean who had nationwide confidence and support. From its inception, however, it was beset by partisanship. The overwhelming majority that elected Rhee was more intent upon controlling his administration than in adhering to his leadership. The Americans, whose support was absolutely indispensible for the new government, accepted Rhee's election reluctantly, only because they could not avoid it. Consequently, his administration from its inception was hamstrung by resistance and opposition from ambitious rivals. As in all pluralistic societies, dissention was institutionalized. In their internal structure the difference between North and South was simple: the one was communistic, the other democratic. Externally, their differences were compounded by the contrasting policies of their sponsors.

The most significant reality was the hostile division of the peninsula and the severe tensions that resulted and intensified. Because the south and the north were in a state of semi-warfare from their beginning, the ideals of freedom and civil rights that both promised were impossible to implement. A second and equally vital reality was the nature of their sponsors, who were challenging one another in an increasingly bitter Cold War, and who had contrary views of the Korean peninsula. The Soviet Union was determined to maintain a strong influence over the "strategic heartland," and therefore granted strong and effective military support to the north. The United States was eager to withdraw and, to make withdrawal feasible, wanted a relaxed calm in the area, for which reason it adamantly denied any military strength to the south. The U.S.S.R. supported dictatorial controls in the north; the United States insisted on political competitiveness in the south. Other realities were impoverishment of the populations, much worse in the south than in the north, and the lack of either a tradition of democracy or any experience with it in both areas.

In the monolithic North a seeming harmony and virtual unanimity prevailed. All "enemies of the state" were either eliminated or isolated and silenced. The most independent-minded of them were allowed to flee into the South. Dissidents who remained had their properties seized, were denied any means of livelihood, and their local and even their family influence was destroyed by severe public denunciations, by imprisonment, or by execution. Quite differently, in the pluralistic South clamorous disagreements and organized opposition were not only inherited but were intensified and nurtured by contentious political parties, by elections featured by acrimonious campaigning among multiple candidates, by competition over properties confiscated from the departed Japanese, and by constitutional division of governmental authority.

When the Russian troops were withdrawn from the North in December, Kim Il-sung was left in undisputed command of a large, well-trained, well-equippped, and battle-experienced army that was supplied with tanks, military aircraft, cannon, and transport facilities, along with being staffed by well-trained and experienced officers and by Soviet advisors. The Americans left to the newly inaugurated Republic of Korea a constabulary of 50,000 members that was denied any formation and field maneuvers, with young and inexperienced officers, and with 472 Americans (including support personnel) organized as the Korean Military Advisory Group, whose principal charge was to prevent the development of an effective army. The major mistake of the United States as it turned over government to the Republic of Korea was that it neither allowed development of a defensive force nor accepted responsibility for defense of the republic.

An equally significant difference lay in the economic circumstances of the two areas. The North, with only a third of the peninsular population, possessed the substantial Japanese-built industrialization that was fueled by an abundance of hydroelectric power and by immediately available coal, iron, and timber resources. As a consequence, the people were fully employed and had a tolerably adequate standard of living. The economy of the South, in sharpest contrast, was in absolute shambles. Twenty-five percent of its workers were unemployed and as many more were under-employed. The three or four million refugees and returnees were without homes or jobs and many of them were without family or friends who could help them to get settled. Farm production was gravely hampered by lack of fertilizer or means to produce it. A vital blow was the abrupt shutoff, on 14 May 1948 of the flow of electric power from the Yalu River hydroelectric plants. Runaway inflation made living doubly difficult. Basically, the inflation derived from the lack of productivity that resulted in a grave shortage of all manner of consumer goods. It was aggravated by the borrowing from the Bank of Korea by the American Military Government of some 44 percent of its operational funds and the borrowing by the Republic of Korea government during 1948–49 from this central bank of 45 percent of its expenses. The cheapness of this printing press money not only boosted prices far more rapidly than wages but also weakened the faith of the people in the effectiveness of their government. As is always true, galloping inflation has heavy political and social as well as economic costs. To make matters even worse, a devastating drought in 1948, for a second year in a row, required heavy imports, rather than the planned export, of food grains.

As a result of these differences, the northern regime was much more efficient than the southern, just as an army is much more disciplined than a mere crowd. Kim Il-sung issued orders and they were carried out. Syngman Rhee had to cajole and persuade acceptance of his policies and procedures by rival politicians whose prerogatives and right of assertive dissent were protected constitutionally and were further supported by U.S. and U.N. insistence on the unfettered processes of opposition. Northern conformity was fully matched by Southern diversity.

Another, less tangible but not less meaningful, difference between the two republics was the effects upon them of foreign opinion. Koreans were necessarily highly sensitive to global opinion because of their long subjection to alien manipulation. The northern population was soothed by streams of approval flowing in from the Communists of Russia, China, and the Eastern European satellites, while adverse news and criticism was excluded by an iron curtain matched in its tightness only by that around Albania. In the South the people were kept in a state of uneasiness by a steady flow of complaints from Americans and Europeans who were disappointed that their sponsorship of the 10 May election had neither unified nor brought peaceful stability and prosperity to the peninsula they had liberated from Japan. The disappointment of their expectations, or hopes, acerbated the feelings of the southerners who read of them in *Time, Newsweek,* and the *New York Times,* heard them on their radios, and listened to both Korean and foreign travellers. They also read a daily barrage of domestic criticisms published in their own newspapers. This is one of the prices of democratic freedom that is borne much more easily in wealthy and well-established nations than in new and impoverished ones.

In many respects the constitutions adopted by the two governments differed fundamentally from one another. This is important because a constitution is designed to express the aims, ideologies, values, and principles of its society. In constitutional law, there are two basic ways of dealing with human and civil rights. One is that human beings have "certain inalienable rights" which must be protected. The other is that citizens of a state have only such rights as the state may extend to them. The ROK constitution was drawn on the first assumption; that of the DPRK on the second. In the Preamble of the ROK constitution, Article 32 sweepingly asserted that "all citizens shall be entitled to a life worthy of a human being." In contrast, the DPRK constitution, in Article 69, equally sweepingly declared that "Citizens must display a high degree of collective spirit . . ., must cherish their collective organizations and establish the revolutionary trait of working devotedly for the sake of society and the people and for the sake of the homeland and the revolution." Like the constitutions of other Communist states, the North Korean constitution, in the name of "democratic centralism," granted absolute power to the executive, with no separation of powers and no independent judiciary. Article 89, defined the powers of the executive as being above control by the legislature, the laws, or the people. He was "head of State and represents the State and directly guides the Central People's Committee." As in the other Communist nations, it was not the government but the party that ruled.

The constitution of the Republic of Korea provided for a strong presidency. The president was granted the considerable power of appointment to office of his cabinet, of the Supreme Court judges, of provincial governors, and of mayors of large cities. The National Assembly had the usual democratic means of restraining executive power, most immediately by its control over the budget and by its adoption of new laws.

One provision of the constitution proved to be by all means the most crucial. This was to reserve to the National Assembly the considerable power of electing the president. In the debate on ratification of the constitution it was posited that this restriction on democracy should continue until the people should somehow find means for demonstrating their capacity to exercise this fundamental democratic right for themselves. This was the factor that proved to be the most disruptive in the legislative-executive relationship. It created tensions that almost destroyed the life of the republic.

The main dispute during the drafting of the constitution, reflecting the political pressures, was over the distribution of power between the legislative and executive branches. Within the Democratic Party the sentiment was strong for the British cabinet system of government, which fuses the two into one. Since this was the majority party, a prime minister and cabinet derived from and responsible to the legislature would have been under this partisan control. Although the presidential system was adopted, there was also provision for a prime minister, whose duties were vaguely defined but who would have administrative responsibility, under presidential authority, and would be subject to confirmation by the Assembly. This was a concession to those who demanded that the Assembly must rule. It proved to be a continuing source of discord. After the government was inaugurated, a large minority of the Assembly tried hard to require that cabinet ministers must be members of the Assembly and must be subject to direct questioning by it concerning government policies and operation. In these respects, disharmony prevailed within the very center of the government from its beginning.

The ROK constitution also provided fundamental provisions for the protection and for the nurture of civil rights. The right to vote and to be elected was assured to all eligible citizens over the age of eighteen. Women were assured full legal and social rights, equally with men, in the sharpest break with the traditional Confucian society. Concubinage was forbidden. Universal education was mandated—even though there were no available means for financing it. Textually, the constitution was one of the most liberal in the world. But harsh realities (partly lack of resources, partly Communist-induced disorder) impeded its normal functioning.

The American Military Government had been unable to reflect effectively the strong anti-Communism of the American people because of the necessity of searching for an agreement with the Soviet Union that would be a mutually acceptable solution for Korea. It had appointed a Coalition Committee, headed by Kimm Kyu-sic and Lyuh Woon-heung, and had given it continuing support. It had appointed representatives of the far left to the Interim Assembly. It had permitted Communist ownership of newspapers and freedom for propagandizing through motion picture theatres and the full spectrum of means of publicity. In two major respects, the AMG laid the groundwork for disruption and rebellion in South Korea by Communist agents. One was to permit the continuance of the widespread network of People's Committees and of their recruitment of new members. The other was to permit, even to encourage, the enlistment in the constabulary and the police of Communists and their supporters, on the principle that the security forces must not be "political." No screening of the beliefs or associations of applicants was permitted. Communists also infiltrated the local, provincial, and national adminstration at all levels, and secured key posts in the vital Communications and Intelligence services.

In addition to these very threatening circumstances, Syngman Rhee, as the founding president, was confronted by many other awesome difficulties and responsibilities. The expectations of the Korean people and of the U.N. sponsors of the government by far exceeded any possibility of attainment. Rhee was expected to create a substructure of working democracy on a foundation of some four thousand years of hierarchy, aristocracy, and monarchy. He was expected to set a high standard of honesty for government officials whose salaries were far too meager for coping with the rapid rate of inflation, and to do so in the face of a long tradition of special privileges and unauthorized remuneration for those with power to punish or to distribute benefits.

The governmental agenda was dominated by threats against national security. But economic needs were equally insistent. With winter approaching, the needs for housing, fuel, food, and distribution of welfare supplies were desperate. The peasants, numbering three out of every four in the population, were trying to support families averaging more than seven members on plots of land that averaged just two and a half acres in size. Half of this land was rented, at rates running above one-third or even half of the annual crop. The money the farmers needed to borrow from private lenders, or "loan sharks," in the spring for fertilizer, seed, and essential equipment, cost them upwards from twenty-five to thirty percent interest.

Coal mines, to provide fuel for cooking and for heating homes and offices, had to be brought into production. Roads, railways, and communication facilities had fallen into grievous disrepair. School buildings had to be constructed, textbooks written and published, and teachers trained and paid. Further, personnel had to be recruited and trained on the job at all levels. Policies had to be determined and procedures developed. All of this required time. And time was not granted.

Strong Communist enclaves had initiated uprisings in and around Pusan and Taegu during the winter of 1946–47 that resulted in wide destruction and the loss of over a thousand lives. The South Korean Labor Party, led by Pak Hon-yong, who was rewarded for his successes by being named Foreign Minister of the DPRK, and the Peoples Committees created a subterranean Army of Liberation that was armed with rifles and ammunition left behind by Japan. The ties of these groups with the Pyongyang regime were close and direct. And their promise to elevate the lot of the poor gave them a following well beyond their membership.

On 3 April 1948, while the AMG was dismantling itself in preparation for the new government, a major revolt broke out on the island of Cheju.[34] During the war Japan had turned Cheju into a military fortress, manned by sixty thousand troops. When the Japanese withdrew, following their surrender, they left behind a huge cache of weapons and ammunition, as well as food and supplies, in the caves of the central mountain which they had enlarged and converted into barracks, warehouses, and a fortification. There the Communists established a strong base immediately upon Japan's surrender. Kim Tal-sam, the Communist Party's general secretary on the island, organized a force of five hundred guerrillas, supported by one thousand civilian auxiliaries. Within weeks, the entire island fell under virtual Communist control, which was little challenged by the AMG.

After the inauguration of the ROK government, the Ministry of National Defense issued new American M-1 carbines to its troops in southeastern Korea but did not immediately reclaim the Japanese rifles and ammunition with which they had been armed. In mid-October, President Rhee ordered the Fourteenth Regiment, which was headquartered in Yosu, to prepare to restore governmental authority on Cheju Island. Instead, on the morning of 18 October, a revolt broke out under the leadership of junior officers. Lieutenant Kim Chi-hoe quickly took command of the rebels. Yosu is a major port city which at that time had a population of seventy thousand, including the well-organized People's Committees. The rebels distributed Japanese rifles and ammunition to the Communist Army of Liberation, which quickly subdued the two hundred-member Yosu police force and took command over the city. The next morning a contingent of the rebels took train to Sunchon, a railway junction twenty-six miles distant. There they were joined by two more mutinous companies of the Fourteenth Regiment. Loyalist troops, seeing many of their comrades among the rebels, withheld their fire and Sunchon was soon captured. More Japanese rifles were distributed to the Army of Liberation. The rebels fanned out across the countryside, murdering police in the surrounding towns and swelling their ranks with members of the People's Committees.

For a few hours President Rhee deliberated whether to send reinforcements to the south or up to the 38th parallel. The decision was not easy. The Army of Liberation was spreading word that Kim Il-sung had already dispatched a force across the parallel, to join up with the rebels. It was impossible to know how much infiltration had occurred among the troops guarding Seoul. World communism had never been stronger. Its "inevitable" triumph was suggested by the Russian blockade of Berlin and by Mao Tse-tung's rapid advances toward final control of China. South Korea's military strength was far from enough.

In the Yosu-Sunchon area, the rebels were terrorizing and murdering non-Communist civilians. They seized the Sunchon chief of police, grouged out his eyes, and dragged him through the streets behind a car until he lost consciousness. Then they shot him, doused his body with gasoline, tied him to a post in the heart of the city, and burned his body. During the first day while the rebels held the town, some nine hundred persons were summarily executed, including four hundred policemen. Dogs maddened by the taste of human flesh added to the terror by running wild. An American attached to KMAG, Captain James Hausman, flew from Seoul to Kwangju, from which he reported that "all hell had broken loose and we had nothing at hand to stop the onslaught."

Within a few hours President Rhee ordered the Fourth Regiment, from its base in Kwangju, to launch an attack against the rebels. Led by Major Paek In-yop, in the afternoon of 22 October these troops entered and captured Sunchon. President Rhee decreed martial law for the area and government troops recaptured Yosu on 26 October. Battle lines were nonexistent; it was virtually impossible to tell foes from friends. Discrimination between those who were obviously guilty and others who were merely suspected of guilt was sometimes sacrificed by the need for immediate action. Emotions ran fever high and mistakes of judgment were made on all sides, by government troops as well as by Communist rebels. As Hausman phrased it, "all hell had broken loose."

After order had been restored to some degree it was possible to assess the situation. Radio Pyongyang's assessment was that 2,326 persons were "murdered by the police." The principal Yosu newspaper, *Chayu Sinmun,* in its 9 November issue reported that

> The entire city . . . is in ashes, still surrounded by horrors and terrors. All kinds of notices cover the walls of the town in the form of orders, appeals, and threats, issued by both sides. Dead bodies and broken pieces of furniture are scattered over rice fields and town lots. People are roaming over the debris without any particular purpose except, it appears, looking for something, either their lost children and relatives or lost property. . . . Everywhere in town there is blood and dead bodies and in one spot we saw deep blood stains on the ground where the rebels seem to have executed innocent people and those they believed to be rightists. . . . The only business in town seemed to be writing such forms as identification cards and passports and other documents.

The ROK Ministry of defense conducted an investigation and issued at the end of November a report on the whole affair, including mopping-up operations. It declared that some five thousand people were arrested, stripped to their underwear, and searched. Many were beaten and some were summarily executed. Seventeen hundred persons, including fifty civilians, were charged with participation in the rebellion. In subsequent court trials, 866 were found guilty of treason and executed; 541 were found innocent; the remainder were sentenced to prison terms. The writers of this report found that at least some good had resulted from all the horrors: the revolt unveiled the depth of infiltration into the ROK armed forces and led to the cleansing out of traitors. The report concluded: "If the Yosu-Sunchon incident had not taken place [which caused the army to take action against Communists in the armed services], the Republic of Korea would have been Communized." KMAG's assessment was that "the purge appeared to have a very profound effect up and down the chain of command and it produced the much needed and desired improvements at all levels."

Communist guerrilla disorders continued for many months. Some two hundred rebel troops, well-armed and with ample ammunition, escaped from the Yosu-Sunchon area into the nearby Chiri Mountain complex, the most precipitous in all Korea, and continued to attack and harass the surrounding area. Rebels ensconced in Cheju Island's mountainous interior also continued to launch forays against the seaside towns, while distributing leaflets that read: "Fight the American imperialists and their lackey, Syngman Rhee. You should side with the people. Fight with the guerrillas who are protecting your country, your homes, and your parents and brothers. Try to be patriots and men of honor!" What they meant by patriotism may be defined statistically. In March of 1949, a report on Cheju listed fifteen thousand people killed by the guerrillas. Three-quarters of the island's four hundred villages lay in ruins. More than twenty thousand houses, thirty-four schools and fourteen local government office buildings had been burned down. About a third of the population had sought safety by crowding into Cheju City, where food supplies were perilously low. By April Cheju was largely pacified and President Rhee spent several days visiting around the island, including a trip into the mountain, to reassure the people of their safety.

The political problems of setting up the new government in South Korea were almost as difficult as was the military problem of defending it. There was no precedent of political party discipline. There was no tendency by either the legislature or the press to accord to the new president a "honeymoon period" for getting his administration in order. The National Assembly members were keenly aware that the president depended on them for his election and they were determined to assert the mastery that was implicit in this arrangement. As newcomers in the political situation that was taking form, they had to sort out their responsibilities, loyalties, personal ambitions, perquisites, and their relationships both with the executive branch and with their own constituencies. The members of the cabinet and the entire administrative personnel had similar problems to solve. Across the whole spectrum of the government, duties were inadequately performed, largely from lack of funds; a lingering inefficiency was the result of lack of experience and lack of any established system of operation. Outside the government, the society was not sure what it wanted but there was inevitable disappointment that independence did not bring with it a much better life.

The 1948 Communist uprisings led to passage, in November of that year, of a National Security Law that defined treason so broadly and so ambiguously as to give the government virtually unlimited power to arrest its critics. The continuing daily incursions back and forth across the 38th parallel line, the sharpening of charges that land reform was being undermined by the influence of pro-Japanese collaborators, and the resentments aroused by the inefficiencies and corruptions of the widespread bureaucracy combined to threaten a dangerous destabilization of the society. The response by the government was to commence a sweep of presumed Communists from positions in the military, in schools, in business and in government itself. The judicial system yielded to the pressure for stern measures, so that in the spring of 1950 the prisons were crowded with some sixty thousand inmates, more than half indicted under the National Security Law. That the instability was Communist-instigated was unquestionable; but it was also inevitable that the arrests were the result of hasty and inadequate investigation. The need to strengthen security was real. But as often happens in times of near-panic, the measures adopted went well beyond the need. To judge the circumstances in perspective, it is helpful to bear in mind the similar action by the United States government of sweeping all Japanese residents of the Pacific coastal states into concentration camps after the Pearl Harbor attack. Anger and fear are nowhere safe guides.

There was an admixture (by no means a blend) in the society of old-style conservatism, with its emphasis upon hierarchy, ritualism, and Confucian ethics; of pride and participation in the heritage of Korea's long history; of Marxian emphasis upon equality and rebelliousness against "capitalistic" authority; and of Western (primarily American) individualism and eagerness for material comforts. There were mixed feelings about modernity—including a determination to speed its promotion of civil rights and of ever-increasing consumption; and a questioning of its pandering to self-interest and breakdown of family ties and of social cohesiveness. Since the first advent of Westernization, Koreans had had all too little opportunity to contemplate its effects or to deal with it on their own terms. Now they could salute their own flag, sing their own national anthem, and celebrate their own commemorative holidays. But they had not yet worked out the pattern by which they wanted to shape their lives. And the severe economic stresses, the cruel onslaughts of guerrillas, and the puzzling enigmas of politics precluded orderly development of new social values. Their chief preoccupation was how to survive.

Donald Macdonald, a long-time American foreign service Korea-watcher, in his 1988 book *The Koreans: Contemporary Politics and Society* posited that success for the new government depended on three factors. First, "the rightists" should do what is seldom if ever accomplished by political leaders anywhere; namely, surrender their own individual and group interests in order "to initiate fundamental democratic reforms and promote effectively unity among patriotic Koreans throughout the country." Second, "sincere opposition elements" should, with equal unselfishness, constitute a "vital and virile" loyal opposition. Finally, "no matter how hard the Koreans work to achieve their goals, Korea cannot become a genuinely independent member of the family of nations as long as the present world-wide Soviet-American deadlock continues." In short, in order to attain success, the entire political spectrum had to exhibit unprecedented selflessness and wisdom. But even if all the people did so, the Cold War, over which they had no control, would prevent fulfillment of their hopes.

The first two requisites were met about as well as could be expected under the disruptive, impoverished, and inexperienced conditions. President Rhee was criticized for some of his cabinet appointments, for some of his policies, and for stubborn determination in pursuing his own course; just as other major political leaders, both inside and outside of the government were also charged with allowing personal ambition to interfere with their duties. The Rhee administration was also charged with corruption; though this was never suspected of him personally. This kind of problem plagues all societies and all governments and it has defied solution both in Korea and in all the rest of the world. The persistent factionalism in Korea has been another serious problem. Considering the circumstances of the time, both the executive and the legislative branches struggled through obstacles to achieve much.

Outstanding was the adoption of a land reform measure that ranks as one of the fairest and best attained by any government. Most of the members of the Assembly represented constituencies dominated by landlords—for traditionally landholders were the guiding leaders among the people. President Rhee, too, owed much to the conservative landlords who led the Democratic Party. Even so, the President and the Assembly worked together, not harmoniously, but with full recognition that land reform was the most imperative need of the nation. Emphasizing his determination to solve this problem, President Rhee appointed to his first cabinet as Minister of Agriculture, an ex-Communist, Cho Bong Am, whose devotion to the welfare of the farmers was unquestionable.

In Old Korea, the ownership of the land was vested in yangbans who were thereby local officials. Landlords and tenants were bound together by their common interest in maintaining productivity. When the Japanese took over Korea they soon took ownership of more than 50 percent of the farmland. Absentee ownership became common. The dominant issue was profit for the land owners. Annual rental rates rose to forty and even sixty percent of the crop. Relations between owners and tenants instead of being mutual became hostile.

When the American Military Government was established, reform of the land rental system was given highest priority. Within a month, on 5 October 1945, the AMG Ordinance Number 9 slashed the land rental rates. During the latter part of the colonial period, a 1938 census found that only 19 percent of Korea's 2,554,000 farm families owned the land they tilled. The average farm size was one *chungbo,* or 2.45 acres. Sixty-three percent of the families farmed less than one *chungbo.* As a second stage in reforming the system, the AMG proposed that the government should buy all tenant farms and sell them to the farmers for a price of three times the average annual value of crops harvested over a five-year period, with payments to be extended over fifteen years. The Interim Assembly rejected this plan, insisting that the reform measure should be left for decision after the inauguration of the Republic of Korea. Nevertheless the AMG proceeded, under its Ordinance Number 173, to sell to tenant farmers the land owned by *Shin Han Kongsa,* the successor to the Japanese-owned Oriental Development Company.

In January 1949, as its first major reform effort, the National Assembly adopted a land reform measure that provided for sale to farm tenants of the farmlands still vested in the government, of lands owned by landlords, and of all farmsteads in excess of three *chungbo.* Payment amounting to three times the annual crop value was to be spread over a ten-year period. President Rhee vetoed this measure and, in cooperative study by the Assembly and the Ministry of Agriculture and Forestry, a new law was enacted in June 1949, as Law Number 31. This law, signed by President Rhee, called for payment by tenants over a ten-year period of 150 percent of the annual crop averaged over a five-year period. In order to ease the burden on farmers unable to pay the annual levies, and to insure to former owners payment for the lands they lost, an amendment was promulgated in March 1950 under which farmers could borrow money for the annual payments, with the loans guaranteed by the government. Sales of the land began promptly after the enactment of Law 31, and by June some 38 percent of landlord-owned land had already been sold to its tenant operators. The outbreak of the Korean War interrupted application of the law; but the land sales were resumed in the spring of 1951, while the war continued.

Results of the land reform were impressive. It went a long way toward elimination of land rental farming. It led to transfer of ownership from landlords to tenants of 577,260 *chungbo,* or more than a million and a half acres. This amounted to some 29 percent of all the farmed land in South Korea. The devastation from the war made it impossible for many tenants to make any payments and landlordism was not eliminated. What the farmers most needed was more land, whether owned or rented. The amount of available land could not be measurably increased—and South Korea's population increase was fourth highest among all the nations in the world. This resulted in a constant struggle to maintain, let alone increase, the size of individual farms. After the land reform, only one farm in five was larger than two to five acres. As the population increased rapidly, rural dwellers could not shift from agriculture to industry, for there was little increase in industrialization. As the general economy of the country gradually improved, farm welfare lagged behind. Inflation boosted greatly the cost for fertilizer and all essential supplies, while the price of rice and other grains was necessarily controlled to reduce the hardship of urban consumers. Land reform was not an isolated issue, to be dealt with solely in terms of land ownership; it was integrated in many ways with the total economy.

Neither could the economy of the nation be dealt with separately from the general circumstances. The need for education was desperate. The AMG laid the foundation for modernizing and enlarging educational facilities in South Korea, but it had neither the funds nor the authority to "meddle" much with Korean domestic institutions. Because of the Japanese language policy, a large majority of Koreans were illiterate in their own language.

Schools, teachers, and textbooks all were urgently needed. So was the development of educational goals. For all of these, programs were well under way when the war interrupted them. In order to counter the Japanization policy of the colonial period and the Communization policy of the North, the ROK constitution specified that "freedom and political neutrality of education shall be guaranteed." As is true everywhere, the government did try to shape its youth into "good citizens." But as the "protest spirit" in Korean schools make manifest, students by no means have been subjected to "thought control."

What was accomplished educationally in South Korea before the 1950 invasion may be at least partially measured quantitatively.

1) Primary school enrollment increased from about one-and-a-half million in 1945 to two-and-a-half million; the number of primary school teachers rose from 13,782 to 34,757; and the number of primary schools went up from 2,694 to 3,442.
2) Middle school enrollment increased from 62,136 to 226,960; the number of middle schools rose from 252 to 423; and the number of middle school teachers from 833 to 8,238.
3) College-grade institutions, including two-year community colleges, technical institutes, four-year colleges, and universities with graduate programs increased from 19 to 29; and their enrollment rose from 3,039 to 21,250.
4) An adult education program raised the number who were literate in the hangul script from about one-third of the population in 1945 to an estimated 83 percent.
5) On-the-job technical training programs were developed in government bureaus and in industrial plants, with results that were hard to measure but that undoubtedly raised substantially the level of efficiency.
6) Public health education was a high priority. Thirteen schools for nurses were accredited by the Ministry of Public Health and Welfare, with three-year curriculums that were modelled on those in American institutions. More doctors, whose education took much longer, were desperately needed. In July, 1946, the number of doctors varied from 27 per 100,000 of the urbanized Kyonggi-do Province to a low of 1.7 in rural areas. With an infant mortality rate at the tragic level of 48.8 per 1,000 births in 1945, the need for more and better medical service was urgent.

Urgency, indeed, was the operative term for government during the founding period of the republic. Public security had to be the first priority. After the Yosu-Sunchon rebels were driven into the Chiri Mountains, they continued their forays in force against the civilian population. Even more threatening were the outbreaks of violence along the 38th parallel line. Since this line was purely arbitrary, it sliced close to villages, towns, and two large cities, Haeju on the Ongjin Peninsula, and Kaesong, some thirty miles north of Seoul. The tip of the Ongjin peninsula, held by the South, was important to both governments, since it dominated the entrance to the Han River. Each side launched frequent forays against the other, striving to gain and hold strategic positions. Kaesong was overlooked by a high hill that straddled the parallel, and, again, both sides periodically violated the border, trying to hold it. All along the border similar tactical engagements occurred, averaging more than one a day. Brigadier General William L. Roberts, commanding the KMAG advisory group, cabled to the Pentagon his view that "most incidents on the parallel are due to needling by opposing field forces. Both

North and South are at fault." He was mostly critical, however, of the ROKA, because it ignored his efforts to restrain its border incursions.

The United States, meanwhile, was carrying out its policy of withdrawal from Korea. Anticipating the withdrawal of Generalissimo Chiang Kai-shek from China to Taiwan in September 1949, the American government reviewed its Asia policy and decided to concentrate its attention on Europe, waiting, as the saying was, "for the dust to settle in Asia." Secretary of State Dean Acheson, Chairman of the Senate Foreign Relations Committee Tom Connally, and General Douglas MacArthur all publicly declared that the American line of defense in the Far East ran from the Aleutian Islands down through Japan to the Philippines, notably leaving Korea outside. Owen Lattimore, an influential advisor to the State Department, wrote on 17 July 1949 in the New York *Post* that "the thing to do is to let South Korea fall [to the Communists], but not to let it look as if we pushed it." The Pentagon advised President Truman that militarily South Korea was a liability rather than an asset to the United States—useful neither for an offense against China and Russia nor for defense of Japan. The Congress, beset by demands for the rehabilitation of Europe and by public resentment against raising taxes, first defeated and then barely passed a minimal Korea aid bill. The administration decided to withdraw all American troops from Korea, except for the KMAG advisors, and did so in July 1949.

Meanwhile, Kim Il-sung steadily increased military pressures against the South. He formed the Democratic Front for the Unification of the Fatherland (DFUF), which joined with the South Korea Labor Party to intensify guerrilla-style insurgency in the South. The magnitude of this effort is indicated by the arrest in the South, between 4 September 1948 and 30 April 1949 of 80,710 Communist insurgents and agitators, and the dismissal from the ROKA of fully one-third of its officers who were found to be Communists or to be participants in their plots. Even seven percent of the members of the National Assembly were arrested for conniving with the North against the Southern government. While these efforts were being made to subvert the Republic of Korea, Kim Il-sung went to Moscow in March 1950, where he received a promise of equipment for six infantry divisions, three mechanized units, eight battalions of border guards, twenty reconnaisance aircraft, a hundred fighter planes and thirty bomber planes. On 15 march 1950, Kim said to a conference in the Ministry of Internal Affairs in Pyongyang that

> the South Korean army, which is supported by the Americans, has poor morale and is defending South Korea rather than intending to attack North Korea. Even though the south Korean army attacks, we shall easily repulse that group. In 1949 we defended North Korea only; however, in 1950 we will begin the heroic struggle to merge [the] separated [parts] and we will achieve a glorious, complete independence. The only way to achieve it is to cause disturbances on the 38th parallel line and have the South Korean army devote all of its attention to that area, while four

> guerrilla units attack the enemy from the rear. This is the only way to unify our separated country.

Syngman Rhee, too, understood that the only way to reunite Korea would have to be by war. But he did not receive support from the United States, as North Korea did from the Soviet Union. On 22 October 1949 he wrote: "Our army of 100,000 men is not equipped and armed as it should be. We have not enough ammunition to defend ourselves if the Northern Communist Army should decide to come down. . . ."[35] The KMAG in June of 1949 estimated that "except for national pride, there was little to recommend the ROKA as a military force." Sawyer, in his *Military Advisers in Korea* (p. 67) explains: "The technical service units were embryonic. . . . Training facilities in general were scarce and inadequate, and at all levels there were deficiencies emphasizing a need for better trained officers and non-commissioned officers, more equipment, and all kinds of technical specialists." In November, Ambassador Muccio recommended to Washington that the Korean Air Force should be supplied with forty F-51 fighter planes, but Washington refused to do so. Rhee joined with President Quirino of the Philippines and with Chiang Kai-shek in a strong effort to persuade the United States to join in forming a Pacific Pact for mutual defense, but their pleas were rejected. Still stressing the goal of reunification, on 1 March 1950, celebrating the Samil anniversary, President Rhee assured his audience that "even though some of our friends across the sea tells us that we must not cherish thoughts of attacking the foreign puppet who stifles the liberties of our people in the north . . . we shall respond to the cries of our brothers in distress." He knew what he wanted to do, just as he knew that he could not do it.

On 30 May 1950 the Republic of Korea held its second general election. Some 85 percent of eligible voters went to the polls to elect 210 members for four-year terms to the National Assembly, from a field of 2.054 candidates, most of them running as "Independents." Although the government was under heavy criticism because of the country-wide guerrilla activities, the continued unemployment and the doubling of taxes to reduce the rate of inflation, President Rhee's followers won enough seats to enable them to organize the Assembly. Shin Icky, re-elected as Speaker, introduced a constitutional amendment to make the cabinet responsible to the Assembly rather than to the President. This amendment was solidly supported but fell short of the two-thirds neeed for its adoption. Another political shock was the assassination of Kim Ku on 26 June by a ROK army lieutenant, who charged that Kim Ku's continuing efforts to form an all-Korea coalition government endangered national security. President Rhee had the vice-speaker and fifteen "progressive" members of the Assembly arrested on similar charges. It was obvious that South Korea's political instability was as threatening as its military weakness.

Obvious, that is, except to American policy-makers. ECA Director Paul Hoffman told the U.S. Congress Foreign Relations Committee that economic progress in South Korea was "nothing less than spectacular." Secretary of State Dean Acheson made the hopeful assessment that "despite the problems with which the Republic of Korea is beset, both internally and externally, and despite its necessarily limited experience in self-government and paucity of technical and administrative knowhow, conditions of stability and public order have continued to improve."

This optimism was not shared by President Rhee. On 8 March 1950 he wrote to Chough Pyung-Ok, ROK Observer at the United Nations, and to Ambassador Chang Myun, urging their utmost efforts to secure from the United States both a solid commitment to defend South Korea and more military materiel for the ROK armed forces. His long letter concluded:

> To summarize the whole military problem, we are not after a large army, a large air force, or a large anything. We only want to obtain forces in each branch of the military service which will be adequate for our defense. Even a start on an air corps and a navy would have great psychological effect on the Korean people and our enemies in the North. However, to accomplish this means that the State Department must revise its present interpretation of the American perimeter so that it includes Korea.

Shin Sung-Mo the ROK Minister of National Defense, showed to Ambassador Muccio and to General Roberts intelligence data detailing the huge military buildup of North Korean forces along the 38th parallel, including hundreds of tanks and mobile cannon, along with the construction of roads, communication facilities and air fields. Brushing these reports aside as ridiculous, General Roberts, on leaving Korea at the completion of his two years as commander of KMAG, disingenuously told *Time* magazine that he was leaving to ROK "the best damn army outside the United States." President Truman, assessing the military situation with his advisors, was told by them that they all agreed that South Korea was one of the places which the Communists might attack. He shrugged this off with the response that the same could be said of all Europe, from Norway down to Greece and Iran, and in Asia from the Kurile Islands down to Indochina and Malaya.

Then came the dawn of Sunday, 25 June—or, as it was dated, across the international date line in Korea, 24 June. The unwelcome day of reckoning had come. The Cold War had suddenly become hot. The question that had to be faced by those who had made the policies that led to this tragic culmination was: What must we do about it?

15

The Tragedy of War

The Korean War was fought up and down the peninsula, again and again, from the Korean Straits in the south to the Yalu River. Down and back, down and back, then on up again and back part way, and once again part way up, so that in the grim jesting of macabre humor it came to be tagged "the yo-yo war." But it was sheer, grim tragedy to Korea, as it was also to the American and other U.N. families whose sons, husbands, or fathers were killed or suffered grievous wounds or illness from exposure. Three million Koreans lost their lives, a hundred thousand children were orphaned, ten million people were driven from their homes and there were none others who did not suffer.

This war was waged nationwide, with no place that was safe or saved: fifty-two cities were largely destroyed, four or five thousand farm villages were pillaged and burned. Seoul was captured and recaptured four separate times. The war was fought in the heat and rain and mud of summer and in the bitter cold of the severest winter Koreans had endured for many years. By South Koreans it was fought generally by young untrained soldiers, officered by colonels and generals no more, at most, than thirty or thirty-five years of age. It was fought by South Korean troops without war planes, or tanks, or cannons, armed at best with bazookas so light that their projectiles bounced off the sides of advancing tanks. It was fought by these troops virtually barefooted, victualled with a few handfulls of uncooked grain, and with only the sparsest of medical support.

Alongside RokA fought the trained and well-equipped soldiers of the United States and of some fifteen other member nations of the U.N. From India, the sixteenth nation, came ambulance drivers and other medical aides, as brave and as endangered as the rest. To add irony to the tragedy, the policies and war aims of the allied governments differed so substantially from those of the Republic of Korea that it was as though the two were fighting side by side in different wars.

Despite the probable inevitability of internecine war in the peninsula ever since its division, and despite all that was known of North Korean preparation and mobilization, and despite, also, the premonitory violence of Communist uprisings in the south and of clashes along the border, the invasion, when it was launched was unexpected. In May President and Mrs. Rhee were hoping to take a summer rest from his exhausting duties, in their hillside cottage overlooking Masan Bay at the southern tip of the country. Farmers were gratefully measuring the growth of their rice seedlings, nurtured by ample rainfall for the first time since World War II.

The circumstances and the mood of that time in late June of 1950 may be illustrated by the experiences of a moderately well-to-do housewife, Mrs. Moon In-sil, known to her many American friends as Julia. Mrs. Moon had grown up in Shanghai. She married a doctor who was educated in the United States. One of her brothers-in-law had served as Consul-General in Hong Kong; another was Minister to England. Her eldest brother was Admiral Sohn Won-yil, Chief of Naval Operations. If any family of South Koreans knew of the imminence of war, this one surely would. Instead, this is what happened, as she related in an interview in Pusan in July 1952:[36]

> I was secretary of a young women's business group in the Seoul Y.M.C.A. On Saturday afternoon, June 23, a group of about thirty of us, all around thirty years of age, some with young children, went up to Uijongbu, about eighteen miles north of Seoul, where the "Y" had recently put up a summer cottage. It was our first visit there and we wanted to fix it up. We stayed all night and worked Sunday morning cleaning and decorating the cottage. Up towards the 38th parallel we heard some dull thundering that sounded like guns. The townspeople told us not to worry, for there was often some shooting up that way. But around noon an elderly man came to us looking very worried and said that the road to Seoul was closed to ordinary traffic and was filled with jeeps and trucks loaded with soldiers going north. We went out to look and decided we must hurry back to Seoul.
>
> Like many of the other women, I had two children, my daughter aged six, and my son, aged four. Besides, we all had bundles of food and bed clothing we had brought along. The bus that was to have come for us did not arrive, and we could easily see that it would not be able to come. So we started out to walk. The jeeps went by us like whirlwinds. Sometimes empty trucks were going back south, and in some of them we got a ride part of the way. The drivers were very angry with us, calling us crazy women to be out for a hike at such a time as this. It was night when we got back home, and our families were very worried. By this time Uijongbu had been captured by the Communist armies. . . .

The rest of her story is equally revealing. She hid in a sewer, "so choked with nastiness that I could not breathe." She spent the summer as a refugee until in September the Communist forces fled back across the 38th parallel. Scores of thousands of Koreans had experiences very much like Mrs. Moon's. There is scarcely a family, north or south, that did not lose someone close. As happens when a country is devastated in war, the suffering was widespread, engulfing the elderly, the children, the women, and civilian as well as military men. While the war was in its depths, with Pusan serving as the temporary capital, Education Minister George Paik (Paek Nak-chun) summed up its effects. "Our cities, homes, and factories must be rebuilt after they have been destroyed. These are the outer defenses of our Republic—important and precious to us, but not vital to our existence as a free people. What we must safeguard at all costs is the Inner Citadel."

Then he explained. "The Inner Citadel is the integrity of our people. It is their minds and their morals, their intelligence, their sense of duty, their spiritual resilience. It is their sense of what they are fighting for, and their continuing faith that it can be attained. While this conviction is locked in the hearts and souls of our people, nothing can defeat them. But if ever this Inner Citadel is cracked, Korea may fall into the same apathy of defeatism that swept China into Communist control."

The defense of the Inner Citadel is the untold story of the Korean War. Many volumes have been written about the general course of the conflict—about President Truman's decision that his policy of "containing Soviet aggression" demanded that the assault upon South Korea must be turned back, and about the military operations that were finally ended by the truce signed on 23 July 1953. Little has been written, at least by Western historians or for Western readers, about what the war meant to Korea and how it was fought by Koreans. The great strength of the Korean Inner Citadel was that the people did not abandon their own government even while the seemingly-invincible North Korean armies, and later, the seemingly-endless hordes of Communist Chinese, threatened to make anti-Communism everywhere in the peninsula a capital offense. This is the essential difference between the fighting in the Korean and the Vietnamese wars. This did not preclude, however, the kinds of mistakes that appear to be inevitable in warfare. The most tragic in this war occurred in February 1951, while the Chinese communist army was hurtling southward, far below the 38th parallel and fear was prevalent that all Korea would be overrun. A South Korean Colonel known as "Tiger" Kim surrounded a Korean village of five hundred inhabitants that, he believed, was harboring communists who might be a serious threat to the temporary capital extablished in Pusan, and ordered an attack in which all the inhabitants were killed. This was a notorious incident that did, in fact, resemble atrocities of the later war in Vietnam. In Korea it did not recur. The South Korean people remained true to their own government and their own president. This is why General James A. Van Fleet, who commanded the ground forces in the final months of the war, said of Syngman Rhee: "He is worth his weight in diamonds to our cause." The United Nations forces had a loyal population at their backs and by their sides. Despite the horrors of the war, there was no disintegration of morale.

In moral terms, however, the Inner Citadel was badly battered. Sexual morality had been centrally valued if not always practiced, in Korea's Confucian family-centered culture. When the American army of occupation moved into south Korea in 1945 to establish its military government, the easygoing, socially attractive GIs, with their cigarettes and candy bars and free-spending ways, naturally seduced many Korean girls. Stern Korean family members threw their own wayward daughters or sisters off the bridge crossing the Han River. Conditions during the war were different. Battle-weary U.N. soldiers sought hasty comfort from Korean women; and amid the disruption and devastation of the war, families necessarily accepted what their womenfolk had to do to bring home such supplies and money as they could. Even so, the unwed mothers of unwanted bastard babies were scorned and their numerous offspring were abandoned to die or to survive as best they could. Adolescent disobedience, juvenile crime, and a breakdown of family discipline proved to be wartime casualties that seared the social fabric with deep wounds.

How the war began in Korea determined how it was fought. The North was well-armed; the South virtually unarmed. The Communist bloc was determined to win; the U.S.-U.N. bloc was determined to avoid broader conflict by confining its efforts to what President Truman termed "a police action" in which "victory is not our aim." Until near the end of the war, the Republic of Korea was constrained by the overall U.N. command from developing a real army of its own. It was a war of limits except for the unlimited destruction in Korea. At its beginning, none of this was clear.

The United Nations Commission, from its observation posts in South Korea reported on 25 June to the Security Council (from which the Soviet Union had absented itself in protesting the refusal to give China's seat to the new Communist Chinese regime) that the attack was unprovoked aggression. Formally it itemized support for its judgment:

> First, judging from how the situation is developing at present, the north Korean forces are committing a well-planned, unified and overall invasion of south Korea.
>
> Second, the Republic of Korea forces have been deployed along the 38th parallel wholly for defense purposes; and
>
> Third, the Republic of Korea forces were attacked wholly by surprise.

War always entails the risk of failure, but Kim Il-sung had reason to expect quick and complete success. The United States had plainly insisted that its Pacific Ocean "defense perimeter" excluded Korea. The United States also had rigorously refused to permit its aid funds (or South Korean counterpart funds) to be expended for modern armament. Meanwhile, the KMAG had restricted both the arms and the training of the ROK troops to the minimum needed for internal constabulary operations. The inducement for the Communists to launch the attack was well-stated by John Foster Dulles, addressing an open-air meeting at the Washington Monument on 4 July: the attack was launched because South Korea's society "was too wholesome to be overthrown from within." The North's efforts to arouse and to organize rebellion in South Korea failed. To the leadership of the militarized North, prospects looked good for accomplishing the Communization of the whole peninsula by a whirlwind conquest.

As early as September 1947 General Wedemeyer had informed the Pentagon that North Korea had some 125,000 troops "equipped and trained" by the Soviets, in contrast to the 20,000-man American-organized constabulary supplied only with outmoded Japanese light arms in the south. President Rhee's pleas that a real army, capable of defending the 38th parallel line, should be recruited, trained, and armed, were ignored. Discouragement was inevitable. The monumental labors and disappointments of the founding period, from 1942 on through the initial months of shaping the new government were taking a heavy toll. To a press conference on 24 March 1950, President Rhee said: "I will not be in this position any more than two more years." Then he added: "I often wish I could turn the whole thing over to someone else and just drop out." Shin Sung Mo, the diminutive and fiercely energetic Defense Minister, was daily pleading for more military manpower and equipment, supporting his urgent requests with intelligence reports of a vast and steady buildup along the northern side of the 38th parallel. By the KMAG commander, and the officials in Washington, these reports were brushed aside as exaggerated, self-serving, and untrue.

In sharp contrast, the militarization of North Korea was proceeding apace. From 1946 on, some one thousand young north Korean men were enrolled in Russian military training schools in Siberia, where they were learning the maintenance and use of heavy ordinance, tanks, communication field facilities, and military aircraft. During 1949 two divisions of "Korean volunteers" were transferred from service with the Chinese Eighth Route Army and were integrated into the North Korean Army as its 5th and 6th divisions. They were armed with Russian weapons and their former Yenan-trained Chinese senior officers were replaced with Russian-trained Koreans. During April and May of 1950, the North Korean forces were provided with supplies of weapons, equipment, and reserves adequate for wartime needs. The result was described by U.S. Marine Colonel (Retired) Robert Debs Heinel, Jr., in his *Victory at High Tide:*

> In equipment and organization, and in military style, the army which had been brought into being was as Russian as beluga caviar: 150 T-34 medium tanks; almost a hundred Yak and Stormovik tactical aircraft; 122mm howitzers and 76mm divisional howitzers and guns; 76mm self-propelled guns; 120mm mortars; the whole family of Soviet anti-aircraft weapons; and every requisite infantry weapon from anti-tank rifles to burp guns. Supervising this array were eight USSR advisors per division and many more at higher staff and command levels. When summer came in 1950, the *In Min Gun* [North Korean Army] was, among the armed forces of the Far East, probably better trained and equipped for its intended work than any other army but Russia's.

After the attack was launched, the U.N. Commission reported to the U.N. from Seoul that the invasion was "a calculated, co-ordinated attack, prepared and launched with secrecy." In Pyongyang Kim Il-sung, in a radio address on 27 June, blamed the Republic of Korea for an attempted invasion of the North and concluded: "The war which we are forced to wage is a just war for the unification and independence of the motherland and for freedom and democracy." President Truman was at his home in Independence, Missouri, when news of the invasion reached him and he tarried at home for a day to allow time for the United Nations to prepare its response.

On 27 June the U.N. Security Council, with Russia still absent, voted seven to one, with two abstentions, to "furnish such assistance to the Republic of Korea as may be necessary"; and on that same day President Truman ordered U.S. "air and sea services to give the Korean Government troops cover and support." On 28 June Seoul fell. President and Mrs. Rhee joined the flood of refugees, to establish a temporary command post at Taejon. Korean soldiers, seeking to hold the invaders at bay, ran at the Communist tanks with bottles of gasoline and satchel charges. Some climbed on the tanks and tried to pry open the turrets to drop hand grenades inside.

On the evening of 2 July the first American troops, four hundred men of the first battalion of the 34th Infantry Regiment, arrived at Pusan from Sasebo, Japan. They were lighthearted, telling one another that as soon as the Communists saw them advancing under the United States flag, they would turn and run. They were heartened by an assurance from President Truman that they were not at war but were simply carrying out a police action for the United Nations. They entrenched themselves a few miles to the north, in individual foxholes, filled by heavy rain, and were quickly disillusioned as they saw large tanks bearing down upon them through the rain and mist.

Neither the ROK nor the American troops were able, during the next three weeks, to hold a fixed position. The heaviest fighting was around Taejon, where the American commanding general William Dean was captured by the North Koreans. The situation was saved from complete rout by the fact that the North Koreans outran their supplies and were not given grain, as they expected, by the farmers, who hid it in the hills. In mid-July the U.N. armies established a defense line along the Naktong River, forming a perimeter surrounding the city of Pusan, the temporary capital of the republic, with ROK troops holding the northern segment and American troops the western side. Desperate as the situation was, President Rhee considered the first necessity was to seek agreement on the war's goals. On 18 July he composed a long letter to President Truman, of which the following paragraph was the crucial part:[37]

> The government and the people of the Republic of Korea consider this is the time to unify Korea, and for anything less than unification to come out of these great sacrifices of Koreans and their powerful allies would be unthinkable. I am sure, Mr. President, that you have come to the same conclusion yourself, but I wish to make clear to you the position of this Government. The Korean Government would consider as without binding effect any future agreement or understanding made regarding Korea by any other state without the consent and approval of the Government of the Republic of Korea. From statements which you have made recently, I believe that this is also the position of the Government of the United States.

The need to decide what to do concerning the conduct of the war became urgent when on 15 September General MacArthur staged history's most spectacular amphibious assault, the landing at Inchon of U.N. troops, thereby opening the way for the reoccupation of Seoul. The entire Communist invasion force was fleeing in a panic rout to get back across the 38th parallel. The paramount question at once became: what next? Should the war end or be pushed on north?

South Koreans had no doubt that the war should proceed promptly and decisively to reunite Korea. The government in Washington was reaching the same conclusion. As early as 17 August, Warren Austin, the U.S. delegate to the U.N., stated that "the General Assembly has decided that fair and free elections should be held throughout the whole of the Korean peninsula." Nevertheless, while the U.N. troops were moving from Inchon toward Seoul (only eighteen miles away) the Joint Chiefs of Staff cabled MacArthur that re-establishment of Seoul as the capital city "must have the approval of higher authority." To this MacArthur shot back an angry reply: "This of course involves no re-establishment of government nor indeed any change in government but merely a restoration of the existing government to its constitutional seat." President Rhee strenuously argued with MacArthur for an immediate advance, telling him, "we have to go up now. They will not have time to regroup and there will be little resistance." When MacArthur demurred that he had no such authority, President Rhee told him: "You can wait with your troops until the U.N. has decided the issue, but no one can stop the Koreans from going up. This is their country. If you give air support to our boys, they can make it." Rhee's orders to his army commanders to proceed promptly in pursuit of the enemy met a confused response, for they had been placed under the U.N. command and also were utterly dependent on the U.S. for supplies and for air and artillery support. Even so, they did commence an advance northward on the east coast.

On 27 September, President Truman accepted the Joint Chief's estimate that the North Korean invasion force had lost its military capability and he authorized MacArthur to conduct military operations north of the 38th parallel, "provided that at the time of such operations there had been no entry into north Korea by major Soviet or Chinese Communist forces, no announcement of an intended entry, and no threat by Russian or Chinese Communists to counter our operations militarily in north Korea."

Clarity and agreement seemed to be emerging. On 30 September Warren Austin stated to the United Nations General Assembly what he believed to be the American position: "The aggressor's forces should not be permitted to have refuge behind an imaginary line." On 1 October Chou En-lai, Red China's prime minister, declared that China "will not stand aside should the imperalists want only to invade the territory of their neighbors." MacArthur addressed a radio message to the north Koreans, assuring them that "the early and total defeat and complete destruction of your armed forces and war-making potential is now inevitable." Chou En-lai summoned India's ambassador at Beijing to a midnight conference, in which he said that if U.N. troops entered North Korea, China would enter the war. The United Nation's response was bold and confident. On 4 October the First Committee adopted, and on 7 October the General Assembly approved, a resolution authorizing "the establishment of a unified, independent and democratic government in the sovereign state of Korea." This policy was even more strongly reaffirmed on 22 October in a resolution authorizing the political reorganization of North Korea, where "there is no government that is recognized by the United Nations."

President Truman, on 9 October, cabled General MacArthur, ordering his advance into North Korea, and explicitly defining the nature of his responsibility: "Hereafter in the event of the open or covert employment anywhere in Korea of major Chinese Communist units, without prior announcement you should continue the action as long as, in your judgment, action by forces now under your control offers a reasonable chance of success." Then he added, "In any case you will obtain authorization from Washington prior to taking military action against objectives in Chinese territory."

The United Nations Commission on the Unification and Rehabilitation of Korea (UNCURK), presented to the General Assembly a favorable report on the conduct of the ROK: "The Republic of Korea has stood up to the strains of war remarkably well. The governmental apparatus did not disintegrate, despite difficulties, confusion, and danger. As districts were liberated . . . the civil administration . . . was quickly re-established. . . . The National Assembly, although still inexperienced and sometimes lacking in a sense of responsibility, has remained an active force."

As the United Nations and ROK forces rapidly proceeded into and up through the north, relations between the Republic of Korea and the United Nations command became dangerously strained. General MacArthur took it for granted that as North Korean districts were occupied, their government would be under his jurisdiction. President Rhee was equally adamant in his view that they would automatically come under the jurisdiction of the Republic of Korea government. President Truman and the principal allied leaders, Clement Attlee of England and Jawaharlal Nehru of India, were alike determined that the ROK government should not get control over the north without explicit U.N. approval. The question was sovereignty. Did the ROK constitution mean what it said: that it applied equally to all Korea? The U.N. in its December 1948 approval of the southern government had deliberately left the question ambiguous. It resolved that the ROK was the "only lawful government" in Korea; but it left unsaid "the government of all Korea." The question was not ambiguous to President Rhee. Either Korea was sovereign or it was not.

The issue became crucial as large portions of north Korea came under the control of the rapidly advancing U.N. forces. General MacArthur began appointing governors of the northern provinces. President Rhee had already made such appointments; and his appointees, with their staffs, were ready to assume civilian administration. The United Nations Interim Committee declared that the authority of the ROK government was restricted solely to South Korea. On 15 October President Rhee hotly cabled to MacArthur: "U.N. new Committee resolution not acceptable. Korean people will insist on maintaining their inalienable right." MacArthur's solution was that he would hold the power to appoint governors and other Korean officials in the North, but he would appoint the ones President Rhee nominated. As he told the Senate Committee on the Conduct of the War in its December 1951 hearings: "My understanding was that he [Rhee] could use South Korean officials but not as such. In other words, use them as civilians." This "solution" would have left sovereign control to the U.N. Dr. Rhee refused to agree to it. The issue remained unresolved when the U.N. retreated from the North.

Still another problem roiled Korean-American relations during this period while it appeared that the nation was again to be united. This was a sharpening of the dispute over the expansion of the ROK army. The U.S. Congress in December 1949 had approved (by a slim margin) the setting up of the Economic Cooperation Administration (ECA) to give minimal aid to the badly shattered South Korean economy. President Rhee asked that ROK be allowed to use at least five percent of its counterpart funds to buy military equipment. This request was refused.

As the U.N. and ROK forces moved closer to the Yalu River and it appeared that the war was about over, the United States sought to make it clear to the world, and particularly to the Red Chinese and the Soviet Union, that it had no ambitions in Korea except to get out as quickly as it could. General MacArthur assured the U.N. troops that they would "be home by Christmas." President Truman, following a meeting with MacArthur on Wake Island, issued a statement declaring that the purpose of the United States was "to establish peace and independence" in Korea and then to leave. President Rhee made hurried visits to the Northern cities of Wonsan and Pyongyang, to assure the people that they were already rejoined with their brethren in the South.

Then came what General MacArthur somberly described as "an entirely new war." During the week of 15–20 October, U.S. Army Intelligence reported that some 250,000 Chinese troops were taking up advanced positions near the Korean-Manchurian border, with another 200,000 stationed behind them as a reserve force. On 26 October the ROK Sixth Division engaged in hard fighting with a Chinese Communist force about twenty-five miles south of the Yalu River. The First ROK Division at the same time met stiff resistance from a North Korean contingent that had Chinese Communists in its ranks. The U.S. Eighth Army command ridiculed these reports as being irresponsible. On 30 October Chinese prisoners were taken by the ROKA near Hamhung. The next day MacArthur's headquarters acknowledged that between a regiment and a division of Chinese troops were attacking the ROK Capitol Division. By 3 November it was evident that the entire Chinese Forty-Second Corps was in Korea. MacArthur's Tokyo headquarters described the situation as "not alarming." On 6 November MacArthur cabled the Joint Chiefs of Staff that "men and materiel in large force are pouring across the bridges over the Yalu from Manchuria." He asked for permission to bomb the installations in Manchuria and was ordered to restrict resistance to Korean territory. On 24 November MacArthur ordered a major U.N.-ROK attack designed to drive the Chinese out of Korea.

His northern advance was as ill-planned as his Inchon landing was brilliant. The frontal attack against the incoming Chinese was launched by greatly inferior numbers with scanty supplies. Moreover, the drive into the North was under three separate commands—led by General Walker in the west, by General Almond in the east, and by Il Kwon Chung's Capitol Division (which had no air support and little artillery) in the middle. These three commands had no direct contact with one another but were ordered to communicate through MacArthur's Tokyo headquarters. During the advance north, no reserve positions or supply depots were prepared.

MacArthur's assessment came in a 28 November cable to the Joint Chiefs of Staff: "This command has done everything humanly possible within its capabilities but is now faced with conditions beyond its control and strength." Secretary of State Dean Acheson told a special meeting of the National Security Council that "we should find some way to end it." On 30 November President Truman told a news conference that he was considering using the atomic bomb to beat back the Chinese. Britain's Prime Minister Clement Attlee hastened to Washington and on 4 December he and Truman issued a statement assuring that the atomic bomb would never be used without prior consultation with America's allies. President Rhee, on 7 December, summed up the circumstances: "The present situation is one of chaos and confusion. . . . In Seoul people are moving south, shops are closing. . . . Our division on the east coast is not in a position to join with our forces in the center." The Chinese troops drove south, with the U.N. forces in precipitous retreat, and Seoul was again captured by the Communists.

On 14 December the U.N. General Assembly in effect rescinded its 7 October and 22 October resolutions and set up a Cease-Fire Committee authorized to seek a compromise truce. The U.S. Joint Chiefs of Staff told MacArthur that "we believe Korea is not the place to fight a major war." In the discussion in the General Assembly, Canada's Lester Pearson suggested that the Republic of Korea be disbanded to placate the Communists; and Britain's Sir Gladwyn Jebb said that no solution would work unless it satisfied the Chinese. On 5 January President Rhee asked MacArthur for 500,000 rifles for Korea's soldiers and urged that the U.N. command accept Chiang Kai-shek's offer to send 50,000 Nationalist Chinese troops to Korea from Taiwan. Both requests were refused. The Communist drive into the south was finally halted and on 17 March Seoul was again in ROK possession.

On 10 April President Truman dismissed General MacArthur for publicly asserting that the U.N. should "depart from its tolerant effort to contain the war to the area of Korea." General James A. Van Fleet was brought in to command all ground forces in Korea. He and President Rhee agreed that the U.N. forces should move on from their fixed positions and advance northward as rapidly and as far as the U.N. limits allowed. Van Fleet also agreed that large numbers of Koreans should be trained and equipped—thus he became in President Rhee's words, "the father of the Korean Army." When the advance reached the 38th parallel, Van Fleet was ordered to take it no further, except for a sector on the east coast. Bitter fighting broke out from time to time, but the war was at an impasse. American soldiers complained, "We can't win. We won't lose. And we can't get out." For Koreans the situation was even worse.

What the war cost the Koreans General MacArthur indicated during the hearings of the U.S. Senate subcommittee on the conduct of the war. "The war in Korea," he said, "has almost destroyed the nation. . . . I have never seen such devastation. I have seen, I guess, as much blood and disaster as any living man, and it just curdled my stomach the last time I was there. After I looked at that wreckage and those thousands of women and children and everything, I just vomited."

Most school buildings were either destroyed or taken over by the armed forces, U.N. and ROK, so classes were held out of doors. Seeds for the spring planting were very scarce and fertilizer much more so. A minimum of 500,000 tons was needed, but an ECA shipment was diverted to Formosa (Taiwan) because Korean ports were tied up by military shipping. Slaughter of the remaining cattle was forbidden, so there was no meat. In the recovered area little was left. Houses, animals, fields, and villages were destroyed or stood desolate. Not even vegetables could be grown. The ROK government released 200,000 men from its underarmed forces to allow them to start work in the fields. Neither statistics nor general facts suffice to reveal the horror of the situation. Every family had its own tale of tragedy. Two or three such tales indicate the nature of them all.

In the outskirts of Seoul, beyond the ancient West Gate, near an old Confucian temple, stood the ruins of a large home formerly owned by a Japanese industrialist. A direct bomb hit had blown away much of its roof. To this ruin a sad-faced young Korean named Baek In Cheol (Paek In-chol) brought 130 orphans. These were a portion of some four hundred that he had gathered up, alone and unaided, from the no-man's-land between the fighting lines. Often he crawled into broken huts under gunfire to drag them out. Twice he was wounded, but he kept on with his self-appointed task. American soldiers helped him when they could. They loaded his charges into their empty trucks as they drove back south for more supplies. When Baek got the children to Seoul, he housed them in the wrecks of empty buildings, patching them up as best he could. He also started schools in empty yards or rooms. The children slept on the floor, usually with one blanket for every two or three. Some food was brought to them by American soldiers, enough to keep them alive. Baek sought and found additional help—including Pak Yong-dal, a young professor who had taught in Seoul National University; a black American corporal, Ansul Mattier, from Boston, who scrounged actively for supplies; and three young women, separated from their families, who helped as nurses and caretakers. Similar orphanages were established all throughout the South, with Koreans and Americans working together to save as many children as they could. In Seoul fourteen-year-old Kim Hyo-jun, whose right leg was lamed, sat watching his ten-year-old brother Hyo-ik, who was running about hitting and spitting on other children. Their father had died shortly after the war started; their mother grew ill and died in January 1951. Hyo-jun took his brother Hyo-ik by his hand and started south. They came to the fighting front and clambered across dead bodies and through shell fire. It was then that Hyo-ik lost his mind. On Wolmi Island in Inchon harbor, in September 1950, the mayor of the island's small fishing village, with his family, helped an American marine lieutenant who was landed there to gather data on the tides. When the mayor saw that Communists on the mainland were watching the unusual activities in his village, the lieutenant was taken off the island in a launch by night. In the morning Communists troops arrived. The mayor, his family, and fifty of the villagers were executed. In the village of Kapyang, just east of Seoul, and on the north side of the Han River, young Kyo Woon and his five-year-old sister were living with their well-to-do uncle. The Communist drive separated them from the family and for three months they wandered, begging for food. After the Inchon landing they returned to their home and enrolled in school. Then the Chinese Communist advance separated them again. Kyo Woon was taken to an orphanage by a ROK engineering outfit. He spent his days sitting by himself, hugging his knees, and wondering where his sister might be.

The war was also tragically costly to Korea's U.S. and U.N. allies. The price in lives paid by Americans for their courageous resistance to the Communist armies was exceedingly high. A total of 5,764,143 Americans served in the war. Of these 33,629 were killed in battle; 20,617 died of illness and exposure during the war; and 103,284 suffered non-lethal wounds. Among other U.N. combatants, special praise for great heroism was won by troops from Great Britain, Turkey, Ethiopia, and Australia, along with the Americans.

Throughout the war, the untrained and ill-armed ROK forces fought as best they could.[38] Admiral Arthur Radford, Commander of the Pacific Fleet, summed up his impression of the ROK Navy in an interview on 22 October 1951: "From Admiral Sohn on down they have been reliable, tireless and technically extremely competent." The Navy consisted merely of a handful of small craft, manned by a total force of nine thousand. The ROK Marines numbered ten thousand. When the attack was launched, Admiral Sohn was on his way back from Hawaii with two frigates, the fruit of weeks of negotiation. In the Inchon landing, two small ROK gunboats moved in ahead of the fleet to knock out the guns on Kangwha Island.

The ROK Army was the first U.N. force to cross the 38th parallel in the October 1951 advance and ROK soldiers were the first to reach the Yalu River. ROK troops achieved the most rapid advance of any soldiers on either side when they advanced seventy miles up the east coast in six days. They constituted the largest number of fighting men on the U.N. side. And they endured by far the greatest ratio of casualties. Total Korean casualties, including civilians, could never be counted, but reliable estimates place the number of deaths (South and North) at around three million. The number who suffered wounds and illness caused by cold, hunger, and exposure defies any effort to count them.

Robert K. Sawyer, the official historian of KMAG, clarified the result of the refusal by the United States to permit the development of the South Korean military:

> Now [in July and August, after the invasion began], when time was at a premium and the need for trained men was greatest, the replacements sent to the front were raw troops. Receiving only ten days of quick instruction and seldom firing more than one clip of rifle ammunition, they could not be expected to perform like trained combat soldiers. The lack of training also contributed to their difficulty in holding onto the terrain they were defending and caused them to suffer heavier casualties than their more experienced compatriots.

He might have added, as he did elsewhere, that the ROK troops were grievously underarmed and without air cover. The U.N. troops also suffered needless casualties in the early months of the war by failure of their commanders to realize that before advancing up narrow valleys they should first of all capture the precipitous mountain ridges on which the Communists were entrenched. Despite such basic difficulties, both the ROK and the U.N. troops fought tenaciously and successfully, first to hold the Pusan Perimeter, thereby insuring the failure of the North to secure the quick victorious ending of its assault, and afterwards for the duration of the war.

Major disagreements and misunderstandings roiled the relations between the Republic of Korea and the United States. Publicly President Rhee was unfailingly lavish in his gratitude for the prompt U.S. entrance into the war, for bringing the U.N. in with it, and for persisting against American public opinion and despite heavy casualties until the invasion was beaten back. But he was distraught by the refusal of the Allies to fight on for victory by reuniting Korea. President Rhee was keenly aware that the Truman Doctrine of containing Communism was insurance for the Republic of Korea against defeat. But he disagreed deeply with Truman's limitation of the war to that one single objective. Truman, on his part, actively disliked Dr. Rhee for stubbornly insisting on Korean sovereignty, and he had no intention of allowing him to shape, in any degree, the goal for which the war was being fought. The issue came to a head when the U.S.-U.N. leadership gave up the plan for reunification of Korea following the entrance of China into the war. Dr. Rhee's reaction was a mixture of desperation and defiance. "We will either die fighting or defeat and destroy our enemies," he insisted. "This is our determination and we hope the U.N. has nothing to say against it. They have proved themselves incapable of handling a world crisis such as this." Truman informed the Joint Chiefs of Staff why he refused to permit the arming of ROK troops, even while the war was in its most desperate straits: "I would not agree to what amounted to political units." Political units? What else is an army? General Mark Clark, in his history of the war, noted that "tough old Syngman Rhee . . . was ready to take on anyone, friend or foe, who stood in the way of his strategic concept. . . . I had to admire him. . . . I respected him. . . . personally I liked the man, but I still found him as exasperating an ally as anyone could have." Rhee, on his part, having spent forty years of his life in the United States, and having during the whole of his mature life opposed American policies of avoidance in dealing with Korea, felt perfectly free to express his disagreements and did so vigorously.

A continuing source of troubled relations between Rhee and American top officials was their habitual disregard for Korean sensibilities. To the U.S. top command, civilian and military, the Republic of Korea was not so much an "ally" as a "client," with no honest claim to sovereignty—and certainly not to equal sovereignty. An instance that occurred during the fierce fighting along the Pusan Perimeter illustrates what was typical of their relations. President Rhee prepared a cable he wished to send to the U.N. member nations that had sent their troops into Korea. The U.S. Army, which held complete control over the communication facilities, refused to send the cables. The U.S. information officer explained privately that the reason was Rhee's indication in the cables that the Soviet Union was the instigator of the war. Truman agreed that the Soviet Union was responsible, which is why he approved entry in the conflict—to deny Soviet Communist expansion. But the two disagreed on how to deal with the situation. President Rhee believed that lasting peace demanded a strong stand against the aggressors (similar to John Kennedy's demand that the Soviets remove their missiles from Cuba). Truman and the U.N. Allies believed the way to preserve peace was to "pretend" that the Soviets and the Communist Chinese were not participants in the war but were only North Korea's sympathetic and helpful friends. Domestic politics in both the United States and South Korea reflected the underlying disagreement as to what the war was all about.

In Washington Joseph Martin, the Republican Minority Leader in the House of Representatives, said: "If we are not in Korea to win, then this Administration should be indicted for the murder of thousands of American boys." In South Korea, when the National Assembly was about to exercise its electoral power by defeating Rhee for re-election to the presidency, Rhee decreed martial law and used miliary force to get the constitution amended so that the general populace would have the electoral right. In the ensuing election, he was overwhelmingly re-elected, by a vote of five million against 600,000 for his leading opponent. Many condemned his arbitrary revision of the constitution; but none doubted that he was by a very long range the choice of the people as their leader.

On 8 July, an American delegation went to Kaesong, which was held by the Communist armies, to commence negotiations for an end to the war.[39] Two years later, on 23 July, not a "peace" but a "truce" was signed by the U.N. officials. President Rhee did his best to prevent it by releasing twenty-five thousand prisoners of war who wished to remain in South Korea or go to Taiwan, rather than be taken back under Communist rule. He also refused to sign the truce, though he had to agree to abide by it. Winston Churchill represented the U.N. resentment of Rhee's deviation from its war aims by declaring furiously that "we shall not reconquer north Korea for Syngman Rhee." General James A. Van Fleet expressed the admiration of those who agreed with Rhee that the war should have and could have ended by depriving the Communists of their North Korean base (as did all the American generals who testified in the U.S. Senate's Armed Forces hearings on the unsatisfactory ending of the war) in an article in *Life* magazine, describing Dr. Rhee as "one of the greatest thinkers, scholars, statesmen and patriots of our time."

Four full decades after the start of the war, historians still dispute one another about the degree of its international character. Even those who persist in calling it a "civil war" accept the obvious facts that the North Korean capacity to wage it was provided by the Soviet Union, that its ending without unification of Korea was owing to the massive intervention by the Communist Chinese, and that the war was started by a well-prepared assault by North Koreans across the 38th parallel line.

Nikita Khrushchev, in his memoirs, relates that when Kim Il-sung visited Stalin in Moscow in the winter of 1949–50, he told him that "North Koreans wanted to prod South Korea with the point of a bayonet." "Naturally," Khruschev added, "Stalin couldn't oppose this idea. It appealed to his conviction as a Communist all the more because the struggle would be an internal matter which the Koreans would be settling among themselves." Khrushchev did not himself write his memoirs and they may not fully represent his views. Nevertheless, this passage seems credible since it was the long-term policy of the Soviet Union to fight its wars through surrogates, veiling its own involvement. At any rate, whether civil or international—and obviously it was partly both—the war was fought and was ended leaving the peninsula in ruins and still divided. This was its tragedy.

16

New Faces of Sovereignty: North and South

On 13 July 1953, the Korean War was "halted," not "terminated." The fighting ended with a truce rather than a peace treaty. Since the Republic of Korea refused to sign the truce, the war between the South and the North went on . . . and on. The United Nations ended its military participation and all troops from U.N. member nations were promptly withdrawn, except for an American contingent left to guard against a renewed attack from the North (and as a restraint against any attack from the South). All Korea was in ruins and resources for rebuilding were sparse.

Both North and South were desperately in need of all the help they could get from their allies. Nevertheless, the two governments both were belligerently disappointed, even to the point of outrage, that the outcome of the war was so very short of their needs and demands. Neither was satisfied that their allies had given proper consideration to the aspirations of the Korean people. Both had proven unable to shape—or even significantly affect—the policies that determined the course and the outcome of the war. Their leaders—Kim Il-sung in the North and Syngman Rhee in the South—were humiliated by the very evident fact of their helplessness, as well as angered by what each considered the want of constancy by their allies. Such feelings were mixed with honest gratitude for the sacrifices and contributions by their allies that resulted in a truce rather than in surrender. And both were also absolutely aware of their need for all the material help they could get for the rehabilitation of the catastrophic war damage. Above all else, both governments and both peoples were determined that Korea must and would survive and that it would rise again.

A major concern of both Koreas in the years following the armistice was *chuch'e (juch'e).*[40] It is a term with a cluster of meanings, all expressive of "independence" and it is deeply meaningful in both sections of the peninsula. Independence is a luxury that Koreans had yearned for for generations, as they endured the effects of imperialism, of colonialism, of military governments, and of international tutelage. Their postwar status as "client states" brought benefits but also limitations and humiliations. The tragedy of war sheared away even their means of livelihood; but it strengthened rather than weakened their sense of "Koreanism." What was essential in the meaning of *chuch'e* was their right to govern themselves in their own way. This sentiment emerged strongly, however differently, both in the North and in the South.

In the South, where individualism was rampant, *chuch'e* meant primarily a stubborn determination to go one's own way, regardless of consequences. It meant a reluctance to accept even advice, let alone domination, from any government—whether foreign or their own. It meant not only individualism but also devotion to one's own clan, and faction, and region, and class. One meaning of *chuch'e* is "leave us alone," and this sentiment was felt none the less deeply by individuals who resisted being governed than by their government, in its dealings with its foreign friends, desperate as its need was for foreign aid.

Chuch'e is a term that points in two different directions, one cohesive, one divisive. In part it is a patriotic loyalty to Koreanism, that binds the whole population together with pride in being different from all others. In part it is sheer individualism, a feeling that "I'm as good as you are, if not better." It is this feeling that has been disruptive in Korean history, making it difficult for individual citizens, for leaders, and for political parties to work together harmoniously, to cooperate, or to compromise. It was this mixture of feelings that coalesced after the deeply unsatisfactory truce that was shaped not by themselves but by foreign powers.

The prospects for reunification of Korea remained exceedingly dim. The two power clusters waging Cold War with one another were determined to keep it from turning into a nuclear holocaust; and one of their joint determinations was to reduce the possiblities of a new outbreak of hostilities in Asia. Later, in the 1970s, when detente became their policy, it remained equally urgent that Asian stability not be threatened by altering the status quo in Korea. Both North and South Korea leaned as hard as they could against major policies of their sponsoring allies, in order to pursue the interests of their own peoples, as their leaders perceived them. But in both zones, the needs for external help were so basic as to set limits within which the two Korean governments had to operate.

In North Korea, the growing strength of Mao Tse-tung in China was viewed as an opportunity to lessen its dependence on the Soviet Union. Since the two Communist powers were then closely united, Moscow did not obstruct negotiations for a treaty that Kim Il-sung and Mao Tse-tung signed on 17 March 1949, to provide for a "joint struggle against American and British imperialism." The treaty promised Chinese "arms, materiel, and manpower" to be supplied to North Korea from 1 July 1949 to 3 August 1950. As part of it, twelve thousand Chinese-trained Korean troops were transferred from Chinese territory into North Korea. China got from North Korea some 300,000 kilowatts of electric power from the Supung plant on the Yalu River, and also tungsten and high-grade steel to speed development of Manchurian industrialization.

The renewal of the "brotherly relationship" between Chinese and Korean peoples greatly helped both of them. On 23 November 1953 they signed an "Agreement of Economic and Cultural Cooperation,"[41] by which China granted to North Korea gratis "all supplies given and all expenses incurred in aid to Korea." China also extended to the DRPK $325.2 million to help to restore North Korea's economy. To cover the costs of the Chinese intervention in the Korean War, the Chinese borrowed from the Soviet Union the then enormous sum of two billion dollars. As tensions grew between the two Communist superpowers, repayment of this huge loan was one factor. Another was tensions concerning the economic aid both were extending to North Korea for its rebuilding. Kim Il-sung, viewing the circumstances with more opportunism than gratitude, in December 1955 announced North Korea's independence from both of them. Carefully veiling his meaning in face-saving ambiguity while yet making it clear, he said: "It makes no difference whether we eat our meal with the right hand or the left hand, with a spoon or with chopsticks, as long as the food is fed to the mouth."

The Sino-Soviet split became serious at the 20th Congress of the Communist Party, held in Moscow 14–25 February 1956, in which Khrushchev declared his goal of "peaceful coexistence with states with different social systems," thereby denying the Marxist-Leninist doctrine that "wars are inevitable so long as imperialism exists." At the same time Khruschev also announced a campaign against Stalinism and the personality cult. Red China and North Korea drew closer together to ward off these threats to their systems. The Sino-North Korean tie was further strengthened in 1962, when North Korea approved Communist China's border clashes with India and joined with Mao Tse-tung's denunciation of Khruschev's withdrawal of nuclear missiles from Cuba as "another Munich." The Soviets reacted by refusing to permit North Korean delegates to address a January 1963 Communist Party meeting in East Germany. A climax was reached when Kim's regime openly and strongly criticized Soviet interference in North Korea's internal affairs. An editorial in the 7 September 1964 issue of the Pyongyang newspaper *Rodong Sinmun* sharply rebuked *Pravda's* claim that the Soviets had greatly aided North Korea's economic development ever since the defeat of Japan. Instead, the editorial angrily charged that:

> In the process of providing assistance in rebuilding our factories, you sold us facilities . . . and materials at prices far above the world market, while taking away from us in return many tons of gold, huge quantities of precious metals, and other raw materials at below market prices . . . [and] you took away from us the fruits of our painstaking labor at a time when our life was most difficult for us to bear.

The shift in North Korean rhetoric from depicting the Soviet Union as "our glorious Fatherland" to this kind of denunciation was gradual, over a period of years. It was made possible by the ideological, economic, and military bonds between North Korea and Red China. But it did not bring from China the amount of aid Kim needed and counted on, and it did result in the drying up of Soviet economic aid and the temporary withdrawal of further military aid. The situation changed again when the ousting of Khrushchev from power in Moscow in October 1964 opened the way for renewal of close USSR-DPRK relations. In February 1965 premier Alexei Kosygin spent four days in Pyongyang, during which he and Kim Il-sung agreed to restore and strengthen their ties. From this time, Soviet economic aid to North Korea was considerably increased and military aid, at a high level, was renewed. The Soviets completely re-equipped DPKR's armed forces with submarines, heavy tanks, jet fighters, and ground-to-air missile launchers. How fully the wheel had come full circle was indicated by another editorial in *Rodong Sinmun* on 15 August 1965, extolling the "noble sacrifice of the Soviet people in liberating our fatherland" and neglecting to so much as mention Communist China's crucial role in driving the U.N. forces back across the 38th parallel.

In China Mao Tse-tung was hardening the harshness of his own dictatorship by inflicting on the Chinese people the inhumane Cultural Revolution. The Red Guard, resentful of the renewed ties of the DPRK with the Soviets denounced Kim Il-sung as a "fat revisionist." Peking recalled its ambassador from Pyongyang. Kim retorted that "these are the activities of the big-power chauvinism . . . fundamentally contradictory to the revolutionary ideas and the spirit of self-reliance." At the end of 1958 there had even been threats of a Red Chinese invasion of the North, to seize some territory as recompense for the massive help it rendered in the war. The end of the Cultural Revolution brought a return to cordial relations, leading to renewed diplomatic representation and, in April of 1970, a ceremonial visit to Pyongyang by Chou En-lai. Sino-Soviet relations simmered down and North Korea reaped profits from both. Swelling with pride at being wooed by both the Communist giants, since both needed a friendly North Korea for protection of their flanks, on 5 October 1966 at a convention of the Korean Workers' Party, Kim Il-sung gloated: "Should anyone ask which side we are on, we should answer that we are on the side of Marxism-Leninism. We reject great power chauvinism and we do not blindly follow others but we maintain independence, and we cannot and never will dance to the tune of others."

In addition to profiting from the severe tensions between the neighboring Communist giants, Kim Il-sung had also the great advantage that domestically he had to dance to no tune but his own. The Communist apparatus of controls so thoroughly permeated the society that anyone even suspected of disloyalty—which in North Korean jargon is called "mental illness"—suffered the loss of his home and his job and deprivation of such prized opportunities as entrance to a university and membership in the Party. Moreover, such an array of punishments was visited not only on erring individuals but also upon members of their families. The general public was required to join in, or at least to acquiesce in, veneration of the Great Leader whose genius, they were endlessly told, had accomplished defeat of Japan, the United States, and the imperialist member states of the United Nations.

This was the new face of sovereignty in North Korea. It has proved as damaging to its own people as it remains threatening to the South. In some respects it looks like achievement. Pyongyang is a glittering modern city, with efficient factories, attractive residences, broad streets and, in its center, a towering statue of the Great Leader Who Has Done It All. The poverty and the squalor are in the countryside. The foreign indebtedness grows and foreign trade is minimal. For the people, *chuch'e* does not mean personal independence or self-will.

Syngman Rhee, too, pursued full sovereignty as South Korea's fundamental goal. Meanwhile, the political competitiveness of the Republic's pluralistic society subjected him to a continuous buffetting from which Kim Il-sung was protected. Paradoxically, it was not Kim Il-sung but Syngman Rhee who was subjected to clamorous charges of "dictatorship" in the world press. The conduct of Kim was simply taken for granted, as typical of Communism. President Rhee's efforts to impose unity and discipline in domestic politics were condemned as being "undemocratic."

Among South Korean politicians and in the society generally there were three groupings, each maintaining its convictions with passionate intensity. These were the "extreme rightists" who felt, as did Dr. Rhee, the leader of this group, that any kind or degree of compromise with Communism was impossible. In confronting Communists anywhere—in both South and North Korea, and everywhere else in the world—they felt the choice was clear: to destroy or to be destroyed. In pursuit of this policy, they also dealt unjustly and severely with individuals who were not Communists but were rivals for political power or complainers about conditions. Those who wield power are not notably discriminatory in its use. On the "extreme left" were those who neither dreaded nor feared Communism but, on the contrary, took seriously its claims of seeking a classless society, with justice for all, brotherhood, and world peace, while excusing its ruthless dictatorships as merely a transitional stage. In South Korea these were the members of the People's Committees, the Workers' Party, and the Liberation Army; and they came to include many idealistic youths in the universities. They, too, like the "extreme rightists" resorted to violence in words and actions. In between were the "moderates," the followers of Kim Ku, Kimm Kyu-sic, Lyuh Woon Heung, and after their deaths, of Cho Bong-Am, John Myun Chang, and Shin Icky, who recognized the need of caution in dealing with Communism but were willing to take the risks for the possible potential of reunification.

To govern the country it was necessary to have the support, or at a minimum to avoid the rejection, of the great mass of the people, the peasantry. This three-quarters of the population was by far more interested in how to survive than in politics. They did have a traditionalist conviction that their ancient nation must be reunified, which made them susceptible to Communist promises. While both extremist groups and the moderates contended volubly and connivingly against one another in the cities, where their contention was under the scrutiny and subjected to the criticism of the world press and of the allied diplomats, the vital battleground was in the rural areas. It was with this support base that President Rhee retained his power.

After the enormous destructiveness of the war, the most immediately pressing need was for reconstruction and recovery. This need was met during the seven-year postwar tenure of President Rhee primarily through generous aid grants from the United States, which reached the impressive total of some two billion dollars. However, even this was inadequate, for South Korea suffered at least three billions of dollars worth of destruction from the "yo-yo" character of the war. Also, for substantial reasons, but injuriously for South Korea, the aid was more peripheral than fundamental. Because of first Japanese and then American Military Government policies, South Korea lacked an industrial infrastructure and had a paucity of managerial understanding and skills. Hence, it was difficult to rapidly develop a new industrial base. In addition, the woeful condition of the population amidst the ruins left by the war demanded that primary and continuing emphasis had to be upon relief, to alleviate disease and hunger and to supply clothing and housing. In view of both these circumstances, the ECA (American) and UNKRA (United Nations) aid programs dealt basically with these immediate, rather than long-term, needs.

Moreover, the fundamental Asian policy of the United States was to rebuild and restore Japan, as the keystone of Asian stability. In pursuit of this aim, the United States hastened to negotiate a Japanese Peace Treaty in July 1953, in which America assumed primary responsibility for the defense of Japan and implicitly guaranteed its restoration from the destruction it suffered from the bombing of its cities and industries. Actually, this policy began to take effect immediately after the signing of the surrender document on board the U.S. battleship *Missouri.* But the program burst forth to success during the Korean War. Robert Murphy, the first American ambassador to Japan after the Pacific War, summarized the results in a single sentence, in his autobiographical *Diplomat Among Warriors:* "The Japanese with amazing speed did transform their islands into one huge supply depot, without which the Korean War could not have been fought." In specific terms, through "Special Procurement Orders" the United States purchased from Japan for its Korean aid program, between 1951 and 1953, $746 million annually, which sum accounted for roughly two-thirds of Japan's total exports. As Herbert P. Bix concluded in his study, "Japan and South Korea in America's Asian Policy," "At the highest policy-making level the Korean War provided the first great opportunity for reviving Japanese monopoly capitalism and militarism."

The second great opportunity came through the postwar ECA economic aid program for Korea. Since neither the American Congress nor the public was in any mood at that date to appropriate funds directly for the rebuilding of Japan, there emerged instead a guiding policy of "getting two dollars of benefit from every dollar expended as Korean aid funds." What this meant in practice was to activate Japanese factories from which the products were purchased by America to be distributed to Koreans for their relief. Its effect was to rebuild Japanese industry while only enabling Korea to survive.

In confronting these circumstances and policies, President Rhee was in the paradoxical position of complaining vigorously against the very American aid policies that were bringing indispensable relief funds to Korea. He accepted large sums of largess while protesting both privately and publicly against the way this program was administered. Insisting as strongly as he could that major emphasis should be upon building an industrial base in South Korea, he invoked an old saying, "If you give a hungry man a fish, he will enjoy a meal; if you give him a fishing pole, he will continue to eat." He fumed and fussed in making this point as strongly and as continuously as he could, while U.S.-U.N. aid administrators concluded that he was an obstructionist rather than a cooperative and grateful client.

One of the most perceptive of the American aid administrators, John P. Lewis, presented his assessment of it in a book, *Reconstruction and Development in South Korea,* in which he explained that America simply had lost interest in Korea. "The Korean problem is old hat," he wrote. "We were weary of it long before the Panmunjom truce was signed and have grown wearier since." Europe, profiting from the Marshall Plan, was holding most of America's foreign affairs interest. Without much domestic debate, the United States was able to ignore basic needs in Korea and to proceed quietly to develop its policy of restoring Japan. President Rhee protested as best he could against the exclusion of Korea from the U.S.-Japan peacemaking process. He cited studies by a Special Economic Committee that had been set up by the American Military Government, on which Korean economists were aided by American advisors. The conclusions, as summarized by American-educated Chey Soon-Ju, while he was Director of the Bank of Korea, showed Japanese indebtedness to Korea, for transfers from insurance companies, banks, and various financial accounts, of 49,254,288,000 Yen and of Korean indebtedness to Japan for its capital investments in Chōsen of 8,889,399,420 Yen. The difference of over forty billion Yen was figured in 1945 currency. If it were repaid, even in the highly inflated 1953 currency, the sum would be of enormous help in Korean reconstruction. The United States brushed these claims aside, granting only the Korean right to reclaim certain art treasures taken to Japan. Thus in vital respects the Korean aid funds were entangled and restricted by U.S. guidance of Korean-Japanese relationships.

President Rhee necessarily accepted important restrictions on Korean soveriegnty.[42] He accepted the demand that Korean forces be under the unified command of General MacArthur. After the truce was signed, in order to gain a promise of American guarantee against another Communist invasion, he agreed, as he had to, to leave Korean troops under U.S. command. He agreed to "abide by" the truce only on two conditions: (1) the signing of a U.S.-ROK treaty, on 1 October 1953, in which the United States promised that if South Korea were attacked the U.S. "would act to meet the common danger in accordance with its constitutional processes"; and (2) the holding of a conference in Geneva, Switzerland, in which the reunification of Korea would be sought.

This conference was opened on 28 April 1954 with a speech by John Foster Dulles, asserting that "we are here to establish a united and independent Korea."[43] ROK's Foreign Minister Pyun Yung-tae stated that "the remaining task to be fulfilled for the completion of Korean unification" was for the U.N. "to hold free elections in North Korea." Nam Il, the chief delegate from the DPRK, replied that an "all Korea" election should be held under the auspices of a Korean Commission on which North and South Korea would be equally represented, with each having a veto over plans for the election. On 15 June the Conference adjourned, with a resolution approved by all of the U.N. member nations that had taken part in the Korean War, calling once again for U.N.-supervised elections in all Korea. Its conclusion was somber. "It is clear that the Communists will not accept impartial and effective supervision of free elections. . . . We believe, therefore, it is better to face the fact of our disagreement than to raise false hopes and mislead the peoples of the world into believing that there is agreement when there is none."

To emphasize the continuing close relationship with the United States, in late July President Rhee made a state visit to America. After addressing a joint session of both Houses of Congress, he went on across the country, making half a dozen speeches on the theme that a rollback of communism was needed, not merely its containment. This theme called for the exertion of strong pressures, if not actually a call for war, against the Soviet Union. New warfare did, in fact, break out. But it was in Southeast Asia, with the limited aim of prying Vietnam loose from communist domination. It proved to be immoderately costly, increasingly unpopular, and of no help either to Korea or any people anywhere.

On another problem that appeared to be more minor than it was the United States did also become deeply involved. This was the dispute between South Korea and Japan about fishing in the narrow straits between them. To both peoples, fishing was vital. And it had been a source of continuing dispute and distrust between them for generations. During the colonial period, Japanese fishermen virtually monopolized fishing in Korean waters. After the Korean War erupted, General MacArthur established a line of demarcation in the straits midway between Japan and Korea. He dubbed it the Peace Line, and urged that nationals from both countries avoid navigating across the line, to avoid clashes and also to make it simpler to patrol the Korean waters against

Communist military craft. President Rhee declared that the line also separated the fishing waters between the two countries and forbade Japanese fishing boats to operate on the Korean side. From this time on, the world press called this the Rhee Line and published stories of Korean truculence when their patrol boats turned back or arrested Japanese who persisted in fishing in Korean waters. For several years the issue roiled feelings and intensified ill will in both countries. Once again the United States intervened. John M. Allison, in his autobiographical *Ambassador from the Prairie or Allison in Wonderland,* noted that the Department of State must "make clear" to President Rhee that "Korea is a small nation surrounded by three powerful neighbors, only one of which, Japan, was friendly to the free world." He added, "it is therefore essential that Korea realize that its safety and future progress, as well as that of the West, depends upon the renewal of friendly relations with Japan, and this can come about only through compromise and cooperation on both sides." Korean fishing boats were ordered to stay on their side of the line. President Rhee insisted that "cooperation" meant that the Japanese should cease violating it.

Following the warmth of his American visit, President Rhee was very soon becoming a target of sharp criticism in the American and world press and, privately, by American officialdom. Ever more insistently, disagreements multiplied between Rhee and administrators of the Korean aid program. To ECA officials it appeared that in effect Rhee was insisting: "Give me your checkbook and we'll handle our own reconstruction." To President Rhee it appeared that the Americans were scarcely aware that Korea belonged to the Koreans. He stressed Korean sovereignty; they stressed American oversight. John Lewis, in his *Reconstruction and Development in South Korea,* written from his viewpoint inside the ECA, concluded that the aid program was stumbling and misguided for five major reasons:

1) "Budgetary austerity in Washington has sufficiently stunted the present program to render it incapable of lifting the Korean economy to the measure of health which Korea's needs and our strategic interests both dictate."
2) Refusing to face the fact that building a ROK defense force would be enormously costly, the decision in Washington was to "submerge heavy military support" within the aid program, which meant diverting to military purposes funds that were vitally needed for reconstruction.
3) There was "inadequate joint planning" because "the makers of American policy, it seems fair to say, have not yet solved the problem of how to do business with the Rhee government." The major fault was the regarding of South Korea as a dependent client rather than as a truly sovereign ally.
4) There weren't enough trained and able Korean technicians to deal with the many specialized matters on which joint planning was essential.

5) "Simplest and perhaps most incapacitating of all . . . is the American loss of interest in Korea."

Both the ECA personnel and the ROK officials who worked with them felt frustrated because the needs were so much greater than the resources. Whatever they did appeared inadequate because so much more had to be left undone. The good feelings that were required for effective cooperative planning and working together were soured by cultural and linguistic distance between the Americans and the Koreans, by the dramatic disparity in their living conditions, and by the psychological differences between "helping" and "being helped." Some of the American experts who were brought in were overage or underskilled—men who took much better-paying jobs in Korea than they could get at home. Others were sincere idealists; their very idealism led them to expect unattainable results. Koreans with managerial titles worked with American "advisors" whose salaries were five to ten times greater than theirs. Resentments were heightened by the circumstance that at the end of the workday the Koreans went home to join their families in miserable living conditions while the Americans sought relief from their tensions and disappointments in nightclub entertainment and in the comfortable quarters they built for themselves—notably in the Walker Hill complex—resembling plush American resorts. Ludicrous misunderstandings were inevitable, such as the insistence by an American agricultural expert that his educational speeches to farmers had to be translated for them one word at a time, "to be sure the interpretation was accurate"; and the use of expensive earthmoving imported equipment to build a road high up on the ridges instead of, as a disapproving Korean co-worker complained, "down in the valleys where the people could use it."

President Rhee had earlier, in November 1951, issued a statement of principles and procedures that should govern reconstruction of the ruins. Basically, "to the largest extent practical, Korea should be reconstructed from Korean resources, by Korean labor, through Korean initiative." Then he added a schedule of priorities, calling for restoration of six hundred thousand homes that were destroyed, the reopening of coal and tungsten mines, development of hydro- and steam-generated electricity plants, restoration of damaged textile and rubber shoe plants, the establishment of new fertilizer, rayon, cement, and glass factories, of fish canneries, and of shipbuilding yards. Longer-range rehabilitation, he urged, should concentrate on the development of heavy industries and machine tool plants and on the restoration of "thousands of square blocks of wrecked buildings in our cities, including schools, government buildings, office buildings, new apartment houses and others that will take years to complete." The dredging of rivers and harbors, the start of irrigation, flood control, and farmland reclamation projects, and extensive reforestation were also on the "urgently needed" list. On the principle that those who provide the money should decide how it would be spent, the ECA-UNKRA administrators went ahead with their own plans of what to do and how to do it, with the emphasis upon immediate relief.

The shaky status from which Dr. Rhee sought to enforce his "Korea for Koreans" conviction is indicated by a comment by Walter Robertson, Assistant Secretary of State for Occupied Countries, in an impassioned discussion with one of Rhee's advisors as the Panmunjom Truce talks were nearing their conclusion: "The U.S. has put up with all it intends to from Rhee. If he wants to 'go it alone' that is his privilege; he will be absolutely alone, without a friend in the world, and with no military, economic, or political help of any kind, if that is what he wishes. But he has got to stop making these unreasonable demands." Robertson was referring to Rhee's objections to the truce, but the sentiment extended also to reconstruction differences. Along with the advantages of being a "client state," the Republic of Korea had also to accept the disadvantages.[44]

As a key part of its basic Asian policy, the United States sought to create a cordial working partnership between South Korea and Japan—one that would insure a protective flank for Japan on the peninsula, that would facilitate Japanese investments to rehabilitate South Korea, and that would develop South Korea as a major customer for Japanese products. Neither the Japanese nor the Koreans proved to be cooperative in this endeavor. When the Americans arranged a "peace-making" meeting in Tokyo between officials of the two countries in October 1951, the Korean delegate, Kim Yong-Shik, demanded an apology from Japan for its colonial seizure and rule of Korea—after which the meeting broke up angrily. At another U.S.-sponsored meeting in 1953, Kubota Kanichiro, the Japanese delegate, insisted that Koreans should be grateful for all the "improvements" made by Japan during its rule of Korea. His tone radiated sentiments stated earlier by a member of the Japanese Diet, that "we refuse to stand in silence watching . . . Koreans . . . swaggering about as if they were nationals of victorious nations. . . . it is most deplorable that those who lived under our law and order until the last moment of the surrender should suddenly alter their attitude to act like conquerors." The time for reconciliation had not yet come.

Neither had the time yet come for commencement of a dialogue between the divided segments of the peninsula, let alone for a start toward negotiations aiming toward peaceful relations and eventual reunification. In politics, President Rhee used police power to impose a constitutional change in 1952—election of the president would no longer be by the National Assembly but by all citizens over the age of eighteen. The living conditions of the people, after the destructiveness of the war, remained even worse than they had been at the conclusion of the Pacific War. Illiteracy remained to be overcome and the lack of managerial experience was restraining real economic recovery. The relations of the Republic of Korea with the United

States and its other U.N. allies were worsened by the surging disagreements between them. The conditions, North and South, were far from promising. But they did highlight the point that remains true throughout the course of modern Korean history—that the pursuit of sovereignty is the paramount aim of the Korean people.

17
The Testing of Democracy

The meaning of democracy is not clearcut, but there is general agreement that it is much more than merely desirable—that it is indeed sacrosanct. Just as "communistic" has been used as a term of condemnation to be applied to enemies and undesirables, so is "undemocratic." Part of the usefulness of the term is its lack of precision. Like "atheistic," and "uncultured," and "insensitive," and "stubborn," it is an emotionally loaded pejorative, just as "democratic" is a term of praise. All kinds of nations value it as a label. Communist dictatorships regularly have identified themselves as "people's democracies." In Indonesia Sukarno presided over a personalized rule that he called "guided democracy." Mao Tse-tung, winning his war to seize control over China, informed the Chinese people on 30 June 1949 that under his "democratic" government, "the right of reactionaries to voice their opinions must be abolished, and only the people are allowed to voice their opinions." Among the world powers that created modern democracy, Great Britain developed a system of centralism that unites the executive and legislative authority, with no written constitution to curb its powers. To strengthen still further its centralized rule, the prime minister is authorized to call for elections at any time (within a six-year time span) that is favorable to continuance of the majority party's control. In the United States the founders were sure democracy had to be curbed. They established an Electoral College to choose the President. Senators for the first hundred and fifty years were elected by state legislatures. The ballot was denied to all women and to the twenty percent of the population considered to be colored. Incumbents in Congress have advantages enabling them to win more than 90 percent of subsequent elections over their challengers. All of this is "democratic," at least verbally. True democratic values were added to the constitution as a "Bill of Rights" in the first ten amendments.

Around the globe, the peoples who most ardently and successfully practice democracy interpret its meaning in two distinctly different ways. One stresses *equality,* or "rule by the majority," which points toward surrender of some individual freedoms, to attain "the best for the most." The other stresses *liberty,* or the "right to live one's own life in one's own way," resulting in the inequalities and the contentiousness of free enterprise competition. In Korean history there was no precedent for either kind of democracy and no preparation for it. But both the Korean temperament and the cultural traditions of particularization and localism favored the "leave us alone" interpretation of democracy. Majority rule, to them, is just another form of autocracy. Why should "they" tell "us" what to do?

As the two Koreas, South and North, began painfully to emerge from the ruins of the war, the question was: What next? Would the welfare of the people be improved? Would there be an equality of justice? How about freedom from want, freedom from fear, freedom of speech, and freedom of religion and thought? The testing time had come. It was a test of the leadership but even more a testing of the society, of the culture and traditions, of the people. Had the time for democracy arrived?

In both parts of Korea, the new governments, their respective foreign sponsors, and their most virulent foreign and domestic critics all were agreed that the political systems and the societies were to be democratic—but according to their own differing definitions. The term had become a fetish. Like religious symbols its worth was unquestionable and its meaning transcended definition.

Nevertheless, definitions of one sort or another abound. For South Korea the standard was set high. Typical is the definition by which John Kie-Chiang Oh undertook to identify South Korea's shortcomings in his 1968 study *Korea: Democracy on Trial.* Democracy, he posited, is "a philosophy of socio-political organization and functions in which major public policies are decided on the majority principle and executed by public officials subject to popular control at periodic elections, conducted on the principle of political equality and under conditions of political freedom." Then he added quickly, "one cannot, without qualifications, equate democracy as defined here, with that of the Western world." In short, it was rather more idealistic than the most experienced and advanced peoples have as yet attained. For example, in the highly democratic United States such "public policies" as Franklin Roosevelt's abandonment of his 1932 pledge to balance the federal budget, Johnson's decision to intensify the Vietnam War, Truman's "doctrine" on Greece and Turkey, Reagan's invasion of Grenada, and Bush's entry with military force into first Panama and then the Middle East—all of these and many more important public policies were determined soley by executive fiat, nor were they "subject to popular control." The "principle of political equality" in countries around the world is a rhetorical phrase, not a reality. As Oh himself clearly indicated, abstract definitions of democracy are of little account except to use them to highlight faults and shortcomings in leaders or in policies and practices that are deemed undesirable. Defenders of such leaders, policies, and practices just as readily blame circumstances and conditions beyond the government's control. Nevertheless, Dr. Oh (and many other critics) have used an admittedly idealistic definition as a standard by which to judge. The two goals ambitiously set in 1948 by the Republic of Korea constitution were both impossibly high, far beyond attainment by any society. The first was "to establish a democratic system of government eliminating *evil social customs of all kinds.*" The second, equally sweeping, was "to afford *equal opportunities to every person* and to provide for the *fullest development of the capacity of each individual* in all the fields of political, economic, social and cultural life" [Emphasis added.].

The National Assembly, in confirming the constitution, took care to magnify its own powers. It not only gave itself the right to elect the president but provided also that by a mere fifty-four percent (two-thirds of a quorum, which consisted of two-thirds of the membership) it could override a presidential veto. It was barely restrained from adopting a parliamentary system that would make the presidency a ceremonial office, with executive power exercised by a prime minister who would be the creature of an Assembly majority. Even after this plan was defeated, to satisfy the Assembly's grasp for power, the executive office was to have an ambiguously subordinate prime minister who would administer the government and who was subject to confirmation by the Assembly. The president, under the plan finally adopted, not only nominated the prime minister but also could remove and supplant him, subject always and only to Assembly confirmation. What the prime minister could do was what the president allowed him to do. What made the president an unusually "strong" executive was his power to "issue orders having the effect of law . . . for the maintenance of public order and security." The necessity for such a provision was soon demonstrated by the Yosu-Sunchon uprising and by continuing guerrilla fighting by the Peoples Committees and the Army of Liberation.

As the history of Korea amply demonstrates, Koreans are aggressively individualistic and their society is rent by clannish and regional factionalism. In North Korea these tendencies have been stringently controlled. In the pluralistic society of the South, controversies, antagonisms, competition, and the clashing of personal ambitions have been the rule. In the first generation of independence, out of these diverse systems have emerged economic disaster and severe restrictions on human and civil rights in the North. In the South, sensational economic attainments have been called "the miracle of the Han," while the more narrowly defined political rights have lagged behind expectations. Every successive government has been harshly condemned as "corrupt" and "dictatorial" except one—and that one (not dictatorial but still corrupt) is universally adjudged a failure. How democracy fared during the administrations of Syngman Rhee and John Myun Chang illustrates its problems as a "developing" country.

The failure of John Myun Chang was that he stretched democracy too far and too fast. President Rhee, like his successors in the office, committed specific abuses of democracy and in general, did not extend it broadly enough. However, his administration always had majority support. He was and remained by far the most popular choice of all the Korean presidents.

Elections were sufficiently free so that throughout his presidency Rhee had to contend with opposition majorities or at least with strong minorities in the National Assembly. Moreover, even the anonymous author of the antagonistic *Korea's Syngman Rhee* (published in 1960 under the psuedonym Richard C. Allen) had reluctantly to admit that "the degree of press freedom in South Korea was somewhat remarkable." In addition to the domestic press freedom, which was adjudged by the Associated Press in its annual global reviews to be among the highest in the world, the Republic of Korea was also kept open to an in-pouring of resentful criticisms from the world's Communists—to whom President Rhee was "the puppet of American imperialism"—and also from the allied nations, which (after China's entry into the Korean war) were desperately eager to end the conflict and get out and afterwards set high standards for South Korea in order to excuse lapses in their efforts on its behalf.

The Korean press had much to legitimately complain about—including rising taxes, shortage of consumer goods, unemployment, a living standard among the lowest in the world, and both inefficiency and corruption in the bureaucracy. But even as the people read continuing denunciations of President Rhee's leadership in failing to improve these conditions, they persistently remained loyal to him personally and to the government of the Republic. As to what was being accomplished, the United Nations Commission, composed of delegates from Australia, Chile, Netherlands, Pakistan, the Philippines, Thailand, and Turkey, on 5 September 1951, while the war was taking its first favorable turn against the North Korean invaders, rendered to the U.N. Secretariat a report on its eleven-month study of South Korea's political conditions. The charge that had been given to this commission was to assess "the continuing development of representative government based on the freely expressed will of the people."

The report opened with a warning against expecting too much. "It is wrong to expect to find the institutions of Western democracy reproduced exactly in Korea. The Republic of Korea has the counterpart of many European and American political institutions, but they have been adapted and are still being developed to meet Korean traditions and history." Another warning was a reminder of the conditions under which the government had to operate.

> Before it was properly established, the young State was struck by war and devastation. Continuous emergency conditions have existed. Most of the country has been a battlefield at one time or another. . . . Twice the Government of the Republic had to evacuate its capital and five times the central administration had to be moved and re-established in a different place. Serious problems in administration and internal security had to be faced as they arose, without previous planning or experience. It is therefore not surprising that deficiencies exist today in the Korean government; that abuse of power has sometimes occurred; or that corruption and inefficiency can be found in some places. Such things should not be ignored. But

they must be seen in perspective. Moreover, signs of progress and remedy are clearly to be seen.

The substance of the report consisted of five "grounds for optimism":

> 1) "A sincere effort is being made. . . . Many Korean leaders are trying to raise standards of political conduct and administration."
>
> 2) "The Republic of Korea has stood up to the strains of war remarkably well. The government apparatus did not disintegrate, despite difficulties, confusion, and danger. As districts were liberated from enemy occupation, the civil administration of the Republic was quickly re-established."
>
> 3) "In many countries in wartime the role of the legislature diminishes in relation to the executive, but in the Republic of Korea the National Assembly, although inexperienced and sometimes lacking in a sense of responsibility, has remained an active force."
>
> 4) "Considerable public criticism of the Government is allowed, thus paving the way for correction and reform. Abuses are frequently exposed and denounced in the National Assembly and in the press."
>
> 5) "The Republic of Korea has placed no restrictions whatever upon the observations within the country by international bodies. . . . This willingness to open the Republic of Korea to the outside world, to seek international assistance, and to cooperate in the work of international bodies, is a sign of genuine desire to carry out the purposes and principles of the Charter of the United Nations to the best of the country's abilities."

The report concluded with the hopeful prognosis that Korea "would continue to develop the institutions of democracy." This was before there was any indication that the Chinese Communists would enter the war and, as the term "Korea" indicates, the Commission expected that the combined allied forces would surely win the war and reunite the country. When, instead, the Republic of Korea confronted a continuing need to give its highest priority to defense against a restored and militarily restrengthened North, the need for an executive branch enabled to exercise emergency authority was clear. Both the National Assembly and the general public supported it as a military necessity. But this did not allay the insistence of the Assembly upon its own powers, nor did it submerge the public's primary interest in improving its low living conditions. The United States premised its economic aid upon adoption by the Republic of severe measures to curb and reduce the ruinously high rate of inflation. This required both higher taxes and significant reductions in governmental services. The Assembly voted the required measures but, to avoid being blamed by its constituents, emphasized that it was the administration that demanded them. The public accepted the painful additional burdens and deprivations but could not be happy about them. President Rhee provided additional fuel for attacks upon him by forcing the Assembly to adopt constitutional amendments that enabled him to serve an unrestricted number of terms (thereby avoiding the "lame duck" weakness of limited tenure); by eliminating the ambiguous office of prime minister (thereby centering all executive authority in the presidency); and by granting to the people the right to recall Assemblymen from office by petition (thus keeping them answerable immediately to their constituents).

Attacking President Rhee had become a worldwide habit.[45] It was something the free world and the Communists agreed upon. Rhee was called authoritarian, uncooperative, and stubbornly insistent on having his own way. At the same time he also received praise for being "a true patriot" who was utterly sincere, and who held the government together under extremely adverse conditions.

During the twelve years of Rhee's tenure as president, the Republic of Korea, while recovering from the war, achieved increasing maturity in actualizing its independence. Rhee remained stubbornly insistent upon protecting and promoting vital Korean interests by eliminating the worst aspects of its role as a "client state." He succeeded in getting both needed approval and essential supplies and training for the creation of a strong defense force. In his dealings with the United States, with Japan, and with other nations around the world his "stubborn irrationalism" subjected him to much personal abuse but effectively made the point that even while Koreans were weak in wealth and in military strength they were unyielding in maintaining their national independence. By trading expropriated Japanese industrial and commercial properties to yangban landholders, not only was land reform achieved but also a new free enterprise system was commenced. The deeply implanted hierarchic nature of the society was considerably changed as the aristocratic yangban class was either replaced or converted into businessmen. The status of women and opportunities for their development were substantially advanced. None of these changes was possible without sharp opposition, bolstered by criticism that changes were induced too rapidly or too slowly, and with either too little discipline or too much governmental pressure. The police and judicial systems were modernized (with police training academies established nationally and in every province), amid charges, again, that too much or too little was being done. Gradually, and all too slowly, the bureaucracy was brought into greater efficiency, and cabinet ministries learned how to perform their functions.

One of the controversial aspects of Korean history during the years of its restored independence has been the conduct of the judicial system. Have the judges, the prosecutors, and the police been impartial and independent in protecting the basic rights of the citizens, or have they been instruments of oppression? In Old Korea the king was the source of law and what law meant was "what best serves the king." Law was equated with punishment and was, accordingly, to be dreaded and evaded. This tradition was strengthened during the colonial period, when "the rule of law" meant "rule by and for the Japanese." The police, prosecutors, and judges applied the law to enforce subjection to the state. Defense attorneys were derogated because they were in effect powerless and because defense against indictment was close to treason. Koreans made private agreements and scorned such legal documents as contracts. Promises made to relatives and members of the community were to be strictly kept and failure to do so resulted in "loss of face." What mattered was community sentiment, not law. The law was looked upon as *theirs* not *ours*. One of modern Korea's chief needs has been to develop an overall respect for law.

A democratic law-abiding society is one in which the people are basically content with their lot and feel the advantages of maintaining and stabilizing the status quo. Under a dictatorship, such as that of North Korea, laws are obeyed out of fear. In South Korea protests and dissatisfaction have been rife. There has been freedom enough to allow the people to complain that there was not even more freedom. The laws have not been equally enforced nor have punishments been equally administered. This is not unusual. Even in the United States, for example, blacks and the poor suffer more police harassment and receive harsher judicial sentences than do the comfortably rich and well-educated. Corruption among officials and successful businessmen has not been easily contained, as is true, also, in far more "advanced" nations. As always happens in developing societies, wants and expectations rise more rapidly than they can be satisfied. Balanced advancement is impossible, and the imbalances cause distress and resentment.

In South Korea, this was felt especially sensitively during the 1950s, when rapid growth in education did not lead to better employment. Achievements in education were notable. But their good effects were countered by failure to advance economic opportunities. This disparity was a crucial factor in enhancing public distrust of government. As youths from the farm villages were educated, they looked in vain for opportunities to utilize their exhanced abilities.

The typically Korean hunger for higher and fuller education was met as well as circumstances permitted. In 1954 contracts were signed with the University of Minnesota and with Tennessee's Peabody College providing for exchange of professors with Korean universities and for provision of laboratories and libraries needed for medical, law, engineering, and other professional programs. In 1955 the Ministry of Education cleared 1,179 men and 992 women for study abroad. In 1956, thirty-six degree-granting colleges and universities and thirteen junior colleges were enrolling some twenty-nine thousand male and four thousand female students. Since many of the higher education buildings had been destroyed or severely damaged during the war, many of the classes and laboratories were housed in half-ruined factories and warehouses, while new campus buildings were being erected. Libraries had suffered especially during the war, for the Communists burned many of the English-language books and periodicals. To help in the restoration of library resources, the Ministry of Education in 1956 imported a total of 1,123,726 volumes. It also revised all textbooks and translated them into the hangul alphabet.

President Rhee, sensitive to the urgent need for knowledgeable personnel, was especially interested in the development of higher education. By 1960, South Korea had seventy-three degree-granting collegiate institutions, with an enrollment of some eighty thousand students. Most significantly, education no longer was characterized by "thought control." Ironically, as the students learned more and more about democracy, many of them became activist rebels against the government. Fuelled by natural youthful enthusiasm for justice and brotherhood, some became socialistic. A few came to believe that unification must be the primary goal even if it meant subordination to the Communist North. A general feeling among them was frustration from the lack of economic opportunities. Students drawn to college from rice paddies cannot, after they complete their studies, be sent back to rice paddy labor. The discontent became both sharper and more widespread. Education alone was not enough. To give it social value it had to be accompanied by displacement of deeply implanted social traditions of inequality. And there had to be suitable jobs for graduates.

New visions were stirring much more widely than new opportunities. Especially among the youth, demands for better times were insistent. The young had no memories of either monarchical Korea or even of the colonial period. They did have very vivid and very painful memories of the war. Their feelings were stirred by the Americans in their midst, the soldiers and the aid workers, all of whom complained bitingly of the deprivations of their life in Korea and talked freely of how much better everything was back home in America. American motion pictures and radio programs pictured what prosperity and democratic equality and freedom from pressures could mean. Korean youth felt many pressures. Old Korea's isolationism was completely broken; but static traditionalism was yielding ground only grudgingly. Young parents who wanted to rear their children in modern ways had to take them for frequent visits to the homes of grandparents, where they all were required by custom to kneel down and touch their foreheads to the floor as signs of respect for the old. The whole social as well as the political structure was in ferment, caught between the old and the new.

Utopian literature emerged and became popular. Kim Cha-rim, who was born in 1926 and who became the first woman professional playwright in South Korea, producing her first play in 1959, was a typical literary idealist. Born in Pyongyang, in an upper-middle-class family, she was the third daughter (not really wanted) in a family of nine children. Her father was a university professor, Confucian and conservative. Her mother was Christian and was drawn to Westernized ideas. Her mother wanted to be a writer but was kept sternly at home, away from literary circles, while her husband kept telling her that "a woman's duty is to marry and have children." Cha-rim suffered from the tension in the home between these two conflicting life philosophies. She grew up tough and rebellious. "A slavish life based on docility and submission to men is not a woman's virtue," she wrote. In 1952, at the age of twenty-six, she married a poet (Yang Myong-Mun) at the cost of stormy opposition from her father. The major theme of her twenty plays is that "there are women who are not satisfied with either the past or the present, and thus struggle to find a way out of both." Ewha University, growing to be the largest women's university in the world, exemplified the generational and the male-female struggles. Its students developed broader intellectual horizons and learned much of modern ways, for which they yearned. But if they chose the normal way of matrimony, they found rejection of their ideals not only from their parents but also from the eligible young men, most of whom wanted old-style wives.

Kim Cha-rim was by no means sure that "modernity" is in all ways worth its very real costs. The challenge, she felt, is to make it better.

Along with the virtual elimination of illiteracy and the rapid spread of education, attendance at theatres for both plays and films multiplied. So did reading, especially of novels and poetry. Presently, in South Korea, there are more than twelve hundred actively productive poets. During the economically depressed 1950s their number was rapidly growing. A volume of poetry, often as collected works of a poet or of selections from a particular genre or school of poetry, is currently published on an average of one every day. Such popularity has been accompanied, at times, by profitability. *Seeing You in a Wild Flower* sold half a million copies; *Standing on Your Own Feet* more than a million. Being both talented and (most of them) poor, the poets tended to be alienated from society and hence were highly critical of its abuses and shortcomings. This no doubt added to their popularity, especially among college students and the disadvantaged workers.

The young men, meanwhile, especially those in universities, were reading the utopian literature and the brotherhood promises of Marx and Tolstoi and Gandhi. They were looking futilely for the jobs for which their university study prepared them, seething with the mixed emotions of disappointment and anger. The one obvious target where their wrath could be directed was the government, which clearly was not satisfying their needs and desires. Naturally, they were much more keenly aware of the government's failings than of its efforts and accomplishments.

President Rhee and the National Assembly, as well as the general public, recognized the urgent need for an educational system that would serve both the civic need for political democracy and the personal need for productive skills. In 1954 a six-year plan was instituted to insure educational facilities for 99 percent of six-year old children and for 96 percent of those aged 6–11. The plan succeeded so well that by 1956 more than 91 percent of all children aged 6–11 were enrolled in elementary schools. Unfortunately, the quality of the schooling was restricted by lack of funds. The modest aim of the Ministry of Education was to provide one teacher for every sixty students. But lack of both finances and teachers resulted in average class size of seventy-five in Seoul, seventy in other cities, and sixty-two to sixty-five in smaller towns and rural districts. The total annual cost of about five billion Won was divided fifty-fifty between the national and local budgets. Special provision was made from the national budget for children of refugees and other homeless families. Most families paid the local costs themselves, often at very heavy sacrifice. Emphasis was given to establishing schools in rural areas and to providing schools for girls. By 1956, 588 middle schools with 765 classes were in operation, in addition to 388 private (mostly Christian) missionary schools. Public high schools numbered 148, with 1,524 classes, along with 63 private high schools with 144 classes.

Politics was also maturing. For the May 1956 presidential election the Democratic Party nominated Shin Icky to oppose Rhee, with John Myung Chang named its vice-presidential candidate to oppose the Liberal party's nomination of Lee Ki-pyung. The Democratic candidates waged a vigorous campaign, charging the administration with failure to meet the needs of the people, under the slogan, "We can't make a living; so let's change!" However, Shin Icky died of heart failure after making an impassioned speech to a crowd of 300,000 in Seoul on 5 May, just ten days before the election. Cho Bong-Am, making another try for the presidency, received more than two million votes and another two million were "invalid" ballots cast for Shin Icky. President Rhee was re-elected with a majority of 56 percent of the votes. By a slim margin, amidst charges of ballot-rigging, Lee Ki-pyung lost the vice-presidency to John Myun Chang. For the Assembly, the Democrats won 47 seats, the Liberals 131. Democracy, despite the limitations imposed on it, appeared to be working. The diversity of results supported the U.N. Commission's conclusion that the elections in general represented the people's will.

This election, however, was followed by a sharp decline in Rhee's effectivenss. His declared program of *Yilmin Chuyi,* the principle of equality of all the people—rich and poor, yangban and commoner, men and women, young and old—obviously did not characterize the society. Progress toward it was too slow. Meanwhile, his long tenure in the presidency had resulted in an entrenched bureaucracy of officials who were unwilling to risk losing their privileged prerogatives. Moreover, the Democratic slogan—"We can't make a living so let's change"—was relevant. The accomplishments of the new Republic were submerged by the deep depression of the economy, for which there seemed no end in sight.

The collapse of the First Republic gathered force not only from the continuing economic distress but also from political circumstances that crystalized in the seizure of the National Assembly on Christmas Eve, 1958, by the Liberal Party majority members. After the Democratic minority conducted a week-long sit-down strike in the Assembly to prevent action on pending bills designed to increase the power of the executive branch, three hundred Assembly Guards cleared the dissenters from the chamber. Within minutes the Liberal Party members, remaining in the hall, passed twenty-two bills defining provisions of a new National Security Law, which, in effect, designated dissent from foreign policies as treason, punishable by lengthy imprisonment or death. The bills contained many provisions that gave the administration latitude to prosecute almost any kind of opposition, culminating with a threat of five years of penal servitude for anyone who "benefitted by disturbing the people's minds by openly pointing out or spreading false facts." What facts were "false" was for the government to decide. With these bills, the effort to democratize the society virtually came to a halt.

The pseudonymous Allen's *Korea's Syngman Rhee* blamed the breakdown of democracy on "Rhee's two great shortcomings, his egotism and the inflexibility which characterized his old age." Dr. Oh's *Democracy on Trial* concluded that the partial suspension of democracy occurred because

> it was no longer his [Rhee's] wishes alone that counted in Korean politics. The numerous hangers-on who rode the administration gravy train no longer shared Rhee's assumption that he remained first in the hearts of the gullible *[sic]* portion of his countrymen. Desperately they sought for a means to insure their future for four more years or longer by securing Rhee's re-election and the election of a Liberal Vice-President. Obviously, Rhee was no longer using the people around him as much as these people were using him.

The presidential election of 1960 was a test that democracy failed. With President Rhee in his eighty-fifth year, and with no doubt that he would be re-elected, the office that mattered most was the vice-presidency. With determination to insure that his policies concerning military and foreign policy affairs would continue, President Rhee insisted on nomination to that office of his longtime friend and loyal supporter, Lee Ki-pyung. Lee had served as Rhee's principal secretary, the mayor of Seoul, minister of defense, and prime minister. He was also chairman of the Liberal Party, which he controlled as his personal fief. John Myun Chang, serving as vice-president, was renominated by the Democratic Party. To run against Rhee, the Democrats chose Chough Pyung-Ok. Chough was found to have cancer and was rushed to Walter Reed Hospital, where he died prior to the 15 March election date. The Democrats did not pick a successor nominee. The only issue of consequence in the campaign was which of the two vice-presidential nominees would be elected. Lee Ki-pyung used all the powers of the incumbent administration to register voters, to control the content of broadcasts by the Korean National Broadcast system, and to intimidate voters on election day by stationing police at polling places. Then, adding corruption and stupidity to these advantages of incumbency, Lee's agents seized ballot boxes and grossly miscounted the votes. President Rhee received more than 92 percent of the presidential votes. Lee Ki-pyung claimed 8,221,000 votes, with only 1,844,000 allotted to John Myun Chang. No further proof of fradulent counting was needed.

Announcement of this result was greeted with disbelief and outrage. On

18 April three thousand students, led by those from Korea University (which had been founded as Posung College by Kim Sung-su, founder also of the Democratic Party) surged into the streets, demanding justice. Demonstration turned into riots. Newspapers denounced "police brutality" in dealing with the mobs. A hundred thugs, believed to be hired by the Liberal Party, clubbed and beat students. President Rhee proclaimed martial law and soldiers were brought into Seoul. Then the United States intervened to prevent the complete subversion of democracy.

The State Department spokesman issued a public statement reading: "the Korean government should, in its own best interest and in order to restore public confidence, take necessary and effective action aimed at protecting democratic rights of freedom of speech, of assembly and of the press, as well as preserving the secrecy of the ballot and preventing unfair discrimination against political opponents of a party in power." On the same day that this statement was released, 19 April, some one hundred thousand demonstrators (students and townspeople) surged beyond the Capitol and up the street leading to the presidential office and residence building, Kyung Mu Dai. They broke through two police barricades and when the police tried to stop them with tear gas, they continued on, declaring that they only intended to present a petition to President Rhee. Then the police fired into the crowd. On that day, throughout the city, 125 people were killed and over one thousand were wounded. In other demonstrations, in Masan, Kwangju, Taejon and Pusan, a total (including police) of 183 died and 6,259 suffered wounds. In the evening of 19 April U.S. Ambassador Walter P. McConnaughy went to Kyung Mu Dai to caution President Rhee not to use force. The Korean Army was under American command. Lt. General Song Yo-chan, commanding the martial law troops, informed President Rhee that he would not sanction the shooting of demonstrators. In an effort to save the situation, the cabinet resigned and Lee Ki-pyung also resigned the vice-presidency. President Rhee declared, on 24 April his willingness to hold new elections for both the vice-presidency and the presidency. Two days later the National Assembly demanded Rhee's resignation and he responded that he would resign "if the people desire." On the night of 28 April, Lee Ki-pyung, his wife Maria Park and their two sons, the elder having been adopted by President and Mrs. Rhee, died apparently in a suicide pact, all shot by the older son.

Dr. Rhee had already resigned, on 27 April. He and his wife, Francesca, an Austrian whom he met in Geneva in 1933 and married in 1934, rode to their private home through a cheering throng of a million people who lined the roadway to express their farewell to the man still honored as a lifelong patriot. Dr. and Mrs. Rhee, under arrangements with the United States government, on 15 May flew to Honolulu, taking only a few suitcases of clothes.[46] In Honolulu they were invited by a wealthy Korean, Wilbur Choi, to live in his beachfront cottage. Dr. Rhee lived on until July 1965, supported by contributions by the Hawaiian Koreans. His widow moved back to their home in Seoul, where she was granted a government annuity. Dr. Rhee was buried in a central position of honor in the Korean National Cemetry.

The end of the First Republic, as the tenure of President Rhee came to be known, has been variously interpreted. To some Korean historians, it was "the overthrow of a dictatorial regime." To others, "it appeared that the majority of the students might have been quite satisfied with some nullification of the result of the rigged elections and with fair and clean re-elections." The protests were virtually spontaneous, without leaders, without any organization, and without a specified goal. They were "against" poverty, and bureaucratic corruption, and increasing restriction of free speech. What they were "for" was uncertain. Two years later, a careful study of student opinions in Seoul found that 86 percent of them considered Western democracy unsuited to Korea under existing conditions. What was suitable they did not say.

A major factor in the overturn of the government was foreign influence. The United States officials "had had quite enough of Syngman Rhee." They used their control of the military to insure that he could not stay in office through the use of force if he had chosen to do so. The United Nations Commission for the Unification and Rehabilitation of Korea, in a report rendered to the U.N. on 15 September interpreted the events as "the further growth and spread of an active concern on the part of the Korean people for democratic methods and the safeguard of civil liberties." In any event, what ensued for Korea was not better, but worse.

Arrangements for the Second Republic were made hurriedly. By 15 June a new constitution was drafted and inaugurated by a vote of 208 to 3 in the National Assembly. Its most important provision was adoption of the cabinet system of government. The presidency was made a merely ceremonial office, with executive power vested in a prime minister who was subject to legislative control. The prime minister was to preside over a State Council (the cabinet) which would make executive decisions collectively. Both the prime minister and at least half of the State Council members were to be elected by the lower chamber, the House of Representatives, and were to be members of the Assembly. A Central Election Committee was established to oversee the conduct of fair elections, with nine members—three Supreme Court judges and six members recommended by political parties. This provision caused problems, for a major effect of the political turnover was the proliferation of political parties. The Liberal Party disintegrated. The Democratic Party broke asunder into an Old Faction and a New Faction. Cho Bong-Am's Progressive Party re-emerged as the Popular Socialist Party. Kim Ku's Independence Party revived. Various small splinter parties emerged. As before, many candidates ran as independents.

Politics was in confusion. President Rhee's chief supporters and closest associates were discredited. Pyun Young-tae died; but Kim Young-shik, Ben

Limb, and Han Pyo-Wook all re-emerged later as political mentors of newly rising administrators in the bureaucracy. The most prominent in the post-Rhee leadership were Yun Po-sun, John Myun Chang, and Huh Chung. Yun was a strong-minded scion of a wealthy yangban family, with a curious mix of old and new ideas. He had earned a Ph.D. in political philosophy through rigorous study at the University of Edinburgh. He lived in a Victorian mansion surrounded by walled-in gardens, in central Seoul, in an atmosphere of aristocratic removal from public controversies. He headed the Democratic Party after Kim Sung-soo's death, but his principal political experience was service as mayor of Seoul. He was a gentle intellectual, quiet in manner but fiercely loyal to Korean traditions and dedicated to Korean sovereign independence. Huh Chung was representative of the middle class, formerly a preacher, whose tall angular frame and gentle manners reflected his lack of personal ambition and his cooperative approach to problem solving. He, too, had served as mayor of Seoul and held successively two cabinet positions—first as Minister of Transportation, then as Minister of Social Services—during the Rhee presidency.

During the April turmoil, following the 1960 March election, John Myun Chang resigned as vice-president, Huh accepted the office of Foreign Minister, with the approval of the National Assembly, which made him the temporary caretaker president while new elections were being organized. John Myun Chang, equally middle-class, had served during the latter years of colonialism as Superintendent of a Catholic Middle School. He was, like Huh, a quiet man, conservative in ideas and in manner, with a strong sense of responsibility and a belief in consensus rather than personal leadership. Dr. Rhee appointed him to head the delegation to the Paris meeting of the United Nations in 1948, where the status of the Republic of Korea was determined. Because of Chang's conciliatory temperament, his friendship with John Muccio, the first U.S. Ambassador to Korea, and his reputation for responsible personal and official conduct, President Rhee also named him as ROK's initial Ambassador to the U.S. That is when conflict between the two commenced, for Chang was keenly sensitive to Korea's need for American aid, while Rhee was restive under conditions of Korean subordination to its indispensable ally.

The stringent economic conditions resulted in embarrassing financial restraints. Except at the ambassadorial level, Korea's foreign service personnel were not allowed funds for having their families abroad with them. The kind of restrictions which Chang (and all of them in the foreign service) endured is indicated in an experience that he relayed to President Rhee to support his need for an enlarged budget. He did not yet have an automobile. When he left the Chinese Embassy, during a heavy rainstorm, he had to stand out at the curb for half an hour waiting for a taxicab, while the Chinese could peer out the windows at the spectacle of the rain-drenched Korean Ambassador. This incident clearly illustrates two facts that it is well to understand: first, that when the Republic of Korea undertook responsibility to restore the sovereignty of Korea, the country was still what Yuan Shih-kai, a generation earlier, bluntly called it to King Kojong, "the poorest of nations"; and second, that John Myun Chang, who was to play crucial roles in 1952 and in 1961, had neither ingenuity nor common sense. He so easily could have had a taxi summoned before he left the embassy.[47] Dr. Rhee recalled him, much against Chang's will, to serve during the constitutional struggle of 1952 as prime minister, making Chang the storm center of the bitter controversy. When in 1956 Chang defeated President Rhee's personal choice of Lee Ki-pyung for the vice-presidency, the split between them became decisive. During the next four years, they never met together, had no personal relations, and seldom spoke to one another. Political bitterness in Korea was not the exception but the rule. It is a problem that has proved difficult to transcend. Partisan controversies, often entailing personal animosities, remained fully as contentious after Rhee's presidency as they had been before and during it.

In the election, held on 29 July 1960 in stormy weather, 82.6 percent of eligible voters went to the polls, the lowest percentage for any of the Republic's elections. The Democrats won control of the two houses of the National Assembly, with 175 seats of the 233 in the House of Representatives and with a majority of the 58 members in the House of Councillors. The next largest number consisted of "independents," with a handful of members representing other parties and splinter groups. Yun Po-sun, of the Old Faction Democrats, was elected President and named one of his associates, Kim To-yon, to the executive post of prime minister. This nomination was rejected by the narrow margin of three votes, after which Yun nominated John Myun Chang, from the New Faction. Chang was elected, but only by the same margin of three votes. Thereupon, seventy members of the Old Faction, led by Kim To-yon, resigned from the Democratic Party to join with independents in forming a substantial opposition. Prime Minister Chang's first cabinet choices were rejected and it was not until 12 September that he could put together an acceptable coalition cabinet, comprised of seven New Faction members, five from the Old Faction, and two independents. By 19 October Premier Chang managed to coalesce a bare majority of 118 members of the House of Representatives who were willing to offer him general support. During his nine-month term in office, Chang had to change his cabinet membership three times—in contrast to the twenty-two-month average tenure of cabinet members during Rhee's presidency. Instability had proceeded from being a nuisance to become the rule.

Prime Minister Chang commenced his tenure by stating the right aims—to restore full democratic freedom and to develop the economy. Since the multiple ills of the Republic had been all charged to President Rhee, the people expected not only a full panoply of civil rights but also a notable improvement in their living conditions. Instead, what they got was uncertainty and confusion. In addition to the instability and contentiousness of the political parties, the Chang government had to contend with an unleashed and invigorated public opinion, that manifested itself not only with complaints in the press and in all manner of personal resentments but also in some two thousand demonstrations, with over nine thousand participants, during the brief Chang regime. Students invaded the chamber of the House of Representatives, seized the rostrum, and demanded stiffer punishments for officials of the Rhee period, reparation for individuals killed or wounded in the April uprising, prohibition of "police brutality," and the resignation of Assemblymen who dissented from these demands. In response, the Assembly hastened to adopt another constitutional amendment, giving the government power to suspend citizenship and impose severe penalties on any and all persons who had "committed grave and undemocratic acts" and who had "accumulated properties by unlawful means" prior to the April events. Thereby the National Assembly granted to itself far-reaching powers to punish those whom its majority deemed "traitors to democracy." Police began rearresting many who had been charged and released, and court trials in process were redirected under the retroactive laws. On 31 December a law was enacted to restrict "the civil rights of those who committed anti-democratic acts." Incumbents in nine categories of "special positions" during the First Republic were deemed automatically guilty, without need for trial.

Political reactionism easily merged into lawlessness. When one thousand five hundred students, in mid-November, attacked and ransacked the home of the president of Yonsei University—because he had refused to fire professors who had remained loyal to President Rhee—the police, who had been intimidated and disheartened, stood by, making no effort to restrain them. Calling themselves the "Fourth Branch of the Government," delegations of students regularly demanded, and received, meetings with Prime Minister Chang to submit new demands. "Freedom" became a label for all manner of abuses. Newspapers and periodicals increased from around 600 to nearly 1,600 and employed some 160,000 reporters—many of whom supported themselves by blackmail, threatening to publish stories that would bring public wrath upon their victims. Economic conditions, instead of improving, got worse. Extortionate interest rates as high as 80 percent were charged to farmers for their necessary spring loans. The unemployment rate increased. All government services were threatened before Prime Minister Chang barely managed to win Assembly acceptance of the national budget. The political cynicism that had come to infect the public resulted in a decline to 38 percent participation in 29 December elections for the mayor of Seoul and the governors of the nine provinces.

Anti-Americanism and pro-Communism of rebellious students became rampant. Student rallies and demonstrations demanded reunification with the North, on the naive theory that this could be accomplished through meetings of students from the South and the North in the Armistice building in Panmunjom. Money from Korean Communists resident in Japan poured in to support and enlarge demonstrations. Slogans from Pyongyang's radio were shouted and used as themes for newspaper articles and speeches. Prime Minister Chang answered his critics by saying that all of this proved that Koreans now "enjoyed all the rights and freedom guaranteed by the Constitution." Democracy had degenerated into paralysis and anarchy. Ironically, the 1956 Democratic slogan used against President Rhee became even more appropriate as a denunciation of his successor: "We can't make a living; so let's change." Democracy had failed its test. Military government came quickly to take its place.

18
The Military Takes Over

At 3:30 a.m. on 16 May 1961, while the people of Korea slept, the spearhead of a small force of some 1,600 rebel troops started across the single Han River bridge that served the traffic of Seoul. A quickly alerted force of fifty security guards tried futilely to turn them back. Several were wounded; these were the only casualties in a coup that launched a new era in modern Korean history. Popular democracy was submerged and military government replaced it. Since that date, South Korea's heads of state have been generals.[48]

"The key to the unexpectedly easy success of the military coup d'état," wrote Kim Se-jin, in *The Politics of Military Revolution in Korea,* "lies not so much in the efficiency with which the coup was executed as in the widespread apathy of the populace." This judgment represents two widely-held errors. The Korean people were indeed ready for a change. But their mood was not apathy but anxiety. Moreover, the painlessly easy success of the coup resulted from the carefulness with which it was planned and the personal abilities of the men who led it.

It is axiomatic that when a governing system fails, leaving a power vacuum, another takes its place. This is the easy explanation of what happened in Korea as the incapacity of the Second Republic became unmistakably evident. The confused civilian authorities were replaced by purposive men in uniform. There was virtually no resistance, no struggle, as the transformation took place. Failure has few friends. A nationwide feeling of futility demanded a reaching out, somehow, for a new promise, however ambiguous or uncertain the new prospect might be.

The circumstances that brought about the downfall of both the Syngman Rhee and the John Myun Chang administrations were twofold—political and economic. Both failures were more circumstantial than personal. Democracy is a complex of both attitudes and procedures that involves cultural changes of the whole society; this process requires time as well as energetic and forward-looking leadership. Meanwhile, the barriers to economic improvements—especially the unnatural division of the nation, the ruinous war, and the influx of refugees—could not be surmounted until after the fundamental welfare needs of the population were cared for, and educational growth eliminated the widespread illiteracy and provided a pool of individuals trained in managerial skills. Prior chapters have presented other factors that prevented quick success, either politically or economically. Among the most serious problems were clannish cliquism, competitive individualism, a defensive disrespect for law and for governmental controls, and the absence of both guiding traditions and experience in economic undertakings and in democratic political participation.

Especially during the Second Republic, societal pluralism failed from an excess of diversity and from lack of agreement on rules by which competition among special interests could be controlled. Unbridled rivalry and unrestrained contention became endemic. Politics deteriorated into unregulated struggles for power. The shattered economy sank even lower. During the nine months of the Chang administration, the scant factory productivity declined by another twelve percent; inflation and unemployment (the two economic incompatibles) both sharply increased. Farmers in need of borrowing money for their spring planting were unable to get loans from the government banks and were gouged by loan sharks. The slow and gradual improvement in living standards attained after the war that raised the per capita annual income from less than $100 to more than $300 (measured in U.S. currency) was jettisoned.

Competitive political parties, given reasonable freedom to advocate their policies, and with freedom of choice by the people to pick between them, offer the only means by which the general public can exercise political power. During the first fifteen years after liberation from colonialism, both these freedoms were, in varying degrees, available in South Korea. But the culture had not prepared the people for the operation of principled political parties. Factionalism, based on both regional and clan cohesiveness, was too deeply implanted. Special interests competing with one another are always the lifeblood of politics: but in Korean experience the special interests that mattered were expressive of localized grievances and of loyalty to extended clan and family groupings. The Democratic and Liberal parties were more factional than partisan, for they were more representative of personalities than of principles. When the personal appeal of first Syngman Rhee and then of John Myun Chang dissolved, the chance for democratic political reforms had to be postponed.

Intellectuals well understood that democracy had to be improved, and they knew what had to be done—elimination of the excesses of pluralistic competitiveness, the ending of factionalism, and the regulation of self-centered ambitions of individuals, clans, and regions. But reality is not so simplistic. These kinds of reforms required transformation of the whole society. This had to be a gradual developmental process, needing time measured in decades or even in generations rather than in weeks or months or years. Meanwhile, the necessitous public was more concerned with its very pressing material needs than with methods of goverment.

Such feelings as these, animating the whole society from the top to the bottom, amounted to anything but apathy. Far from it: they constituted an urgent demand for change. The two most obvious and urgent needs were for social orderliness and for improvement of the economy. Neither the established government nor the international aid programs had accomplished either goal. Little faith remained that they would or could. These were the circumstances that made possible the military coup.

The rise of the military in South Korea started from a weak foundation and developed slowly. Under the monarchy the army had not been politically important. During the colonial period there were no Korean armed services. The American Military Government, during its three-year rule, maintained a strict policy of prohibiting the maintenance of military force beyond the requirements of domestic police functions. A National Defense Constabulary was established by AMG decree number 86 on 15 June 1946. It was not until 16 December 1948, after the General Assembly of the United Nations recognized the legitimacy of the Republic of Korea, that this Constabulary was reconstituted as the ROK Army. Even after that, severe fiscal limitations and diplomatic restrictions upon training and supplies restrained the armed services to mere constabulary capacity.

President Rhee, after his inauguration in 1948, gave emphasis to building the strength of the armed services. But what could be accomplished was greatly limited by the lack of resources of the new government, by the welfare needs of the population, and by the refusal of the United States to support or to allow the development of any military force that might threaten or even worry the North. Even so, the number of men in service was promptly increased from twenty thousand up to fifty thousand. At best, however, they constituted only a shadow army. When the Navy was created from the Coast Guard on 5 September 1948, it numbered only two thousand men. The Air Force, with only a few training planes, was nonfunctional.

Senior officers were appointed by President Rhee, who had virtually no reservoir from which to draw. Some few officers proved to be surprisingly proficient in handling their responsibilities. Notable among them was the new Defense Minister, Shin Sung Mo, whose previous experience was limited to serving as captain of a small British coastal trading vessel. Sohn Won Il, named as Admiral of the infant fleet, was trained only in handling small boats; nevertheless, he excelled in organizing an assortment of patrol vessels that guarded the coasts against Communist infiltration. General Chung Il Kwon, a four-star general at the age of thirty-three, earned admiration for his command of the proudly named Capitol Division and served with distinction as Chief of Staff of the Armed Services. Major General Choi Tok-shin also performed effectively as Assistant Chief of Staff for Planning. The army was organized only on the brigade level and had very little training in field maneuvers. Even so, during the war it won distinction in such crucial battles as Old Baldy, Sniper Ridge, White Horse Hill, Triangle Hill, Capital Hill, and Heartbreak Ridge.

After the entrances of the Chinese into the war, as the battle front rapidly collapsed southward, President Rhee hastily formed the National Defense Corps. It consisted of draftees who had virtually no training and who were so ill-supplied that they lacked even sufficient food and straw footwear. During the extreme cold of January and February, while enduring forced marches, uncounted numbers of them died from malnutrition and cold. A presidential investigation revealed that the top command had embezzled funds that were allocated for supply of the troops. After a quick court-martial trial, five of the top generals were executed.

Despite all the handicaps, organizational reforms pushed by both President Rhee and U.S. General James A. Van Fleet resulted in a tremendous buildup that made the ROK army effective as well as the second largest of the anti-Communist forces in the world. It won the commendation of General Van Fleet as "the largest, most loyal, most modern . . . of any Asian nation." By 1958 the ROK Army reached its peak, with 660,000 personnel organized into two field armies, four corps, and twenty divisions. In addition, there were ten more reserve divisions. This enlarged force was partially supplied by grants of over $400 million annually from the United States. Well-staffed Army, Navy, Air Force, and Coast Guard academies were established, with curricular programs similar to those in the United States.

Impressive as these armed services became, their status was ambiguous. They remained under the overall command of the United States and were also dependent on American supplies. Neither were they entirely loyal to one another. The cliquishness of the society was fully matched in the services, especially by the officers. Some of them in high ranks had served in the Japanese army, some in China's Kuomintang, some with guerrilla units in China or in Manchuria. Younger officers who were graduates of the military academies won promotions that placed them above or equal in rank to much older and more battle-experienced officers. Some had received special training in military centers in the United States. Some had liaison duties on American staffs. These latter two groups were by far more proficient in English than were the other groups; they tended to hobnob with American officers during off-duty leave, adopt American behaviors, and enjoy American-style entertainments. These various groupings were divided from one another by jealousies and by resentments. In addition, there were political-minded officers who had close association with civilian leaders and were not immune to the political rivalries. Similar kinds of divisiveness exist also in other national armies. But the newness of the Korean services, their lack of deeply rooted military traditions, and their unnatural dependence on the United States helped to make the divisiveness sensitively felt. What it added up to was a diminution of the trust and comaraderie that creates mutual bonds.

Despite these unfavorable factors, by the end of the decade the armed services had become a strongly influential force in South Korea. Unquestionably they were loyal to the people, but not equally so to the government.

After the Korean War ended, the threat of renewed invasion became less the focus of military concern than the cliquishness, inequalities, and abuses of power within the military, the government, and the society. In 1960, with the concurrence of the American command, the generals in effect told the president of the Republic: "You must go." During the disruptive nine months of the Second Republic, the officer corps, along with the public, realized that the unleashed anarchic democracy that was unable to fulfill its responsibilities also must go.

What happened was distinctly a revolution from the top. It ended not only the John Myun Chang administration but also in effect the subjection of the armed services to the United States. Not less, it was also a blow against the cliquishness that was seriously impairing military effectiveness. All of this was carefully and systematically planned.

Preparation for the coup extended over a full year. It was fueled by widespread dissatisfaction of the military with the misconduct and ineffectiveness of the civil government. But the actual planning group was very small. Major General Park Chung Hee was the authoritative center. He remained obscurely in the background, so completely that his actual leadership was known only to a few. The planning for the coup was carried out by Park's nephew-by-marriage, Lt. Colonel Kim Jong-pil, with the assistance of ten more lieutenant colonels, all of whom were longtime associates as 1949 graduates of the eighth class of the Korean Military Academy. Both Colonel Kim and General Park were primarily "desk men." Both taught in elementary schools before enlisting in the Army. Both had the depth of their military experience in intelligence service, serving in counterespionage, and in headquarters administration. And both were devout believers in strict discipline, along with their conviction that the mission of the armed forces was to protect South Korea not only from external attack but also from internal abuses. In the armed services many of the generals lived in opulent style, some from their embezzlement of budgeted funds, while the privates and junior officers survived at a bare subsistence level—and while back home their families, deprived of their earning power, suffered even more. The colonels and lieutenant colonels were key figures in the services as the critical link between the upper and lower echelons. They performed most of the work of the top command and were also well aware of the hardships of the lower levels. They were also keenly aware of the top-level fraud and mismanagement in the allocation of funds. These factors not only motivated the coup but also expedited its planning.

During the planning period, Major General Park was in Pusan, in charge of logistics, and afterwards was shifted to Seoul. Two other Major Generals, Yi Chu-il, Chief of Staff of the Second Army, and Kim Tong-ha, Commander of the Marine Division stationed at Pohang, were confidants of Park as the plans evolved. The plans they worked out and authorized Lt. Colonel Kim Jong-pil to execute commenced as merely an effort to "purify" the armed services, chiefly by rectifying the misuse of its funds and by restoring unity among its cliquish groups. Because of their key role, the colonels were confident of their power to attain these ends. They were a deeply dissatisfied group, partly because the war had left the top command overloaded with generals, thereby blocking their own promotion to that rank. Colonel Kim readily persuaded his associates to join with him in submitting to the Army Chief of Staff, General Song Yo-chan (commonly known as Tiger Song), a set of five bold demands: (1) to punish senior officers who had helped Lee Ki-pyung's Liberal Party politicians in the fraudulent 1960 election; (2) to bring to justice generals who had robbed the services to enrich themselves; (3) to purge the ranks of incompetent and corrupt officers; (4) to eradicate both factionalism and political activism from the services; and (5) to provide improved pay and living conditions for servicemen. Far from accepting these demands, General Song had six of the colonels detained for two days of severe questioning concerning their "plotting of rebellion"—a charge that might have led to their execution. Nevertheless, Song quickly resigned and left Korea for "special study" in Washington, D.C. His resignation, and the failure to bring charges against the colonels, encouraged further action by the rebellious group.

When the Second Republic was launched, Prime Minister Chang appointed a presumed reformist, Hyon Sok-ho, as Defense Minister. The colonels promptly demanded to talk with him. Instead, Minister Hyon had them taken to the Provost Marshall, who severely reprimanded them for their presumption. That evening nine of the colonels met with General Park Chung Hee, in which meeting they decided that reform of the armed services was hopeless and that what was needed was a revolutionary overthrow of the government. On 24 September a group of sixteen confronted the new Chief of Staff, Lieutenant General Choe Yong-hi, and demanded his resignation. For this presumption, one of the colonels was dishonorably discharged and three more, including Kim Jong-pil, were remanded to reserve status.

The planning for the coup intensified during the winter months. Adherence to it was gained from officers of the First Army and other units stationed in Seoul, from officers in various reserve divisions, and, most importantly, from Major General Kim Tong-ha and Brigadier General Kim Yun-gun. The group grew to include at least 250 high ranking officers, involving direct participation by 3,500 men—and yet, despite this enlargement of the participating group over a period of several months, no warning reached government officials, testifying to the superb ability of the planning group to conduct clandestine operations.

The Army Chief of Staff, Lt. General Chang Do-yong, learned of the coup plan at 11:00 p.m. on 15 May, just as it was about to be launched; but the only action he took was to have fifty military police dispatched to protect the Han River bridge. When the rebels commenced their crossing of the bridge at 3:20 a.m., General Chang telephoned Prime Minister John Myun

Chang to inform him of the "disturbance." At 4:10 a.m. he phoned Chang again, this time to warn him to flee to safety. Prime Minister Chang and his wife hastily left their residence in his jeep, accompanied by a single bodyguard, a police sergeant. The Changs drove to the American Embassy and found it closed, after which they went on to the refuge of the Carmelite convent in northeastern Seoul.

The Korean citizenry was awakened that morning by a radio broadcast stating that a Military Revolutionary Committee composed of five generals had taken over "the executive, legislative and judicial branches of the government" and that martial law was in effect. It was further announced that all bank assets were frozen, that airports and harbors were closed, that strict censorship of all publications would be rigorously enforced, and that any public meetings were forbidden. As the Seoul daily *Times* cautiously reported, "the citizens just watched." The Revolutionary Committee also broadcast a series of pledges—promising to "eliminate corruption and eradicate other social evils," to "provide relief for poverty-stricken and hungry people," to "devote our entire energies toward the development of a self-sustaining economy," and, "after we have completed our mission" to "restore the government to honest and conscientious civilians." During the afternoon of 16 May further radio broadcasts declared that the military had taken over the entire government; that the National Assembly and all provincial counsels were dissolved; that no political or social activities were permitted; that all cabinet members and vice-ministers were to be arrested; that the Revolutionary Committee was taking over all "state organizations"; and that any acts of violence would be severely punished.

The coup was not only a revolution against the Second Republic of Korea but also a repudiation of South Korea's "client state" relation to the United States. One of the pledges broadcast by the Military Revolutionary Committee was that "we shall respect and observe the United Nations Charter and strengthen our relations with the United States and other Free World nations." Nevertheless, the coup was in fact a negation of the supervisory role of the United Nations and a flat violation of the subordination of the ROK military to the overall command of the United States as provided in the 1953 Mutual Defense Treaty. Anti-Americanism was by no means absent in the Korean armed services, particularly in its senior ranks. The reasons were similar to those that caused all the cliquish divisions in the services. Since the military academies were modelled on their American counterparts, promotions and favorable assignments went disproportionately to those Korean officers who most fully adopted American ways and who were proficient in the English language. The coup was plotted and brought into effect by officers who willfully ignored the treaty provision that placed them under American command.

The sixteenth of May, the decisive day during which the coup was effected, was crowded with action. At 5:00 a.m. the takeover was announced to the public, in the name of the Army Chief of Staff, Lt. General Chang Do-yong. At 9:00 a.m. martial law was proclaimed, also on his order. That afternoon, at 4:30 p.m., the public was informed that General Chang was chairman of the Military Revolutionary Committee. His role was crucial, since the army units, wherever stationed, were subject to his command. It was his acceptance of nominal leadership of the coup that avoided intramilitary confrontations that might well have become civil war.

General Carter M. Magruder, commander of all U.N. (and Korean) forces in Korea, and Marshall Green, chargé d'affaires of the U.S. Embassy, met together at 5:00 a.m. and decided, without waiting to consult with Washington, D.C., that they should attempt to reverse the revolution. Magruder telephoned to General Chang and asked for his assessment of the situation, to which Chang replied, "I don't know whether it's mutiny or revolution." The American Embassy made strenuous efforts to locate Prime Minister Chang Myun, without success. At 11:00 a.m. General Magruder broadcast a statement over the Voice of America radio facilities calling for restoration of the government to the constitutional authorities and for "order . . . in the armed forces."

President Yun Po-sun, after listening to this radioed statement, urgently summoned Magruder and Green to a meeting in his residence. Marsall Green made it "emphatically clear that the United State supports the constitutional government." Magruder said to Yun that he was prepared to utilize contingents of American troops and of the ROK First Army to subdue the rebellion. This plan President Yun vetoed, telling the two Americans that he "had believed revolution to be inevitable." Yun, in effect, sponsored the coup as soon as he learned of it. As head of state, even if merely ceremonially, he had unwillingly bowed to the marginal majority of the Assembly that demanded that he name Chang Myun as prime minister. During the next months he had watched glumly and helplessly the virtual disintegration of the government. He was glad to see it overthrown. After his meeting with Magruder and Green, he sent by military planes his own instructions to Korea's service commanders. "Our nation's fate," his message read, "is dependent upon how well we handle this sudden and grave situation which has already caused domestic and international reverberations. . . . Mindful of the well-being of the citizens, the military must meet this situation with equanimity. . . . In closing, I am emphasizing again that there must be no bloodshed in bringing this situation under control."

Yun's role, like that of General Chang, was critical. Even though his presidency was without power, he was the head of state and by issuing such a restraining message he averted the necessity for military officers to accept personal responsibility for yielding to the coup. Beyond this, by remaining in office for another ten months, as he did, he made it possible for other governments to continue unbroken diplomatic relations with the Republic without having to undergo the embarrassment of endorsing the coup. Moreover, the remainder of the ROK government found it expedient to follow his example. On 18 May Prime Minister Chang Myun was brought to the capitol from the Carmelite convent, to preside over a last meeting of the cabinet, in which he and all the ministers resigned.

On that same day, General Chang sent a message to President John F. Kennedy urging continuance of "the most friendly ties" between their two governments. In his message Chang cited "ill practices and corruption" as reasons why the military had "embarked upon the sacred revolutionary task of overthrowing the corrupt and inefficient regime." He added a pledge "to uphold democracy, based on liberty, equality and good neighborliness." President Kennedy forebore to reply; but the State Department sent a terse statement that the interest of the United States was "to help the Korean people to achieve, through democratic processes, stability, order, and the rule of law." The Department also noted "with satisfaction the expression of intention to return the Government to civilian control." With this acceptance by the United States of the coup as a *fait accompli,* the success of the military revolt was sealed.

A rapid period of consolidation commenced. The Military Revolutionary Committee was transformed into the more civilian-seeming Supreme Council for National Reconstruction. General Chang was its chairman and, for the first time, General Park Chung Hee emerged openly into leadership as vice-chairman. Membership of the Council was designed to give representation to the Manchurian-experienced generals, the native-based southeastern Korean generals, and the lieutenant colonels who had carried out the coup and who were awarded a full third of the Council membership. Within six weeks the intramilitary feuds were settled. General Chang Do-yong and forty-five of his close associates were arrested on charges that they were plotting to assassinate General Park Chung Hee. Chang, instead of being executed, was sent into exile in the United States. The top-ranking officers who had refused to participate in the coup were purged. Grimly the Supreme Council issued assurance to the public that "law is being enforced. It is no longer possible to bribe police or prosecutors. Malefactors, rich or poor, receive the same treatment from the police and the courts." Tax evaders were granted a brief period of amnesty in which to come forth with admissions and payments. To insure full control of the country by the Supreme Council, and to root out subterranean opposition, a Central Intelligence Agency (the first ever in Korea) was set up, under the direction of Colonel Kim Jong-pil. There was no longer any danger of popular or military resistance to the new regime.

Park Chung Hee did not come into public notice until after his acceptance of the vice-chairmanship of the Supreme Council. After that he quickly promoted himself to lieutenant general in August, and to general in November. He seemed an unlikely prospect for national leadership. His personality was reclusive, without a trace of charisma. He wore dark glasses to conceal his expression and he seldom smiled. He had neither the special ability nor the right temperament for public speaking. He had a few friends rather than many acquaintances, and he avoided the casual comradeship of the officer's clubs. Born 30 September 1917 in the small village of Sangmo in North Pyongsang Province, neither his personality nor his family connections offered him any advantages. He grew up as a normal farm boy, the fifth son in a family of eight children. He was quiet and studious; and he was too small, reaching only five feet four inches at maturity, to show promise as a farmer. For these reasons he alone of the eight children was enrolled by his parents in the Taegu Normal School. After graduating in 1937, he spent three years as a primary school teacher. Hating this mode of earning a living, he enrolled in Japan's Manchurian Military Institute, from which he was admitted to the prestigeous Tokyo Imperial Military Institute. He was then attached to the Manchuria-based Kwantung Army, rising in rank from second to first lieutenant. When the war ended he returned to Korea and remained unemployed for a year. In 1946 he was admitted to the Officers Candidate Constabulary School and in September of that same year was graduated with the rank of captain.

During the Yosu-Sunchon uprising, he was suspected of sub rosa sympathy for the Communists and was one of the hundreds who were purged from the army. Nevertheless, under the protection of Chung Il Kwon, he was assigned as a civilian to intelligence duties in Army Headquarters in Seoul. When Seoul fell to the Communists on 28 June 1950, Park led entrapped members of the staff to safety and was rewarded with restoration of his rank as captain. His subsequent career during the war and afterwards was markedly varied. After serving for three months in the Intelligence Bureau, he was shifted from one post to another for a total of twenty-five times in the years between 1951 and 1961. His most rewarding assignments were to the U.S. Army Artillery School in Ft. Sill, Oklahoma in 1953, and to the ROK Army Command and General Staff School in 1957. At the time of the coup, with the rank of major general, he was in Seoul as Deputy Commander of the ROK Second Army.

Factors that led to his success included, paradoxically, his unsocial personality—for this kept him aloof from the various military factions. Other characteristics that contributed substantially to his progression were his undoubted intellectual superiority, his ability to learn quickly, his habit of hard work, his abstention from self-indulgence, and his singleminded devotion to what he conceived to be the good of the nation. In contrast to too many top politicians and high-ranking armed service officers, he was scrupulously honest, as well as puritanical in his tastes and behavior. Even his prejudices were of a kind to win wide approval. He identified so wholly with rural Korea that he worked in short stints in the rice paddies for recreation. With his roots and his affections in the countryside, he remained suspicious of city-dwellers and frequently described urban life as "filthy" and "rotten."

He disdained Western movies and music and was fond of Korean folk music and traditional dances.

Despite these preferences, his artillery training and his exposure to life in America convinced him of the values of technology. The importance of machinery, of large-scale productivity, and of well-coordinated management he understood and thoroughly accepted. Above all other considerations, he was clearly and centrally a militarist, with firm beliefs in discipline, obedience, and the hierarchical chain of command. What motivated him to seize control of the government was no doubt partly personal ambition but even more his distress at the disorderly inefficiency of the Chang Myun government. Despite his frequent and emphatic protestations to the contrary, by no means was he temperamentally democratic. His guiding instincts were to set goals, to tell people what to do, and to oversee their accomplishment.

His rationale was set forth clearly in a special publication of the Ministry of Foreign Affairs, aimed to both the domestic and international audience, published on 1 July 1961, which explained that:

> The Korean people and their present military leaders are fully aware of the dangers inherent in military government. However, there is universal acceptance of these facts: (1) The Armed Forces, hitherto aloof from politics were the only remaining organizations which retained the respect of the people; (2) The Armed Forces, by virtue of their training in organizational matters, were alone capable of reorganizing the Government into an efficient body functioning for the welfare of the nation rather than the private interests of officials and civil servants; (3) The Armed Forces were the only force strong enough to eliminate corrupt and self-serving interests which had brought the country to the verge of disintegration; (4) Only the Armed Forces, in the existing emergency, were able to stop increasing Communist infiltration and subversion and the growth of pro-Communism among some irresponsible elements of the people.

If not himself democratic, General Park well realized the Korean's yearning for democracy. He also well understood the commitment of Korea's indispensable allies to democratic values. Hence he repeatedly professed that it was for democracy that he labored and fought. To enforce this message, unbookish as he was, his primary attention after the coup succeeded was to issue three books that proclaimed him the champion of popular rights. These were *Chijodado (The Ways of a Leader), Uriminjokui nagalkil (Our Nation's Path)* and *Kukkawa hyongmyongkwa na (The Country, the Revolution and I).* The function of these books was to portray Park as a patriotic purist. Their main theme, however, was to interpret him as the undaunted champion of democracy. Quickly translated into English, they were aimed at both the Korean and foreign audiences. It is not unjust to measure his performance as the nation's top executive by the standards he himself proclaimed.

The military coup, he claimed, was accomplished in order "to overthrow the anti-democratic system" of the inept libertarian John Myun Chang and to restore "true, free democracy" to Korea. Emphatically he insisted that "certainly it was not for the establishment of a new dictatorship and totalitarianism." Then he asserted his personal faith that "leaders must strive to breathe together with the people of the nation and exert the maximum effort to infuse the people with the spirit of true freedom and democracy."

Park and his associates had no need to persuade the Korean people that democracy as they had been experiencing it had been tested and found wanting. Of this there was little doubt. Pluralism had become irresponsibly excessive. For fifteen years democracy had been more ardently praised than effectively practiced, so that after its demise its distorted image more condemned than mourned. But its spirit was far from dead. It survived as a wistful hope for the future, enlivened by angry student demonstrations that are reminiscent of the uprisings of the Righteous Army of earlier days. For sound reasons, the protests have been sporadic and superficial rather than widespread and revolutionary. One reason is that the undemocratic restraints have been accompanied by South Korea's sensational economic advancement. Among all the civil rights for which people contend, the right to live well is by no means the least. Secondly, the continuing division of the country and the militancy of the North are accepted reasons for governmental exercise of emergency powers. A major reason for Koreans' acceptance of the military regimes is that they are, after all, Korean—unlike the foreign rule imposed on the preceding generation. But the ultimate fact is that the people have accepted the new militarism because they had no choice. They had to. Park, however, cited additional reasons.

In his principal book, *Our Nation's Path,* issued in 1962, Park Chung Hee's dominant feelings and ideas emerge clearly. "Our modern history," he asserted, "has been a record of failures, national ruination and confusion. Our masses, the creators of history, lacked autonomy and were characterized by flunkyism and subjected to the control of foreign powers." The two evils that he set himself to eradicate were factionalism and poverty. "First," he insisted, "each of us will have to discard his selfishness and unite for the common good. . . . Second, we must liberate the people from poverty and establish a self-reliant economy." He stated his goal in general terms as "establishment of the independent, self-supporting Korea on the basis of an austere, diligent and honest society—this has been my life-long ambition."

Warning the people that democracy could not be imported but must grow from domestic roots, he termed the methods he would use "Koreanized democracy." What this meant to him was loyalty to the nation, subordinating personal interests. It was "ceaseless factional strife," he pointed out, that had opened the way to annexation by Japan.

As a professional soldier, General Park interpreted civilian life essentially in military terms. The rules of permitted—indeed, of required—behavior must be clear. People must work together as an integrated team, not only for themselves but for all. There must be orderliness, and, to insure it, orders must be obeyed. This was the new broom with which the fragmented Korean politics and society were to be swept clean. At the time of the coup, General Park was unknown to the public. But for those who read his books with care, the forthcoming "nation's path" was predictable. Freedom of choice would have to give way to discipline.

For two decades his was the ruling authority in South Korea. During that time the country underwent fundamental changes—politically, economically, diplomatically, and socially. Much was gained; some of the gains were costly, particularly in the vital areas of human and civil rights. The effects, good and bad, of policies and practices he set in motion are still working themselves out. To depict what they were, and to interpret their course requires consideration for all the remaining history of Korea, up to the present day. For along with closing the door, decisively, on Korea's immediate past, Park Chung Hee was unquestionably the directing force of the vast and fundamental changes for which his revolution paved the way.

19
The Military Revolution Takes Form

The coup itself was not revolution; it was what made revolution possible. The revamping began with the prompt purging of the military, quickly followed by purgation of the politics. In the words of Park Chung Hee, there had to be a clearing away of the "remnants of the old order." Within a month the military government peremptorily confiscated almost six billion *won* from fifty-nine individuals who it charged had accumulated "illicit fortunes" from operation of the "military-industrial complex." Park signalized his satisfaction with the success of the takeover, in his *The Country, the Revolution, and I,* with the declaration: "We can only march ahead with a single-hearted determination to establish a welfare state in the Orient, in which justice has its way, in which truth breathes, in which activity and newness are rewarded and in which hope and ideals abound."

To encourage the "hope and ideals" that would salve the anxieties of both the Korean people and South Korea's allies on 12 August 1961, just a month after openly taking charge as chairman of the Supreme Council, Park made two promises: (1) that the constitution would be basically amended; and (2) that after approval of the new constitution in a referendum that was scheduled for May of 1963—giving him two years, meanwhile, for preparatory measures—the military would relinquish power to civilian authorities. The highly respected *Hanguk Ilbo,* a longtime sturdy supporter of democracy, boldly editorialized in its next-day issue that "the military must more widely employ civilian talent and must learn to respect civilians." In November General Park made an official visit to the United States and Japan, sealing their acceptance of his authority.

Returning home after assuring his principal ally that justice and democracy were his aims, On 15 March 1962 Park had his Supreme Council enact a Political Activities Law to defang opposition by prohibiting any form of political activity by 4,369 individuals who were identified as "old politicians," including his benefactor, Chung Il Kwon. The law allowed any who chose to do so to appeal for exemption, and 1,336 of them won the right to continue public activities by attesting that they were and would continue to be loyal to the new order. President Yun Po-sun was virtually the only "remnant of the old order" who was exempted from the purge. But a year later, on 22 March 1962, he resigned from the presidency in protest against the measures to extinguish political opposition.

The basically amended constitution greatly expanded the powers of the presidency. The National Assembly, with little of its authority remaining, was reduced to a single chamber. The legislature's power of the purse, which is its ultimate weapon, was essentially eliminated by the provision that if the annual appropriation for the budget was delayed, or if it was deemed by the president to be either inadequate or excessive, he could decide what public officials should be paid, and how much; which agencies would continue to receive funding; and which governmental projects would be funded. The judiciary was brought directly under presidential control by empowering the president to appoint Supreme Court Justices without review by the Assembly and by appointment of all lower judges by the presidentally-appointed Chief Justice (whom the president could remove from office at his own will). The Supreme Court was further authorized to dissolve any political party which in its judgment was not serving the public interest.

The new constitution affirmed that the ROK "shall be a democratic republic," that "all state authority shall emanate from the people," and that all public officials shall be "servants of the entire people." The source from which power really "emanated" was not left in doubt. The heads of opposition parties were to be paid governmental stipends, thus in effect making them employees of the state. A system of self-censorship was established. The press was to be free and public assemblies were permitted unless the police authorities decided that their news or views were infringing on "public morality and social ethics." If the president became worried about public order, he could declare a state of siege and take "special measures" to suspend the habeas corpus and to curb freedom of the press, of speech, and of assembly.

The president was to be elected by popular vote. He was given the power to name the prime minister and the cabinet without legislative assent. He was empowered to issue on his own authority emergency decrees that gave him direct control over martial law and also over financial and economic measures and conditions. Even more broadly, he was authorized to "issue ordinances having the effect of law."

The referendum on the constitution was conducted ahead of schedule on 17 December 1962, and it was approved by the overwhelming majority of 78.8 percent of the voters. One reason for this majority was that opposition was effectively curbed. But there is also no doubt that the public genuinely wanted to avoid repetition of the overly-permissive excesses of the Second Republic. Park Chung Hee, thanking the people, assured them that "the voting was carried out in an atmosphere of freedom and fairness unprecedented in the political history of Korea." There was not, however, any effective supervision or observation by the United Nations Commission as there had been during the First and Second Republics.

A few weeks later, in January, Kim Jong-pil was accused of using the power of the CIA to build a new political party. Charges of major corruption revolved around the duty-free import and sale of Japanese-made automobiles; the import and use of 880 pinball machines; the excessive costs of building the Walker Hill Resort complex; and the irregular issuance of stocks and bonds. As a result of these "Four Major Cases of Grave Suspicion," Kim Jong-pil resigned from the chairmanship of the CIA and also of the new Democratic Republican Party. No charges were brought against him. Nevertheless, on 25 February he left Korea on an eight-month foreign tour. Major General Kim Dong-ha, commander of the Marines, and Lt. General Park Im-hang, commander of the First Field Army, who were Kim Jong-pil's principal accusers, were both court-martialed and dismissed from the military in April. By this time only six of the original members of the Supreme Council remained in their posts, the remaining twenty-six having been either imprisoned or exiled. *Hanguk Ilbo* somberly warned the military leadership that "the violation of fundamental rights by those who should have defended them" might lead to yet another revolution.

Partisan politics became active during the first weeks of 1963, following Park's announcement that a presidential election would be held as soon as conditions warranted it, with himself as a candidate. This led to widespread anxiety and objections within the military. On 5 March soldiers led by junior officers massed before the capitol building and demanded that military rule be continued. Eleven days later Park acceded to this demand by withdrawing plans for an election, explaining that he needed more time to "complete the revolutionary tasks" and to assure "the birth of a sound civilian government." These circumstances led to an outpouring of alarm and resentment. Huh Chung, who was living in genteel retirement, after having served briefly as interim president in 1960, charged that "the prolongation of military rule is a major tragedy for the Korean people." Yun Po-sun, after resigning his presidency, asserted that "Park had burned the democracy which had just begun building." The U.S. Department of State cautiously announced its hope that "the junta and major political groups in Korea can work out together a procedure for transition to civilian government." The *New York Times* correspondent in Korea reported that "Park and others are under counter-pressure from several groups of angry young [army] officers." The *Times* editorialized that Park "faces mounting agitation from civilian politicians and sections of the public."

Park Chung Hee readily agreed with this analysis of his difficulties. He well realized that he was on the defensive and he rushed into print with his book on the revolution, to justify his coup. "The Army does not want any part in politics," he claimed. "Neither can it have any!" But, he added—and it was an emphatic "but"—

> But patience and indifference are two different things. There had to be a limit! It was impossible for them to continue to do nothing. Must the Army adhere to

> the ostensible duty of national defense, patient and looking on, while the national economy breaks into pieces and is tampered with, society is confounded to its extreme by the rashness and crimes of former politicians, and the nation is threatened with imminent danger of ruin?

This was his interpretation of his role; and it was this image that he consistently sought to maintain.

On 17 August Park resigned from the army and accepted nomination for the presidency as a civilian, saying wearily that he hoped that "never again will any soldier be forced along such an unfortunate pathway as the one I have trod." Then he reiterated his guiding motivation: "to eliminate the unfortunate legacies from our ancestors of mutual hatred and factionalism, waste, confusion, indolence, and dishonesty and to put an end to this contaminated national history, in order to construct the independent, prosperous fatherland of tomorrow." The change from a uniform to civilian clothing did not greatly change Park Chung Hee's character or personality or leadership methods. Throughout the eighteen years of his authoritarian rule over South Korea, he manifested a statesmanlike grasp of the complexities of the goal he set for the nation, but neither did he deviate from the discipline he believed was necessary for attainment of that goal. His "administrative democracy" was strictly authoritarian.

He lost no time in hastening to put in effect his plans for economic development. Immediately after taking command in July 1961 he established the Economic Planning Board, charging it to create and maintain an industrialization strategy. Its powers were extremely broad. The chairman of the EPB was also to be the Deputy Prime Minister. He was assured of funds and of authority for building a bureaucracy sufficient to coordinate the functions of the ministries of Finance, of Commerce and Industry, of Transportation, of Agriculture, of Health and Social Affairs, and of Science and Technology.

The plans of the EPB were comprehensive. The first need was to secure long-term capital that would be allocated for use of those particular segments of industry that the government deemed to be the foundation for generalized growth. To achieve this end, the commercial banks were nationalized. Their available funds were increased by the Bank of Korea, which expanded the amount of currency in circulation. With these new resources, the nationalized banks put into effect an "over loan" policy whereby selected industrial concerns were granted loans in excess of their net worth, at low interest rates. Tax concessions were also granted to the approved industries. To encourage public acceptance of the system of variable taxation and of the inflation that was unleashed, Park encouraged use of the slogan "My Prosperity"—meaning that it promised benefits for everyone. This broad scale EPB program was launched officially in January 1962, labelled The First Five Year Economic Development Program.

The Supreme Council described this program as "economic policies based upon the principles of free enterprise, respecting the freedom and originality of private citizens." Actually, the plans were neither free enterprise capitalism nor state socialism but a carefully integrated combination of the two. They were launched on what was, considering Korea's circumstances, a daringly massive scale, requiring the investment from governmental, foreign, and private domestic sources of some two and a half billion dollars (measured by the 1962 value of U.S. currency). Such a goal was so bold as to seem foolhardy. Where was the money to come from? Risk capital was desperately scarce. The domestic savings rate was miniscule. U.S. aid grants were in sharp decline and were earmarked mostly for the military. Public support was also minimal because of the rise of inflation, and because the largely rural population resented the industrialization that cost them higher prices and produced little that was suited to their needs.

Park Chung Hee's daring vision was supported with the iron discipline he had learned as a professional soldier. The vision itself was somewhat modelled on the state-business partnership that was working well in Japan. But whereas in Japan the initiative came largely from business, there was no business community in Korea capable of assuming the burdens of leadership. Hence in Park's planning the development was government-led, with industry required to do largely what it was told. A further basic component of the Park formula was that it emphasized "Growth first, distribution later," the exact opposite of the "My prosperity" theme. Belt-tightening was the order of the day. The system emphasized controlled free enterprise, with material rewards for individuals and companies that demonstrated superior ability to produce. Yet it was not market-oriented. What developed was a unique relationship between state bureaucracy and private business, with private enterprise supplying the operating units but always under close governmental supervision and assisted by governmental support. The system was an intertwining of politics and economics. It worked because of the strength and single-mindedness of Park's leadership and because it rewarded individual enterprise that advanced the governmental goals. To get the plans started, the government provided 53 percent of the funds required, in addition to generous loans and tax provisions.

Park Chung Hee's aim was to convert South Korea from an agricultural to a manufacturing economy. To accomplish this goal considerable structural changes were needed. The overblown bureaucracy was reduced during the early 1960s by nearly one-third. The cost of government was cut back, by this means, from 23.7 percent of the GNP in 1962 to 16.1 percent in 1964. In this same period, the amount of taxes collected was reduced by roughly 20 percent. Clearly, Park was applying to the civilian society two cardinal military maxims: "neat and trim," and "sacrifice for efficiency."

From the beginning the results were spectacular. At the time of the coup primary goods (raw materials and agricultural products) constituted more than 80 percent of exports, and exports accounted for less than five percent of the GNP. During the first two years, 1961–63, even as the plans were still taking form, the value of exports increased from $41 million to more than

$85 million. Coal output grew from under six million tons in 1961 to almost nine millions in 1963. And cement production went up from just over five hundred thousand tons in 1961 to almost eight hundred thousand in 1963.

The economic effects were far from uniform. The competitive market structure was distorted. Mistakes in the central planning led to misallocation of some resources. The sharp inflationary growth, to the level of 20 percent annually, caused dislocations in the industrial structure as well as severe hardships for the population. Middle-sized industries, the backbone of an industrialized society, declined and heavy and chemical industries were overly developed.

A few big family-owned enterprises built large private fortunes, while the general living conditions lagged and in some respects declined. Urban population, swollen by industrial employment, went up so rapidly that housing became alarmingly difficult, both in availability and in cost, even as real estate development and exploitation created more fortunes for a wealthy few. Labor unions were prohibited, while wages fell well behind in the race with inflation. Working conditions—especially in textile mills and in urban "sweat shops" that employed young girls and women—were deplorable. While the rich were decidedly getting richer, the poor were also making material gains, but slowly. "Growth first, distribution later" was an effective if harsh guideline.

The validity of the old principle "no gain without pain" was abundantly illustrated. The gain was fundamental; the pain was widespread. The traditional wealthy class—the yangbans who basically were landlords—was replaced. Some landowners, when the land reform program was effected, invested the proceeds from sale of their lands in factories; but most of them had neither taste nor talent for industrial or commercial management. The new industrialists were men skilled in political maneuvering. Needing the investment capital they could get only through favored loan provisions, and not being hampered by labor union protection of their employees, they achieved efficiency partly at the cost of neglecting humanitarianism. The traditional Korean respect for education similarly underwent renovation. Schools and universities multiplied, making education universal. Its quality, however, was questionable. Some colleges became in effect little better than diploma mills. Graduation was essential for entry-level jobs in the burgeoning industries, but the kind of education that mattered was learned on the job. Displacement was a chief characteristic of the society, as daughters left home in their early teens to work in textile plants and to live in company barracks, and young men left home pursuing factory employment. Many middle-aged couples also found better opportunities in cities, where they could readily find employment in service jobs or could open small shops of their own. The population of the cities, notably of Seoul and Pusan, doubled and then quadrupled in a decade. The effects of economic and social change were felt most vitally in the north-south corridor from Pusan to Seoul, where rail and highway transport was most available. As a result, Korea's regional rivalries and resentments became intensified. Regional favoritism increased rather than declined. Between 1961 and 1985, for example, all nine army chiefs of staff came from Kyongsang province, which was the family home of Park Chung Hee, Chun Doo Hwan, and Roh Tae Woo. The heads of the great industrial combines were also from this same area.

Rapid economic changes induce paradoxical results. The high inflation rate bore heavily upon the poorer segments of the population. Yet the inflation rose rapidly in part because the living condition of the masses was improving. Between 1962 and 1988, the per capita gross national product increased at a steady rate of nine percent annually, from $520 to $5,000, in U.S. currency adjusted for inflation. The beneficial effects to the public, however limited by the inflationary spiral, were dramatized by the fifty percent devaluation of the currency in May 1964 from 130 to 255 *won* to the U.S. dollar, giving consumers more buying power.

A major cause of inflation is the excess of demand over supplies. As South Korea entered into its new era of industrialization during the years of Park's rule, goods became strikingly more plentiful. But so did the demand for them. The increase of urban population occurred as poor farmers, or some of their family members, left their rice paddies and villages for better jobs with higher incomes in the cities. At first they moved into shoddy shacks that were massed in grubby slums. But with conditions steadily improving, the slums developed into middle-class residential districts. Production multiplied. Inflation was brought down to the low level of three and four per cent. Consumer goods of all kinds were purchased, with telephones, radios, and then television sets becoming commonplace. Statistical measurements merely hint at the social transformation. Surveys found about 20 percent of the urban population identifying themselves as middle class in 1960, with a rise to 30 percent in 1970 and 48 percent in 1980. By 1987, according to *Donga Ilbo,* the percentage of the population considering themselves to be middle class reached 65. Inflation continued but the rate of personal savings also rose rapidly. The people were better off. But rising expectations kept well ahead of the welfare level. Wants increased far beyond the ability to satisfy them.

How the public was feeling about the coup was first tested in the presidential election that was held on 15 October 1963. Park Chung Hee had had two and a half years to consolidate his position and to produce results. Opposition had been virtually silenced. As the campaign developed, Park's Democratic Republican Party faced a major challenge only from a newly organized and scantily financed Civil Rule Party, which Yun Po-sun dominated and for which he was the unopposed nominee. Several splinter parties represented differing kinds of discontent. A massive turnout of more than eleven million voters indicated the depth of feeling with which the mass of the people sought to shape their government. Park defeated Yun—but by the narrowest of margins. Of the 12,985,015 registered voters, 85 percent went to the polls, with the lowest turnout in the big cities, Seoul, Pusan and Kwangju. Park received 46.7 percent of the total vote, with his major support coming from the rural areas; and Yun, best supported in the cities, got 45.1 percent. A political analyst, Sung Joo Han, noted "an undercurrent of dissent capable of manifesting itself as a formidable movement." The people had come a long way from the traditional Confucian pattern of conformity and acceptance of the established order and of the ruling authority. This was far from apathy. This was democracy. What was lacking was adequate opportunity for competing political parties to present their programs and candidates for the people's choice. Kim Se-jin posited that Park's victory was a "blessing"— for "if he had lost it can be safely assumed that the military would have ignored the electoral outcome and continued its rule." The question remains of whether the deeply divided military forces might not have engaged in a struggle among themselves. Despite the purges, Park's support base, either military or civilian, was not yet secure. In any event, Park's election assured his continuance in power; and with this assured, the subsequent election, six weeks later, for the National Assembly, gave Park's Democratic Republican Party a commanding majority of 110 seats, as against 65 scattered among four opposition parties.

In a July campaign speech Park had interpreted his goals as two-fold: "The revolutionary government, having purified the political world as the primary step, concentrated its energy on economic improvement as the second step." When he was inaugurated on 17 December as the republic's third president, he stressed his pledge "to establish a strong economic and social foundation."

The social and economic revolution that President Park termed "Koreanized democracy," and which may more definitively be termed "administrative democracy," was tightly centered. But it differed significantly from the totalitarian regime in the North. Park did not, as did Kim Il-sung, create a "personality cult" that portrayed a Great Leader as the fount of all wisdom and of all goodness, as well as of all power. He did not emulate North Korea's "brainwashing" system of implanting idolization of the leader and of subordination of the self to society. Instead, he persistently called for exertion and self-reliance to secure material benefits for individuals. Moreover, the mechanism of state controls that Park devised imposed a military-style discipline that assisted, rather than curbed the profit motive. Lee Chong-sik, a leading interpreter of Korean nationalism, traced the differences to the force of world public opinion. In testimony presented to the U.S. House of Representatives subcommittee on international organization, in the fourteenth year of Park's rule on 12 June 1975, Dr. Lee argued that

> . . .the North Korean Communists have built an effective totalitarian-mobilization system under which the people have been indoctrinated to believe in the legitimacy

> and effectiveness of the Korean Worker's Party and its leader, Kim Il-song. This is a system built in a completely isolated environment through a long period of coercion, indoctrination, and persuasion. Such a system cannot be built in South Korea, whose windows are open to the West, the economy is oriented toward capitalistic markets in and out of Korea, and where people have been educated in and once enjoyed Western libertarian values.

What was brought to pass in South Korea after the coup was an intertwining of two facts: the considerable curbing of civil liberties and concurrent remarkable economic progress. How these factors were related, and whether the prosperity could have been attained without the authoritarian severity is the historical conundrum that demands interpretation. In any event, their coexistence is indisputable, and the effects of both can readily be traced.

The relationship of labor and capital was a basic factor in the implementation of the First Five Year Plan. It was distinctly capital-oriented. The labor union movement in Korea was both new and weak; and such as it was, it was tainted by political motivations and connections, as well as being strictly restrained by political controls. Under the monarchy there had been no occasion for labor union organization, for there were no large-scale industrial or commercial employers. During the colonial period, the organization of workers was largely an underground opposition to the Government-General. The South Korean Worker's Party, which rose to prominence in the years of rule by the American Military Government, was a Communist political organization. The only rival for the Communist Worker's Party was a feeble Federation of Korean Trade Unions, the *Taehan Nochong*. The AMG did not seek to develop a democratic labor union movement, as MacArthur did in Japan, for a variety of reasons. Among these was its lack of policy-making authority, its shortage of funds, and the virtual limitation of its operations to the prevention of hunger, disease, and disorder. And unlike Korea, it was considered paramount in Japan to prevent the restoration of the war-making potential of huge monopolistic businesses.

In 1953, when the war ended, President Rhee's administration initiated the development of a genuine labor union system of a quasi-American style. Three guiding laws were enacted. A Labor Union Law guaranteed to workers the right to organize, to bargain collectively, and to strike if agreements were not reached through negotiation. A Labor Standards Law was enacted to prescribe minimum working conditions that employers must maintain or exceed. Thirdly, a Labor Dispute Adjustment Law gave the government emergency power to intervene by requiring mediation or arbitration if a strike was prolonged. On paper, these laws assured that the rights of labor would be protected. But the laws were ahead of their time. They were so unrealistic in terms of the distressed and undeveloped economy of the 1950s that they were largely ignored. They ameliorated some problems and prevented general strikes or widespread disorders, in a time of mass unemployment and resentment by laborers who were underpaid and overworked, often under unhealthful and sometimes dangerous conditions. Through the provisions in these laws for government oversight, they paved the way for "sweetheart" labor-management agreements, whereby union officials, employers, and government bureaucrats could find mutually agreeable ways of avoiding laws that were too unrealistic to be enforced. After the coup, Park Chung Hee at first banned labor unions altogether. Under the First Five Year Plan they were permitted, though with such strictly limited power that labor disputes had to be settled through collective bargaining conducted by the government. As was true of Park's administrative policies generally, "discipline" took priority over "rights" in order to expedite progress.

President Park's economic program was not equitable in the spread of its benefits and was not meant to be. As he repeatedly insisted, what was needed was production, with fairness of distribution to be accomplished later. To justify the pains that were part of the adjustment period, he used the analogy of a surgical operation. The unhealthy aspects of the economy must be cut away before economic health could be restored. Any justification for the inequities lay in what was achieved. As Wade and Kim put it in their 1977 study *The Political Economy of Success,* "the startling rapidity with which the Republic of Korea has been transformed from the desperately poor and undeveloped country it was in the 1950s to the highly literate, industrialized, and modern society it is today is unique in world history." More soberly, if not "unique," the South Korean "economic miracle" (as it is commonly called) makes it one of the "four little dragons" of eastern Asia, along with Hong Kong, Taiwan, and Singapore. It also provides a pattern for what is needed in Eastern Europe and the Soviet Union, if free enterprise is to prevail.

Fully matching the socially painful and politically costly character of Park Chung Hee's domestic economic policies was his dramatic shift of official South Korean policies toward Japan from suspicion and hostility to accommodation and conciliation. The effects of this shift were beneficial to both countries and were essential for South Korea's breakthrough to economic development. But so fundamental was the antagonism of the Koreans toward Japan and of Japanese toward Korea, that the change from hostility to cooperation could not have been accomplished without the centralist power system that Park instituted. It was another example of not doing what the public wanted but of ordering from the center what must be done.

Korea's resentment against Japan, matched by Japanese disparagement of Koreans, was the most deep-seated explosive issue in its modern history. Syngman Rhee's popular support was enhanced by his well-publicized anti-Japanese sentiments. John Myun Chang made a start toward reconciliation with Japan but did not have time to pursue it before his administration was overthrown. Park Chung Hee "bit the bullet" and made rapprochment with Japan one of the principal policies with which to accomplish the economic advancement of South Korea. What was absolutely essential, he understood, was the input of very substantial international investment in Korea. He also realized that the most dependable source for such investment was Japan. The Japanese were eager to develop a Korean market for their products. Despite such favorable attitudes, there were formidable barriers between the two peoples—but there also were pockets of good will to serve as bridges.

Both Chang and Park had been educated under the Japanese, spoke the language fluently, had many Japanese friends, and had advanced successfully in their careers during the colonial period. In Japan there was a considerable group of prominent political leaders who favored cooperative relations with South Korea. In April 1960 they organized the Round Table on the South Korean Problem to search for reconciliation measures. In 1961 the Korean Businessmen's Association began to lobby for a Korea-Japan treaty. Chang Myun invited the Foreign Minister of Japan to Seoul and sent one of his close friends to Tokyo to initiate mutual steps of conciliation. Korean public protests against these moves were wide spread and bitter. The need for rapprochment was felt more keenly in Japan than in Korea. The influential *Asahi Shimbun,* evaluating "five phases" of the relationship in its issue of 29 September 1965, cited what it considered to be the major factor: "If the ROK is controlled by North Korea and if Pusan is covered by red flags, Japan will be flooded by mountainous waves of Communist forces." Former Prime Minister Kishi Nobusuke cautioned the government that "Japan must normalize its relations with the Republic of Korea, provide economic aid in conjunction with the United States and thereby build South Korea's economic foundation." To Park Chung Hee this appeared not merely a desirable but an essential development. But he well knew it was both politically difficult and also risky to undertake it.

The Korean public's resentment of Japan was not merely centered on past history. In Japan the Korean minority of eight hundred thousand was deprived of citizenship and suffered many forms of social, political, and economic discrimination. Until 1990 all Koreans in Japan were finger-printed by the police. Moreover, Japan legalized the Communist Party, eagerly expanded its economic ties with North Korea, and permitted the Korean Communists in Japan to conduct a full-scale propaganda warfare against the South. The adult Koreans' hatred of Japan was not only nationalistic but also deeply personal, for they had lived through the humiliation of all the abuses of colonialism. Finally, Park's Japanese connections, which helped him to establish dealings with Japan, had the negative connotation of "collaborationism" (a bitterly derogatory term) among Koreans.

In addition to attitudes, there were also substantive barriers to reconciliation. The fisheries line between the two countries continued to be maintained, and Korean Coast Guard patrols continued to arrest Japanese fishermen who transgressed over it. For both countries fishing was important not only for dietary and economic reasons but also culturally—both nationalities were "people of the seas." Economic issues pointed favorably and negatively. Obviously great advantages to both sides would result from opening Korean markets and investment to the Japanese. But in Korea there was widespread fear that Japanese economic involvement would lead to Japanese control. An important favorable influence was the sustained effort by the United States, exerted in both Japan and Korea, to bring about reconciliation.

Park Chung Hee lost no time in initiating moves toward this end. In September of 1961, a Korean economic envoy suggested to Japan's Foreign Minister that the ROK would compromise on the fishing line if Japan would invest heavily in Korea, to the amount of two billion dollars—which he subsequently reduced to eight hundred million, and to which the Japanese side cautiously responded with an offer of fifty million. This encounter opened the way for a cordial and prestigious welcoming reception for Park in Tokyo in November, on his way to the United States. Korean suspicions burst to new heights a few weeks later, when Kim Jong-pil, back from his exile, took charge of the Korean negotiating team and when the Japanese foreign office spokesman angered Koreans by claims that Koreans owed Japanese for industrial and other properties left behind when the Japanese were summarily ejected from Korea in 1945. Kim Jong-pil reported that he was nearing agreement with Japan on the fishing line and on property claims. But agreement among the negotiators was not supported by the public. In the face of Korean anger at the "inadequacy" of any available settlement, Park Chung Hee sent Kim Jong-pil into a second exile. Emotions in Japan were also exacerbated by renewed and impassioned recital by Koreans of the "evils" of its treatment of Korea.

In April 1965, with Lee Dong Won (Yi Tong-won) appointed by Park as Foreign Minister with explicit instructions to normalize relations with Japan, and with issuance of an "apology" *(hansei)* by Japan's Foreign Minister for the history of Japanese-Korean relations, the negotiators agreed on a Treaty on Basic Relations. Some issues were settled, some were sidestepped. The fisheries line was replaced with mutual acceptance of twelve-mile limits along their coasts. As a "gesture of goodwill"—but emphatically not as "reparations"—Japan awarded some $300 million to the ROK, along with short-term and long-term loans amounting to another $500 million. On the disputed issue of the status of Koreans resident in Japan, the Japanese agreed to give them "residency" but not citizenship. The central issue between the two countries was postponed, as Japan recognized the sovereignty of the ROK only in the South and insisted on maintaining its economic and social relations with the North. In both countries, the major opposition parties and large segments of the public denounced the treaty terms with agitated oratory and violent demonstrations. Nevertheless, on 22 June it was ratified.

In view of the absolutely crucial importance of the relationships between

Korea and Japan, not only to themselves but to all of eastern Asia, it is worthwhile to review the major factors both before and also resulting from that 1965 treaty:

- On 4 January 1949, SCAP permitted the ROK to establish a quasi-diplomatic "mission" in Tokyo.
- In March-April of 1949 the United States reversed its former policy by permitting Japan to use a "special account" fund with which to finance reconstruction of factories to produce military materiel.
- In connection with the 1951 American-Japanese treaty, Japan sought to checkmate Syngman Rhee's demands for "reparations" by asserting its own claim to repayment for the industrial and transport facilities it had built in Korea. It asked the ROK to drop its demands and, instead, to agree to "economic cooperation."
- In 1951–53, through "special procurement orders" the United States purchased some $740 million worth of military and other supplies annually from Japan for allocation to Korea.
- On 23 March 1960 General Lemnitzer, Chief of Staff of the U.S. Army, testified to the Senate Foreign Relations Committee that the eighteen ROKA divisions provided "more security" for both South Korea and Japan, at "less cost per dollar," than any other troops in any part of the world.
- By March of 1970, with South Korea situated within Japan's economic sphere, Japanese controlled less than half the stock in some 50 percent of Korean-Japanese enterprises in Korea; more than half in 22 percent of them; and 100 percent in a quarter of them all. By that time, Japanese held controlling interest in ninety percent of Korean fertilizer plants; 64 percent of chemical fibre plants; 48 percent of glassmaking and cement plants; and 43.5 percent of South Korea's chemical industries.
- In April of 1970, Park's administration signed another treaty with Japan which assured the Japanese cheap land and cheap labor in return for Japanese capital and advanced technology. Korean factory workers at that date received less than one-sixth the wages paid to Japanese factory workers in Japan. This was largely because Japanese labor in Japan was helped by improved technology to produce four times as much per capita as did Korean laborers in Korea. President Park proclaimed a new ordinance denying to Korean workers in foreign-owned plants the right to strike.

Evaluation of these facts, like Japan's colonial policies in 1910–45, is subject to widely varying interpretations. Overall, the treaty arrangements have been extremely helpful to both nations. In some political respects Korea got the worst of the bargain. The political cost that Park paid is indicated in the scorching judgments condemning it: "Park has voluntarily handed the nation back to Japanese control as a quasi-colony, a unique phenomenon of self-demolition unheard of in modern annals of man and nations."[48] Realistically, it is apparent that the input of Japanese capital and technological aid has proved as essential to South Korea's remarkable economic advancement as Japanese military supplies were vital in the conduct of the Korean War. This, at least, was the view of President Park. And it was his policies that prevailed.

South Korea's exceptional growth record from the early 1960s is the beneficiary heritage Park Chung Hee left to the Korean people. The countervailing losses are also notable. For one thing, the dualism that discredited Japan's colonial government of 1910–45 was revived. Economic inequality became marked. Political controls over opposition groups increased in stringency. Social discrepancies, such as the subordination of women, the breakdown of family unity, and the discontent manifested through sporadic protest demonstrations were not adequately addressed. The alarming industrial pollution was largely ignored. Democratic political maturity was reversed. Park's military-style discipline, aimed to enhance and enforce social unity, resulted in severe restrictions of human and civil rights. These are factors that are also parts of the Park heritage.

The hyper-growth of the economy was directly owing to Park's "guided capitalism." This system included the selection of specified segments of the economy to be developed, with these segments assisted by favorable loan and tax provisions, and by a virtual guarantee of profits to private entrepreneurs with good production records, while holding down their labor costs with a frankly avowed policy of attaining growth at the expense of low wages. The rapid and steady increase in exports was accomplished in part by government subsidies to counterbalance inflation-caused unfavorable currency exchange rates; and a steady domestic market was assured by restriction of imports. Economic growth profited greatly from the substantial and indeed essential in-flow of funds and of management from Japan and from the United States, as well as from the global economic upswing in the years prior to the 1973 oil crisis. Even more decisive was the "trade-off" agreement between President Park and Lyndon Johnson, whereby the Republic of Korea sent its troops to fight the Vietnamese and in return the American government bought from South Korea basic materials required for American troops in Vietnam. This arrangement was fully as economically stimulative to South Korean industry as was the value to Japan of the earlier American policy of buying from Japan goods needed for Korean relief during 1945–48 and military supplies to use in the Korean War. Part of the credit for the "miracle of growth" must be granted also to Korean cultural traditions that favored hard study, endurance of hard living conditions, and acceptance of authority. The control system had to contend against such factors as the stubborn insistence by Koreans upon their self-worth, as well as their entrenched factionalism, regional rivalries, and clan-centered disunity. Without

President Park's "strongman" characteristics, his economic goals could not have been attained.

Alice Amsden, in her book *Asia's Next Giant,* cites South Korea as the prime example of how industrialization is coming to developing countries in the twentieth century. England, as the founder of the Industrial Revolution, accomplished its rapid industrialization, she explains, by invention. The United States attained an even broader and fuller industrial pattern by innovation. South Korea, entering the lists very late, set an example for other third world countries, Amsden concludes, by industrializing itself through learning. This may be true, but it smacks a little too neatly of what long was said about the success of Meiji Japan, that it arose from borrowing and imitating. There have to be other reasons.

What is certain about the South Korean development success is that it was truly exceptional. There has been a plethora of authoritarian regimes in developing countries, none of which has even remotely approached South Korea's economic success. This is despite the facts that South Korea was severely handicapped by the 38th parallel division, by the devastation of the Korean War, and by the continuing hostility between the North and the South. Essentially, what South Korea has had as the major asset in its competition for world markets is the "added value" of its products provided by the skills and diligence of its people. Until it could develop technology, it had to compete by using cheap labor. This President Park understood, and he imposed methods that made this resource effective.

There were heavy moral, social, and political costs exacted by his militaristic rule. And despite the economic gains, there were also such negative economic factors as lack of balance and distortion in production, along with the acknowledged imbalance in distribution. It is these disparities that must be put on the scales of judgment in assessing the quality and the long-range effects of Park Chung Hee's eighteen-year rule. Upon what course was Korea set? Where is it trending? These are the weighty questions of principal concern.

20

A Decade of Contrasts

History does not develop in a straight line from one point to another, but rather in a zigzag of contending changes that, in the perspective of time, have more direction than is immediately apparent. This certainly was true of the decade of changes in Korea from 1968 to 1979. The changes have been interpreted and evaluated in many differing ways, because they involved a bewildering complex of contradictory factors within both the North and South zones—and especially between them. Both the Korean governments demonstrated more strength of will than clarity in their dealings with one another.

Contradictions abound: but even so there was direction and significant changes were taking place. Thumbnail summaries conceal more than they reveal. Nevertheless, like a sailboat tacking against uncertain winds and pummelled by crosscurrents, there is departure and there is arrival, and the general direction can be drawn in a simple straight line. The general direction of the decade was that Kim Il-sung clung strictly to his purpose of reunifying Korea under his conditions but sporadically shifted his strategy between force and diplomacy. Park Chung-Hee, de-emphasizing reunification, relentlessly pushed ahead with his basic plan to propel South Korea into advanced prosperity but met with increasing resistance because, instead of relaxing his militaristic discipline over the society, he increased it.

Throughout the decade, Kim Il-sung bewilderingly intermingled violence and diplomacy until, finally, he concluded that violence was proving to be counterproductive. Park Chung Hee learned that material success does not build a supportive consensus when some of the methods for its attainment violate the self-respecting sentiments of dignity, civil rights and justice. Living conditions in North Korea remained at minimally tolerable levels and in South Korea increased impressively for some and more slowly for the general population. In neither zone did realities accord with expectations.

In South Korea the people got much but wanted more. The acceleration of resentments in a time of significant improvements was far from unique to the Republic of Korea. Protests and even rebellions commonly occur when expectations arise faster than they are satisfied. If, to restrain them, controls are tightened, unrest grows. When a people is told what to do and is punished for lapses in the doing of it, they tend to complain and to resist. Democracy, with all its faults, is the system that works best. Partial or pseudo democracy doesn't work. Like oil and water, "some freedom" and "some suppression" don't mix. In the prescient words of Abraham Lincoln, "This nation must become all one thing or all the other." President Park's "half way house" of civil rights was too unstable to persist.

The government of North Korea proved to be definitely more stable and less disorderly than that in the South. The reasons why can readily be itemized. North Korea's control system remains the strictest of any Communist country since the death of Joseph Stalin. Any form of resistance is punished by imprisonment, confiscation of property, denial of employment, or exile to isolated and desolate villages. Radio dials have been fabricated so that they can be tuned only to government broadcasts. Emigration is forbidden and trips to foreign countries, except to Japan, including other Communist countries, are restricted to trustworthy officials. Informants are so numerous that the people are suspicious of even close associates. Discussion of public affairs or of officials was unthinkable, even within families or between friends. Isolation from world news and from foreign ideas was at least as complete as it has been in Albania. With a thoroughness reminiscent of George Orwell's nightmare fantasy, the minds of the people were subverted by control of communication by what might well be called a "Ministry of Truth."

With his personal authority unrestricted at home Kim Il-sung set about shedding his obligations to North Korea's sponsoring powers. Celebrating the twenty-fifth year of liberation from Japan on 15 August 1970 the official newspaper *Rodong Sinmun* editorialized that Pyongyang, not Moscow or Peking, was the judge of how Communism should work in Korea. "The Communists should always do their own thinking and act independently, maintaining their own identity," while scorning "big-nation chauvinism," the editorial asserted. Kim had already, in the preceding April, attended the Bandung Conference in Indonesia, where he assured the third-world delegates that North Korea had become a model pointing toward "the revolutionary development of the world."

Countering the strong assertiveness of Kim Il-sung's foreign pronouncements, North Korea's economic condition was bad and was becoming worse. The one-year goals set by the economic plans for 1947, 1948, and 1949–50 had aimed only to restore the levels of food, clothing, and shelter that had been undermined by the departure of Japanese management and by the plunder of factories and other resources by the Russians. The war was so destructive that in its aftermath the only goal was reconstruction. A five-year economic program announced in 1957, followed by a seven-year plan proposed in 1961, professed no higher aim than to "put flesh on the skeleton."

The standard of living was very low but it was at least endurable. There was no unemployment, for under the socialist system everyone was employed. Such educational and medical resources as were available were shared. Inflation was not a problem. Prices were fixed for the 80.2 percent of retail trade that was conducted through the state-operated stores. Cooperative stores, in effect also state-operated, conducted 19.2 percent of retail sales. What was left, merely 0.6 percent of trade in consumer products, consisted of privately-caught fish and privately-produced eggs and vegetables, which were sold in small farmers' markets or, in the cities, through black market operations.

By 1960, industrial production had generally attained prewar levels—except in the vitally important sectors of salt and fertilizers. During the 1960s the rate of growth slowed in both light and heavy industries, and in agriculture it actually reversed. The Soviet Union and the People's Republic of China both reacted to Kim Il-sung's bellicose assertions of independence by restricting their aid. The domestic losses of productivity resulted in part from mistakes in planning, and in part from the lack of incentives for personal effort by farmers and workers.

Even more significantly, the civilian economy suffered by diversion of resources to the military. The cost of national defense soared upwards from 5.6 percent of the national income (a very heavy burden) in the decade of 1955–65 to the staggering rate of 31.2 percent during 1967–70. Meanwhile, as measured in 1967, the per capita income averaged just $220 annually, in terms of American currency. This low figure was despite the 47.5 percent increase in the number of urban factory workers, as North Korea industrialized.

These were the conditions in the North when Kim Il-sung launched a new wave of violence, which he hoped would destabilize the government and the population in the South and would persuade the United States to withdraw from its costly commitment to the defense of the Republic of Korea. During the night of 21 January 1968, a gang of commandos that had infiltrated across the Demilitarized Zone was intercepted by ROK security guards just a mile from President Park Chung Hee's Blue House residence in Seoul. Two days later, North Korean naval vessels captured the unarmed U.S. intelligence ship, the *Pueblo,* in waters off Wonsan harbor. The crew of eighty-three was taken to Pyongyang, where they were held imprisoned for the remainder of the year. Commando landings on South Korea's east coast were intercepted and turned back. On 15 April 1969 an American reconnaisance plane flying in the Sea of Japan, some ninety miles off the North Korean east coast, was shot down by a North Korean air patrol, with the loss of all thirty-one of its crew. Three or more North Korean infiltration tunnels were blasted out beneath the Demilitarized Zone (the first discovered by the U.N. Command on 15 November 1974), each large enough for use by light vehicles and artillery, and by troops proceeding three abreast. Amid continuous heated propaganda against dominance by "American imperialists" over the "puppet government of South Korea," on 18 August 1976, two American soldiers who were obeying orders to remove small trees that obscured the view of Communist installations were hacked to death by ax-wielding North Korean troopers.

While the DPRK was conducting these acts of violence, with little repercussion except protests from Seoul and Washington, Kim Il-sung was concurrently conducting a wholly different strategy, through diplomacy and conciliation. In a speech to the Third People's Assembly on 23 October 1962, he said that

> Whether the ideal of communism is realized in South Korea or not is a matter to be decided by the South Korean people themselves, and no one can impose it on them. . . . To oppose unification of the country on the pretext of fearing the "communization" of South Korea is to go against the entire people's earnest desire for reunification and to betray the vital interests of the whole nation.

What Kim Il-sung really meant, however, and what the leaders of the South never doubted that he really meant, was stated in a 1958 speech that he regarded so highly that he had it republished in the 16 December 1989 issue of the official *Pyongyang Times*:

> The completion of socialist construction in the northern half will not mean the end of our work. There still remains the tasks of reunifying our country and then carrying out democratic reforms such as agrarian reform and the nationalization of industries in South Korea. The fulfillment of the tasks of democratic revolution in the southern half should be followed by the continuing task of building socialism, and after the completion of socialist construction, our country will gradually have to move towards communism. Only when all these tasks are carried out with success will we be able to say that we have fulfilled our duties in the world revolution.

The significant portions of this statement are Kim's emphasis upon communizing the South and also on his declaration of adherence to the Communist International's aim of communizing the whole world. But what he meant was in sharp contrast to what he was insisting in 1962 and subsequently. His whole aim, he then insisted, was the patriotic determination to free the South Koreans "from the yoke of imperialism." The only contest between the divided segments of the people, he declared, was between "patriots and traitors." To emphasize this view officially, the DPRK constitution, as revised in 1972, affirmed in its Article 5 that the DPRK "strives to achieve the complete victory of socialism in the northern half, while driving out "foreign foes" in order to "reunify the country peacefully."

Both North and South Korea devoted a significant share of their scarce resources to establishing their legitimacy as firmly as possible in the worldwide diplomatic community. In 1948–49 this effort was aimed to emphasize the support each had from its communist or anti-communist friends and supporters. In the early 1960s this turned into an almost frantic outreach for diplomatic relations with any nation willing to establish them, without regard for ideology or for any discernible material advantage. What the DPRK wished was to cancel the U.N. approval of ROK as "the only lawful government in Korea." What ROK sought was to undermine or to counter any advantages the North could have from widespread recognition. This was a competition in which South Korea readily came out ahead. As a direct result of the United Nations approval of the founding of the Republic of Korea, permanent embassies were established in twenty-five countries. By 1965 ROK also had nonresident ambassadors accredited to an additional forty-three nations, and in 1966 it opened diplomatic offices in five more. North Korea's diplomatic relations, by 1966, reached to twenty-six countries, most of them communist, along with several newly independent nations in South Asia, Africa, and the Middle East. It also had trade relations with India, Burma, Ceylon, Uruguay, Iraq, and Austria. Most significantly, it had growing economic ties with Japan and was enabled inside Japan to operate a large and influential propaganda organization that spread worldwide the claim that only the DPRK truly represented the Korean people.

Even the Republic of Korea government abandoned any claim to being Korea's "only lawful government." In sharp contrast to the one-nation emphasis by Kim Il-sung, for President Park Chung Hee, even as early as 25 June 1966, reunification was cited as a "distant goal . . . feasible only after the intermediary objectives of self-reliance and modernization have been attained." A few years later, as Park professed on 18 January 1974, his efforts were directed not to regaining the North but to "peaceful coexistience with it." To Park, nothing was more important than to develop South Korea's economic prosperity, and he refused to be diverted from it. He was also influenced by radical shifts in the global international order.

The heightening of the Vietnam War in the mid-sixties and its apparently aimless continuance into the seventies sharpened world tensions. Because of worried allies and a rising tide of antiwar sentiment in the United States, President Richard Nixon and his foreign policy mentor Henry Kissinger felt obliged to seek a realignment in international relations. Established alliances were being re-examined. Whether democracy, always difficult to define, should be or could be the guiding standard governing global affairs, was being questioned. More specifically, the validity of directing national policies by the basic test of anti-communism was being seriously challenged.

These shifting views had considerable influence on both South and North Korea. President Nixon's surprise visit to China in February 1972 sent a wave of uneasiness all through eastern Asia. Japan openly displayed its anger and anxiety in not having been consulted, or even informed, of the preparatory negotiations. The Republic of Korea equally openly expressed its concern that the United States might abridge its guarantee against renewed invasion from the North. This concern was heightened when Nixon reduced

American troop strength in South Korea by twenty thousand, down to thirty-eight thousand. North Korea was alarmed by the weakening of China's anti-Americanism. Kim Il-sung interpreted the changing scene to the people of the North on 6 August 1971 by prophesizing: "As the U.S. imperialist aggressors who had suffered a defeat in the Korean War in the past came to Panmunjom with a white flag, so Nixon is, in the end, going to turn up in Peking with a white flag." To buttress confidence in his leadership, he reiterated his often repeated assurance that "all facts show that the collapse of imperialism is progressing at great speed in our era." After Nixon's arrival in Peking (renamed Beijing), North Korea's controlled press truculently sneered at Nixon as "a mendicant with a white flag in one hand and a beggar's bowl in the other."

The uneasiness aided President Part Chung Hee to intensify his dominance over South Korea's politics, economy, and indeed over the whole society. By the 1970s South Korea came more and more to resemble a police state. But unlike Kim Il-sung, Park did not possess absolute authority. He was restrained by South Korea's prior democratic experience. There also were constitutional guarantees of at least restricted political rights, including the holding of elections. Moreover, Park had designed and set in operation economic policies that were based on partly-free enterprise. Perhaps most significantly of all, South Korea was open to observation, to criticism, and to pressure from indispensable allies who premised their support on at least the prospect of the restoration of democratic freedom and rights.

President Park's political circumstances were complicated. The remarkable success of his economic program was bringing better living conditions and offered substantial hope for the future. During the first, second, and third five-year plans, up to 1973, real wages (adjusted for inflation) rose at the rate of 8.9%. The bottom 40 percent of workers received 44 percent as much income as the top fifth, a pattern of distribution that compared favorably with that of France and the United States. The income of workers varied, naturally, from one industrial group to another. Such skilled workers as those in petroleum refineries, industrial chemicals, mining, printing and publishing, and iron and steel plants were paid at the highest rate, around $280 (251,291 *won*) per month. Textile workers and those making clothing (predominantly girls and women) received about $190 (190,000 *won*). For the next five years, during the world-wide crisis, wages declined. But then, after 1980, during Chun Doo Hwan's presidency, they rose again, at an average rate of 16.5 percent annually. Regionalism, however, significantly influenced the welfare of workers. Wages were much higher in the industrial corridor from Pusan to Seoul than in the largely rural southwest. In Kwangju, for example, girls working in textile plants were earning during this latter period only $124 per month—and only about 30 percent of that was in basic wages. More than two-thirds of the annual income came from bonus payments, which meant that workers could not quit or get themselves fired without suffering an intolerable income loss. The textile workers were provided with free quarters in barracks-like buildings. They worked long hours, ate in mess halls, and had neither time nor energy for recreation. But they had jobs and were able to save enough to help, when they married, to establish comfortable homes.

Even so, dissatisfactions were multiple and were increasingly eruptive. Even the good works of Park's administration were marred by the rigidity and authoritarianism of the administrators. The mayor of Seoul, for example, rapidly and vastly transformed the city to render it suitable for its burgeoning population, by creating greatly needed traffic arteries, by building more bridges (seventeen in all) across the Han River, and by initiating the construction of first scores and then hundreds of modern apartment buildings. Despite the very obvious benefits, however, he was unpopular because he arbitrarily rode roughshod over property rights and ignored "due process." Political favorites were helped to attain wealth, particularly through real estate transactions.

There were other causes of dissatisfaction, equally disruptive. Favoritism in the granting of loans and building permits assured quick wealth for only the favored few. As Japanese investments multiplied, so did fears that South Korea was becoming a quasi-colony of its traditional enemy. The dispatch of troops as hired mercenaries into "America's war" in Vietnam was not popular, even though, for the economy, it was profitable. The power of the CIA and the police to make arrests on mere "suspicion" of "treasonable" intents or words, the holding of those arrested without trial or even indictment, and the use of torture to exact confessions nurtured an atmosphere of both fear and anger. After Park won re-election in 1967 and 1971 he determined that he would not again risk popular rejection. Controls over the people became even stricter.

In the early morning hours of 27 December 1971 the Democratic Republic majority in the National Assembly, during a protest boycott by opposition members, passed a "Special Law for National Protection." Its provisions severely limited citizens' rights of mobility, prohibited public assembly and demonstrations, further curtailed freedom of speech and press, and prohibited collective bargaining. Park also strengthened his control over his own partisans by purges of office holders and by dismissal or reassignment of top ranking army officers. The cabinet ministries were reduced to mere administrative functions. Since dissent still persisted, on 17 October 1972 Park declared martial law, abolished the constitution, dissolved the National Assembly, outlawed political activity, and temporarily closed all the universities.

Park then promulgated a new *Yushin* or revitalization constitution, declaring that "we can no longer sit idle while wasting our precious national power in futile endeavors." This new constitution provided for selection of the president by a National Conference for Unification, consisting of 2,560 members, half appointed by the President, the other half elected from a presidentially-approved list of candidates. The President's term of office was set at six years, with unlimited right of re-election. One third of the membership of the National Assembly was to be presidential appointments, with the remainder to be elected under rules that ensured a governmental majority. The National Assembly was restricted to annual meetings of two weeks. As a final guarantee of presidential power, the president was authorized to "temporarily restrict civil liberties" whenever he deemed there was a "national emergency."

House arrests and disappearance of critics was climaxed on 9 August 1973, by the kidnapping in Tokyo by CIA agents of Kim Dae-jung, who had won an impressive minority of votes in the 1971 presidential election. Spirited secretively back to Seoul by the KCIA, Kim was held under such severe house arrest that he could not even go to the hospital for treatment of injuries that had resulted from torture. A respected poet, Kim Chi-ha, who boldly criticized the dictatorship, was repeatedly arrested, held without trial, and beaten in prison. Outraged protests from foreign civic groups, religious organizations, and the mass media of allied nations were countered by organization of the Korean National Salvation Evangelical Corps, a pseudo-Christian movement headed by Park's younger daughter, that denied any such abuses were taking place and appealed for international anti-communist support. On 15 August, during an official celebration of the twenty-ninth anniversary of Korea's liberation, a Korean from Osaka, Japan, attempted to kill President Park; instead, his shots fatally wounded Mrs. Park. In 1977 a Korean businessman, Park Tong-son, was accused of undertaking to bribe American officials, using money supplied by the ROK government. American criticism of Park's rule sharpened, but the U.S.-Korean alliance remained strong.

America's interest in Korea and South Korea's recognition of the crucial importance of continuing American friendship resulted in visits by Park with President Kennedy in Washington, D.C., 14–15 November 1961; with President Johnson in Washington, 16–17 May 1965; with President Johnson in Honolulu, 18 April 1968; with President Richard Nixon in San Francisco, 20 August 1969; and in visits with Park Chung Hee in Seoul by President Gerald Ford, on 22 November 1974; and by President Jimmy Carter, 29 June–1 July 1979. The treaty with Japan, even more than the dispatch of Korean troops to Vietnam, was hailed by the Johnson administration in Washington as evidence of Park's high statesmanship. These developments, President Johnson attested (on 22 November 1966) "had contributed significantly to the achievement of an atmosphere of further unity and stability" in Asia. A decade later, when U.S. Secretary of State Henry Kissinger proposed that Korean reunification be sought in a four-power conference of the United States, the People's Republic of China, South Korea, and North Korea, and when President Jimmy Carter (in March 1977) proposed the phased withdrawal of the American troops from Korea, these proposals were not intended by Washington nor interpreted by Seoul as American disengagement from its promise to help restore Korean unity under a free and democratic government, but rather as confidence that progress toward that goal was advancing.

By the many Koreans who resented and, as best they could, resisted the Park administration's violations of civil rights, this American approval was interpreted as support for oppression. This feeling led to noisy anti-Yankee demonstrations. The ROK administration, grateful as it was for American support, also made clear its rejection of any paternalistic U.S. oversight. The Republic of Korea had decisively shed its subordinate status as a client state. It was also emerging steadily from its undeveloped condition to industrial and commercial maturity. Its political faults were not much improved. Attention, both domestically and internationally, was diverted from them, however, by developments of a new kind between the North and the South.

Both Kim Il-sung and Park Chung Hee commenced cautiously but earnestly to search for ways of dealing constructively with the destructive division of the Korean nation. Despite the history of Communist subversion in the South and the renewed truculence of the North, on 15 August 1970 President Park, as part of the celebration of the twenty-fifth anniversary of the end of the colonial period, declared his willingness to open gradual contact with the DPRK if it would renounce the use of force. This was, for the first time, from either zone, a call for a new era of "peaceful competition in goodwill." It was also a momentous shift in ROK policy, from its unvarying stance of being the only lawful government in Korea and from its determined pursuit of reunification. In effect, both of these positions were replaced with the new goal of "peaceful competition."

Kim Il-sung, for his part, was confusingly intermingling the renewal of violence against the ROK with protestions that his plans for reunification did not include the communization of the South. After the delay of a year, he responded to Park's proposals by suggesting, on 6 August 1971, a summit meeting with Park and also inter-Korean meetings of the heads of political parties and social organizations. The Korean National Red Cross proposed talks to arrange for the reunion of separated families. As these Red Cross talks began in September at Panmunjom, they were stymied by Northern insistence on free travel between the zones by individuals looking for family members and by Southern insistence that such travel be restricted to individuals who already had located family members. The Southern stance was based upon the well-founded expectation that Communist agents would use such free travel to disrupt the society and to attempt the overthrow of the Park government.

While this disagreement was fomenting, President Park secretely sent the ROK CIA director, Yi Hu-Rak, to Pyongyang for discussions with Kim Il-sung. The result of these talks was the establishment, in November 1972, of a South-North Coordinating Committee, charged to initiate joint programs and steps toward peaceful reunification. The subsequent meetings of this committee intensified hostility rather than reduced it. The ROK saw North Korean proposals as thinly disguised plans for the subversion of the South; and, from all appearances, the Northern delegates may have become alarmed lest the population of the North would break out of its bondage in a rush to embrace open exchanges with the South. The North Korean delegation proposed that South Korea suspend its laws that limited public discussion of communism and the ROK delegates responded with a demand that the North cease its efforts to subvert the ROK government. Proposals and counterproposals continued, with virtually no constructive discussion of them. Kim Il-sung sought a quick solution of the division of the nation by having all United States troops and military support withdrawn, after which reunification, as "an internal affair of our nation, should be solved not by the interference of outside forces, but by the efforts of the Korean people themselves." Park, quite differently, postponed the efforts for reunification in order to pursue a "step by step" program of cultural and economic exchanges that would bring the two sides into closer accord. Meanwhile, he continued the policy of retaining American troops as a guarantee against renewed attack and sought also to seek for unification through "the U.N. formula alone," meaning "genuinely free elections throughout Korea under U.N. supervision." An essential difference between the two sides was Kim's continuing emphasis on removal of all "foreign interference" (meaning the U.S. and U.N. influence), whereas Park's principal emphasis was upon elimination of North Korean interference in South Korea.

The United Nations commenced a gradual lessening of its commitments to South Korea after the 1961 military coup. In December 1963 it invited "both Korea's" to participate in the annual General Assembly discussion of the Korean problem, with the proviso that the DPRK "unequivocably accept the competence and authority of the U.N." Two years later the U.N. discontinued the UNCURK, thereby ending its sponsorship of the Republic of Korea.

With the United Nations recommitted to neutrality on the Korean question, and with both South and North having, in effect, given up any claim to being the "only" Korean government, in June 1973 the North-South Coordinating Committee recognized that it could not find a basis for agreement. The ROK delegates summed up their position by calling for creation of permanent subcommittees on economic and on sociocultural affairs. North Korea insisted on additional subcommittees to deal with political and with military problems. It also repeated its demand for withdrawal of all U.S. troops from the South, for reduction of the ROK armed forces, and an end to its imports of military materiel. On 23 June Park called for recognition of "two Koreas" and for the admission of both to the U.N. On the same day, Kim demanded creation of a Great National Congress, the unification of

Korea under a confederation in which the North and South would have equal authority, and admission to the United Nations of this "confederal Republic" of Korea. In the face of this uncompromising disagreement, further discussions between the two zones were indefinitely postponed. Eighteen years were to pass before both governments became U.N. members.

It is impossible to understand Korea without understanding the depth of the tragedy of its division—with families separated from one another and unable to communicate, not knowing who was living and who was dead, or how they lived; and not knowing what prospect, if any, there was that their broken nation might be made whole again. Part of the dread feeling was helplessness, of not being able to do anything about it. Neither in the North nor in the South were the people able to take any part in the decision-shaping process; in neither zone were there elections in which reunification strategies were voted upon.

The difference between the tightly closed North and the relatively open South cannot be overemphasized. For the maintenance of stability and order, the advantage was with the North. Its public remained ignorant and quiescent—on some occasions and in some degree even enthusiastically supportive of its leadership because of the all-inclusive propaganda apparatus. In the South, obedience to the government was enforced but resentments ran deep and wide. The militaristic discipline that Park and his associates enforced works within the armed forces because they are themselves a "closed society," in which the enlisted personnel have neither the right nor real opportunities to exert their personal will. The effort to apply this type of discipline to the civilian population was a patchwork of contradictory or conflicting measures that fostered disunity and dissent. This was President Park's great dilemma as he sought to implement his "guided capitalism" and "Koreanized democracy" in the attainment of his economic goals.

As one means for dealing with this problem, in 1971 Park Chung Hee launched the *Saemaul Undong,* translated as the New Village or New Community movement. For its first two or three years, the former translation was the more accurate, since it was aimed specifically for improvement of the rural areas. Afterwards, it expanded to include the nationwide "community of workers" in the factories as well as in the fields. To this movement Park gave a considerable share of his own attention. The stated purpose was the rapid upgrading of rural living conditions. Its earmarks were hard work, self-sacrifice, and intensely loyal devotion to the government. At the same time, it was also a fanatic political organization. In its operations, it consisted partly of ambitious practical programs and partly of evangelistic "re-education" to replace factionalism with enthusiastic support of Park's administration. In its initial phase it represented the fervor of a religious revival, somewhat akin to the secular aspects of Chondogyo. Through it, Park hoped to bring to the farms and villages—and subsequently to the industrial work-force—an enlivening and creative advancement that would parallel his stimulation of industrialism. On another level, he utilized it also as a political campaign organization through which villages and urban workers were tightly controlled.

For the farming class (which, though greatly shrunken, still comprised a quarter to a third of the total population) what Park's economic miracle could do was limited. Between 1965–70 the retail price of rice increased 20–25 percent annually, but the rice-growing farmers did not profit materially. During this period farm income rose from $411 to $445 annually, per farm family, while urban family income rose from $413 to $782. In subsequent years this disparity continued. The principal economic policies, including diverse taxation, loan, and supply allocation to productive segments deemed critical, bore heavily on the unsponsored and nonpreferred small rural factories and on agriculture. Inflation, a serious burden for urbanites, was even more grievous for the small-plot farmers. By 1970, among South Korea's 33,000 villages, only 3,400 had telephone service. Few had doctors or nurses. These factors were problems that President Park simply had to solve. They were a personal concern of his because he felt keenly his own ties with the rural poor. But his concern was more than personal. As the years passed following his ascension to power, these conditions became increasingly politically costly. Something had to be done to win the support of the alienated poor.

Rural improvement campaigns were stressed in many developing countries. But nowhere else were they so comprehensively organized or so definitely a cardinal aim of government policy. In a very much broader context, the Saemaul Undong drew from the Korean tradition of guild cooperation and perhaps even more from the Confucian teachings of respect for authority and of subordination of self to the group. The farmers were not only ready but eager for some kind of program that would assure them their fair share in the nation's rapidly improving economy. During the second Five-Year Plan, 1967–71, the gap between urban and rural income widened, as the value of agricultural products increased by only 2.5 percent, while the overall GNP rose annually by 10.5 percent. As a result, the cities suffered from a surplus of population moving in from the countryside that disrupted traffic, overwhelmed housing, increased unemployment, stimulated street crime, and stirred political unrest. Corollary results in the rural villages were separation of families and loss of productivity as farm labor increasingly became feminine, very old, or very young. Leadership in the villages deteriorated as the more capable individuals left to seek better opportunities.

As part of the Third Five-Year Economic Development Plan, the government allocated some two billions of dollars to rural improvements. Well-trained government agents, skilled in speaking and in the conduct of meetings, spread out through the countryside with inspiring exhortations about what the villagers could do, with government guidance and financial support, to help themselves. Complaints and emotional depression were challenged by admonitions that "we, too, can prosper if we work hard and cooperate with one another." Cooperative societies were launched and expanded. The existing Four-H Clubs, Boy Scouts, and Girl Scouts were invigorated. Money was brought into the communities by government speakers who outlined plans for replacing the straw-thatched huts with modern homes that had tile roofs, plumbing, safe water, and Western-style kitchens. Rural electrification brought telephones, radios, and then television into most of the homes. Rutted streets were paved. City halls were constructed. Arable land area was significantly expanded through flood control dams and by diking along riverbanks and ocean basins. Training programs were established to develop village leaders. Village affairs were unified through election by each village of two leaders, a man and a woman. For individual projects, such as home construction, families were given no funds but received encouragement and technical guidance. Loans, subsidies, and grants were available for village and for inter-village projects. Citizens were encouraged to volunteer their own labor and such money or supplies as they could. Farm cooperatives joined fields into large units and modern machinery was brought in to supplement or replace hand labor. Village schools adopted practical, local-oriented vocational training programs.

The results have been almost as impressive as was the industrial program. The countryside has been transformed, with villagers having most of the facilities available to apartment-dwelling urbanites, as well as more expansive living quarters and an environment much freer from pollution. The Saemaul Undong has accomplished within two decades an agricultural revolution that in many parts of the world takes a full century or simply hasn't happened. Many thousands of rural area leaders from more than 125 countries have come to South Korea to study the Saemaul Undong, and hundreds of them have taken the leadership training program. As years passed, the need for it diminished and maladministration further weakened it. Its prestige was shattered when its operations were corrupted after Chun Doo Hwan's brother became its administrator. The effort to expand it into cities and factories has not been successful. Dwellers in new multistory urban apartment complexes lack the social unity of long established rural villages and it is harder for families to see benefits from volunteer cooperative endeavors. Moreover, the rise of effective labor unions has provided for urbanites a different kind of benefit-enhancement system.

Then, sensationally, the troubles and the triumphs of the confused decade of contrasts came to an end. Park Chung Hee was assassinated. A new military coup brought to South Korea a new government. Transition by revolution once more occurred. And the people of Korea confronted suddenly yet another change of government.

21

The Clouded Tenure of Chun Doo Hwan

The sudden news that Park's eighteen-year rule had been ended by his murder was received by the Korean people without much visible evidence of shock. In a sense, this was emblematic of the confident maturity that the nation, under Park's leadership, had attained. It was also a reflection of widespread feeling that his leadership had lasted too long, that the ordinary citizens were not getting their share of the widely-heralded prosperity, and that it was past time to end the severity of the restrictions he imposed upon civil rights. It was time for a change—even if this was not the right way to bring change about, and even if they had no way of knowing what kinds of change were to follow.

After a brief interlude of uncertainty, the most visible changes, and those that bore most directly upon their lives, were not for the better but rather were shockingly for the worse. Nor were the changes of a kind over which the people had, or felt that they had, any control. The democracy that they needed, and that they were ever more insistently demanding, was sharply curtailed. Other more beneficial changes were to come: but the aftermath of the Park presidency proved to be a time of sharpening discontent. Their successor president was not the people's choice, nor was he the kind of executive they would have chosen if they could.

The subsequent eight-year rule of General Chun Doo Hwan over the republic of Korea is obscured by scandal. Neither the personality of the man nor the means by which he rose to power emerged into clear public view. Some achievements of his presidency were notable. The prosperity of the republic rose to new heights. Economic reforms that he instituted considerably reduced the centralist controls Park had established, thereby pointing the way toward the present free market system. Except for the quiet retirement of Interim President Huh Chung, Chun was the first top national executive to turn over his office to an elected successor. Credit for this progress toward democracy is reduced, however, by the fact that his retirement was obviously reluctant, forced by circumstances beyond his control, and that he manipulated the choice of his successor.

What deeply marred Chun's presidency, and what will always be bitterly remembered about it, was the harsh authoritarianism of his rule and the shameless corruption that involved himself, his brothers, his wife, and her family. Indisputably, his record is deeply besmirched.

Nevertheless, a balanced examination of his administration unveils substantial advancements. For one thing, the republic's international stature was strengthened. Foreign trade and South Korea's status with the global community of nations were significantly enhanced. For the mass of the people there were substantial gains in their living standards. This, in turn, unleashed a strengthened spirit of robust self-confidence. Because of this, when confronting Chun's abuses, the people ultimately proved to be stronger than their corrupt, authoritarian, and militaristic government.

Chun's presidential tenure ended in dramatic disgrace. He was forced to go before the National Assembly to confess his breeches of moral and legal conduct and to apologize to the nation he had ruled. After this, instead of being brought to trial, he and his wife were sent into exile in the remote Paektam Buddhist monastery on the steep slopes of Mr. Sorak, some 125 miles northeast of Seoul. Deprived of the luxuries that had been provided for them during his presidency (with its plethora of attendants to cater to their every want) they had to live in small and sparse quarters, where they were served simple food, and no entertainment, and were unprotected from the winter cold. After two years, the Chuns were permitted to return to their private family home in Seoul—though the title was claimed by the government as partial restitution for money the two had embezzled. There they lived in seclusion, dishonored and long unnoticed, punished primarily by being ignored.

The rise of Major General Chun began with the fall of President Park. The assassination of Park Chung Hee, in the early evening of 26 October 1979, was an opportunistic and unplanned climax of a personal vendetta. Chun Doo Hwan, who most directly and most largely profited from it, was not a party to it, either as a direct participant or as an accomplice. He did not directly succeed to the presidency but won it by subterfuge over a period of ten months, during which he systematically gathered to himself the necessary power.

How the presidency became available to him is a story that reveals the way the military was functioning internally and the role it held in the government. Park had seized the power of the presidency from outside; Chun knit together the essential processes of burrowing within. The interrelationships emerged clearly in the events leading up to the assassination and in its aftermath.

That day in October had been a good one for President Park. It came in South Korea's best season, known as "the time of high skies and fat horses." The weather was sparklingly good and the people were happily celebrating the harvests with the traditional farmers' festivals. President Park spent the afternoon down the west coast, dedicating a large tidal dike that added much needed acreage for the rice growing. The event was a great personal satisfaction reflecting his lasting desire to improve the lot of the farmers and the living conditions for the villagers.

After the return of Park and his entourage to the presidential quarters, *Chong wha dae,* in Seoul, Park's pleasant mood was sharply terminated. His longtime friend and chief of his bodyguards, tough-minded Cha Chi-chol, seized the occasion to urge the immediate dismissal of the KCIA director Kim Chae-gyu. For weeks Cha had been repeatedly warning President Park that the demonstrations of protest against the government could and should have been prevented if only the KCIA had done its duty by controlling dissenters. It was afterwards reported that he told Park that if Pol Pot had killed two million Cambodians, the government need not worry about killing a few hundred thousands of students to end the rioting. Park agreed to conduct a disciplinary session. Cha thereupon telephoned Director Kim to inform him that the president would arrive at the KCIA headquarters at 6:20 p.m. to take dinner in its private dining room. Accompanying Park was his presidential secretary, Kim Kye-won, along with Cha, two other staff officials, and five bodyguards.

Only Cha and Kim Kye-won joined with President Park and Director Kim Chae-gyu for dinner, leaving the others in the anteroom. Cha, not bothering to eat, launched immediately into a heated denunciation of Director Kim. Kim, saying nothing, excused himself and went out. He spoke with his protocol chief, Park Sunho, and his personal secretary, Park Hung-ju, telling them, "I will kill Park and Cha today." He ordered them to bring a KCIA security force and to kill Park's bodyguards and the two civil officers when shots were heard from the dining room. Then he went upstairs to his office and slipped a pistol under his belt. When he rejoined the dinner party, Cha was continuing his abusive harangue. Kim listened without making any reply for a few minutes. Then at 7:30 he left again, to make sure that his aides were ready to carry out his orders. Returning to the dining room, without speaking he drew his pistol and shot first Cha, then Park; then he shot each of them again. Outside, the KCIA security agents killed the presidential guards and officers.

Park's secretary, Kim Kye-won, picked up a phone and, unmolested by Director Kim, reported the murders to General Chung Seung-hwa, who was both the Chief of Staff of the armed forces and commander of martial law. General Chung had not only Kim Chae-gyu but also Kim Kye-won held for questioning. In a subsequent trial, Director Kim was found guilty of murder and was promptly executed. Kim Kye-won was found guilty of complicity and was sentenced to life imprisonment. A few months later, he was released as an act of presidential clemency although not cleared of the charge.

In this flurry of events, it was General Chun Doo Hwan who took charge. He held the key office of Chief of Integrated Investigation Headquarters, which gave him unrestricted investigative power. Promptly he affirmed his own authority, independent of General Chung Seung-hwa. Others who might have questioned Chun's authority were restrained by fear of being themselves charged with either complicity or laxity in Park's murder. The "others" could have been numerous, for hatred of Park had been well-fueled in influential quarters. Ex-KCIA director Kim Hyong Uk, who had testified that Park was personally responsible for the attempted bribing of American political leaders (and who compounded his criticism by writing a book of memoirs detailing abuses of the Park Chung Hee presidency), had reportedly been kidnapped in Paris, brought back to Seoul and tortured until he died in the cellar of the presidential residence. Other critics of Park had been expelled from the National Assembly. Still others, in the army and in the civil government had been passed over for promotions or demoted for alleged or suspected anti-Park sentiments.

Immediately upon release of the news of the assassination, later that same evening Prime Minister Choi Kyu-hah declared himself Acting President and issued a reassuring announcement to the public: "We cannot afford to be lost in sorrow. . . . I call upon the nation to have confidence in the government and the military." General John A. Wickham, Jr., Commander of the US-ROK Combined Forces, also immediately issued a statement aimed both to the North, to forestall an attack, and to the people of the republic, assuring South Korea of "unwavering American support." In a formal message to Acting President Choi, General Wickham reaffirmed United States "total dedication to the national security," then added:

> The republic's loss is grievous. President Park was responsible for stimulating and directing the economic miracle that moved the Republic of Korea to the forefront of developing industrialized nations.
>
> The legacy he leaves to the nation he loved and served so well is long and distinguished. His achievements will remain an inspiration.
>
> The mark of his leadership is an indelible part of Korean history. The nation united under your leadership ensures that the fabric of Korean society will not be torn by this tragic event.

The reactions of the public were similar to those expressed by Choi and Wickham—neither shock nor great surprise, but a mingling of respect and appreciation for what Park accomplished along with acceptance and adjustment to the need for a change. Buddhist commemorative services were conducted in temples and in public squares, attended by crowds of sorrowing people. Nevertheless, shops remained open and workers reported to their jobs as usual. Park's body lay in state in *Chong wa dae,* where Park's eldest daughter Miss Park Keun-hae, his official hostess, welcomed the many dignitaries, foreign and domestic, who came to pay their last respects. The reaction of the military was typically cautious. Martial law was proclaimed and colleges and universities were closed. An especially close watch was maintained in Kwangju, the political base of Park's chief critic, Kim Dae-jung, for its population was angrily resentful of the treatment of Kim and also of its exclusion from the prosperity of the Pusan-Seoul industrialized corridor.

The legacy Park Chung Hee left to the Korean people was complex. Democracy was reduced rather than developed. But other kinds of benefits abounded. By many kinds of measurements, between 1961 and 1979 South Korea was transformed. The material standard of living, however inequitable, was greatly improved. Seoul became a massive beehive of activity, swollen in population and extending its suburbs all the way to Inchon and Suwon. A newly-built subway and elevated highway system crisscrossed Seoul, and seventeen new bridges were constructed across the Han River. But all of these were still inadequate to serve the hugely expanded traffic. Multistoried department stores and large shopping malls provided the public with access to a wide variety and an ample amount of consumer's goods. Schools, utilities, and medical services were all multiplied but still lagged behind the greatly expanding needs. Quantitatively, as measured by statistics of life expectancy, literacy, average per capita income, rate of savings, gross national income, and availability of modern facilities, the living conditions of South Korea were tremendously improved. Six-story apartment buildings were erected quickly and thickly, providing for the inhabitants of Seoul and other large cities the amenities of healthful water, electrified kitchens, air conditioning, television, and garbage collection. Before Park's death, a full half dozen world-class hotels in Seoul matched those of metropolitan centers in the West. By these and other standards, South Korea had become an industrialized success.

As was happening around the world, there were also qualitative losses along with the substantial gains. Serious pollution of the air and of rivers and streams became a threat to health as well as undermining comfort. Noise, traffic congestion, street crime, juvenile delinquency, and daily difficulty in getting back and forth between homes and workplaces were inevitable blotches on the progress. Despite such problems, unquestionably the standard of living in South Korea had greatly improved and was still improving.

Some political circumstances, under a brief interim presidency, improved immediately and substantially after Park's death. On 6 December Choi Kyuhah was confirmed as South Korea's President by the National Conference on Unification. Choi, like Huh Chung, was mild-mannered and liberal-minded. He was a foreign service professional, who had risen to the top through the diplomatic service. Korean commentators have generally denounced him for lack of will and even for cowardice for failing to control the military. Actually, Choi had no political base from which to exercise any real power. He was well intentioned but virtually helpless. Although Chun Doo Hwan's control over the military restricted Choi to a shadow presidency, he undertook to liberalize and democratize both the government and the society. One of his first acts was to restore full civil rights to 684 politicians, including Yun Po-sun and Kim Dae-jung, whose political activities had been proscribed. To reduce North-South tensions, President Choi negotiated plans for joint meetings of the prime ministers of the two governments. On 13 March he inaugurated a Constitution Revision Committee, charged to end the *Yushin* system and return democratic control to the people. These promising measures encouraged the public to demand also better living conditions. Confidence in President Choi, never high, fell rapidly. The worldwide economic decline that resulted from curtailment of Middle East oil supplies was particularly severe in South Korea. Many small and middle-sized industrial plants went into bankruptcy, with resultant unemployment and widespread curtailment of wages. In protest, a major coal miners' strike erupted in April into a four-day riot.

Behind the scenes, in ways unknown to the public, General Chun Doo Hwan was exercizing the real governmental power. Public indignation boiled over against what was termed *angae chonggook,* or the "foggy political situation." Chun Doo Hwan used his unchecked investigatory powers ruthlessly. In what came to be known as the "12-12" incident, he arrested Army Chief General Song Sung-hwa the night of 12 December. Then at 3:30 in the morning he awakened President Choi and secured his signature on a grant of authority. Along with his close associates, Major Generals Roh Tae Woo and Chong Ho-yong, Chun seized total command over the armed services. Generals commanding crucial security forces in Seoul were arrested. Major General Roh ordered his Ninth Division troops into Seoul and in a bloody seven-hour battle captured the ROKA headquarters and the Ministry of Defense. Chun then named Roh commander of the Capitol Garrison and Chong commander of Special Forces.

In April Chun made his power secure by illegally naming himself Director of the KCIA, while retaining his generalship. He also required President Choi to create a National Security Council, with power to govern without constitutional constraints, and he took chairmanship of the Standing Committee of the Council, which exercised full powers in continuous session. Widespread angry protest demonstrations broke out, climaxing on 15 May in a march through the streets of Seoul by some 100,000 students from thirty universities. In an effort to prevent bloodshed, the students called off their demonstration. But it was too late.

On 17 May martial law was proclaimed, nationwide, under the direct command of General Chun Doo Hwan. All political parties were ordered to suspend their activities. Kim Dae-jung was arrested on the charge that he instigated anti-government disorder. Protest demonstrations were staged in Kwangju and to suppress them Chun sent in the toughest military force, the airborne paratroop regiment. Immediately, on 18 May, these troopers opened fire on demonstrators and as many as two hundred were killed. In response to this severity, tens of thousands of Kwangju students and other residents defended themselves as best they could. More troops, commanded by Roh Tae Woo, were rushed in. Small clashes quickly erupted into general fighting, which continued through 27 May. This "Kwangju Massacre" became a major and long-continued political issue. The government reported that some two hundred rebellious rioters were killed. Kwangju spokesmen said the true figure was more than two thousand. Tight and severe martial law was maintained throughout the nation, with tanks stationed at the street corners of the cities and with military units policing both governmental and civilian affairs.

On 16 August Choi Kyu-hah resigned as president; on 27 August Chun Doo Hwan was elected by the National Council on Unification to succeed him. President Chun was inaugurated on 1 September declaring that his seven-year term would be dedicated to creating a "Just Society." He further defined the aims of his presidency as threefold: to maintain social order and national security; to spread the benefits of the economic progress more equitably; and to recast the political and social nature of the society in accordance with Korea's (undefined) traditional culture. In addition to trying as best he could to justify the martial law and the severity of dealing with the Kwangju demonstrations, Chun's goals pointed toward a restructuring of both the economy and the politics of the country.

Politically and socially, he declared, the society was paying too high a price for its remarkably rapid economic growth. "Traditional virtues, morals and manners," he charged, had given way to "rampant materialism, irregularities, injustices, corruption and a climate of universal distrust." There had been a period, he said, of absorbing Western influences "faster than they could be assimilated," leading to "spiritual indigestion."

Chun's remedy for these ills was not more but less social and political freedom. Under government pressure, more than seven hundred journalists were dismissed; many newspapers and radio-television broadcasting operations were merged and placed under government control. Press freedom was sharply restricted. In a major "purification" move, some eight thousand civil service employees were purged. Critics of the administration were put into severely disciplinary *Samchong* re-education camps. As a means for reducing the anger of the people, Chun pledged that he would voluntarily retire from the presidency upon completion of his one term. In the meantime his emphasis was upon "efficiency" rather than "equity." During the closing years of his administration, his call for the restoration of "traditional virtues and morals" was abrogated by financial scandals.

As Chun's presidency was nearing its end, the National Assembly launched inquiries into alleged widespread corruption into his and his wife's families. Embezzlement of major proportions was charged against her, her uncle, Lee Kyu-dong, and her younger brother, Lee Chang-suk. In subsequent court trials they were found guilty and sentenced to long prison terms. Chun's own brothers Chun Ki-hwan and Chun Kyong-hwan (who headed and corrupted the Saemaul Undong) along with Chung's long-time security chief, Chang Se-dong, were also found guilty of fraudulently accumulating large and very expensive Seoul properties. An equally notorious scandal concerned establishment of an Ilhae Foundation that raised enormous amounts of money through threats, coercion, and grants of government favors, presumably to be used by Chun for his political campaigning but actually diverted to the personal accounts of Chun, his family, and some associates.

Despite his autocracy and the dishonesty of his family and of some close associates, President Chun made fundamental and substantial contributions to South Korea's economic progress. He undertook to free the economy from the centralized governmental controls that had at first stimulated rapid growth and later handicapped it. As a first step, he turned the banking system back to private enterprise. In 1981 Chun commenced denationalizing the nation's commercial banks. The following year the government abolished the system of preferential lending rates and lower taxes to favored industries and companies. Joint ventures between Korean and foreign banks were authorized. In 1983 the government completed the restoration of banks to private ownership. Most importantly, the interest rates were freed to become market-oriented, without favoritism.

A Fair Trade Law, promulgated in 1981, included a broad array of reforms. Anticompetitive mergers were prohibited. Unfair and deceptive advertising was forbidden. The tariff system was re-examined, with a commitment to reduce both import duties and subsidies for exports—a process that has led to continuing negotiations, year after year, with South Korea's international trading partners. The most notable achievement was reduction of the high rate of inflation from its peak of 18 and 20 percent annually down to the level of three and four percent. As the economic structure was gradually shifted from government controls to market-oriented free enterprise, new problems, as well as benefits, developed.

What Chun's administration failed to accomplish was revision of the legal system to serve the basic needs of a free economy. Neither did it achieve sufficiently its promised spread of benefits through high wages and improved working conditions. Hence, its proclaimed "private sector industrial guidance model" proved inadequate to end the state-guided economy. As bankruptcies multiplied, the government ordered banks to issue relief loans. Embezzlement scandals, involving some Chun associates and family members, precipitated the insolvency of some commercial banks. Other firms were deprived of funds needed for capital investment, leading to failures of companies to meet their contractual obligations. These problems became especially severe for trading companies, shipping companies, and some of the firms that were doing what had been profitable business as construction contactors in the Middle East and in Southeast Asia.

Aside from the damaging corruption, the shift from centralized governmental controls to free enterprise proved to require such a complicated restructuring of laws, practices, and attitudes that disarray made the situation worse before it could become better.

When Chun came into the presidency, he issued a statement denouncing the liberalizing of the Choi Kyu-hah administration. Ironically, his criticism of Choi also fairly described his own tenure: he understood the problems of the country better than he knew how to solve them. "We must learn from our experiences since the death of President Park Chung Hee," Chun said.

> This incident created a power vacuum, and the country began to drift aimlessly, like a kite cut off from its string. The discipline of the administration slackened, the grass-roots New Community Movement began to wither, and worst of all the economy registered a minus growth, though this was of course influenced by a worldwide recession.
>
> Society, in other words, came to a nearly total standstill, and political agitators, opportunists, deluded idealists and cynical manipulators came to the forefront, since there was none to stand in their way, none to refute their claims, none to raise the voice of reason and prudence.

In the eighties, as the world economy recovered from the recession caused by the energy crisis, South Korea resumed its very rapid economic advancement. By 1986 unemployment fell to the low level of 3.9 percent. The GNP rose to the impressive level of $80 billion. Exports increased during the first quarter of that year by 22.9 percent. The import liberalization policy opened South Korea's markets to 1,400 new foreign products. The promised "spread of benefits," however, did not automatically occur. Workers became first dismayed and then angry, resulting in a wave of strikes that closed many factories. Labor gained enough power to force a 62.5 percent average increase in wages. Major factories speedily commenced to automate their production, confronting the trade unions with the threat of lost jobs. Once again, as in the first decades of the republic, labor and management confronted one another with resentment and anger. Still the economy surged on upwards. Across the nation material gains were substantial. But the labor front confrontation, occurring while President Chun was coming under a barrage of public charges of corruption, soured the temper of the society.

South Korean literature recast itself to enact the role of social critic. Novelists, poets, journalists, and religious leaders alike became outspoken critics of the political irrationally that plagued the society. Perhaps the most popular of these poets was a rebel named Kim Nam-ju, who wrote steadily during nine years of imprisonment for his political activism. In "The Poem's Cradle," he stated his credo:

> You ask
> Why are my poems so cruel and fierce
> Like a woodsman chopping firewood
> I can only return your question like this.
>
> Isn't that what a fight is all about?
> Once you've started the voices soar like steeples
> And curses you'd never think of using burst out.

A factory worker, Pak No-hae, published an anthology of poetry written by laborers entitled *The Dawn of Labor,* which he dedicated to "my fellow workers who live and work with gusto, never forgetting hope and laughter despite their miserable living conditions, low wages, and long working hours." The literary community was swept by a "Pak No-hae storm," which resulted in a veritable flood of labor poetry.

Social protest and criticism marked the novels as well. One of the most popular young novelists, Yi In-song, wrote a novelette in 1980, *Into a Strange Time,* relating the experience of a college student who was drafted into the army as a punishment for taking part in demonstrations. Because of the sudden death of his father, the student is discharged early. Returning home, he concludes that if he had remained in college his father would not have died. Overcome by guilt, he tried to commit suicide. Similarly cheerless are the stories of Miss Yan Kwi-ja, whose collection of short stories, *A Blind Bird,* published in 1986, deal mostly with the materialistic greed and selfishness that characterized the working place. Choi Su-chol published psychological novels dealing with loneliness and alienation because of the impossibility of attaining genuine communication among individuals. Other novels, like those by Choi In-hoon, depict the Korean War as a struggle between Soviet communism and American democracy, with Korea crushed between them. Still other novels deal ironically with the theme of stress and internal conflicts in the generation following liberation from Japan.

The prevailing unhappiness in these literary productions found a sufficient echo in the feelings of the people so that book stores did a rousing business. Several anthologies of poems and of stories sold over two hundred thousand copies during the decade of the eighties, and one sold more than a million. South Korea, like other lands and places, suffered even during a time of vastly improving conditions from the fact that present gains are dwarfed by rising expectations.

A tremendous lift to the spirits of the Korea people resulted from the choice of the republic to host the Asead Summer Games in 1986 and the Summer Olympic Games in 1988. This global approval of the elevated status of the Korean republic not only induced a tremendous construction boom in Seoul but also insured that, under the steady observation of the world community, as well as the outrage and anger of the Korean public against his corruption, President Chun's pledge to retire from office at the end of his term was kept. Even this was marred, however, by his obvious desire to remain in office if only he could.

22

Roh Tae Woo's Reach for Democracy

The next presidential election in South Korea is, at this writing, scheduled for December 1992. Many in Korea feel that it will give them another chance to reach a level of democratic rights that has thus far eluded them. General Roh Tae Woo (who calls himself Noh Tai-woo) has never been the popular choice. His close association with the most autocratic acts of Chun Doo Hwan deeply stained his reputation. His election as president by just over a third of the votes cast was far from a mandate. His conduct of the presidency has been marred by broken promises and by long delays in implementing electoral reforms.

Countering these heavily negative factors, President Roh has followed a course of reasoned restraint in dealing with the continuing protests and demonstrations by university students, laborers, political opposition, intellectuals, and of urbanites, especially those in the southwest, who feel they are deprived of their share of well-being and of just treatment. Under Roh's presidency, South Koreans have manifestly enjoyed more democracy than in any prior period except that of the ill-starred tenure of John Myun Chang. Meanwhile, their prosperity has continued to mount and has very greatly spread its benefits. Articulate critics continue to complain, however, that the government does not do enough. The situation illustrates what Robert Browning meant when he wrote that *A man's reach should exceed his grasp.* The people, and Roh himself, have reached for more than they have as yet been able to get.

The reach that Roh Tae Woo set for himself when he announced his candidacy for the presidency on 29 June 1987 was "to make this country a more mature, developed democracy." In advancing toward this goal, even Roh's severest critics grant that significant progress has been made. And even his strongest supporters admit that progress has been too little and often too late.

Part of the explanation for this mixture of contrary sentiments is that always, in times of progressive improvements, expectations leap ahead of what has been achieved. But beyond this, there remain serious problems that have not yet been solved. In varying degrees these problems arise from the continuing hostile division of the nation. Like a festering cancer, the effects of this division directly and indirectly affect virtually every aspect of the society. These effects were intensified when the breakdown of communist totalitarianism in Eastern Europe and then in the Soviet Union did not spread to include North Korea.

Questions abound and answers are elusive. Who and what are to blame? Is the fault wholly the intransigence of North Korea's Kim Il-sung? Must reunification await his death or removal from office? To what degree, if at all, does the "military-industrial complex" in the South reject northern overtures in order to serve its own interests of protecting its power and prosperity? Will the North accept nothing less than control? Unquestionably, the traditional homogeneity of the peninsula has been damaged by the deeply implanted economic, ideological, and cultural differences that now exist between the two zones. Even if, on both sides, there was goodwill and a desire to do so, fitting these disparities back together would be staggeringly difficult. Beyond such domestic problems, increasingly many Koreans, and particularly those too young to remember the Korean War, are wondering why American troops are kept on in South Korea. Does their own government favor it because of psychological and economic as well as military values? Why is this also the policy of the United States? Is it wholly an unselfish commitment to the goal of a reunited Korea under its wholly independent democratic government? Or are there economic, diplomatic, and strategic military reasons as well? All of these questions merit extensive public discussion and debate. All of them are, in fact, freely and deeply explored by Korean scholars in their own conferences and publications. But they are not publicly equally freely discussed. One of the limitations on democracy in South Korea is that it is precisely these questions on which the freedom of speech is restricted. The insistence of Koreans that they must discuss them is the major reason for the continuing maintenance of the National Security Law.

Never yet, since the liberation of the peninsula from Japanese control, has the country been free from a pervasive atmosphere of emergency. It is as though, in militaristic terms, the whole population is required to remain totally on alert. National security is everywhere the first consideration. In Korea it is the justification for periods of martial law, with their suspension of civil rights. It is why complete freedom of speech and press remain restricted or threatened, even when censorship has been banned. It is why local autonomy, the grass-roots foundation for full democracy, remains a promise still only partially fulfilled. As the republic has grown enormously stronger both militarily and economically, the reason for such restraints becomes increasingly dim.

President Roh's presidency is marked to an unprecedented degree by openness and candor. But it is also marked by his personal history of close identification with ex-President Chun and with the military. Like Park and Chun, Roh's whole career was in the army. He was a classmate of Chun's in the Military Academy, and they rose together through the ranks as professional soldiers. When Chun's presidency in its closing years was undermined by a rising clamor of denunciation, General Roh was selected by the ruling circle of the Democratic Justice Party to become Chun's successor. The bond between the two men was too real to be concealed. To help Roh win public notice and favor, Chun removed the veteran diplomat Kim Young-shik from the highly prestigious post as Chairman of the preparatory Committee for the Olympic Games, in order to bestow that position upon Roh Tae Woo. When President Chun resigned as head of the DJP, Roh was named to succeed him. His nomination as the party's presidential nominee assured his campaign of the full support of the incumbent administration. While this obviously was a great advantage, it also had the serious disadvantage of linking him very closely, in the view of the public, with Chun Doo Hwan.

What was very clear was that the election of 1987 would result in a definitive change of direction in the republic's politics. This was assured by the strong tide of public resentment against outgoing President Chun. Moreover, both the direction and the extent of the changes to come were substantially influenced by the focusing of worldwide attention upon South Korea as it prepared to host the Summer Olympic Games. Roh Tae Woo was enabled by the ruling party to take the key role of shaping the nature of the necessary changes by guiding the revisions for the new constitution. The drive for such revision had already been stimulated primarily by Kim Dae-jung. It began in May, with mass demonstrations by tens of thousands in all the major cities as a nationwide "Grand March for Peace and Democracy." On 29 June, in announcing his candidacy for the presidency, Roh Tae Woo gave his approval to this movement, in effect claiming it as his own. The provisions in the new constitution represented the common determination by all the major political leaders that South Korea must have, in candidate Roh's words, "a more mature, developing democracy." The phrase meant what it said—that the new reach for democracy must be "more mature," but "developing," rather than absolute. The people were unwilling to accept this limitation.

Getting the constitution revised took longer than its proponents hoped or expected. Kim Dae-jung and Kim Young-sam, heads respective of the two opposition parties, the Peace and Democracy Party and the Democratic Reunification Party, were the natural leaders of the reform movement. But they proved to be disappointingly ineffective. Their disputes between themselves, as well as with Roh Tae Woo, delayed agreement on the terms of the revision for several weeks, while the presidential campaign was gathering force and bitterness, making urgent the need for clarification of what the constitution would provide. As the two Kims cancelled one another's leadership potential, Roh Tai Woo developed an eight-point program of changes and was able to win interparty agreement to its provisions. The National Assembly adopted the revised constitution on 12 October and when it was referred to the people in a referendum on 27 October, it was overwhelmingly approved. Its greatest merit was that it ended the *Yushin* system that gave to an incumbent president, and to his political party, power with which to remain indefinitely in office.

This constitution was a commitment to popular democracy. The president was to be elected by a direct popular vote, as had been done from 1952 through 1963. The presidential term was to be for five years, without the right to re-election. To restore the balance of governmental powers, the courts were shielded, at least in substantial degree, from presidential influence; and the powers of the National Assembly were considerably increased. Censorship of the press was banned. Freedom of speech was guaranteed, and so were the rights to assemble in public meetings and to form associations to promote causes. Workers were guaranteed the rights to organize, bargain collectively, and strike. The armed forces were charged to remain politically neutral. An office of prosecutor-general was created, with responsibility and authority to prevent or to punish judicial abuses. But the "emergency powers" of the presidency were retained.

Kim Jong-pil entered the presidential campaign at the end of September by reviving the defunct Democratic Republican Party; but the time was too late for him to launch an effective organized effort. Kim Dae-jung and Kim Young-sam held meetings designed to coordinate their opposition to Roh. But these proved to be futile, for neither of them would renounce his own ambitions or support the other's candidacy. In the closing days of the campaign Roh Tae-Woo seized the initiative by making two dramatic promises. The first was that if elected president he would no longer allow ideology to rule the republic's foreign affairs but would undertake to establish diplomatic relations with the People's Republic of China. His second pledge was that, if elected, as soon as the Olympic Games were completed he would hold a national referendum to ask the people for a "national vote of confidence."

On election day, 16 December, twenty-six million voters went to the polls. The result was a virtual standoff. Roh Tae Woo headed the field; but he received only 36.3 percent of the votes cast. There was no provision for a runoff, and Roh was declared the winner. To quiet the nationwide uneasiness, close to outrage, over his very dubious electoral "victory," Roh promised that within a year he would conduct a plebiscite to permit the people to either affirm or deny his election. This promise he never kept. There never was a time that was quite right for it, he explained. Finally, he declared there was no need for such a plebiscite and the plan was dropped.

Despite the bitterness of the campaign and Roh's slim margin of victory with just over one-third of the votes, the concentration of attention on the forthcoming Olympic Games made him the first president of the republic to enjoy a brief "honeymoon" period, free, for a brief time, from substantial criticism. Roh's inauguration, under the new constitution, took place on 25 February.

The subsequent months through September were, with some notable exceptions, a time for jubilant celebration in South Korea. In March the British Royal Ballet came to Seoul's Sejong Cultural Center to present the famous *Swan Lake.* In early September, with even greater excitement, the Soviet Bolshoi Ballet presented its performance. The Federation of Artistic and Cultural Organizations in Seoul proposed that an annual all-Korea art festival be held alternately in South and North Korea. In late August the International PEN Congress opened its 52nd annual Congress in Seoul, with an attendance of nine hundred writers from thirty-seven countries, including communist nations. The Ministry of Education announced that henceforth Korean college and university students would be granted passports for study in East-bloc nations. The Education Minister proposed a goodwill students' sports meeting and exchange of visits between the North and the South. The National Council of University Students resolved to go ahead with an interstudent all-Korea conference on 15 August. Italy's famed la Scala Opera company came in August and performed *Turandot.* The Foreign Ministry removed the few remaining restrictions on travel abroad by ordinary citizens. The Korea Public Performance Ethics Committee ended its ban on movies and plays from Japan and from East-bloc countries. On many fronts, and in many ways, it was a season for goodwill and general satisfaction. Even before the opening of the Olympic Games, South Koreans were feeling themselves to be fully and successfully participants in all manner of world affairs.

Roh Tae Woo promptly fulfilled the first campaign promise he had made, to separate foreign affairs from ideology. On 1 March he commenced actively to promote trade and diplomatic relations with China, the Soviet Union, and other communist countries. In April agreement was reached between the republic and Yugoslavia for the opening of trade offices in each other's countries. China's State Council agreed to develop trade and personnel exchanges with South Korea. Trade with Hungary commenced in June and with Yugoslavia in July. In August six Soviet diplomats arrived to open consular offices. The only bitter note in foreign relations was between the North and the South. Kim Il-sung demanded that the North be co-host for the Olympic Games, which he said, should be held in Pyongyang as well as in Seoul. His demand was rejected by both South Korea and the International Olympic Commission. Seoul's invitation to North Korean athletes to participate in the games as members of all-Korea teams was angrily refused. In an apparent effort to frighten foreigners from attending the games, on 29 November 1987 a Korean Airlines plane was destroyed in the air over Burma by North Korean agents and all on board, 104 passengers and eleven crew members, were killed. The United States added North Korea to the list of nations guilty of fostering international terrorism.

The next July President Roh issued a detailed plan to ease tensions between the two Korean zones and pave the way toward peaceful reunification. Kim Il-sung responded in September by reiterating his proposal that the

North and the South should discuss reunification as a "confederal republic," which "could be achieved only after the withdrawal of U.S. forces in Korea and the signing of an inter-Korea non-aggression pact." President Roh offered to go to Pyongyang for talks with the Northern leader. Three days later, on 7 October, the government announced a new policy of opening trade with the North, allowing North Korean commercial ships to dock in South Korean harbors. On 18 October, in an address before the General Assembly of the United Nations, President Roh proposed the holding of a consultative conference to settle a broad range of Northeast Asian problems, with the members to be North and South Korea, China, Japan, the United States, and the Soviet Union. This suggestion North Korea rejected. At the end of the year, the Seoul government proposed to Pyongyang a meeting between the prime ministers of the two zones to organize a summit meeting to consider this and any other matters that would promote harmony between them. The suggestion was rejected.

President Roh's goal of eliminating ideology from ROK's foreign policy has been pursued steadily. Against the intransigence of North Korea it could not be completely successful. Kim Il-sung's policies appeared to be little affected by the collapse of communism in the Soviet Union and in Eastern Europe. He continued to insist on creation of a "confederal" government for a reunited Korea—a government to be headed by two co-chairmen, each with a veto over decisions by the other, and with a National Assembly in which the North, with one-third of the population, would have an equality of membership with the South. Reaching his eightieth birthday in 1992, Kim persisted in fortifying by all available means the plan to turn over the presidency to his son, Kim Jong Il. In late 1991 he named his son commander-in-chief of all North Korean armed service.

Coincidentally, in November 1991, a dramatic breakthrough in South-North relations was achieved. Kim Il-sung suddenly accepted President Roh's frequently reiterated plan for admittance of "both Koreas" into the United Nations. Without delay, the General Assembly of the U.N. voted them both into its membership. Shortly afterwards, representatives of the Seoul and Pyongyang governments, meeting at Panmunjom, where the 1953 truce was signed, joined in a pledge of nonagression. They also agreed to "denuclearize" by having the U.S. withdraw all of its nuclear missiles from Korea, together with a pledge by North Korea to discontinue its development of an atomic bomb. The nuclear missiles were promptly withdrawn from the South, but so far North Korea still refuses to permit inspection of its atomic research and development facilities.

Relations between the North and South have clearly become more relaxed. Trade between them, and the movement of persons across the demilitarized zone, have at least become a hopeful prospect. As confidence mounts, it appears probable that in both the enormously costly burden of militarism may be reduced. If these accomplishments are indeed achieved, restrictions of civil rights in both areas should be eased. The relaxation of tension veils the fundamental fact that the claim of each government to sovereignty over all Korea, or at the least "the only lawful government in Korea," have been swept into the dustbin of history. They are as completely ignored as were the October 1951 resolutions of the General Assembly of the United Nations, which authorized the reunification of Korea by force of arms, to be followed by a U.N.-supervised election of a unified government. Whether this will be the next stage in Korea, or whether there will be continuance of the two governments by mutual acceptance remains for the future to decide.

While the two Koreas were still eyeing one another truculently, the Olympic Games opened in Seoul on 17 September. They proved to be impressive but no more than a partial success. The games were marred by unsportsmanlike actions by Korean athletes and also by disrespectful behavior of American athletes. Consequently, the customary celebration of the games was offset by disappointment that harmony did not prevail. The capacity of the Republic of Korea to host the games was amply demonstrated. A huge assemblage of 9,257 athletes participated, representing 160 nations. The sports and hotel facilities proved to be ample and of excellent quality. They remain as testimony to the high level of accomplishment attained by South Korea.

On other fronts, economic and political, developments also were mixed. The per capita income in South Korea mounted that year to $3,728. The GNP reached an annual growth rate of 12.1 percent, the highest in the world. In 1988 the annual savings rate reached 38.1 percent of income, another world record. In the first half of 1990 the rate slipped to 33.1 percent, not due to lower income or higher prices but to the temptations of the expanding marketplace. Domestic consumption, a sound measurement of social well-being, increasd by 8.1 percent, while exports were increasing at a rate of 26.5 percent and farm production expanded by 8.43 percent. Despite these very substantial improvements, the labor unions actively promoted still higher gains for the industrial workers. In addition to the 62 percent gain in average wages already won, the unions were determined for still more, to make up for the hardship in the sixties and seventies, during which economic advancement was at the price of cheap labor. Workers at such major plants as the Korean Heavy Industries and Construction company and the Daewoo Heavy Industries Company went on general strike and across the nation more strikes were threatened. The settlement reached granted a net additional 20 to 25 percent wage increase, along with health insurance, housing, and improved work conditions as important fringe benefits. Businesses and industries of all types across the nation were forced to curtail their costs and increase their per-unit productivity. The Seoul Stock Market went through a troubled period of falling equity prices; but general stability was maintained and Korean exports remained competitive in the world markets.

In politics, President Roh's promise of hastening the maturation of democracy appeared increasingly dubious. For one thing, after several months of vaccilation, he reneged on his promise to hold a "vote of confidence" referendum to determine whether he could raise his support level to at least 50 percent. For another, he delayed implementing changes that had been agreed upon by the several political parties to liberalize the National Security Law and to grant local autonomy to the provinces, towns and villages—citing as a reason for the delays both the danger of communist-caused social disorder and the high cost of holding elections. The politically liberalizing factors in the society were outrunning his leadership. Industrial democracy, requiring a highly educated and self-motivated workforce, was growing steadily and its effects spread throughout the society. As the general public enjoyed an ever-higher standard of living, it became increasingly conscious of its power and more insistent upon a panoply of civil rights.

The parliamentary elections held on 26 April 1989 reflected these political dissatisfactions and aspirations. Of the 224 seats in the Assembly, President Roh's Democratic Justice party won only 87. Kim Dae-jung's Party for Peace and Democracy won 54, Kim Young-Sam's Reunifican Democratic Party won 46, and Kim Jong-pil's New Democratic Republican Party garnered 27. Responding to the disappointing results of this election, President Roh entered into a series of behind-the-scenes negotiations with the most conservative of the opposition leaders, Kim Young-sam and Kim Jong-pil. These three startled the nation with an announcement that their three parties were merged into one—thereby creating a political situation similar to that which has prevailed in Japan, namely the unchallengeable domination of a single party. Under this system, realistic political competition is transferred from inter-party struggles to intra-party negotiation, compromises, and confrontation between factions and individuals within the one dominant party. Under such conditions, the opportunity of the public to choose for itself what policies to reject or support is minimized. This is the political circumstance as the party strategists position themselves for the next presidential election.

Education is not only the foundation of democracy but also the key indicator of long-term developments. Along with steadily increasing prosperity, the Koreans continue their unusually earnest quest for education. By the close of 1990 nearly eleven and a half million students, at all levels from kindergarten through graduate study in universities, were enrolled in schools in South Korea. This means that almost one in every four of the nation's inhabitants had become a full-time student. More than a million of them are collegians, and four million and eight hundred thousand are elementary school students. These numbers impose a continuous burden upon the resources of the state. They also reflect the faith in learning that inspires parents and family members to make heavy sacrifices—which they regard as an investment in their childrens' future—to keep this many in school.

Education is not only universal; it is also steadily, if slowly, improving.

The number of four-year universities in the republic reached 107 in 1990, as compared to 71 in 1970 and 85 in 1980. The number of students in graduate courses increased thirteen-fold during the past two decades, from 6,640 in 1970 to 86,900 in 1990. Salaries of teachers have risen to compare favorably with pay for comparatively skilled work in business or industry, with the result that over 40 percent of elementary school teachers have remained in their posts for more than twenty years. Interestingly, the percentage of women teachers continues to increase, reaching more than fifty percent. In the cities the proportion of women teachers in elementary classes is 71.5% in Seoul, 67.5% in Pusan, and 52.7% in Inchon. As these figures attest, the women in Korea are approaching to nearly equal educational opportunities with men, except in graduate programs.

Measuring the quality of education is uncertain; but it is evident that textbooks, libraries, and laboratories are vastly improved over these past decades, although they remain far below desirable levels. It is equally evident that the increasing sophistication of technology in industries, in businesses, and in the military requires further improving of education.

The educational statistic that is least encouraging is the steady decline in the teacher-student ratio. During the past twenty years there has been a 450 percent increase in the number of university professors, but a 960 percent rise in the number of their students. In 1970 there was an average of 20.45 college students for each professor, with the numbers changing to 30.07 in 1980, and to 43.86 in 1990. This same disparity extends all through the system, indicating an urgent need for a greatly expanded educational budget. What this would entail is indicated by a study of California's school system in early 1990, in which it was found that to decrease average class size by just one student would cost the state a billion dollars. The steady decline in South Korea's birthrate offers some amelioration of this problem, as is shown by the decline in number of elementary pupils in South Korea by 880,000 from 1970 to 1990.

This decline in birthrate is a significant indication of the modifications modernization have brought to Korea, for in 1945 it had one of the highest birthrates of any country. By 1990 the concern of the government was that the rate was too low. With the current average of 1.6 children per family, in another generation South Korea's population will peak at around 51.14 million, and then will decline. Thirty per cent of the population will be over sixty-five; and those aged fifteen or younger will decline by four million. The current goal is not further reduction of family size but an increase to 1.8 children per family.

Statistics are building blocks, but what they represent is more than and different from mere numbers. Education in Korea, from its middle history, has been the most significant social differential—more important than wealth, and central in defining social status. The yangban aristocracy was an aristocracy of scholars. This cultural conviction has not faltered. Democracy, the great leveler, demands that educational opportunities must be equal. But for Koreans, as for peoples everywhere, the desire of families and individuals is to rise in the social hierarchy; to become special rather than to remain ordinary. And in their view, the only sure route to progressive advancement is education. This is one reason why the educational goal of the Roh presidency is to increase the industrial research and development investment from its level of 2.1 percent of the GNP as it was in 1988—a fair figure as compared with that in industrially matured countries—to the lofty level of 3 or even 4 percent by the 1995 completion of the current Five-Year Plan. Only by such endeavors can Korea lead rather than lag behind in the new Age of Technology.

The evolution of modern Korea is awesome. From being impoverished, disease-ridden, helpless and dependent, the South, at least has become a major industrial power. The North lags far behind in economic well-being and in diplomatic clout. The reunification of the peninsula is certain to come sooner or later and there is every indication that it will not be much longer delayed. North Korea is mired in debt, has lost its only powerful allies, and its prospects are dismal. South Korea, on the contrary, has become in economics and in international standing an impressive success. Straw-thatched, muddy-street farm villages, without sanitation facilities and with few contacts outside their borders have become agri-business centers, with modern electricized homes, with large fields farmed with oil-driven machines, with good schools for the children and with effective political clout to ensure and extend their manifest benefits. Once dependent upon the United States and a few other allies for its survival, the Republic of Korea government has offered to extend some two billion dollars in aid to its once worst enemy, Russia; it has also entered into diplomatic relations with long-domineering China. Korean interests and influence encircle the globe. Its people—who for centuries "had nowhere to go"—now "go everywhere" as virtual partners in the building of a new world community. The modernizing process never will be complete, for change has replaced stagnation as its manifest trademark. But wherever and however modernity is measured, the Republic of Korea rates high. Out of their long past, Koreans are entering with confidence into a brilliant future. Instead of international imperialism, domestic politics has become the people's principal remaining concern. And this, too, is coming ever more surely into their own hands.

Notes

1. The historical background of Old Korea is well presented by Carter J. Eckert, Ki-baik Lee, Young Ik Lew, Michael Robinson and Edward W. Wagner, in *Korea Old and New: A History* (Cambridge: Korea Institute, Harvard University, 1990); and by Wanne J. Joe, *Traditional Korea: A Cultural History* (Seoul: Chungang University Press, 1972). Under the *taedong* law all, rich and poor, were subject to a single uniform tax on land; and the tax was to be paid in cotton cloth or in rice. Equality of treatment was the key feature.

2. Elaborations of the meanings of *jen* and *li* abound, for they are crucial in all Asian history. My own interpretation is found in Robert T. Oliver, *Communication and Culture in Ancient India and China* (Syracuse, N.Y.: Syracuse University Press, 1971), particularly in chapter 9, "The Rhetoric of Behavior, Ceremony, Etiquette, and Methodology," pp. 145–60.

3. A comparative view of the embracing importance of Confucian influence in Chinese society is found in Oliver, *Ancient India and China,* chapter 6, "China: The Rhetorical Milieu," pp. 84–99.

4. The broad meanings of Silhak (sometimes spelled Sirhak) and its importance as an energizing force in Korea are elaborated by Michael C. Kelton, in "An Introduction to Silhak," *Korea Journal* 15 (May 1973): pp. 29–46.

5. Yi Ik, an eighteenth-century liberal, illustrated his view of what these disaffected *sonbi* were teaching in his *Trivial Essays of Songho:*

> Suppose there are ten hungry men thrown together for a meal sufficient for only one. Before they finish it, a quarrel or two may occur among them. They might accuse one another of impolite words or impudent attitudes. People, not familiar with the situation, might think of quarrels as caused by mismanaged words or manners, but the real cause lies in the inadequacy of the meal. If ten men were given ten meals, would they not eat their meals in a happier mood?

Note the derogation of arguing and the stress upon harmony, which is central in Korean ethics.

6. An equivalent phrase would be "looking up to authority."

7. "The nobility is to blame for the tragic fate of the nation. Noblemen did everything they pleased to us. Noblemen killed many of us of low birth, wrested wealth from us if we were rich, made our wives their concubines if our wives were pretty. How could a man of low birth like myself have served his country well when he was completely at the mercy of noblemen for his life, his wealth and his wife? How could he have exercised his rights in a society where noblemen threatened to chop off his knees or elbows, or condemn him to exile for the slightest wrong-doing?"

Three things are of special interest in this quotation. (1) The low-bred commonality was assumed to have an equality of rights, even if they could not enforce them; (2) Yi-Ik assumed a general desire to serve the country well and regarded exile even from this unjust society as among the greatest of deprivations; and (3) the evil behavior of Korea's noblemen was much like that of French nobles prior to the French Revolution.

8. For a discussion of divergent interpretations, see Haksul Chongmo Daewoo, *Chong Tasan Yongu ui Hyonhwang* (The Present Situation in Chong Tasan Studies) (Seoul: Minum-sa Pub. Co., 1985).

9. Lillian Underwood's account of the Korea she knew in the latter two decades of the nineteenth century is both vivid and faithful, even if biased by Christian evangelism. "The majority have very little faith in any religion. Confucianism, otherwise a mere philosophical system of morals, has the strongest hold upon the people in the laws it enjoins for ancestor worship. This custom, enforced by the strongest and most widespread superstitions in the minds of the Koreans binds them with fetters stronger than iron. If ancestors are not worshipped with most punctilious regard for every smallest detail of the law, dire calamities will befall, from the wrath of irate and neglected spirits. The servitude thus compelled is hard and wearisome, but not one jot or tittle must be omitted, and woe to the wretch who, embracing another doctrine, fails to perform these rites. He or she is looked down upon as more than a traitor to home and friends, false to the most sacred obligations." *Fifteen Years Among the Top-Knots, or Life in Korea* (New York: American Tract Society, 1904).

10. A typical Korean interpretation of this disturbed period is that by Wanne J. Joe, in his *Traditional Korea: A Cultural History* (Seoul: Chungang University Press, 1972), pp. 421–22: "The *sŏwŏn,* now heavily parasitized by *yangban*-riffraff, also lorded it over the masses. And those small-time, low-class cheats who purchased high-priced petty clerkships in alliance with magistrates became the most notorious tormentors of the common masses. They imposed the land tax on land that never was and the military tax upon infants or dead men. They mixed a half bushel of unhulled rice with a half bushel of chaff to make one. These are only a few widely practised methods for extortion of extra-legal fees and tributes from the peasantry and defrauding the government of its revenue."

11. Professor Lew Young Ik soundly explored the period of Yuan Shih-k'ai's residency and the Korean Enlightenment Movement (1885–94), *Journal of Korean Studies,* December 1977, pp. 21–62.

12. After ratification of the U.S.-Korean treaty by the United States in May 1883, King Kojong sent a mission to America headed by Prince Min Yong Mok, to gain knowledge of the culture of the West and, more urgently, to make manifest the independence of Korea from Chinese control. The mission members were treated with high respect and honorific hospitality in San Francisco and in Chicago during their leisurely trip by train across the United States. They were greeted by President Arthur, who praised their "beautiful peninsular country," and assured them that "the ocean which intervenes between our respective nations has, by means of the introduction and perfection of steam navigation, become a highway of convenient and safe intercourse—you are our neighbors." The mission members also visited New York and Boston. Prince Min, vice-minister Hong Yong Sik and So Kwangbom, secretary to the mission, were escorted as honored guests back to Korea on the *Trenton,* in a long journey that included stopovers in Paris and London. Hong and So busied themselves learning all they could of Western ways, but Prince Min "secluded himself with copies of the Chinese classics." Harold J. Noble, "The Korean Mission to the United States in 1885," *Transactions* of the Korean Branch of the Royal Asiatic Society, vol. 8, 1929, pp. 14–21.

13. Homer B. Hulbert, whose many contributions to Korea are summarized later in this chapter, presented many vignettes, along with much pertinent data, to show how Japan dealt with Koreans. For further personalized accounts, see Channing Liem, *America's Finest Gift to Korea—the Life of Philip Jaisohn* (New York: William Frederick Co., 1952); Horace A. Allen, *Korea Fact and Fancy* (Seoul: Methodist

Publishing House, 1904); Younghill Kang, *The Grass Roof* (New York: Scribner's 1932); James A. Gale, *Korea in Transition,* (New York: Board of Foreign Missions of the Presbyterian Church, 1909; and Agnes Davis Kim, *I Married a Korean* (New York: John Day, 1953).

14. A further study by Professor Young Ik Lew, "Korean-Japanese Politics behind the Kabo-Ulmi Reform Movements, 1894–1896," analyzes the Taewongun's motives as including "his desire for revenge against Queen Min as well as his sense of mission to save the Korean people from suffering." In the *Journal of Korean Studies* 3 (1981): pp. 39–82.

15. "Japanese records show that the Japanese themselves first learned from Koreans the cultivation of the silkworm, the weaving cloth, the principles of architecture, the printing of books, the painting of pictures, the beautifying of gardens, the making of leather harnesses, and the shaping of more effective weapons. . . . The Koreans invented metal type in 1403. [Actually in 1234.] They used a phonetic alphabet in the early part of the fifteenth century. They saw the significance of the mariner's compass in 1525. . . . Money was used as a medium of exchange in Korea long before it was employed in northern Europe. They used cannon and explosive shells in attacking the invading Japanese in 1502. The first iron-clad warship in the world was invented by a Korean, Yi Sun sin" (Arthur Judson Brown, *The Mastery of the Far East*).

16. The development of public speaking in modernizing Korea was as important in Korea as it was in Japan, and as it had been in ancient Greece and Rome, and in modern England and the United States. It proved to be the bloodstream of democracy, making democratic government a reality. It is for this reason that President Rhee authorized in 1955 the writing of a textbook *Effective Speech for Democratic Living* that was published by the Ministry of Education and for two decades served as a guide and stimulus to self-expression in the elementary and middle schools in South Korea. Philip Jaisohn's recognition of this value led him to emphasize debating in the Independence Club. As he explained, "The subjects discussed were mostly political and economical questions but religion and social questions were not overlooked. In the beginning the Koreans were shy about standing up before an audience to make a public speech, but after a certain amount of coaching and encouragement I found very effective speeches. I believe the Koreans have a natural talent for public speaking." Cited by F. A. McKenzie, *Korea's Fight for Freedom* (New York: Flemming H. Revell, 1920).

17. Rhee descended through seventeen generations from Prince Yi Yang-yong, grandson of the founder of the Choson or Yi dynasty. When family fortunes declined, Rhee's grandfather, Yi Hwang, moved from their ancestral estate in Seoul, in the Haeju District, to the Ongjin Peninsula.

18. Of equal importance, though with very different impact, it should be added that no communicant, whether speaker, writer, listener or reader, can ever have certain and complete understanding of the meaning of the other. Hence, even users of the same language have ample misunderstandings among themselves—though in different ways and with differing effects—than have users of differing languages. It is not inaccurate to say that when individuals communicate misunderstandings are the rule and complete mutual understanding is only an occasional happy accident. Despite their linguistic homogeneity, it must be noted that Koreans often do misunderstand one another (as do we all).

19. Published by Scribner's in 1947.

20. Searching studies into the main issues have indeed been conducted by scholars in Korean and American universities. Specialist scholars who merit special mention include Chong-Sik Lee, Dae-Sook Suh, Robert A. Scalapino, Michael Robinson,

Kenneth W. Wells, Hyung Chan Kim, Frank Hoffman, Frank Baldwin, and a dozen more whose studies appear in compilations edited by Andrew C. Nahm, C. I. Eugene Kim, and Doretha B. Mortimer.

21. Saitō added both a promise and a hope, neither of which came to pass. "There will be many more changes even if many of these cannot be carried out immediately. However, I believe that if these measures are implemented rapidly, it will end the domestic and foreign criticism of our Korean policy and make the annexation of Korea complete."

22. These data are assembled by Dr. Han Y. Rim in his doctoral dissertation "Development of Higher Education during the Japanese Administration." Columbia University, 1951.

23. Chiang said this while two-thirds of China was held by apparently invincible Japanese troops, after England and the United States had closed the vital supply route of the Burma Road, and while Japanese victories in South Asia and in the Pacific seemed to signal its eventual victory. The speech is reported by David Nelson Rowe, *Modern China* (Princeton: Van Nostrand, Anchor Books, 1959), pp. 136–37. Earlier, in 1937, Madame Chiang Kai Shek, addressing the American people by radio, vented a harsh judgment that could as well have been spoken by a Korean during the years of Japanese oppression of the peninsula: "Tell me, is the silence of Western nations in the face of such masscres, such demolitions of homes and dislocations of businesses, a sign of the triumph of civilization with its humanitarianism, its code of conduct, its chivalry, and its claim of Christian influence? Or is the spectable of the first-class Powers, all standing silently in a row as if so stupified by Japan that they do not utter a reproach, a forerunner of the collapse of international ethics, of Christian guidance and conduct, and the death knell of the supposed moral superiority of the Occidental?".

24. This letter, which is obviously important for assessing American policy toward Korea, is reproduced in full in Robert T. Oliver, *Syngman Rhee and American Involvement in Korea, 1942–1960: A Personal Narrative* (Seoul: The Panmun Press, 1978), pp. 95–98.

25. The full text of this long and bitter letter itemizes reasons for resentment at how the U.S. dealt with Korea. It is presented in full in ibid, pp. 107–12. It is also an effective proof that Rhee and his associates were not, as Communists and their cohorts charge, "American puppets."

26. E. Grant Meade, *American Military Government in Korea* (New York: King's Crown Press, Columbia University, 1951).

27. For an overview of the roles of Rhee, the other Korean leaders, and member nations of the U. N. see Oliver, *Syngman Rhee and American Involvement in Korea,* chapter 6, pp. 119–39.

28. This account, unpublished, shifts blame for south Korea's difficulties from the AMG to Korean "dissidents." It is in the files of the Department of Defense, Washington, D.C. After admitting that the 38th parallel division resulted from an international agreement, the author argues that failure by the Korean leaders, mostly members of the Democratic Party and Dr. Rhee, to "cooperate" in U.S. efforts to win Soviet agreement is what led to continuance of the division.

29. Presented first as lectures sponsored by the Charles E. Walgreen Foundation, the book was published by the University of Chicago Press and republished as a Mentor Book by the New American Library. The quotation, taken from p. 47 of the Mentor edition, follows the author's argument that the "loss of China" was not caused by American irresolution, since we "had little control or influence" over either Soviet or Japanese imperialism in the area, and concluded that "it is easy to exaggerate the latitude our statesmen enjoyed."

30. Oliver, *Syngman Rhee and American Involvement,* chapter six.

31. Ibid., p. 134. This paragraph is my summary of a long letter from Rhee.

32. Ibid., see pp. 141–43 for an account of a mistake by Harold Noble that resulted in mis-reporting, thereby intensifying international derogation of Dr. Rhee.

33. How the constitution was drafted and then approved, is explained in ibid., pp. 176–77 and 182–183.

34. In the main the account of this rebellion adheres to the excellent reconstruction by John Merrill, *Korea: Peninsular Origins of the War* (Newark: University of Delaware Press), pp. 98–129.

35. The text of this letter, which was read in full over the Pyongyang radio, from the text taken by the Communists after the capture of Seoul, is presented in Oliver, *Syngman Rhee and American Involvement in Korea,* pp. 271–72. Although it very obviously reveals Rhee's anguish that the U.S. did not permit any action against the North, it was cited by the Soviets and the North Koreans as "proof" that Rhee planned an attack.

36. For the full text of Mrs. Moon's account, see Robert T. Oliver, *Verdict in Korea* (State College, PA.: Bald Eagle Press, 1952), pp. 60–64.

37. Oliver, *Syngman Rhee and American Involvement,* pp. 297–98. Although President Truman made no acknowledgement of this letter he understood very well the significance of the difference between his war aims and those of President Rhee, according to Averill Harriman, who discussed the differences with him. See Harry S. Truman, *Memoirs,* II, p. 351.

38. The New York *Times* for 28 June 1953 carried a story filed by one of its correspondents in Korea, Robert Alden, reporting that "one of the purposes of the present Communist offensives is believed to be to embarrass the Republic of Korea forces and give the impression to the world that the South Koreans are not able to hold their own on the battlefield. This is just not the case. For well over a year now they have been manning their part of the fighting front—they now hold more than two-thirds of the entire front—without giving any ground to speak of to the battle-experienced Chinese armies [who are held in check by] the fearless, ferocious counter-attacks launched by South Korean infantrymen."

39. The difficulties in negotiating the truce are related vividly by Admiral C. Turner Joy, who headed the U.N. negotiating team at Panmunjom, in his book *How the Communists Negotiate* (New York: Macmillan, 1955). An extensive account of the whole period of U.S.-U.S.S.R. efforts to resolve their differences over Korea is presented in Kenneth T. Young, *Negotiating with the Chinese Communists* (New York: McGraw-Hill, 1968).

40. Oliver, *Syngman Rhee and American Involvement,* pp. 408–9.

41. How Mao Tse-tung's dictatorship was strengthened by his claim of achieving victory over the major armies of the Western World, as Communist propaganda interpreted the war in Korea, is explained by Professor Myoungsoon Kim in his article, "China's Foreign Relations with North Korea, 1949–1975," in *Korea Observer* 24 (Winter 1979): pp. 390–404.

42. For an explanation of how reluctantly this decision was reached (roughly akin to the forced agreement of King Kojong to accept the Japanese protectorate) see *ibid.,* chapter 19, pp. 411–31.

43. See *The Korean Problem at the Geneva Conference, April 26–June 15, 1954* (Washington, D. C.: the United States Department of State publication 5609, October, 1954).

44. See Oliver, *Syngman Rhee and American Involvement,* pp. 427–28.

45. See ibid., pp. 15, 32, 50, 131, 201, 220, 235, 300, 327, 342, 346, 351, 369, and 397.

46. The circumstances of President and Mrs. Rhee's departure for Hawaii are described vividly by Acting President Huh Chung in his biography *U-Nam, Rhee Syngman* (Seoul: Tae-Kuk Pub. Co., 1970), pp. 403–6. An English translation is included in Oliver, *Syngman Rhee and American Involvement,* pp. 489–491.

47. This incident was related to me by ambassador Chang in order that I might cite it to President Rhee, to support a plea for an enlarged expense account. For my interpretation of Chang's personal qualities, see ibid., p. 207.

48. T. C. Rhee, "American Policy in Korea in a Tokyo-Peking-Pyongyang-Moscow Quadrangle," in Yung-Hwan Jo, ed., *U.S. Foreign Policy in Asia: An Appraisal* (Santa Barbara, CA, 1978). Even more bitterly, Dr. Rhee added what many Koreans believed, that "what has generally marred Park's 'economic miracle' is not so much the inequities, which are not found in the North, as Park's 'lack of nationalist ethos,'—his 'unrestrained embrace' of Japan in total 'insensitivity' to the 'political meaning' of Japan's benighted colonial rule as well as his inglorious part in it."

49. For this and the subsequent chapters, my interpretation of the circumstances is based upon many visits to South Korea, supplemented with press accounts (Korean and foreign) and correspondence with various friends in Korea. For further information I have consulted scholarly studies listed in the References.

50. Even popular novelists are noting Korean achievements. *Vide,* a fragment of conversation: "Do you know what city has the highest number of Ph.D.'s per capita in the world?" "Boston?" "Seoul, Korea." From Michael Crichton, *Rising Sun* (New York: Knopf, 1992), p. 178.

51. Joon-Mann Kang, "The Explosion of Television in South Korea," *Asian Pacific Parliamentarians' Union* 16 (Autumn 1988): pp. 67–76. Embittered, however, by the slowness of ROK's progress toward democracy, Kang belittles the "myth" of the "Korean Miracle." *Journal of Contemporary Asia* 19 (1989): p. 480.

References

Documents

Aid to the Republic of Korea, 81st Congress, First Session, Senate Report 748. Washington, D.C.: 1949.

Carnegie Endowment for International Peace, Division of International Law. *Korea, Treaties and Agreements.* Washington, D.C.: 1921.

Coles, Harry L., and Albert K. Weinberg. *Civil Affairs: Soldiers Become Governors.* Washington, D.C.: Office of the Chief of Military History, 1964.

Conlon Associates, Ltd. *United States Foreign Policy—Asia: A Study Produced at the Request of the Committee on Foreign Relations.* Washington, 1960.

Correspondence, President and Madame Rhee with Robert T. Oliver, 1945–1960. Originals of Rhee letters in Rhee Memorial Collection, Rhiwachang, One Rhiwha-dong, Chongro-ku, Seoul; photocopies in the Archives, of the ROK Ministry of Foreign Affairs, in the East-West Center Library, Honolulu, and in the Library of the University of Southern California, Korean Heritage Collection.

Documents on Korean-American Relations, 1943–1976. Editor, Kim Se-Jin; Associate Editor, Yu Suk-Ryul. Seoul: Research Center for Peace and Unification, 1976.

Economic Cooperation Administration. *Economic Guides of Republic of Korea.* Washington, D.C.: January, 1950.

Evans, D. J., ed. *The Korean Conspiracy Trial: Full Proceedings.* Kobe, Japan: 1913.

Far East Command, Office of the Chief of Military History. *History of the North Korean Army.* Washington, D.C.: U.S. Department of Defense, 1952.

Government-General, Korea. *Annual Reports on the Administration of Chosen.* In English. Compiled by H.I.J.M.'s Residency-General, 1908–1909; and by the Government-General of Chosen, 1909–1910 to 1921–1922.

Hapdong Yon'gam (Korean) and *Korea Annual* (English). Seoul: Hapdong News Agency, annually since 1964.

Headquarters of the Far East Command. *History of the Occupation of Korea.* Tokyo, 1947; plus unpublished manuscripts in the Office of the Chief of Military History, Washington, D.C.

House of Representatives Committee on International Relations, *Selected Executive Session Hearings.* Vol. 7, part 2, *Korean Assistance Acts,* 1976.

Investigation of Korean-American Problems. Report of the Subcommittee on International Relations of the Committee on International Relations. U.S. House of Representatives, 31 October 1978.

The Korean Problem at the Geneva Conference, April 26–June 15, 1984. Washington, D.C.: Department of State, 1954.

Laws of the Republic of Korea. Translated, edited, and published by The Korean Legal Center. 3d ed. Seoul: January 1975.

Lee, Yong-Hee, ed. *Catalogue of Foreign Diplomatic Documents Relating to Modern Korea.* Seoul: National Assembly Library, 1979.

McCune, George M., and John A. Harrison, eds. *Korean-American Relations: Documents Pertaining to the Far Eastern Diplomacy of the United States.* Vol. I, *The Initial Period, 1883–1886.* Berkeley and Los Angeles: University of California Press, 1951.

Ministry of Foreign Affairs, Republic of Korea. *The Military Revolution in Korea.* Seoul, 1 July 1961.

Mitchell, C. Clyde. *Final Report on the History of the New Korea Company, Limited.* U.S. Army Military Government in Korea, National Land Administration, 1948.

The Papers of Horace N. Allen, 1858–1932. Manuscript and Archives Division, New York Public Library, 1974.

Paulley, Edwin W. *Report on Japanese Assets in Soviet-Occupied Korea, To the President of the United States.* Washington, June 1946; declassified 1949.

Tewksbury, D. G., ed. *Source Materials on Korean Politics and Ideologies.* New York: International Secretariat, Institute of Pacific Relations, 1950.

The United States and the Korean Problem, Documents, 1943–1953, 83rd Congress, First Session, Document #74, Washington, D.C.: 1953.

United States Department of State. *Korea's Independence.* Publication 2933. Washington, D.C.: October 1947.

———. *North Korea: A Case Study in the Technique of Takeover.* Publication 7118. Washington, D.C.: 1961.

———. *Papers Relating to the Foreign Relations of the United States.* Washington, D.C.: Government Printing Office. For the years 1871–72, 1881–1910, 1942ff.

Wedemeyer, Lt. Gen. A. C. *Report to the President, Korea, September, 1947.* Washington, D.C.: Defense Department, declassified 1951.

Selected Dissertations

Baldwin, Frank Prentis, Jr. "The March First Movement: Korean challenge and Japanese response." Columbia University, 1969.

Bang, Hung-Kyu. "Japan's Colonial Educational Policy in Korea, 1905–1930." The University of Arizona, 1972.

Chai, Jae-hyung. "The Military and Modernization in Korea." Western Reserve University, 1972.

Ch'en, Tieh-min. "The Sino-Japanese War, 1894–1895: Its Origin, Development, and Diplomatic Background." University of California, Berkeley, 1944.

Cheung, Joong-gun. "Japanese Colonial Administration in Korea, 1905–1919." Claremont Graduate School and University Center, 1971.

Chung, Myoung Ja (Wilson). "History of Public Speaking in Korea During the Independence Movement, 1910–1945." Pennsylvania State University, 1969.

Hahn, Bae-ho. "Factions in Contemporary Korean Competitive Politics." Princeton University, 1971.

Han, Sung-joo. "The Chang Myon Government (1960–1961) in South Korea: a case study of failure in political democracy." University of California, Berkeley, 1970.

Kang, Han-mu. "The U.S. Military Government in Korea, 1945–1948: an analysis and evaluation of it policy." University of Cincinnati, 1970.

Kang, Soon-heung. "The Problem of Autonomy for Korea Amid Rivalries of Great Powers: the search for a new order." University of Iowa, 1974.

Karl, Hongkee. "A Critical Evaluation of Modern Social Trends in Korea." University of Chicago, 1934.

Kim, Dong Koo. "American Influence on Korean Educational Thought during the Period of the U.S. Military Government, 1945–1948." University of Connecticut, 1984.

Kim, Hak-joon. "Korean Unification in the Asian Balance of Power." University of Pittsburgh, 1972.

Kim, Yong-shik. "Taewongun, the Catholic Movement, and the Role of Religion in Transitional Politics." Brigham Young University, 1971.

Ledyard, Gari. "The Korean Language Reform of 1446." Columbia University, 1965.

Lee, Young-ho. "The Political Culture of Modernizing Society: political attitudes and democracy in Korea." Yale University, 1969.

Macdonald, Donald Ross Hazelton. "Russian Interest in Korea to 1895: The Pattern of Russia's Emerging Interest in the Peninsula from the Late Seventeenth Century to the Sino-Japanese War." Harvard University, 1957.

Merrill, John Espy. "American Official Reactions to the Domestic Policies of Japan in Korea, 1905–1910." Stanford University, 1954.

Oh, Se-jeung. "Dr. Philip Jaisohn's Reform Movement, 1896–1898: a Critical Appraisal of the Independence Club." The American University, 1971.

Park, Young-June. "Land Reform in South Korea." Temple University, 1974.

Rhee, Jae-han. "Inflation and Agricultural Development in Korea." Pennsylvania State University, 1971.

Rim, Han Y. "Development of Higher Education During the Japanese Administration." Columbia University, 1951.

Shin, Roy W. "The Politics of Foreign Aid: A Study of the Impact of U.S. Aid in Korea from 1945 to 1969." University of Minnesota, 1969.

Son, Po-gi (Sohn Pow-Key). "Social History of the Early Yi Dynasty." University of California, Berkeley, 1963.

Thompson, William Randall. "Explanations of the Military Coup." University of Washington, 1972.

Vinocour, S. M. "Syngman Rhee: Spokesman for Korea." Pennsylvania State University, 1953.

Weems, Benjamin Norwood. "The Korean Reform and Independence Movement (1881–1898)." Columbia University, 1954.

Wheatly, Charles W. "Military Coups and Political Development: a Comparative Exploratory Study." Columbia University, 1968.

Yang, Sung-chul. "Revolution and Change: a Comparative Study of the April Student Revolution of 1960 and the May Military Coup d'etat of 1961 in Korea." University of Kentucky, 1970.

Yim, Yong-soon. "Politics of Korean Unification: a Comparative Study of Systemic Outputs in Two Different Political Systems." Rutgers University, 1974.

Books

Addleman, Irma, ed. *Practical Approaches to Developmental Planning: Korea's Second Five Year Plan.* Baltimore: Johns Hopkins University Press, 1969.

Allen, Richard C. (pseud.). *Korea's Syngman Rhee, An Unauthorized Portrait.* Rutland, VT: Charles E. Tuttle Co., 1960.

Amsden, Alice. *Asia's Next Giant: South Korea and Late Industrialization.* New York and London: Oxford University Press, 1989.

An, Tai Sung. *North Korea in Transition: From Dictatorship to Dynasty.* Westport, CT: Greenwood Press, 1983.

Baik, Bong. *Kim Il Sung: A Poliical Biography.* 3 vols. New York: Guardian Books, 1970.

Baldwin, Frank Prentis, Jr. *Without Parallel: The American-Korean Relationship Since 1945.* New York: Pantheon Books, 1973.

Barnet, Richard J. *Intervention and Revolution: The United States in the Third World.* New York: World Pub. Co., 1968.

Barnett, A. Doak, ed. *Communist Strategies in Asia.* New York: Praeger, 1963.

Barringer, Herbert R., and Man-gap Lee, eds. *A City in Transition: Urbanization in Taegu.* Seoul, 1971.

Bartz, Patricia M. *South Korea.* London: Oxford University Press, 1972.

Bergman, Sten. *In Korean Wilds and Villages.* London: John Gifford, 1938.

Bevin, Alexander. *Korea: The First War We Lost.* New York: Hippocrene Books, 1986.

Bishop, Isabella Lucy (Bird). *Korea and Her Neighbors: A Narrative of Travel, with an Account of the Vicissitudes and Position of the Country.* London: John Murray, 1898.

Brandt, Vincent S. R. *A Korean Village between Farm and Sea.* Cambridge: Harvard University Press, 1971.

Brown, Arthur Judson. *The Mastery of the Far East: The Story of Korea's Transformation and Japan's Rise to Supremacy in the Orient.* New York: Charles Scribner's Sons, 1919.

Burchett, Wilfred G. *Again Korea.* New York: International Publishers, 1968.

Cavendish, A. E. J. *Korea and the Sacred White Mountain.* London: George Philip and Son, 1894.

Chang, Joseph, ed. *Patterns of Economic Development: Korea.* Kalamazoo: Western Michigan University Press, 1965.

Chang, Myun. *Sashil ui chonu rul kisul handa* (All Truths Are Told). Seoul: Nuimang ch'ulp'ansa, 1966.

Ch'en, Jerome. *Yuan Shih-k'ai.* 2d ed. Stanford, CA: Stanford University Press, 1961.

Chien, Frederick Foo. *The Opening of Korea: A Study of Chinese Diplomacy, 1876–1885.* Hamden, CT: The Shoe String Press, 1967.

Chindan, Hak'hoe, ed. *Han'guk sa* (Korean History). 7 volumes. Seoul: Uryu Munwha Sa, 1959–1964.

Cho, Hang-nae. *Kaehanggi tae-Il Kwan'gyesa yon'gu* (A study of Korean-Japanese relations in the opening of Korea). Taegu: Hyongsol ch'ulp'ansa, 1973.

Cho, Soon Sung. *Korea in World Politics, 1940–1950.* Berkeley and Los Angeles: University of California Press, 1967.

Choe, Ching Young. *The Rule of Taewongun, 1864–1873: Restoration in Yi Korea.* Cambridge: Harvard University Press, East Asian Research Center, Harvard University, 1972.

Ch'oe, Chun. *Han'guk sinmun-sa* (History of Korean Journalism). Seoul: Ilchogak, 1960.

Choi, Chongko. *Han'guku soyang-bop suyong-sa* (The Reception of Western Law in Korea). Seoul: Pagyongsa, 1982.

Choi, Ho-jan. *An Outline of Korean Economic History.* Seoul: Pommungak, 1962.

Chong, Kyo. *Taehan Kyenyon'sa* (History of the Last Years of the Yi Dynasty). 2 vols. Seoul: Kuksa P'yonch'an Wiwonhoe, 1957.

Chong, Yon-sok. *Miguk ui Tae Han chongch'aek, 1945–1980* (American policy toward Korea, 1845–1980). Seoul: Ilchogak, 1979.

Chung, Chong-Shik, and Jae-Bong Ro, eds. *Nationalism in Korea.* Seoul: Research Center for Peace and Unification, 1979.

Chung, In-taek. *An Appraisal of the Unification Policies of the Korean Government, 1948–1970.* Seoul: Korea University, Asiatic Research Center, 1971.

Chung, Joseph S., ed. *Patterns of Economic Development: Korea.* Kalamazoo: Western Michigan University, 1965.

———. *The North Korean Economy: Structure and Development.* Stanford, CA: The Hoover Institution, 1974.

Chung, Kyung Cho. *Korea Tomorrow: Land of the Morning Calm.* New York: Macmillan, 1960.

———. *New Korea.* New York: Macmillan, 1962.

Chung, Nam-ku, and Heung-keun Oh. *An Introduction to Korean Agriculture.* Seoul: The American-Korean Foundation, 1962.

Clements, Kenneth A., ed. *James F. Byrnes and the Origins of the Cold War.* Durham, NC: Caroline Academic Press, 1982.

Cochran, Bert. *Harry Truman and the Crisis Presidency.* New York: Funk and Wagnalls, 1964.

Cole, David C., and P. N. Lyman. *Korean Development: The Interplay of Politics and Economics.* Cambridge: Harvard University Press, 1971.

Conroy, Hilary. *The Japanese Seizure of Korea: 1868–1910: A Study of Realism and Idealism in International Relations.* Philadelphia: University of Pennsylvania Press, 1960.

Cook, Harold F. *Korea's 1884 Incident: Its Background and Kim Ok-Kyun's Elusive Dream.* Seoul: Korea Branch, Royal Asiatic Society, 1972.

Culin, Steward. *Korean Games.* Philadephia: University of Pennsylvania Press, 1895.

Cumings, Bruce. *The Two Koreas.* New York: Foreign Policy Association, 1984.

———. *The Origins of the Korean War: Liberation and the Emergence of Separate Regimes, 1945–47.* Princeton: Princeton University Press, 1981.

Curzon, George Nathaniel. *Problems of the Far East, Japan-Korea-China.* London: Longmans Green, 1894.

Daewoo, Haksul Ch'ongso. *Chong Tasan Yongu ui Hyonhwang* (The Present Situation in Chong Tasan Studies). Seoul: Minum-sa Publishing Co., 1985.

Dallet, Charles. *Histoire de L'Eglise de Coree.* Two volumes. Paris: Victor Palme, 1874.

———. *Traditional Korea.* New Haven, CT: Human Relations Area Files, 1951.

Dayal, Shiv. *India's Role in the Korean Question.* Delhi: S. Chand and Co., 1959.

De Bary, Wm., and Jayhyun Kim Haboush, eds. *The Rise of Neo-Confucianism in Korea.* New York: Columbia University Press, 1985.

Denison, Edward F. and William K. Chung. *How Japan's Economy Grew So Fast: The Sources of Postwar Expansion.* Washington, D.C., 1976.

Deuchler, Martina. *Confucian Gentlemen and Barbarian Envoys: The Opening of Korea, 1875–1885*. Seattle: University of Washington Press, 1977.

———, ed. *The Chinese World Order: Traditional China's Foreign Relations*. East Asian Series, no. 32. Cambridge: Harvard University Press, 1968.

Dobbs, Charles M. *The Unwanted Symbol: American Foreign Policy, the Cold War, and Korea, 1945–1950*. Kent, OH: Kent State University Press, 1981.

Dore, Francil. *Les Regimes Politique en Asia*. Paris: Presses Universitaires de France, 1973.

Duverger, Maurice. *Political Parties: Their Organization and Activity in the Modern State*. Translated by Barbara and Robert North. New York: John Wiley and Sons, 1963.

Eckert, Carter J., Ki-baik Lee, Young Ik Lew, Michael Robinson, and Edward W. Wagner. *Korea Old and New: A History*. Seoul: Ilchokak Publishers, for Harvard University, Korea Institute, 1990.

Eckhardt, Andreas. *A History of Korean Art*. Translated by M. M. Kindersley. London: Edward Goldston; Leipzig: Karl W. Hiersemann, 1929.

Esthus, Raymond A. *Theodore Roosevelt and Japan*. Seattle: University of Washington Press, 1967.

Feis, Herbert. *Between War and Peace: The Potsdam Conference*. Princeton: Princeton University Press, 1960.

———. *Churchill, Roosevelt, Stalin; The War They Waged and the Peace They Sought*. Princeton: Princeton University Press, 1957.

Gale, James A. *Korea in Transition*. New York: Board of Foreign Missions of the Presbyterian Church, 1909.

Gardner, Lloyd C., ed. *The Korean War*. New York: Quadrangle Books, 1972.

Gati, Charles. *Containment and the Cold War*. New York: Bobbs-Merrill, 1974.

Gitovich, A., and B. Bursov. *North of the 38th Parallel*. Shanghai: Epoch Pub. Co, 1948.

Goldman, Eric F. *The Crucial Decade; America, 1945–1955*. New York: Alfred A. Knopf, 1956.

Goodrich, Leland M. *Korea: A Study of U.S. Policy in the United Nations*. New York: Harper and Row, 1956.

Gordenker, Leon. *The United Nations and the Peaceful Unification of Korea: The Politics of Field Operations*. The Hague: Martinus Nijhoff, 1959.

Grajdanzev, Andrew J. *Korea Looks Ahead*. New York: Institute of Pacific Relations, 1944.

———. *Modern Korea, Her Economic and Social Development Under the Japanese*. New York: Institute of Pacific Relations, 1944.

Griffis, William Elliott. *A Modern Pioneer in Korea*. New York: Fleming H. Revell, 1912.

———. *Corea, The Hermit Nation*. New York: Charles Scribner's Sons, 1897; reprint, 1907.

Grintner, Lawrence, and Young Whan Kihl, eds. *East Asian Conflict Zones: Prospects for Regional Stability and Deescalation*. New York: St. Martin's Press, 1987.

Halpern, Abraham M. et al, eds. *The Future of the Korean Peninsula*. New York: Praeger, 1977.

Hammond, Thomas T., and Robert Farrell. *The Anatomy of Communist Takeovers*. New Haven: Yale University Press, 1971.

Han, Sung-jo, ed. *After One Hundred Years: Continuity and Change in Korean-American Relations*. Seoul: Asiatic Research Center, Korea University, 1982.

———. *The Failure of Democracy in South Korea*. Berkeley: University of California Press, 1974.

Han, Tae-su. *Hanguk chongdang-sa* (A History of Korean Political Parties). Seoul: Sin Taeyang-sa, 1961.

Harrington, Fred Harvey. *God, Mammon, and the Japanese: Dr. Horace N. Allen and Korean-American Relations, 1884–1905*. Madison: University of Wisconsin Press, 1944.

Heinl, Robert Debs, Jr. *Victory at High Tide: The Inchon-Seoul Campaign*. Philadelphia: J. B. Lippincott, 1968.

Heller, Francis H., ed. *The Korean War: A 25-Year Perspective*. Lawrence: Regents Press of the University of Kansas, 1977.

Herlihy, Francis. *Now Welcome Summer*. Melbourne, Australia: The Hawthorne Press, 1946.

Ho, Takushu. *Meiji shoki Nis-sen kankei no kenkyu* (Japanese-Korean relations in the early Meiji period). Tokyo: Hanawa Shobo, 1969.

Hoare, James, and Susan Pares. *Korea: An Introduction*. London and New York: Kegan Paul, 1988.

Honey, W. B. *Corean Pottery*. New York: Van Nostrand Co., 1948.

Hong, So-min. *Yogol Minbi* (A great woman, Queen Min). Seoul: Samjungdang, 1958.

Hong, Wontack, and Anne O. Kreuger, eds. *Trade and Development in Korea*. Seoul: Hanguk Kaebal Yonguwon (KDI) 1975.

Hong, Yi-sup. *Korea's Self Identity*. Seoul: Yonsei University Press, 1973.

Hsiao, Gene T., ed. *Sino-American Detente and Its Policy Implications*. New York: Praeger, 1974.

Huh, Chung. *U-Nam, Syngman Rhee*. Vol. VII of the Modern Korea Biography Series. Seoul: TaeKuk Pub. Co., 1970.

Hulbert, Homer B. *The History of Korea*. 2 vols. Seoul: Methodist Publishing House, 1905; reprint ed. with introduction and notes by Benjamin B. Weems, Indianapolis: Hillary House, 1962.

———. *The Passing of Korea*. New York: Doubleday, Page & Co., 1906.

Hwang, In Kwan. *The Korean Reform Movement of the 1880's: A study of Transition in Intra-Asian Relations*. Cambridge: Schenkman Pub. Co., 1978.

Itani, Zenichi. *Chosen Keizaishi* (Economic History of Korea). Tokyo, 1928.

Japan Times. *Economic Development of Korea and Manchuria*. Tokyo: Japan Times Pub. Co., 1923.

Jo, Yung-Hwan, ed. *Korea's Response to the West*. Kalamazoo, MI: Korea Research and Publications, 1971.

———, ed. *U.S. Foreign Policy in Asia*. Santa Barbara, CA, 1978.

Joy, Admiral C. Turner. *How Communists Negotiate*. New York: Macmillan, 1955.

Johnson, E. A. J. *American Imperialism in the Image of Peer Gynt*. Minneapolis: University of Minnesota Press, 1971.

Kang, Younghill. *East Goes West*. New York: Scribner's Sons, 1937.

———. *The Grass Roof*. New York: Scribner's Sons, 1932.

Kang, Young Hoon, and Young Soon Yim, eds. *Politics of Korean Reunification*. Seoul: Research Center for Peace and Unification, 1978.

Kendall, Laura, and Griffin Dix. *Religion and Ritual in Korean Society.* Berkeley: University of California, Institute of East Asian Studies, 1987.

Kennedy, Edgar S. *Mission to Korea.* London: Derek Verschoyle, 1952.

Kikuchi, Kenjo. *Kindai Chosenshi* (Modern Korean History). 2 vols. Tokyo: Dairiku Kenkyūsho, 1940.

Kim, Agnes Davis. *I Married a Korean.* New York: John Day, 1953.

Kim, Changsoon, ed. *The Culture of Korea.* Honolulu: Korean-American Cultural Association, 1945.

Kim, C. E. Eugene, eds. *Korea: A Pattern of Political Development.* Ann Arbor: University of Michigan Press, 1964.

——— and Doretha E. Mortimore, eds. *Korea's Response to Japan: The Colonial Period, 1910–1945.* Kalamazoo: Western Michigan University, Korean Studies Center, 1977.

——— and Han-kyo Kim, eds. *Korea and the Politics of Imperialism, 1876–1910.* Berkeley: University of California Press, 1967.

Kim, Eul Han. *'I Chose Freedom'—A Story of the Korean War in Connection with a Best Seller.* Seoul: The International Cultural Association of Korea, n.d. [1958?]

Kim, Hak-Joon. *The Unification Policy of North and South Korea.* Seoul: Seoul National University Press. Distributed by University of Hawaii Press, 1984.

Kim, Helen Kiteuk. *Rural Education for the Regeneration of Korea.* New York: Columbia University, 1931.

Kim, Hyung-chan. *Letters in Exile: The Life and Times of Yun Ch'i-ho.* Oxford, GA: The Oxford Historical Shrine Society, 1980.

Kim, Il-sung. *Jojak Sonjip* (Selected Works of Kim Il-song). Pyongyang: Korean-Workers Party, 1968.

Kim, J. Ilpyung. *Communist Politics in North Korea.* New York: Praeger, 1975.

Kim, Joungwon Alexander. *Divided Korea: The Politics of Development, 1945–1971.* Cambridge: Harvard University Press, East Asian Research Center, 1975.

Kim, Hey-Hiuk. *The Last Phase of the East Asian World Order: Korea, Japan, and the Chinese Empire, 1860–1882.* Berkeley and Los Angeles: University of California Press, 1980.

Kim, Kwan Bong. *The Korea-Japan Treaty Crisis and the Instability of the Korean Political System.* New York: Praeger, 1971.

Kim, O-song, ed. *Chidoja kunsang* (The Leaders). Seoul: Taesong chulpan-sa, 1946.

Kim, S. H. *Foreign Capital for Economic Development: A Korean Case Study.* New York: Praeger, 1970.

Kim, Se-jin. *The Politics of Military Revolution in Korea.* Chapel Hill: University of North Carolina Press, 1971.

——— and Cho Chang-hyun, eds. *Government and Politics in Korea.* Silver Springs, MD: The Research Institute of Korean Affairs, 1972.

———, eds. *Korea: A Divided Nation.* Silver Springs, MD: The Research Institute on Korean Affairs, 1976.

Kim, Tai-jin, ed. *A Bibliographical Guide to Traditional Korean Sources.* Seoul: Korea University, Asiatic Research Center, 1976.

Kim, Ui-hwan. *Footprints of the Korean Envoys: Correspondence to Japan.* Seoul: Chonggum Munhwasa, 1985.

———. *Study of the Modern History of Korea's Relations with Japan.* Seoul: Tongmungwan Pub. Co., 1965.

Kim, Won-mo. *Kundae Hanmi Kyuosopsa* (The Early Korean-American Relations, 1852–1871). Seoul: Hongsongsa, 1980.

Kim, Young C., ed. *Major Powers and Korea.* Seoul: Research Institute on Korean Affairs, 1973.

Ko, Yong-hwan. *Kumil ui chonggaektul* (Today's Politicians). Seoul: Tonga Ilbo-sa, 1949.

Koh, Pyung Chul. *The Foreign Policy of North Korea.* New York: Praeger, 1969.

Kokin Kinekai. *Kim Kyoku-kin den* (Biography of Kim Ok-kyun). Tokyo: Keio Shuppan sha, 1944.

Kolko, Gabriel. *The Politics of War: The World and United States Foreign Policy, 1943–1945.* New York: Vintage Books, 1968.

Komatsu, Midori. *Chosen Heigo no Rimen* (Background of the Japanese Annexation of Korea). Tokyo: Chugai shimonsa, 1920.

Koo, Jae-suh. *A Study of the Regional Characteristics of Korean Agriculture.* Seoul: Korea University, 1967.

Koo, Youngnok, and Dae-sook Suh, eds. *Korea and the United States: A Century of Cooperation.* Honolulu: University of Hawaii Press, 1984.

Korean History Research Society. *An Introduction to the Study of Korean History.* Seoul: Chisik sanopsa, 1981.

Korean National History Compilation Committee, ed. *Hangul tongnip undong sa,* (History of the Korean Independence Movement), Seoul: National History Compilation Committee, 1965–

Kuno, Y. S. *Japanese Expansion on the Asiatic Continent.* Berkeley and Los Angeles: University of California Press, 1937–40.

Kwak, Tae-Hwan, John Chay, Soon Sung Cho, and Shannon McCune. *U.S.-Korean Relations, 1882–1982.* Seoul: Kyungnam University Press, 1982.

Ladd, George T. *In Korea with Marquis Ito.* New York: Scribner's Sons, 1908.

Land Economics Research Center. *A Study of the Land Tenure System in Korea.* Seoul, 1966.

Langes, George Alexander. *Balance of Intrigue: International Rivalry in Korea and Manchuria, 1884–1899.* 2 vols. Tallahassee: University Presses of Florida, 1982.

Leckie, Robert. *Conflict: The History of the Korean War, 1950–53.* New York: Putnam's Sons, 1962.

Lee, Changsoo, ed. *Modernization of Korea and the Impact of the West.* Los Angeles: University of Southern California, East Asia Studies Center, 1981.

Lee, Chong-Sik. *Japan and Korea: The Political Dimension.* Stanford, CA: Hoover Institution Press, 1985.

———. *Kim Kyu-sik ui saengae* (The Career of Kimm Kyu-sic). Seoul: Singu Munwha-sa, 1974.

———. *Korean Workers' Party: A Short History.* Stanford, CA: Hoover Institution Press, 1978.

———. *Materials on Korean Communism, 1945–1947.* Honolulu: Center for Korean Studies, 1977.

———. *The Politics of Korean Nationalism.* Berkeley and Los Angeles: University of California Press, 1963.

Lee, Hahn Been. *Korea: Time, Change, and Administration.* Honolulu: University of Hawaii Press, 1968.

Lee, Hoon Koo. *Land Utilization and Rural Economy in Korea*. Chicago: The University of Chicago Press, 1936; Shanghai: Kelly and Walsh, 1936.

Lee, Hyo-Chae, and Joo-Sook Kim. *The Status of Korean Women*. Seoul: Ewha Women's University, 1975.

Lee, Yur-Bok. *Diplomatic Relations Between the United States and Korea, 1866–1887*. New York: Humanities Press, 1970.

———. *West Goes East: Paul Georg von Möllendorff and Great Power Imperialism in Late Yi Korea*. Honolulu: University of Hawaii Press, 1988.

——— and Wayne Patterson, eds. *One Hundred Years of Korean-American Relations, 1882–1982*. University: University of Alabama Press, 1986.

Ledyard, Gari. *The Dutch Come to Korea: An Account of the Life of the First Westerners in Korea, 1653–1666*. Seoul: Royal Asiatic Society, Korea Branch, 1971.

Lensen, George Alexander. *Balance of Intrigue*. Gainesville: University Presses of Florida, 1982.

Lewis, John P. *Reconstruction and Development of South Korea*. Washington, D.C.: National Planning Association, 1955.

Li, Mirok. *The Yalu Flows: A Korean Childhood*. London: Harvill Press, 1954.

Liem, Channing. *America's Finest Gift to Korea: The Life of Philip Jaisohn*. New York: William Frederick Press, 1952.

Lim, Un (pseud). *The Founding of a Dynasty in North Korea: An Authentic Biography of Kim Il-song*. Tokyo: Jiyuisha, 1982.

Longford, Joseph H. *The Story of Korea*. London: Fisher Unwin, 1911.

Lowell, Percival. *Chosen, The Land of Morning Calm*. Boston: Ticknor, 1886.

Macdonald, Donald Stone. *The Koreans: Contemporary Politics and Society*. Boulder and London: Westview Press, 1988.

Malozemoff, Andrew. *Russian Far Eastern Policy, 1881–1904*. Berkeley and Los Angeles: University of California Press, 1958.

Matray, James Irving. *The Reluctant Crusade: American Foreign Policy in Korea, 1941–1950*. Honolulu: University of Hawaii Press, 1985.

McCune, Evelyn. *The Arts of Korea: An Illustrated History*. Rutland, VT: Charles E. Tuttle, 1962.

McCune, George. *Korea's Postwar Political Problems*. New York: Institute of Pacific Relations, 1947.

———. *Post-War Government and Politics in Korea*, Gainesville: University of Florida Press, 1947.

McCune, George and Arthur L. Grey, Jr. *Korea Today*. Cambridge: Harvard University Press, 1950.

McCune, Shannon. *Korea: Land of Broken Calm*. Princeton: D. Van Nostrand, 1966.

———. *Korea's Heritage: A Regional and Social Geography*. Rutland, VT: Charles E. Tuttle, 1956.

McKenzie, F. I. *Korea's Fight for Freedom*. New York: Fleming H. Revell Co., 1920.

———. *The Tragedy of Korea*. New York: E. P. Dutton, n.d.

McNeill, William H. *America, Britain, and Russia: Their Cooperation and Conflict, 1941–1946*. New York: Johnson Reprint Corp., 1970.

Meacham, Stewart. *Korean Labor Report*. Seoul: United States Armed Forces in Korea, 1947.

Meade, E. Grant. *American Military Government in Korea*. New York: King's Crown Press, Columbia University, 1951.

Merrill, John. *Korea: Origins of The Peninsular War.* Newark: University of Delaware Press, 1989, and London and Toronto: Associated University Presses.

Min, Tae-won. *Kapshin Chong-byon-gwa Kim Ok-kyun* (The Coup d'Etat of 1884 and Kim Ok-kyun). Seoul: Kukche Munwha Hyophoe, 1947.

Moore, Barrington, *Social Origins of Dictatorship and Democracy.* Boston: Beacon Press, 1966.

Moose, Robert J. *Village Life in Korea.* Nashville: The Publishing House of the M.E. Church, 1911.

Moreley, James W. *Japan and Korea: America's Allies in the Pacific.* New York: Walker and Co., 1965.

Morris, Ivan. *Nationalism and the Right Wing in Japan.* New York: Oxford University Press, 1960.

Murphy, Sunny, and Yi Myung-whi, eds. *Koreana Collection.* Seoul: Yongsan Library, U.S. Army Recreation Services Operation, 1982.

Nagai, Yonosuke, and Akira Iriye. *The Origins of the Cold War in Asia.* Tokyo: The University of Tokyo Press; New York: Columbia University Press, 1977.

Nahm, Andrew C., ed. *Korea and the New Order in East Asia.* Kalamazoo: Western Michigan University, Center for Korean Studies, 1973.

———. *Korea Under Japanese Colonial Rule.* Kalamazoo: Western Michigan University Center for Korean Studies, 1973.

———. *North Korea: Her Past, Reality, and Impression.* Kalamazoo: Western Michigan University, Center for Korean Studies, 1978.

———. *Problems of Korean Unification.* Vol. I. Seoul: Research Center for Peace and Unification, 1976.

———. *Studies in the International Aspects of Korea.* Kalamazoo: Western Michigan University, Center for Korean Studies, 1969.

———. *The United States and Korea: American-Korean Relations, 1866–1976.* Kalamazoo: Western Michigan University, Center for Korean Studies, 1979.

Nam, Koon Woo. *The North Korean Communist Leadership, 1945–1965.* University: University of Alabama Press, 1974.

National Academy of Sciences, Republic of Korea, ed. *Introduction to Korean Studies.* Seoul: Daekwan Printing Co., 1986.

Nelson, M. Frederick. *Korea and the Old Orders in Eastern Asia.* Baton Rouge: Louisiana State University Press, 1945; reprint ed., New York: Russell & Russell, 1967.

Oh, John Kie-chiang. *Korea: Democracy on Trial.* Ithaca: Cornell University Press, 1968.

Okonogi, Masao. *North Korea at the Cross-Roads.* Tokyo: Japan Institute of International Affairs, 1988.

Oliver, Robert T. *The Case for Korea: A Paradox of United States Diplomacy.* Pamphlet. Washington, D.C.: Korean American Council, 1945.

———. *Divided Korea: Its Economic Resources, Potentials and Needs.* New York: Citizens Conference on International Economic Union, 1947.

———. *Korea, Forgotten Nation.* Washington, D.C.: Public Affairs Press, 1944.

———, ed. *Korean Report.* Annual volumes, I–VI, 1948–52, 1952–53, 1954, 1955, 1957, 1958. Washington, D.C.: Korean Pacific Press—Korean Research and Information Office.

———, ed. *Korea's Fight for Freedom.* 2 vols. Washington, D.C.: Korean Pacific Press, 1951, 1952.

———. *Leadership in Twentieth Century Asia: The Rhetorical Principles and Practices of the Leaders of China, Korea, and India.* University Park: Center for Continuing Liberal Education, Pennsylvania State University, 1966.

———. *Leadership in Asia: Persuasive Communication in the Making of Nations, 1850–1950.* Newark: University of Delaware Press, 1989; and London and Toronto, Associated University Presses.

———. *Syngman Rhee and American Involvement in Korea, 1942–1960: A Personal Narrative.* Seoul: Panmun Books, 1978.

———. *Syngman Rhee: The Man Behind the Myth.* New York: Dodd Mead, 1954, 1955.

———. *The Truth about Korea.* London: Putnam, 1951.

———. *Verdict in Korea.* State College, PA: Bald Eagle Press, 1952.

———. *Why War Came in Korea.* New York: Fordham University Press and MacMullen Co., 1950.

Olsen, Edward A. *U.S. Policy and the Two Koreas.* Boulder, CO: Westview Press, 1988.

Oppert, Ernest. *A Forbidden Land: Voyages to the Corea.* New York: Putnam's, 1880.

Osgood, Cornelius. *The Koreans and Their Culture.* New York: Ronald Press, 1951.

Padelford, Norman J., and Leland M. Goodrich, eds. *The United Nations in the Balance: Accomplishments and Prospects.* New York: Frederick A. Praeger, 1965.

Paek, Chong-gi, *Hanguk Kundaesa yongu* (Studies on Korean recent history) Seoul: Pakyongsa, 1981.

Paik, L. George. *The History of Protestant Missions in Korea, 1832–1910.* 2d ed. Seoul: Yonsei University Press, 1971.

Paige, Glenn D. *The Korean Decision, June 24–30, 1950.* New York: Free Press, 1968.

———. *The Korean People's Democratic Republic.* Stanford, CA: The Hoover Institution on War, Revolution and Peace, 1966.

Pak, Chi-Young. *Political Opposition in Korea, 1945–1960.* Honolulu: University of Hawaii Press, 1980.

Pak, Ki-hyuk, et al. *A Study of the Land Tenure System in Korea.* Seoul: Land Economics Research Center, 1966.

———. *Three Clan Villages in Korea.* Seoul: Yonsei University Press, 1963.

Palais, James B. *Politics and Policy in Traditional Korea.* Cambridge: Harvard University Press, 1975.

——— and Bruce Cumings. *Human Rights in Korea.* New York: Asia Watch Committee, 1986.

Pannikar, K. M. *In Two Chinas: Memoirs of a Diplomat.* London: Allen and Unwin, 1955.

Park, Chung-Hee. *Our Nation's Path.* Seoul: Kwangmyong Pub. Co., 1962.

Park, Myung-Seok. *Communication Styles in Two Different Cultures: Korean and American.* Seoul: Han Shin Pub. Co., 1979.

Park, Tong-Un. *Pukhan Tongchi Kigu Ron* (The Government Structure in North Korea). Seoul: Center for Asiatic Studies, Korea University Press, 1964.

Paullin, Charles Oscar. *Diplomatic Negotiations of American Naval Officers, 1778–1883*. Baltimore: Johns Hopkins University Press, 1912.

Pihl, Marshall, ed. *Listening to Korea*. New York: Praeger, 1973.

Pyun, Yung-tae. *Korea—My Country*. Washington, D.C.: Korean Pacific Press, 1953.

Reeve, W. D. *The Republic of Korea: A Political and Economic Study*. London: Oxford University Press, 1963.

Reitzel, Wm., Morton A. Kaplan, and Constance G. Coblenz. *The United States Foreign Policy, 1945–1955*. Washington, D.C.: Brookings Institute, 1956.

Reischauer, Edwin O. *Wanted: An Asian Policy*. New York: Knopf, 1949.

Rhee, Syngman. *Ilminju ui kaesol* (Outline of the One People's Principle). Seoul: Ilminjuui po'gup-hoe, 1949.

———. *Japan Inside Out*. New York: Fleming H. Revell, 1942.

Riley, John W., Jr., and William Schramm. *The Reds Take a City*. New Brunswick, NJ: Rutgers University Press, 1951.

Robinson, Michael Edson. *Cultural Nationalism in Colonial Korea, 1920–1925*. Seattle: University of Washington Press, 1989.

Rose, Lisle A. *Dubious Victory: The United States and the End of World War II*. Kent, OH: Kent State University Press, 1973.

Rostow, W. W. *The United States in the World Arena: An Essay in Recent History*. New York: Harper and Brothers, 1960.

Rudolph, Philip, ed. *North Korea's Political and Economic Structure*. New York: Institute of Pacific Relations, 1959.

Sawyer, Robert K. *Military Advisors in Korea: KMAG in Peace and War*. Washington, D.C.: Office of the Army, 1962.

Scalapino, Robert A., ed. *The Communist Revolution in Asia: Tactics, Goals, and Achievements*. Englewood Cliffs, NJ: Prentice-Hall, 1969.

———, ed. *North Korea Today*. New York: Frederick A. Praeger, 1963.

——— and Chong-Sik Lee. *Communism in Korea*. 2 vols. Berkeley and Los Angeles: University of California Press, 1972.

——— and Sung-joo Han, eds. *United States-Korea Relations*. Berkeley: University of California Institute of East Asian Studies, 1986.

Schatsneider, E. E. *The Semi-Sovereign People*. New York: Holt, Rinehart, and Winston, 1960.

Shaw, William. *Human Rights in Korea*. Cambridge: Harvard University Press, 1985.

Shin, Yong-ha. *Choson Toji Chosa Saop Yon'gu* (A Study of the Land Survey Project in Korea). Seoul: Chisik sanop-sa, 1982.

Shoemaker, James. *Notes on Korea's Postwar Economic Position*. New York: Institute of Pacific Relations, 1947.

Sia, Kuk-chu. *Kindai Chosen gaiko shi kenkyu* (Studies on diplomatic history of modern Korea). Tokyo: Yushindo Publishing Co., 1966.

Simmons, Robert E. *The Strained Alliance: Peking, P'yongyang, Moscow and the Politics of the Korean Civil War*. New York: The Free Press, 1975.

Sin, Yong-ha. *Tongnip hyophoe yon'gu* (A Study of the Independence Club), Seoul: Ilchogak, 1976.

Soh, Chung Hee. *The Chosen Women in Korean Politics: An Anthropological Study*. New York: Praeger, 1991.

Sohn, Hak-Kyu. *Authoritarianism and Political Opposition in South Korea*. London and New York: Routledge, 1989.

Son, In-ju, *Hanguk kundae kyoyuk-sa* (History of new education in Korea, 1885–1945). Seoul: Yonsei University Press, 1971.

Song, Chun-Duk, ed. *Hanguk Sinmunsa* (History of Korean newspapers). Seoul, 1955.

Spanier, John W. *The Truman-MacArthur Controversy and the Korean War.* Cambridge: The Belknap Press, Harvard University Press, 1959.

Stairs, Denis. *The Diplomacy of Constraint: Canada, the Korean War, and the United States.* Toronto: University of Toronto Press, 1974.

Stueck, William W. *The Road to Confrontation: American Policy toward China and Korea, 1947–1950.* Chapel Hill: University of North Carolina Press, 1981.

Suh, Byong-Cho. *Jukwonja ui chungon: Hanguk daeui chongch'i sa* (Testimony by a Sovereign: A History of a Representative Government). Seoul: Moumsa, 1964.

Suh, Dae-Sook, ed. *Documents of Korean Communism, 1918–1948.* Princeton: Princeton University Press, 1967.

———. *The Korean Communist Movement, 1918–1948.* Princeton: Princeton University Press, 1967.

——— and Chae-Jin Lee, eds. *Political Leadership in Korea.* Seattle: University of Washington Press, 1976.

Suh, Sang Chul. *Growth and Structural Changes in the Korean Economy, 1910–1945.* Cambridge: Harvard University Press, Council on East Asian Studies, 1978.

Sunoo, Harold H. *American Dilemma in Asia: The Case of South Korea.* Chicago: Nelson-Hall Pub., 1979.

Swartout, Robert R., Jr. *Mandarins, Gunboats, and Power Politics: Owen Nickerson Denny and the International Rivalries in Korea.* Asian Studies at Hawaii, No. 25. Honolulu: University Press of Hawaii, 1980.

Synn, Seung Kwon. *The Russo-Japanese Rivalry over Korea, 1876–1904.* Seoul: Yuk Phub Sa, 1981.

Takahashi, Kamekichi. *Kendai Chosen keizairon* (A Study of Current Korean Economy). Tokyo: 1935.

Thompson, Reginald. *Cry Korea.* London: MacDonald, 1952.

Tsuboe, Senji. *Choson minsoku dokoritsu undo hishi* (The Undisclosed History of Independence Movements of the Korean Nation). Tokyo: Gennan-do, 1966.

Underwood, Lilian H. *Fifteen Years Among the Top-Knots.* New York: American Tract Society, 1904.

Van Buskirk, James D. *Korea: Land of the Dawn.* New York: Missionary Education Movement, 1931.

Wagner, Edward W. *The Korean Minority in Japan, 1904–1950.* Vancouver: University of British Columbia, 1951.

Wales, Nym and Kim San. *Song of Ariran: A Korean Communist in the Chinese Revolution.* San Francisco: Ramparts Press, 1973.

Weale, B. L. *The Coming Struggle in Eastern Asia.* Lonson: Macmillan, 1908.

Weems, Benjamin Norwood, ed. *Hulbert's History of Korea.* 2 vols. New York: Hilary House Pub., 1962.

———. *Reform, Rebellion, and the Heavenly Way.* The Association for Asian Studies: Monographs and Papers, No. XV. Tucson: University of Arizona Press, 1964.

Weems, Clarence N. *Korea: Dilemma of an Underdeveloped Country.* New York: Foreign Policy Association, 1960.

Whiting, Allen S. *China Crosses the Yalu: The Decision to Enter the Korean War.* New York: Macmillan Co., 1960.

Wright, Edward W. *Korean Politics in Transition.* Seattle: University of Washington Press, 1975.

Yang, Sung Chul. *Korea and the Two Regimes: Kim Il Sung and Park Chung Hee.* Cambridge, MA: Schenkman Pub. Co., 1981.

Yang, U-chong. *Yi taet'ongnyong t'ujaeng-sa* (History of President Rhee's Struggle). Seoul: Yonhap Sinmun-sa, 1949.

Yanghi, Choe-Wall, ed. and trans. *Memoirs of a Korean Queen by Lady Hong.* London and New York: KPI, 1987.

Yi, Chae-O. *Perceptions of Korea-Japan Historical Relations.* Seoul: Hangminsa, 1984.

Yi, Hyong-hui. *Han'guk Yosong Kaewha-sa—Uri Yosong-ui Koroon Kil* (A History of Modernization of Korean Women—The Path of Our Women). Seoul: Iu Ch'ulp'an-sa, 1978.

Yi, Kwang-su. *Tosan An Ch'ang-ho* (Biography of Ahn Chang-ho). Seoul: 1956.

Yi, Kyu-tae. *Modern Transformation of Korea.* Translated by Sung Ton-man et al. Seoul: Sejong Pub. Co., 1970.

Yi, Sang-baek. *Han'guksa: Kunse hugi p'yon* (History of Korea: late modern period). Seoul: Uryu munhwasa, 1965.

Yi-Son-gun. *Han'guksa: Hyondaep'yon* (History of Korea: modern era). Seoul: Ullyumunhwasa, 1964.

Yi, Yong-hyop. *Han'guk hyondae t'oji chedo-sa yong'gu* (Studies on the History of the Modern Land System in Korea). Seoul: Pomun-gak, 1962.

Young, Kenneth T. *Negotiating with the Chinese Communists: The United States Experience, 1953–1967.* New York: McGraw-Hill, 1968.

Yun- Ki-bong. *North Korea as I knew It.* Seoul: North Korean Research Institute, 1974.

Zabriskie, Edward. *American-Russian Rivalry in the Far East, A Study in Diplomacy and Power Politics, 1895–1914.* Philadelphia: University of Pennsylvania Press, 1946.

Zaichikov, V. T. *Geography of Korea.* Translated by Albert Parry. New York: Institute of Pacific Relations, 1952.

Journals

Allen, Richard C. (pseud.). "South Korea: The New Regime." *Pacific Affairs* 34 (Spring 1961): 54–55.

Au, Pyong-uk. "Tosan (Tasan): The Man and His Thought." *Korea Journal* 11 (June 1972): 33–42.

Anonymous. "The Amended Constitution of South Korea." *Review of the International Commission of Jurists* 26 (June 1981): 17–23.

Barr, John M. "The Second Republic of Korea." *Far Eastern Survey* 29 (September 1960): 129–32.

Bernadou, J. B. "Korea and the Koreans." *National Geographic Magazine* 2 (1898): 232–42.

Borton, Hugh. "Korea: Internal Political Structure." *Department of State Bulletin,* 14 November 1954.

———. "Occupation Policy in Japan and Korea." *Annals of the American Academy of Political and Social Science* 255 (January 1948): 146–55.

Bradbury, John. "Sino-Soviet Competition in North Korea." *The China Quarterly* 2 (April-June 1961): 15–28.

Bradner, Stephen. "Korea: Experiment and Instability." *Japan Quarterly* 8 (October-December 1961): 412–20.

Breidenstein, Gerhard. "Capitalism in South Korea." In Frank Baldwin, ed., *Without Parallel,* pp. 233–70. New York: Random House, 1973.

Briggs, Walter. "The Military Revolution in Korea: On Its Leader and Achievements." *Korean Quarterly* 5, no. 2 (Summer 1963): 17–34.

Bunce, Arthur C. "The Future of Korea, Parts I and II." *Far Eastern Survey,* 19 (April 1944 and 17 May 1944).

Chan, Kwon. "The Leadership of President Rhee." *Koreana Quarterly* (Spring 1971): 31–48.

Chandra, Vipan. "The Concept of National Sovereignty: So Chae-pil and Yun Chi-ho." *Korea Journal* 21 (April 1982): 4–13.

———. "Sentiment and Ideology in the Nationalism of the Independence Club (1896–1887)." *Korean Studies* 26 (1986): 13–34.

Cho, Chi-hun. "Motives and Essence of Enlightenment Movement." *Korea Journal* 9 (March 1969): 24–34.

Cho, Soon-sung. "Hodge's Dilemma." *Korean Affairs* 4 (1965): 58–74.

———. "Japan's Two Koreas Policy and the Problems of Korean Unification." *Asian Survey* 7 (October 1967): 703–25.

———. "Politics of North Korea's Unification Policies." *World Politics* 19 (January 1967): 218–41.

Choe, Yong-ho. "The Kapsin Coup of 1884: A Reassessment." *Korean Studies* 6 (1982): 105–24.

———. "Sino-Korean Relations, 1866–1876, Tributary Relationship to China." *The Journal of Asiatic Studies* 9, no. 1 (March 1966): 131–84.

Choi, Chong-Ko. "The Reception of Western Law in Korea." *Korea Journal* 20 (May 1980): 35–45.

Choi, Moon Hwan. "A Review of Korea's Land Reform." *Koreana Quarterly* (Spring 1960): 55–63.

Choi, Myung-Hyung. "Korean-British Amity and Its Historical Significance." *Korea Journal* 24 (April 1984): 9–22.

———. "The Onslaught of Imperialist Powers and Its Influence on Korea." *Korea Journal* 24 (March 1984): 4–23.

Choi, Syn-Duk. "Social Change and the Korean Family." *Korea Journal* 15 (November 1975): 4–113.

Chong, Chae-in. "Japanese Language-Literature in Korea." *Korean Journal* 25 (November 1985): 42–47.

Chong, Chang-yol. "Disputes and Tasks in the Research on the Thought of Silhak." *Korea Journal* 22 (November 1982): 4–12.

Chong, Chin-Sok. "E. T. Bethell and the Taehan Maeil Shinbo." *Korea Journal* 24 (April 1984): 39–44.

Chu, Yong-bok. "I Was in the Invading Army in Korea." *Korean Survey* 13 (October 1958): 3–4, 11.

Chung, Joseph Sang-Hoon. "North Korea's Economic System and the New Constitution." *Journal of Korean Affairs* 3 (April 1973): 28–34.

Chung, Chin O. "The Central Government and Power Structure of North Korea." *Journal of Korean Affairs* 1 (October 1971): 3–11.

———. "The Six Year Plan (1971–76) of North Korea: Targets, Problems, and Prospects." *Journal of Korean Affairs* 1 (July 1971): 15–26.

Chung, Young-iob. "Korean Investment and Confucian Personality under Japanese Rule." *Korea Journal* 17 (March 1977): 22–36.

Chung, Kae H. "Industrial Progress in South Korea." *Asian Survey* (May 1974): 439–55.

Clippinger, Morgan E. "Kim Chong-Il in the North Korean Mass Media: A Study of Semi-Esoteric Communication." *Asian Survey* 21 (March 1981): 289–309.

Deuchler, Martina. "The Opening of Korean Ports." *Korea Journal* 9 (January 1969): 11–20.

DeWeerd, H. A. "Lessons of the Korean War." *Yale Review* 40; 592–603.

Douglas, William A. "Korea Students and Politics." *Asian Survey* 3 (December 1963): 584–95.

———. "South Korea's Search for Leadership." *Pacific Affairs* 37 (Spring 1964): 20–36.

Dubin, Wilbert B. "The Political Evolution of the Pyongyang Government." *Pacific Affairs* 23 (December 1950): 381–92.

Earl, David M. "Korea: The Meaning of the Second Republic." *Far Eastern Survey* 29 (November 1960): 169–75.

Flanz, Gisbert. "Korea and Vietnam—Two Constitutional Experiments." *St. John's Law Review* 42 (1967): 18–37.

Ginsburg, George. "The Citizenship Status of Koreans in Pre-Revolutionary Russia and the Early Years of the Soviet Regime." *Journal of Korean Affairs* (July 1975): 1–19.

Guins, George C. "The Korean Plans of Russian Imperialism." *The American Journal of Economics and Sociology* 6 (October 1946): 71–86.

Gupta, Karunakar. "How Did the Korean War Begin?" *China Quarterly* (October-December 1972): 699–716.

Hahm, Pyong-Choon. "Korea's Mendicant Mentality: A Critique of U.S. Policy." *Foreign Affairs* 33 (October 1964): 165–74.

Hahn, Bae-ho and Kim, Kyu-taik. "Korean Political Leaders (1952–1962): Their Social Origin and Skills." *Asian Survey* (July 1963): 305–23.

Hamilton, A. H. "Origin of British Interest in Korea in the 19th Century." *Korea Journal* 14 (May 1975): 25–33.

Hamilton, Andrew W. "The Komundo [Port Hamilton] Affair." *Korea Journal* 22 (June 1982): 20–33.

Han, Nae Bok. "Rice Crisis in South Korea." *Far Eastern Economic Review* (18 July 1963): 164–69.

Han, Sung-Joo. "An Assessment of the Ho Chong and Chang Myon Governments." *Korea Journal* 22 (May 1982): 4–13.

———. "South Korea, 1977: Preparing for Self-Reliance." *Asian Survey* (January 1978): 50–51.

———. "Syngman Rhee: The Political Entrepreneurship of a Conservative Nationalist." *The Journal of Asiatic Studies* 22 (January 1979): 97–103.

———. "The Korean-American Relations during the Post-World War II Period." *Korea Journal* 22 (December 1982): 4–21.

Han, Tai Yon. "Impact of Western Democracy on Modern Korea." *Koreana Quarterly* (Spring 1960): 11–21.

Han, Yong-u. "Chong To-jon: His Political Reform Thought." *Korea Journal* 14 (July 1974): 46–51; and 15 (August 1974): 56–61.

———. "Chong Yak-yong: The Man and His Thought." *Korea Journal* 11 (August 1971): 24–35.

Hellman, Donald C. "Basic Problems of Japanese-South Korean Relations." *Asian Survey* (May 1962): 19–24.

Henderson, Gregory. "Chong Ta-San: A Study in Korea's Intellectual History." *Journal of Asian Studies* 16, no. 3 (1957): 377–86.

Hitchcock, Wilbur N. M. "North Korea Jumps the Gun: Did Kim Il Sung or Stalin Plan the Korean War?" *Current History* 20 (March 1951): 136–44.

Hoare, James. "Britain and Korea, 1881–1983." *Korea Journal* 24 (April 1984): 4–8.

Holubnychy, Vsevolod. "Soviet Economic Aid to North Korea." *Bulletin of the Institute for the Study of the U.S.S.R.*, Munich, 4 (January 1957).

Hong, Chong-hyuk. "The Historical Background of Korea's Division." *Koreana Quarterly* (Autumn 1972): 10–32.

Hong, I-sop. "Between ROK and Japan: A Thought on Cultural Exchange." *Korea Journal* 2 (April 1962): 5–9.

———. "Eastward Advance of Western Culture and the Process of Modernization in Korea." *Korea Journal* 4 (1964): 23–32.

Huang, Sung-mo. "Whither the Revolution?" *Korean Affairs*, no. 1 (1963): 44–50.

Hwang, Won-gu. "Korean World View through Relations with China." *Korea Journal* 13 (October 1973): 10–17.

Jung, Yong-suk. "A Critical Analysis on the Cause of the Korean War." *Pacific Affairs* 23 (December 1950): 381–92.

Kalinov, Kyril. "How Russia Built the North Korean Army." *The Reporter* 26 (26 September 1950): 4–8; and (10 October 1950): 17–20.

Kalton, Michael C. "An Introduction to Silhak." *Korea Journal* 15 (May 1973): 29–46.

Kang, Man-gil. "Silhak Thought and Its Reflection in Policies." *Korea Journal* 14 (May 1975): 4–13.

Kang, Thomas Hosuck. "Confucian Behavior toward the Modernization of Korea, 1864–1910." *Korea Journal* 13 (August 1974): 4–15.

———. "The Changing Nature of Korean Confucian Personality under Japanese Rule." *Korea Journal* 17 (March 1977): 22–36.

Kim, C. I. Eugene. "Korea at the Crossroads: The Birth of the Fourth Republic." *Pacific Affairs* 46 (Summer 1973): 218–31.

———. "The Big Power Detente and the Structure of Peace in the Korean Peninsula." *Korea Observer* 10 (Autumn 1979): 259–72.

Kim, Chun-kon. "Korean Communist Guerrilla Warfare (1948–1950)." *Journal of Korean Affairs* (1975): 27–33.

———. "The Detente and the Future of South Korean Democracy." *Pacific Community* 7 (1976): 283–95.

Kim, Dong-Hyun. "The Development of Indigenous Science and Technology Capabilities in Korea." *Korea Journal* 30 (February 1990): 20–27.

Kim, Hak-chun. "The South-North Dialogue in Historical Perspective." *Korean Journal* 20 (August 1980): 30–40.

Kim, Ilpyong J. "Constitutional Development in North Korea." *Journal of Korean Affairs* 2 (January 1973): 31-38.

Kim, Jin-Wung. "American Policy and the Korean Trusteeship, 1943–1947." *Korean Journal* 25 (April 1985): 19–35.

Kim, Joungwon A. "The 'Peak of Socialism' in North Korea: The Five and Seven Year Plans." *Asian Survey* 5 (May 1965): 255–69.

Kim, Kyu Taik. "The Behavior Patterns of the Rulers and Ruled in Korean Politics." *Korean Affairs* 1, no. 3 (1962): 319–26.

Kim, Pyoung-hoon, "Korea-Japan Rapproachment." *Korean Affairs* 4 (May 1965): 14–18.

Kim, Roy U. T. "Sino-North Korean Relations." *Asian Survey* 8 (August 1968): 708–22.

Kim, Se-jin. "Korea's Involvement in Vietnam and Its Political and Economic Impact." *Asian Survey* 10 (June 1970): 519–32.

Kim, T'ae-gil. "A Study of Values as Presented in Contemporary Korean Novels: With an Emphasis on the Political Consciousness of the Intellectuals." Translated by Sol Sun-hong. *Korea Journal* 21 (May 1981): 4–20.

Kim, Tae-ho. "The Ruling System of the North Korea Regime." *Korean Affairs* 2, no. 2 (1963): 174–86.

Kim, Uchang, Nak-chung Paik and Dong-il Cho. "The Direction of National Literature, in the 1990s." *Korea Journal* 32 (Summer 1992): 5–21.

Kim, Won-mo. "American 'Good Offices' in Korea." *Journal of Social Sciences and Humanities* 41 (June 1975): 93–139.

Kim, Yong-ho. *"Hanmal soyang ki sul ui suyong"* (The Acculturation of Western Techniques in the Late Period of the Yi Dynasty). *Asea Yongu* 31 (September 1968): 295–343.

Kim, Yong-mo. "Social Background and Mobility of Landlords under Japanese Imperialism in Korea." *Journal of Social Sciences and Humanities* (June 1971): 87–100.

Kim, Yschol-su. "Comparison of the Constitutions of South and North Korea." *Korean Journal of Comparative Law* 10 (1982): 1–18.

Kimm, Kyu-sik. "The Asiatic Revolutionary Movement and Imperialism." *The Communist Review* 3 (July 1922): 137–47.

Ko, Seung Kyun. "Communist China's Intervention in the Korean War." *Korea Observer* 4 (April 1972): 216–35.

Koh, B. C. "Dilemma of Korean Unification." *Asian Survey* (May 1971): 47–96.

———. "North Korea and the Sino-Soviet Schism." *The Western Political Quarterly* 22 (January 1969): 18–27.

Koh, Pyung Chul. "North Korea and Its Quest for Autonomy." *Pacific Affairs* (Fall-Winter 1965–66): 294–306.

Kohn, Yeong Kyeong. "Land Reform and Agricultural Structure in Korea." *Korean Affairs* 1, no. 4 (1962): 428–39.

Kong, Man-gil. "How History is Viewed in the North and in the South: Convergence and Divergence." *Korea Journal* 30 (February 1990): 4–12.

Korea Journal (Issue devoted to studies of British-Korean relations.) 24 (April 1984): 4–59 and 76–77.

Korea Journal (Issue devoted to studies of Japan-Korea relations.) 25 (December 1985): 4–82.

Koreana (issue devoted to nature and influence of Shamanism in Korean history). Vol. 6 (Summer 1992).

Kum, Chang-Tae. "Tasan on Western Learning and Confucianism." *Korea Journal,* 26 February 1986, pp. 4–16.

Lattimore, Owen. "Rebuilding our Policy in Asia." *Atlantic Monthly* (January 1950): 21–23.

Ledyard, Gari. "The Dutch Come to Korea." *Transactions* of the Royal Asiatic Society, Korea Branch, 1971.

Lee, Bae-Yong. "A Study on British Mining Concessions in the Late Choson Dynasty." *Korea Journal* 24 (April 1984): 23–38.

Lee, Chong-Sik. "Evolution of the Korean Workers' Party and the Rise of Kim Chong-Il." *Asian Survey* (May 1982) 434–48.

———. "The Detente in Korea." In William E. Griffith, ed., *The World and the Great-Power Triangles.* Cambridge: Harvard University Press, 1975.

———. "Kim Il-Sung of North Korea." *Asian Survey* 7 (June 1967): 374–82.

———. "Korea: Troubles in a Divided State." *Asian Survey* (January 1965): 25–28.

———. "Korean Communists and Yenan." *The China Quarterly* 9 (January-March 1962): 182–92.

———. "South Korea in 1980: The Emergence of a New Authoritarian Order." *Asian Survey* (January 1981): 126–29.

———. "The 'Socialist Revolution' in the North Korean Countryside." *Asian Survey* 2 (October 1962): 9–22.

——— and Oh Ki-wan. "The Russian Faction in North Korea." *Asian Survey* 8 (April 1968): 270–88.

Lee, Han-Key. "Constitutional Developments in South Korea." *Hong Kong Law Journal* 4 (1974): 41–51.

Lee, Hong Yung. "Korea's Future: Peking's perspective." *Asian Survey* 18 (November 1977): 1088–1102.

Lee, Hu-rak. "Why Is a Pan-National Party Necessary?" *Koreana Quarterly* 5 (Summer 1963): 11–16.

Lee, Kuk-Hong. "Missionary Activity in Korea 1889–1904." *Korea Journal* 24 (April 1984): 45–49.

Lee, Kwang-rin. "Newspaper Publication in the Late Yi Dynasty." Translated by Choe Yung-ho. *Korean Studies* 12 (1988): 62–72.

———. "The Rise of Nationalism in Korea." *Korean Studies* 10 (1986): 1–12.

Lee, Pong S. "Overstatement of North Korea's Industrial Growth, 1946–1963." *Journal of Korean Affairs* 1 (July 1971): 3–14.

Lee, Tong Won. "How the United Nations Failed in Korea." *Koreana Quarterly* (Summer 1961): 28–41.

Lee, Yur-Bok. "Establishment of a Korean Legation in the United States, 1887–1890: A Study of Conflict between Confucian World Order and Modern International Relations." *Illinois Papers in Asian Studies,* vol. 3. Urbana: University of Illinois, Center for Asian Studies, 1983.

Lew, Young Ick. "Japanese Challenge and Korean Response, 1870–1910: A Brief Historical Survey." *Korea Journal* 25 (December 1983): 36–51.

———. "Korean-Japanese Politics behind the Kabo-Ulmi Reform Movements, 1894–1896." *Journal of Korean Studies* 3 (1981): 39–82.

———. "Minister Inoue Kaoru and the Japanese Reform Attempts in Korea During the Sino-Japanese War, 1894–1895." *Journal of Asian Studies* 27, no. 2; 145–86.

———. "The Reform Efforts and Ideas of Pak Yong-hyo, 1894–1895." *Korean Studies* (December 1977): 21–62.

———. "Yuan Shih-kai's Residency and the Korean Enlightenment Movement (1885–94)." *Journal of Korean Studies* 5 (1984): 63–108.

Lhee, Ho-jeh. "Diplomatic Activities and Proposals of Syngman Rhee following Withdrawals of US Armed Forces in 1949." *Korea Observer* (July 1970): 22–48.

Liem, Channing. "United States Rule in Korea." *Far Eastern Survey* 18 (April 1949): 77–80.

Lin, T. C. "Li Hung-chang: His Korean Policies, 1870–1885." *Chinese Social and Political Science Review* 19 (July 1935): 203–33.

Loh, Keie Hyun. "Self-Dependent Line of North Korean Foreign Policy." *Korea Observer* (Spring 1974).

McCune, George M. "Korea—The First Year of Liberation." *Pacific Affairs* 20 (March 1947): 3–17.

———. "Occupation Politics in Korea." *Far Eastern Survey* (February 1946): 33–37.

———. "Post War Government and Politics in Korea." *Journal of Politics* (November 1947): 605–23.

———. "The Japanese Trading Post at Pusan." *Korean Review* 1 (1948): 11–15.

McCune, Shannon. "The Thirty-eighth Parallel in Korea." *World Politics* 1 (1949): 223–32.

Merrill, John. "The Cheju-do Rebellion." *Journal of Korean Studies* (1980): 139–98.

Min, Benjamin H. "The Revolutionary Strategy of North Korea." *Pacific Community* (Tokyo) 2 (January 1971): 354–68.

Min, Byung-Ki. "Problems in Korean-Japanese Relations." *Koreana Quarterly* 6 (Spring 1964): 39–45.

Mitchell, Clyde C. "Land Reform in South Korea." *Pacific Affairs* 22 (June 1949): 144–54.

Mitchell, C. R. "Civil Strife and the Involvement of External Parties." *International Studies Quarterly* 14 (June 1970): 166–94.

Mok, Chon-gyun. "The Centripetal and Centrifugal Functions of the Tonghak Movement: With Reference to Communication in the Tonghak Group." *Korea Journal* 18 (May 1979): 50–63.

Mosely, Philip E. "Soviet Policy and the War." *Journal of International Affairs* 6 (Spring 1952): 107–42.

Mun, Hwan Choi. "The Path to Democracy: A Historical Review of Korean Economy," *Korean Quarterly* 3 (Summer 1961): 59–61.

Nahm, Andrew C. "Kim Ok-kyun and the Reform Movement of the Progressives." *Korea Journal* 24 (December 1984): 38–62.

———. "Korean-American Relations, 1866–1978: A Critical Examination." *Korea Journal* 18 (December 1979): 14–25.

———. "The Impact of the Taft-Katsura Memorandum on Korea—A Reassessment." *Korea Journal* 25 (October 1985): 4–17.

———. "Korean Nationalism: Its Origins and Transformation." *Korea Journal* 23 (February 1983): 19–37.

———. "Studies on United States-Korean Relations in the English Language: A Bibliographical Survey." *Korea Journal* 22 (December 1982): 33–43.

Noble, Harold J. "The Korean Mission to the United States in 1883: The First Embassy Sent by Korea to an Occidental Nation." *Transactions* of the Korean Branch of the Royal Asiatic Society 18 (1929): 1–21.

———. "The United States and Sino-Korean Relations." *Pacific Historical Quarterly* 2 (1933): 292–304.

Noh, Hee-bang. "Communication Systems during the Choson Dynasty, 1392–1910." *Korea Journal* 25 (October 1985): 44–53.

Oh, John Kie-chiang. "Post-coup Korea on a Treadmill: A Political Analysis." East-West Center Review 2 (October 1965): 1–15.

———. "Role of the United States in South Korea's Democratization." *Pacific Affairs* 13 (Summer 1969): 164–77.

———. "The Political Role of the Korean Military: The Making of the Third Republic." In *Studies of Asia,* pp. 71–86. Lincoln: University of Nebraska Press, 1967.

Oliver, Robert T. "Brief for Korea." *Annals* of the American Academy of Political and Social Sciences (July 1954), pp. 33–41.

———. "The American Stake in Korea." *U.S. National War College Publications* 21, no. 653 (1958): 6.

———. "Buddhism and Democracy." In Lee Sun Keun and Rhee Ki Yong, eds., *Buddhism in the Modern World,* pp. 12–22. Dongguk University Press, 1976.

———. "Crisis in Korea." *The Standard* (November 1948): 47–54.

———. "The Crux in Korea." *The Christian Century* (February 1948) 234–36.

———. "Diplomatic Efforts to Restore Korean Sovereignty." *Korea Journal* 23 (February 1983): 48–59.

———. "Korea: A Bastion of Freedom in Asia." *United Asia* (October 1949): 153–57.

———. "Korea: The Key to Peace in the Orient." *Vital Speeches of the Day* (15 March 1947): 329–32.

———. "Korea: A People Betrayed." *The New Leader* (18 August 1945): 6–7.

———. "Korea: A Progress Report." *Current History* (September 1949): 132–36.

———. "Korean Culture and Democracy." *Free World Forum* (Winter 1959–60): 10–14.

———. "The Confucian Rhetorical Traditional in Korea during the Yi Dynasty." *Quarterly Journal of Speech* (December 1959): 363–73.

———. "Northeast Asia: Vital Flank in the Cold War." *Discourse: A Review of the Liberal Arts* (April 1959): unpaged.

———. "The Speech of Diplomacy: Appearance and Reality." *Colorado Quarterly* (1964): 353–74.

———. "Transition and Continuity in American-Korean Affairs, 1945–1982." *Korea Journal* (November 1982): 27–31.

———. "Young Nation Appraised." *Stars and Stripes,* Pacific edition, three parts, 10, 12, 13 August 1958; also distributed by United Press International.

O'Rourke, Kevin. "The Korean Short Story of the 1920's and Naturalism." *Korea Journal* 17 (March 1977): 48–63.

Pae, Yong-su. "A Bibliography on Korean-American Relations." *Korea Journal* 22 (December 1982): 44–50.

Paik, Wan-ki. "Merits and Demerits of Public Administration in Korea's Modernization." *Korea Journal* 23 (February 1983): 38–48.

Pak, Chan-sung, et al. "Historical Research on Latter Choson Period." *Korea Journal* 28 (September 1988): 4–15; and (October 1988): 5–20.

Pak, Chung-sok. "Concept of International Order in the History of Korea." *Korea Journal* 18 (August 1979): 15–21.

Pak, Kyong-sok and Nam Shi-uk. "Factions in Korean Political Parties." *Shindong-A* (February 1967): 198–209.

Pak, Hen En. "Seoul Documents on Rhee Invasion Plans." *Soviet Russia Today* (December 1950): 19–20, 20–27, and 35.

Pak, M. N., with Wayne Patterson. "Russian Policy toward Korea before and during the Sino-Japanese War of 1894–95." *Journal of Korean Studies* 5 (1984): 109–20.

Pak, Pyong-ho. "The Legal Nature of Land Ownership in the Yi Dynasty." *Korea Journal* 18 (August 1979): 15–21.

Pak, Seong-rae. "Introduction of Western Science in Korea, 1876–1910." *Korea Journal* 21 (May 1981): 29–38.

Pak, Un-sik. "Independence Movements in Uiju and Chinju: March 1–May 31, 1919." *Korea Journal* 21 (March 1982): 35–38.

Pollard, Robert T. "American Relations with Korea, 1882–1895." *Chinese Social and Political Review* 16 (1932): 425–71.

Reischauer, Edwin O. "Is it Time to Disengage?—The Korean Connection." *New York Times Magazine,* September 1974.

Rho, Kwang-ane. "The United Nations and the Founding of the Republic of Korea: A Reappraisal." *Koreana Quarterly* (Spring 1960): 65–74.

Robinson, Michael. "National Identity and Thought of Sin Chaeho: *Sadaejuui* and *Chuche* in History and Politics." *Journal of Korean Studies* 5 (1984): 121–42.

Scalapino, Robert A. "Moscow, Peking and the Communist Parties of Asia." *Foreign Affairs* (January 1963): 323–43.

———. "The Nature of the North Korean Regime: An Assessment." *China Report* 8 (January-February, March-April 1972).

———. "Korea: The Politics of Change." *Asian Survey* 3 (January 1963): 31–40.

Schram, Wilbur, and John W. Riley, Jr. "Communication in the Sovietized State, as Demonstrated in Korea." *American Sociological Review,* 16 (December 1951): 757–66.

Schufeldt, Robert W. "Opening of Korea: Admiral Shufeldt's Account of It." Edited by Henry G. Appenzeller. *Korean Repository* 1 (February 1892): 57–62.

Shim, Hyun-Nyo. "Yun Chi-ho and the Independence Club." *Korea Journal* 30 (October 1990): 27–43.

Shim, Jung Soon. "Torn Between Self and Tradition: The Image of Women in the Plays of Kim Cha-rim." *Korean Culture* 2 (Summer 1990): 32–37.

Shin, Ki-suk. "International Relations with Respect to the Coup d'etat of 1884." *Korea Journal* 24 (December 1984): 22–37.

Shin, Myungsoon. "China's Foreign Relations with North Korea, 1949–1975." *Korea Observer* 10, no. 4 (Winter 1929): 390–404.

Shin, Susan S. "Tonghak Thought: The Roots of Revolution." *Korea Journal* 19 (September 1979): 11–20.

Shin, Yong-ha. "Landlordism in the Late Yi Dynasty." *Korea Journal* 18 (June 1978): 25–32.

———. "Land Reform in Korea, 1950." *Bulletin* of the Population and Development Studies Center, Seoul National University, 5 (September 1976): 14–29.

———. "The Revolutionary Movement of the Tonghak Peasant Army of 1894: Seen *vis-a-vis* the French Revolution." Translated by Koh Myung-shik. *Korea Journal* 29 (October 1989): 28–34.

———. "The Thought of the Enlightenment Movement." *Korea Journal* 24 (December 1984): 4–21.

Simmons, Robert R. "China's Cautious Relations with North Korea and Indochina." *Asian Survey* 11 (July 1971).

———. "North Korea: Year of the Thaw." *Asian Survey* 12 (January 1972).

Sin, Il-chol. "Tonghak Movement and Modernization." *Korea Journal* 6 (May 1966): 16–21.

Sin, Sung-gwon. "Korean-Japanese Relations, 1894–1904." *Korea Journal* 21 (February 1981): 12–25; and (March 1981): 4–20.

———. "The Russo-Korean Relations in the 1880s." *Korea Journal* 20 (September 1980): 21–30.

———. "Russian Policy toward Korea, 1894–1895." *Korea Journal* (November 1981): 47–57, 65.

Sin, Yong-ha. "The Life and Thought of Pak Un-sik." *Korea Journal* 21 (March 1981): 21–30.

Smith, Joseph B. "The Koreans and Their Living Space: An Attempted Analysis in Terms of Political Geography." *Korean Review* 2 (September 1949): 45–52.

Soh, Jun-chull. "The Role of the Soviet Union in Preparations for the Korean War." *Journal of Korean Affairs* 3 (January 1974): 3–14.

Son, Young Ho. "The Search for Ethnic Identity in America: Politics of Korean Nationalism." *Korea Journal* 29 (August 1989): 4–18.

———. "Korean Response to the 'Yellow Peril' and Search for Racial Accomodation in the United States." *Korea Journal* 32 (Summer 1992): 58–74.

Stevens, Durham White. "China and Japan in Korea." *North American Review* 159 (1894): 308–16.

Stuek, William. "Cold War Revisionism and the Origins of the Korean Conflict: The Kolko Thesis." *Pacific Historical Review* 42 (1973): 537–75.

Sunoo, Hag-Wo'n. "Notes on the Korean Language." *Korean Review* 2 (September 1949): 53–67.

———. "A Study of the U.S.-Korean Treaty of 1882." *Korean Review* 2 (September 1949): 25–44.

Thomas, S. B. "The Chinese Communist's Economic and Cultural Agreement with North Korea." *Pacific Affairs* 27 (March, 1954).

Tiwari, D. K. "India's Participation in the Korean Crisis: An Assessment." *Korea Journal* 28 (December 1988): 14–22.

Tralim, Hankum. "Land Reform in North Korea." *Amerasia* 11 (February 1947): 55–62.

Treat, Payson J. "China and Korea." *Political Science Quarterly* 49:506–43.

Trollope, Bishop M. "Corean Books and their Authors." *Transactions,* Korean Branch, Royal Asiatic Society, vol. 16 (1932): 1–105.

Unruh, Ellen Salem. "The Case of the Landowning Slave: a Korean Phenomenon." *Korea Journal* 16 (April 1977): 27–34.

Vinocour, Seymour M. "A Brief Sketch of the South Korean Interim Legislative Assembly." *Korean Review* (September 1949): 18–24.

Wagner, Edward E. "Failure in Korea." *Foreign Affairs* 40 (October 1961): 129ff.

———. "The First Century." In *Reflections on a Century of United States-Korean Relations, Conference Papers, June 1982,* pp. 17–27. Lanham, NY, and London: University Press of America for Academy of Korean Studies and the Wilson Center, 1983.

Walker, Hugh D. "Traditional Sino-Korean Diplomatic Relations: A Realistic Historical Appraisal." *Monumenta Sinica* 24 (1965): 155–69.

Wan, Hyok-pu. "The History of American Aid to Korea." *Koreana Quarterly* (Summer 1961): 71–96.

Wang, Se Hoon. "Political Turmoil Marked a Hectic Year." *The Korean Republic Weekly,* 14 August 1963, pp. 2–3.

Washburn, John N. "Russia Looks at Northern Korea." *Pacific Affairs* 20 (June 1949): 144–54.

———. "The Soviet Press Views North Korea." *Pacific Affairs* 22 (June 1947): 144–54.

———. "Soviet Russia and the Korean Communist Party." *Pacific Affairs* 23 (1950): 59–65.

Weems, Clarence M. "Washington's First Steps Toward a Korean-American Joint Action (1941–1943)." Unpublished paper presented at the East Asian Studies Center of the University of Southern California, 11–13 November 1988, p. 47.

Wolf, C. J. "Economic Planning in Korea." *Asian Studies* 2 (December 1962): 22–28.

Won, Yu-han. "Different Periods in the History of Money during the Late Yi Dynasty." *Korea Journal* 16 (August 1977): 42–58.

Yang, Sung Chul. "Korean Reunification: A Functional Model." *Journal of Korean Affairs* 2, no. 2 (1972): 8–20.

———, guest ed. "The Korean Question in the Post Cold War Era." *Korea Journal* 22 (July 1989): 4–58.

———. "The Politics of Cult in North Korea." *Political Studies Review* 2 (1985): 27–52.

Yang, Tae-jin. "On the System of Beacons in Korea." *Korea Journal* 11 (October 1972): 34–35.

Yarovoy, B. "Korea: Forgotten Nation." *New Times* (Moscow), 15 August 1945, pp. 26–27.

Yi, Hui-dok. "Formation of Confucian Ethics in Korea." *Korea Journal* 13 (February 1974): 10–16.

Yi, Kyu-ho. "The Ideals and Development of National Education." *Korea Journal* 18 (April 1979): 48–56.

Yi, Pyeng-Do. "The Impact of the Western World on Korea in the Nineteenth Century." *Cahiers d'Histoire Mondiale* 5 (1960): 957–74.

Yi, Tong-Hwa. "Yo Un-hyong and the Preparation Committee for the Reconstruction of the Nation." *Korea Journal* 26 (November 1986): 41–61.

Yim, Seong-hi. "Modern Newspapers Got Start in Twenties." *The Korean Republic Weekly,* 4 September 1963, p. 8.

Yong, Pyong-u. "Korea in World History." *Korea Journal* 20 (October 1981): 19–24.

Yoon, Ho-Byeong. "Modern Korean Poets' Concepts of Poetic Language in an Age of National Crisis, 1910–1945." *Korea Journal* 29 (December 1989): 4–16; and 30 (January 1990): 28–37.

Yoon, Young Kyo. "United Nations Participation in Korean Affairs: 1947–1951." *Koreana Quarterly* (Spring 1960): 22–54.

Yu, An-jin. "Child Education in Traditional Korean Society." Translated by Chon Sung-bok. *Korea Journal* 21 (May 1981): 21–28.

Yu, Hong-yol. "Korea's Cultural Independence." *Korea Journal* 5 (January 1966): 16–21.

Yu, Kwang-yol. "Last Reminder of National Humiliation." *Korea Journal* 2 (August 1962): 6–7.

Yum, June Ock. "The Impact of Confucianism on Interpersonal Relationships and Communication Patterns in East Asia." *Communication Monographs* 55 (December 1989): 374–88.

Yun, Pyong-sok. "Korean Resistance to Imperial Japanese Aggression." *Korea Journal* 24 (March 1984): 24–39.

Zagoria, Donald S. "Korea's Future: Peking's perspective." *Asian Survey* (18 November 1977): 1103–1112.

Subject Index

"The subject of history is the life of peoples and of humanity."
—Leo N. Tolstoi, *War and Peace*

Name Index*

"An individual is really of consequence."
—Thomas Carlyle, "Burns"

*The plethora of foreign names accurately reflects the enormous influence of foreigners in the modernizing period in Korea.